*The Strife of Systems*

# The Strife of Systems

An Essay

on the Grounds

and Implications of

Philosophical

Diversity

## Nicholas Rescher

*University of Pittsburgh Press*

Published by the University of Pittsburgh Press, Pittsburgh, Pa., 15260
Copyright © 1985, University of Pittsburgh Press
All rights reserved
Feffer and Simons, Inc., London
Manufactured in the United States of America

Library of Congress Cataloging in Publication Data

Rescher, Nicholas.
　The strife of systems.

　Includes indexes.
　1. Methodology—Addresses, essays, lectures.
　2. Philosophy—Addresses, essays, lectures.
I. Title.
BD241.R44 1985　　　101　　　84-21958
ISBN 0-8229-3510-4

*For Lorenz Puntel*
*in cordial friendship*

# Contents

Preface   xi

1. *The Problem of Philosophical Diversity*   3
   1. The Strife of Systems   3
   2. The Problem Is Itself a Focus of Diversity   6
   3. The Untenability of the Platonic Ideal   9
   4. Is Disagreement an Illusion?   13
   5. A Fatal Flaw?   15

2. *Philosophy and Paradox: The Pivotal Role of Aporetic Clusters*   17
   1. The Task of Philosophy   17
   2. Antinomies and Cognitive Overcommitment   21
   3. How Apory Engenders a Diversity of Resolutions   25
   4. Antinomies Structure the Issues   28
   5. Can Different Schools Debate the Same Issues?   31
   6. Consequences of Incommensurability   34
   7. Why Not Simply "Live with Inconsistency"? The Imperative of Cognitive Rationality   38

3. *Why Antinomies Pervade Philosophy*   45
   1. Philosophical Concepts Are Fact Coordinated   45
   2. Clarificatory Pressures and Antinomy   49
   3. Fact-Coordinated Concepts Resist Purely Theoretical Clarification   52
   4. Philosophy Cannot Abandon the Concepts of Presystemic Experience   57
   5. Philosophy and the "Limits of Experience"   60

4. *Escaping Inconsistency via Distinctions*   64
   1. Removing Inconsistency Through Curtailments   64
   2. The Role of Distinctions   65
   3. Dialectical Development   69
   4. A Historical Illustration   70

5. Intimations of Imperfection  72
6. Some Important Forms of Philosophical Inventiveness  75

## 5. Developmental Dialectics    78
1. The Convergence of Traditions  78
2. The Growth of Complexity and its Dialectical Ramifications  80
3. A Glance Backwards: Hegel and Herbart  84
4. The Structure of Philosophical History  85
5. Sic Transit  88
6. The Burden of History  90

## 6. Cognitive Values and Antinomy Resolution    95
1. The Problem of Evaluative Selection  95
2. The Pivotal Role of Analogy and the Role of Cognitive Values  98
3. Philosophizing Hinges on Cognitive Evaluation  105
4. The Loss of Objectivity  111

## 7. Orientational Pluralism: The Inevitability of Value Diversity    116
1. Doctrinal Diversity Reflects a Diversity of Values  116
2. The Import of Orientational Pluralism  122
3. The Inevitability of "Schools of Thought" and the Unattainability of Consensus  125
4. Whence Cognitive Values? The Key Role of "Experience"  129
5. Are Philosophical Problems Pseudoproblems?  132
6. The Persistence of Conflict  133
7. A Review of the Argumentation  137

## 8. The Range of Reason    139
1. The Infeasibility of a "Neutral" Basis of Philosophical Appraisal  139
2. Against Indifferentism: Orientational Pluralism Does Not Make the Choice Among Positions Into "a Mere Matter of Taste"  145
3. Does Orientational Pluralism Support Irrationalism?  151
4. Pluralism and the Impetus of Reason  154
5. The Rational Imperative  156

## 9. What Orientational Pluralism Means for Philosophy    159
1. The Individual and the Community  159
2. In Philosophy We Cannot "Rise Above the Battle"  160
3. Is Philosophy a Guide to Life?  161
4. Are Orientationally Bound Positions Worth Having?  165

    5. Does the Relativity of Philosophical Claims Undermine the Worth of the Enterprise? 168
    6. The Values Underlying the Present Account Itself 170

## 10. Truth and Reality: Ramifications of Relativism     173
    1. Views Regarding Our Cognitive Access to Reality 173
    2. Where Orientational Pluralism Stands 177
    3. Against Absolutism 179
    4. Does Its Relativism Undercut Orientational Pluralism Itself? 180
    5. The Pursuit of Truth 186
    6. Relativism and the Problem of Protagoras 191
    7. Does Orientational Pluralism Mean We Must Abandon the Pursuit of Truth? 196

## 11. Is There Progress in Philosophy? The Problem of Unattainable Consensus     202
    1. The Complexity of the Question in the Absence of Consensus 202
    2. The Balance Sheet: Technical vs. Doctrinal Progress 203
    3. Abandoning Consensus as a Prime Desideratum 207
    4. The Contrast of Scientific Consensus 210
    5. Progress in the Absence of Consensus 217
    6. Is Consensus Dispensable? 219

## 12. Reactions to Pluralism     221
    1. An Inventory of Responses 221
    2. Scepticism 224
    3. Arationalism 230
    4. Historical Convergentism 233
    5. Rationalistic Doctrinalism in Its Absolutistic and Orientational Versions 235
    6. Syncretism: Against the Averroist Theory of Multiple Truth 236
    7. Coda 238

## 13. More on Scepticism and Syncretism     241
    1. The Kinship of Scepticism and Syncretism 241
    2. Agnostic Scepticism 241
    3. Scepticism in Its Neo-Hermeneutic Guise 245
    4. Why Not Abandon Philosophy? A Reply to the Sceptic 248
    5. Syncretism 252
    6. A Critique of Syncretism 257
    7. The Flight from Commitment 258

## 14. Prescriptive Versus Descriptive Metaphilosophy     261
    1. Modes of Metaphilosphy 261
    2. Orientational Pluralism is Not at Odds with Doctrinal Commitment 265

3. On Replacing Philosophy with Its Own History   267
4. Does Orientational Pluralism in Metaphilosophy Carry Lessons for Philosophy Itself?   271

*Name Index*                                                                279
*Subject Index*                                                             282

# Preface

It is notorious that philosophers disagree. This book develops a theory that accounts for this phenomenon in terms of the very nature of the subject. It argues that the cause of philosophical disagreement ultimately lies in conflicting "cognitive values" that relate to such matters as importance, centrality, and priority, and set the standards in whose terms philosophers appraise the analogies that determine the plausibility of the fundamental contentions of their systemic positions. It thus traces disagreement regarding philosophical *doctrines* to a disagreement regarding *values* and concludes that philosophers will never actually settle their disputes. An orientational pluralism is bound to prevail.

In the light of this analysis, the book argues that, despite the inevitable strife of systems, scepticism regarding traditional philosophy is not warranted. Because values—cognitive values included—are important to us as individuals, philosophy remains an important and worthwhile enterprise, notwithstanding its inability to achieve a rationally constrained consensus on the fundamental issues. Indeed, given the nature of the enterprise, consensus is simply not a sensible goal, and failure to achieve it is not a defect. The abandonment or revision of traditional philosophy along lines recently proposed by Richard Rorty and Robert Nozick are considered at length and criticized in depth.

Only in part does the book grind its own theoretical ax, however. Most of its discussions are devoted to providing a clear view of why philosophical problems arise and how philosophers go about addressing them. Through the mechanism of aporetic clusters it provides a useful (and substantively unprejudiced) way of considering the interrelations of philosophical problems and of forming a clearer view of the issues at stake.

The view of philosophy set out in this book owes much to three great German masters of the last century: G. W. F. Hegel, Johann Friedrich Herbart, and Wilhelm Dilthey. Yet it also departs sharply from their positions. They all thought that philosophy could somehow exploit its history to transcend its own historicity. This is a view I cannot share. They all thought that philosophy could defeat pluralism by embracing pluralities. This too I do not believe. The reasons for these convictions will be examined in the book itself. But the reader should be put on notice from the outset that much of the tenor of the view of philosophy propounded here is historicist, pluralistic, and "relativistic." It sees philosophical tendencies as perennial, but philosophical systems as time-bound and standpoint-conditioned artifacts that never represent more than one alternative among others. That the project still is eminently worthwhile as an intellectual enterprise is a perhaps surprising but nevertheless important conclusion whose basis is well worth closer consideration.

The book developed from a paper titled "Philosophical Disagreement: An Essay towards Orientational Pluralism," originally published in *The Review of Metaphysics* in 1978 (vol. 32, pp. 217–51). On further reflection it became clear that the ideas of this paper both required and deserved a more systematic development, and the present deliberations are the outgrowth of this perception.

The substance of the book was presented in a series of public lectures titled "The Nature of Philosophy," which I delivered at Bowling Green State University during the winter term of 1983. An abbreviated version of these lectures was delivered during Trinity Term of 1983 in the School of Literae Humaniores of the University of Oxford at the kind invitation of the Sub-Faculty of Philosophy. I much appreciate the hospitality of Corpus Christi College in affording me an academic home away from home on this as on many previous occasions.

I am grateful to Geoffrey Sayre McCord and to Diego Marconi for reading the book in draft form and offering useful suggestions for its improvement. And I wish to thank Linda Butera, Donna Williams, and Christina Masucci for the patience with which they managed to produce a presentable manuscript through innumerable revisions.

Pittsburgh
*February 1984*

*The Strife of Systems*

# 1

# The Problem of Philosophical Diversity

*1. The Strife of Systems*

The ranks of philosophy are in serious disarray. Theory confronts theory, school rivals school in implacable opposition. Disagreement and controversy prevail to such an extent in this discipline that one can safely endorse the quip: "If two people agree, one of them isn't a philosopher."

This view is not the cynical reaction of a jaded twentieth-century observer but something philosophers have long recognized. At the very dawn of philosophy, Xenophanes of Colophon (born ca. 565 B.C.) prophetically wrote:

No man knows, or ever will know, the truth about the Gods and about everything I speak of. Even if he should chance to speak the complete truth, yet he himself knows it not. But all may have their opinion.[1]

The ancient Sceptics made the doctrinal clash of philosophical conflict a cornerstone of their own teaching. Sextus Empiricus informs us:

That nothing is self-evident is plain, they the skeptics say, from the controversy which exists amongst the natural philosophers regarding, I imagine, all things, both sensibles and intelligibles; which controversy admits of no settlement because we can neither employ a sensible nor an intelligible criterion, since whatever criterion we may adopt is controverted and therefore discredited.[2]

Descartes, the founding father of modern philosophy, complained as follows:

---

1. Fragment 34 in H. Diels, *Die Fragmente der Vorsokratiker*, 3rd ed. (Leipzig, 1912).
2. Sextus Empiricus, *Outlines of Pyrrhonism*, bk. I, 178. The conflicting teachings of the philosophers were the very first of the five *tropoi* or sceptical arguments (*rationes dubitandi*) by which Agrippa sought to support a sceptical position (ibid., 95).

# THE STRIFE OF SYSTEMS
*The Problem of Philosophical Diversity*

I shall not say anything about philosophy, but that, seeing that it has been cultivated for many centuries by the best minds that have ever lived, and that nevertheless no single thing is to be found in it which is not subject of dispute, and in consequence which is not dubious, I had not enough presumption to hope to fare better there than other men had done. And also, considering how many conflicting opinions there may be regarding the self-same matter, all supported by learned people, while there can never be more than one which is true, I esteemed as well-nigh false all that only went so far as being probable.[3]

In the eighteenth century, David Hume deplored philosophy's chaotic lack of consensus in these terms:

Want of coherence in the parts, and of evidence in the whole, these are everywhere to be met with in the systems of the most eminent philosophers, and seem to have drawn disgrace upon philosophy itself. . . . Even the rabble without doors may judge from the noise and clamour, which they hear, that all goes not well within. There is nothing which is not the subject of debate, and in which men of learning are not of contrary opinions. The most trivial question escapes not our controversy, and in the most momentous we are not able to give any certain decision. Disputes are multiplied, as if every thing was uncertain; and these disputes are managed with the greatest warmth, as if every thing was certain. Amidst all this bustle 'tis not reason, which carries the prize, but eloquence; and no man needs ever despair of gaining proselytes to the most extravagant hypothesis, who has art enough to represent it in any favourable colours. . . . From hence in my opinion arises that common prejudice against metaphysical reasonings of all kinds, even amongst those, who profess themselves scholars.[4]

A century later Wilhelm Dilthey wrote (in 1867):

[Many think that] the development of philosophy encompasses through all those various systems a succession of systems which approaches a single perfected system in unending approximation. However in reality every age manifests the strife of all these systems among one another. This includes the present age, which shows no sign that this strife of systems is diminishing.[5]

---

3. René Descartes, *Discourse on Method*, pt. I; trans. E. S. Haldane and G. N. T. Ross (Cambridge, 1911).

4. David Hume, *A Treatise on Human Nature*, Introduction. When one considers the sorry history of the efforts of philosophers to produce recognizable truth, Hume's sceptical confrère Montaigne writes, one must conclude that philosophy is little better than sophistical fable-making: "Et certes la philosophie n'est qu'une poésie sophistiquée" (*Les Essais de Michel de Montaigne*, ed. Pierre Villey, vol. III [Paris, 1922], p. 279).

5. Wilhelm Dilthey, *Gesammelte Schriften*, vol. V (Stuttgart and Göttingen, 1960), p. 134. He observed that the tendency of his time was "to treat the systems of these great philosophers as a series of delusions, akin to a bad dream which, on awaking, one had best forget altogether" (p. 13), and he remarked that "the anarchy of philosophical systems is one of the most powerful supports from which scepticism draws ever-renewed nourishment. A contradiction arises between the historical realization of their boundless multiplicity and the claims of each to universal validity which supports the sceptical spirit more powerfully than any theoretical argumentation" (p. 75).

In the late 1920s Moritz Schlick gave expression to a similarly discouraging view:

> But it is just the ablest thinkers who most rarely have believed that the results of earlier philosophizing, including that of the classical models, remain unshakable. This is shown by the fact that basically every new system starts again from the beginning, that every thinker seeks his own foundation and does not wish to stand on the shoulders of his predecessors. . . . This peculiar fate of philosophy has been so often described and bemoaned that it is indeed pointless to discuss it at all. Silent scepticism and resignation seem to be the only appropriate attitudes. Two thousand years of experience seem to teach that efforts to put an end to the chaos of systems and to change the fate of philosophy can no longer be taken seriously.[6]

The litany of dismay echoes through the ages: complaints regarding unsettled issues, unresolved controversy, unending disputes, and unachieved consensus. For more than two millennia, philosophers have grappled with "the big issues" of man and his place in the natural and social scheme of things without resolving anything. The consequence, as one observer remarks, is that "the history of philosophy has been, to a very great extent, a history of impressive failures, of large conceptions whose particular deficiencies have finally been laid bare for all to behold."[7] We look in vain for one consolidated and generally acknowledged item of philosophical "knowledge"—one "philosophical fact" on which the philosophical community at large has reached a settled consensus. As Husserl somewhere remarked, philosophy is in a state of conflict and confusion: "To be sure, we still have philosophical congresses. The philosophers meet but, unfortunately, not the philosophies."

What Dilthey calls "the strife of systems" has always been a matter of dismay and embarrassment to philosophers. As one recent commentator puts it: "In Descartes, in Kant, in Hegel, in Husserl, in Wittgenstein . . . one finds the same disgust at the spectacle of philosophers quarreling endlessly over the same issue."[8] Doctrines are no sooner proposed than attacked, theories no sooner constructed than contested. Lord Herbert of Cherbury began his great work *De veritate* (ca. 1630) with a picture of the sorry state of contemporary learning, the chaos of beliefs, and the prevalence of controversy.[9] And this situation has prevailed throughout: wherever we turn in philosophy, we see a

---

6. Moritz Schlick, "The Turning Point in Philosophy," *Logical Positivism*, ed. A. J. Ayer (New York, 1959), pp. 53–54 (originally published as "Die Wende der Philosopie" in vol. 1 of *Erkenntnis* [1930]). Compare also Kant, *CPuR*, Preface to the First Edition, A viii–x; and Charles Sanders Peirce, "The Fixation of Belief," *Collected Papers*, vol. V, ed. C. Hartshorne and P. Weiss (Cambridge, Mass., 1934), sec. 5.383.

7. Joseph Margolis, ed., *An Introduction to Philosophical Inquiry* (New York, 1968), p. 10.

8. Richard Rorty, *The Linguistic Turn* (Chicago, 1967), p. 1.

9. Trans. M. H. Carré (Bristol, 1937).

battlefield. Yet why should it be that—as one writer picturesquely puts it—"systems lie about us like the ruins of gigantic castles" without our being able to build one solid and defensible structure from this ample debris?[10]

And so we come to the question that the practitioners of the discipline have faced time and again: "Must Philosophers Disagree?" (to quote the title of F. C. S. Schiller's perceptive 1933 essay).[11] Why are philosophers chronically incapable of reaching agreement regarding the problems they have debated for well over two millennia? Why is philosophy locked into a condition of endless and apparently irresolvable controversy?

## 2. The Problem Is Itself a Focus of Diversity

Interestingly enough, the problem of philosophical disagreement itself exemplifies the phenomenon at issue. For even in addressing this very question of the grounds of diversity, philosophers have achieved no settled consensus. Diverse accounts have been proposed, primarily the following:

(1) *Methodological explanations* that attribute the historical failure to reach consensus to a fundamental deficiency in the previously used mechanisms of philosophical practice. Descartes saw the deficiency of earlier philosophers in their failure to achieve a proper *method* of investigation. Hume saw the futility of prior philosophizing in its failure to uncover appropriate *first premises* as a basis of reasoning.[12] Peirce and others saw the failure of consensus to result from the absence of agreed *definitions* of terms, resulting from the lack of an adequate theory of meaning. Theorists of a historicist persuasion tend to

---

10. Karl Heim, *Das Weltbild der Zukunft* (Berlin, 1904), p. 1. This book is by no means the first, however, to have "the strife of systems" (*der Streit der Systeme*) as its central theme. Hegel aside, it was anticipated as of the 1860s in Wilhelm Dilthey's unfinished masterpiece, *Weltanschauungslehre* (*Gesammelte Schriften*, vol. VIII, [Stuttgart and Göttingen, 1960]), where "the anarchy of philosophical systems" (*die Anarchie der philosophischen Systeme*) is the central issue. The problem-stage of his discussion is set by the fact that "a profusion of philosophical systems trails behind us and spreads out on every side, boundaryless and chaotic. In every time since their origin, they have excluded and contested one another, and there is no sign of hope that a decision among them can ever be realized" (p. 75). He goes on to speak of the "boundless expanse of ruins" of purportedly established philosophical systems (*ein unermessliches Truemmerfeld demonstrierter Systeme*, p. 76).

11. F. C. S. Schiller, "*Must* Philosophers Disagree?" reprinted in his anthology of the same title (London, 1934). Schiller's paper was initially published in the Aristotelian Society's *Supplementary Volume* for 1933.

12. Among recent discussions, the infeasibility of proving results in philosophy is urged with lucidity and vigor by Frederick Waismann. See his essay "How I See Philosophy," in *Contemporary British Philosophy: Third Series*, ed. H. D. Lewis (London, 1958), pp. 447–90.

ground philosophical conflict in differences regarding the basic assumptions of presuppositions of workers in the field. Various moderns locate substantive disagreement in a divergence of views about standards of proof and criteria of sound argumentation—different ideas regarding the nature of probative rationality itself. In general, the contention is that philosophers have failed to agree because they have heretofore taken an incorrect approach to the foundations of reasoning in their field. They have used different, divergence-producing methods, postulates, assumptions, definitions, probative criteria, or the like—which is not surprising, since the basis (*archē*) of rational knowledge itself lies beyond rationalization. (Aristotle, *Anal. Post.*, 100a10)

(2) *Epistemological explanations* that attribute disagreement to different "logics" or different criteria of acceptability (different standards for "good reasons") or different inferential paradigms (e.g., S. C. Pepper's "root metaphor" theory).[13]

(3) *Psychological explanations* that ground philosophical disagreement in the differences of psychological make-up among diverse thinkers, perhaps in point of differences in temperament or personality (this is the line taken by William James[14] and F. S. C. Schiller, among others) or in point of more deeply and

---

13. Stephen C. Pepper, *World Hypotheses: A Study in Evidence* (Berkeley and Los Angeles, 1942).

14. William James characterized the differences at issue as ultimately temperamental in character. In his classic essay on "The Present Dilemma in Philosophy" he wrote:

The history of philosophy is to a great extent that of a certain clash of human temperaments. Undignified as such a treatment may seem to some of my colleagues, I shall have to take account of this clash and explain a good many of the divergencies of philosophers by it. Of whatever temperament a professional philosopher is, he tries, when philosophizing, to sink the fact of his temperament. Temperament is no conventionally recognized reason, so he urges impersonal reasons only for his conclusions. Yet his temperament really gives him a stronger bias than any of his more strictly objective premises. It loads the evidence for him one way or the other. ("The Present Dilemma in Philosophy," in J. J. McDermott, ed., *The Writings of William James* [Chicago and London, 1977], p. 363)

This stance was echoed by James's pragmatist congener F. C. S. Schiller, who saw philosophical differences as rooted in differences of *personality* and thus pictured philosophical commitment as the "legitimate offspring of an idiosyncracy":

Actually every philosophy was the offspring, the legitimate offspring, of an idiosyncracy, and the history and psychology of its author had far more to do with its development than *der Gang der Sache selbst*. . . . . The naive student insists on viewing the system from the outside, as a logical structure, and not as a psychological process extending over a lifetime. And he thereby throws away, or loses, the key to understanding. . . . the great types of philosophic diversity, the great problems on which philosophers disagree, are very persistent, and exemplify themselves from generation to generation in different philosophies. They carry on an inconclusive and unending warfare, precisely because neither side has hitherto penetrated to the psychological core of its opponents' creed. (Schiller, "Must Philosophers Disagree?" pp. 10–12)

The view of these pragmatists that the basis of philosophical diversity is ultimately rooted in differences in temperament and psychological disposition was also maintained (before their day) by Wilhelm Dilthey. See his *Gesammelte Schriften*, vol. VIII, pp. 9, 78, 81, et passim.

darkly subconscious, psychoanalytically grounded diversities (a line supported especially by M. Lazerowitz).[15]

(4) *Sociological explanations* such as the contention that the reward system of the discipline countervails against agreement. Substantial credit only accrues to one who launches out in a distinctive direction of his own; otherwise, a philosopher is regarded as a mere exegete or syncretist rather than "a real contributor to the subject who deserves to be taken seriously." Philosophers do not agree with one another because no professional benefits can accrue from doing so. Or again, they disagree because they do not understand one another since professional self-protection invites deliberate obscurity.[16]

(5) *Cultural explanations* that ground disagreement in differences in upbringing, educational exposure, experiential conditioning, or overall mode of life (as in Dilthey's *Lebensphilosophie*).

(6) *Eliminative explanations* that dismiss the entire discipline as illegitimate. The issues of philosophy are improper pseudoproblems. They are not real questions and do not admit of any sensible answers. Inquiry does not arrive at a stable consensus in this field because philosophical issues just do not admit of any significant resolution at all.

None of these explanations itself gets the matter quite right, though each carries a grain of truth and contributes something positive to a more complex whole. The ultimate ground of philosophical discord must be sought at a deeper level—in the structure of philosophical inquiry itself, in the nature of the conceptual issues with which the discipline deals.

If this is so, then it is not a "scandal of philosophy," but a *fact of life*—an intrinsic and inevitable aspect of philosophy as an intellectual discipline. Disagreement is simply a feature of "the logical structure of philosophical thought," to use R. G. Collingwood's phrase.[17] This, at any rate, is the view to whose defense the present book is dedicated.

There is a variant view of the pervasiveness of philosophical disagreement that will clearly *not* do the job, namely an explanation that pivots on the *inherent complexity and difficulty* of philosophical issues. One recent writer puts the matter as follows: "I would suggest that

---

15. See Morris Lazerowitz, *The Structure of Metaphysics* (London, 1955), and *Studies in Metaphilosophy* (London, 1964).

16. "The obscurity of many philosophers is notorious and indisputable; but it may be explained as a defence-reaction. They write obscurely in order to be respected by academic colleagues who dare not criticize what they are not sure they have understood, and in order not to be found out." Schiller, "*Must* Philosophers Disagree?" p. 14.

17. "No one philosopher's system can be acceptable to another without some modification. That each must reject the thoughts of others, regarded as selfcontained philosophies . . . is due not to causes in taste and temperament but to the logical structure of philosophical thought." R. G. Collingwood, *An Essay on Philosophical Method* (Oxford, 1933), p. 192.

there are . . . several factors which need to be considered, all of which are connected with the complexity and difficulty of metaphysical thinking . . . which seems to me to provide the basic key to ineradicable disagreements among metaphysicians."[18] Such an invocation of complexity, difficulty, intricacy, subtlety, sophistication, or the like, surely cannot provide an acceptable explanation. For it can hardly be contended that the problems that confront philosophers are inherently more complex than those that confront their colleagues in other fields—mathematics or physics or medicine or engineering—where agreement and consensus are very much the rule. That the problems of philosophy are more intractable than those of science—less amenable to generally acceptable resolution—is doubtlessly true. But that this is so because they inherently are more complex seems very doubtful indeed. (After all, philosophical reasonings are almost never even remotely as intricate as those one encounters in mathematics or natural sciences.) Some further, discipline-specific factor is going to have to be invoked to provide a viable account of the matter.

## 3. The Untenability of the Platonic Ideal

Philosophy began in hopefulness. The Platonic ideal of the philosopher as the possessor of true insight into the real nature of ultimate reality exerted its potent force throughout classical antiquity. We were assured that when the work of philosophy is properly done, we will be in possession of an intellectual vision of the real truth—apprehensible by and convincing to all suitably prepared minds. The conception of the philosopher as a wise guide to his less insightful fellows stood thus at the forefront—then and often since. He claimed to have "all the answers," and his claims were generally viewed with respect and often accepted.

In the brief preface to his *Tractatus Logico-Philosophicans*, (1921), Ludwig Wittgenstein wrote that "the *truth* of the thoughts that are here communicated seems to me unassailable and definitive. And so I believe myself to have found, in essentials, the final solution of the problems." Every generation sees the dawning of a hopeful new approach whose author claims, as Hans Reichenbach claimed in 1951, to have "found the tools to solve those problems that in earlier times have been the subject of guesswork only. To put it briefly: this book is written with the intention of showing that philosophy has proceeded from speculation to science."[19] Generation after generation, young hopefuls

---

18. Frank B. Dilley, "Why Do Philosophers Disagree?" *The Southern Journal of Philosophy*, 7 (1969): 217–28; see p. 225.
19. Hans Reichenbach, *The Rise of Scientific Philosophy* (Berkeley and Los Angeles, 1951), p. vii.

step forth in ever-renewed optimism of now at last turning philosophy "from speculation to science." With Ayer, they insist that "the traditional disputes of philosophers are, for the most part, as unwarranted as they are unfruitful. The correct way to end them is to establish beyond question what should be the purpose and method of a philosophical inquiry."[20] The problem is simply to give philosophy the right sort of turn—to introduce more of this or less of that.[21] The attitude that "heretofore they didn't have the right method [or "the right starting point"], but now that I'm here, . . ." seems never to run out of steam. It is the secret hope of every philosopher that his own work will prove decisive—that it will carry everyone along and put an end to "the strife of systems." With the coming of logical positivism, Schlick hopefully proclaimed: "I am convinced that we now find ourselves amidst an altogether definitive transformation in philosophy and that we are objectively justified in seeing the fruitless conflict among the systems as finished. I maintain that the present is already in possession of the methods that render every such conflict unnecessary; it is only necessary to employ them resolutely."[22] In every age philosophers write books with prefaces saying: "Heretofore all has been indecisive and chaotic. Heretofore philosophers have failed to recognize the significance of X. But now that I'm here to put matters in proper perspective and give X the central place that is its due, we can finally put a stop to all this confusion and see matters aright." But this optimistic expectation invariably and swiftly comes to grief. Philosophers glibly point out "the fundamental error" that vitiates the work of all their predecessors—only to fall victim themselves to a similar move on the part of their successors.

Not without pain do philosophers read the mockery of William James's complaint that

> In philosophy the absolute tendency has had everything its own way. The characteristic sort of happiness, indeed, which philosophies yield has mainly consisted in the conviction felt by each successive school or system that by it bottom-certitude had been attained. "Other philosophies are collections of opinions, mostly false; *my* philosophy gives standing-ground forever,"—who does not recognize in this the key-note of every system worthy of the name? A

---

20. A. J. Ayer, *Language, Truth, and Logic* (Oxford, 1936), p. 1.
21. Edmund Husserl, for example, thought at one stage that he could render philosophy into a rigorous science by orienting it away from "Weltanschauungs-philosophie", away from its traditional preoccupation with grandiose world views ("Philosophie als strenge Wissenschaft," *Logos* 1[1910–11]: 289–95). The idea that philosophers get confusing answers because they ask confused questions has always been prevalent.
22. Schlick, "The Turning Point in Philosophy," pp. 53–54.

system, to be a system at all, must come as a *closed* system, reversible in this or that detail, perchance, but in its esential features never![23]

Philosophy's ruling passion has always been the yearning for absoluteness. Virtually every philosopher has seen himself as a seeker for truth, engaged in a quest for the authentic answer to the problems of the field—that decisive and definitive resolution that is rationally compelling for all reasonable minds. For there can be no doubt about the transcendent significance of the issues at stake. The problems of chance vs. necessity, permanence vs. transiency, right vs. wrong, of accident and design, law and freedom, thing and person, and the like, set the stage for our understanding of our place in the world's scheme and our relations to our fellow creatures within it. Without some satisfactory answers to the whys and wherefores of existence, we are lost in a dark labyrinth of ignorance, baffled by incomprehension and confusion. We have deep questions and want, indeed *need*, to have answers to them.

Yet while the philosopher seeks hopefully for THE answer—and, often as not, persuades himself and his friends that he's found it—the cold, cruel light of subsequent history inexorably shows that he does no more than add yet one more theory to the rubble heap; yet one more doctrine that does not produce communal consensus but simply the assent of a few followers. We are constantly mocked by the paradox of "the conflict between the absolutistic demands of philosophy and the multiplicity of its historical versions, which have agitated philosophers for generations."[24] Philosophy never seems to find its foothold on Kant's "sure road of a science." It seems to be in the paradoxical position of a subject whose legitimacy is undermined by the course of its own history. We look back across a virtually limitless plain filled with the ruins of "scientifically" (*wissenschaftlich*) developed metaphysical doctrines and "demonstrated" systems that have come to grief.

Bertrand Russell has written:

As soon as definite knowledge concerning any subject becomes possible, this subject ceases to be called philosophy, and becomes a separate science. The whole study of the heavens, which now belongs to astronomy, was once included in philosophy; Newton's great work was called "the mathematical principles of natural philosophy." Similarly, the study of the human mind, which was a part of philosophy, has now been separated from philosophy and has become the science of psychology. . . . Those questions which are capable of definite answers are placed in the sciences, while those to which, at present,

---

23. William James, *The Will to Believe and Other Essays in Popular Philosophy* (New York and London, 1899), pp. 12–13.
24. See Lucien Braun, *Histoire de l'histoire de la philosophie* (Paris, 1973), pp. 287–88.

no definite answer can be given, remain to form the residue which is called philosophy.²⁵

Russell's perspective gives a hopeful augury for the future. In the eighteenth century "natural philosophy" (=physics) emigrated; in the nineteenth century "political philosophy" (=economics); in the twentieth century "mental philosophy" (=psychology) and "linguistic philosophy" (=semantics). Gradually perhaps epistemology, ethics, and the other branches of philosophy will join the ranks of "definite knowledge" until the philosopher has worked himself out of a job altogether because all his problems will have been resolved satisfactorily. We can look forward expectantly to the day when definitive "scientific" solutions to the residual problems of all these fields are in hand.

But that's just not the way it is. The definitive and final solution to philosophical problems seems ever beyond our grasp. The big philosophical issues that arise within natural science, political philosophy, psychology, and other fields—the range and limits of our knowledge about the nature of physical reality, of the basis of the authority of the state, the nature of human happiness, and the like—were put on the agenda in classical antiquity and are still with us, the subject of just as much disagreement now as then. The great Platonic issues of appearance and reality, nature and artifice, the good and the right, knowledge and mere opinion, language and thought are all still with us and give every indication of immortality. To all appearances, philosophical problems just do not admit of final, definitive solutions in the mode of a "definite knowledge" that can compel assent from all rational minds.

Yet somehow it has never really sunk in that agreement will *never* come about—that there is no consensus now and that there never will be. The practitioners of philosophy seem to have an insuperable reluctance to admit that diversity and discord are ineliminable facts inherent in the very nature of the enterprise. To all appearances, each system of philosophy excludes every other; each refutes the rest; none is conclusively demonstrable. History does not afford the picture of the amiable discussion portrayed in Raphael's "School of Athens"—itself the product of the receptively syncretistic spirit of those open-minded times. On the contrary, the opposition between the growth of historical diversity and the philosphers' demands for universal validity has steadily hardened.²⁶ Diversity and disagreement are, as best we can tell, the

---

25. Bertrand Russell, *The Problems of Philosophy* (Oxford, 1912), p. 240. Émile Boutroux similarly remarked earlier (in 1911) that once we have found a definitive resolution to a problem we thereby show, retrospectively as it were, that it was not a *philosophical* problem at all—it is the persistence of philosophical problems that marks them as such. Quoted in Franz Kröner, *Die Anarchie der philosophischen Systeme* (Leipzig, 1929; rpt. Graz, 1970), p. 185.

26. Compare Dilthey, *Gesammelte Schriften*, vol. VIII, p. 76.

eternal destiny of this discipline, lying not just in human foolishness and folly, but deep in the very nature of the subject.

## 4. Is Disagreement an Illusion?

To be sure, the very phenomenon that concerns us—philosophical disagreement—is sometimes denied. Philosophers, we are told, never really disagree, they just *misunderstand* one another. X never actually disagrees with Y, he *constructs* a convenient Y' and disagrees with *him*—a fiction of his own devising. Everything that every "real" philosopher says is perfectly correct—when philosophers apparently conflict, they are actually answering different questions. If we could penetrate deeply enough into the thought realm of a philosopher we would see that everything he actually intends to say is perfectly correct and acceptable all around. To understand is to accept: *tout comprendre c'est tout accepter*. If X really understood Y, then he would be bound to agree with him. Disagreement is always merely *seeming* disagreement, based on outright misinterpretation or on an overly literalistic interpretation that dwells narrow-mindedly on the letter rather than the spirit of a philosopher's declarations.[27] All those discordant-seeming philosophical systems are actually so many idiosyncratically different attempts to give expression to the same underlying truths. Like Leibnizian monads, each system is like a glass that mirrors the same reality differently—from varying "points of view."

Now admittedly, misunderstanding is frequent. Dr. Johnson sought to contradict Berkeley by kicking a stone; G. E. Moore endeavored to consternate the idealists by waving his hand; Russell "refuted" Bradley by examining the railway timetable; Carnap rebutted Heidegger by mocking the strange machinations he attributed to "nothing." None of these reactions emerges from a serious attempt at understanding the views so glibly rejected. There is no denying the plain fact that philosophers often misunderstand one another. But this is quite beside the point. For what is now at issue is not simply that philosophers often fail to understand each other, but the more far-reaching contention that they always misunderstand whenever they disagree. And this stronger contention is problematic in the extreme. For there is little evidence that philosophers "at bottom agree." Indeed, they are generally *motivated* in their work by

---

27. Schelling condemned such (mis)-interpreters as *Buchstabenphilosophen* or again as *Philosophen ohne Geist*. True philosophers, he insisted, are bound to agree in fundamentals. He sees the philosophical "disagreements" of different ages or epochs in typically Romantic fashion as no more mutually inimical than the different parts or phases of an organism. Diverse systems are like so many flowers on a plant, all nourished and supported by one common stem. For a compact account see Braun, *Histoire de l'histoire de la philosophie*, pp. 289–90.

# THE STRIFE OF SYSTEMS
## The Problem of Philosophical Diversity

disagreement with one another's views. It is precisely because they understand (or insofar as they understand) another position that they devise their own. Any realistic account of philosophical history must recognize that adequate understanding itself often provides the basis for disagreement. Disagreement is not something we can conveniently brush under the rug as the venial product of imperfect comprehension.[28] True enough, philosophers often argue in ways that indicate that they are reasoning at cross purposes. They appeal to very different sorts of probative considerations. But the conclusions to which their arguments supposedly lead are in clear conflict.

Yet another approach takes the line that disagreement roots not in illusion but in self-deception. There is in fact only one valid and authentic position in philosophy, and that is that all variant doctrines are based on delusion, self-deceit, and what Marxists deplore as "false consciousness"—a lazy failure to find our way through to the common underlying truth. But this line does not have much potential for acting like oil on troubled waters. For it does little good to insist that there is one single answer in circumstances where no one can convince anyone else of what that answer is. Where rival beliefs come into conflict, one cannot settle matters by extolling the virtues of "true believers."

It is sometimes maintained that philosophical disagreement is an optical illusion that results from looking at the issues from too great a distance. Only by regarding matters in their roughest outlines—only by abstracting from the mass of detail—can one maintain those oversimple generalities that put some philosophical doctrine into conflict with another. If this superficiality could be avoided and philosophical doctrines could be viewed in their concrete fullness, all discord would be eliminated and everything would fall into place in overarching systemic coherence.

But such a view fails to be true to the facts. It is infeasible to end the strife of competing doctrines by blending them all into a single superdoctrine. They are *designed* to conflict—Aristotle sets out to disagree with Plato, Kant's theory of causality is devised to refute Hume's. Philosophical positions are tailor-made to correct or contradict one another—not to supplement but to deny. To "reconcile" them is to emasculate them, to make them over into something they are not. For they are based on a deliberately conflicting vision of things, and there just is no way to "have it both ways." To deprive them of their contra-

---

28. Sometimes it is maintained that philosophers cannot disagree for a different sort of reason: not because they at bottom agree, but because they differ so radically that no real contact can be established between them at all. This view will be discussed at length in chapter five below.

riety is to deprive them of their substance—*omnis affirmatio est negatio*. The supersystem that synthesizes philosophical theses does so at the cost of their own life. Its peace is the peace of the grave. The more closely philosophical positions are examined the more clearly their differences emerge. The view that all philosophers at bottom agree is openminded to the point of emptymindedness. To strip philosophical positions of their contrariety is to strip them of their doctrinal bite, to impel them into bland vacuity. Disagreement is a very real—and important—fact of life in this domain, both in its pervasiveness and in its persistence.

## 5. A Fatal Flaw?

Still, this seems baffling. How can legitimacy be maintained in the face of the fact that intelligent and reasonable people addressing the same range of questions always propose such different and divergent answers? How can a discipline lay claim to serious attention when its practitioners have carried on the same old controversies and debates for over two millennia? Surely a field whose questions are *that* problematic rests on fallacious basis, manifesting its own illegitimacy through this very fact.

More than any other factors, the strife of systems and the unattainability of consensus explain the recurrence of deep disillusionment with the discipline. There is little doubt that the proliferation of conflicting philosophical systems is viewed by many with deep discontent and dissatisfaction. Omar Khayyam wrote:

> Myself when young did eagerly frequent
> Doctor and saint, and heard great argument
> About it and about; but evermore
> Came out by the same door as in I went.[29]

Profound disillusionment with the pluralistic situation of philosophy and dissatisfaction with the entire subject are ongoing facts of life that each succeeding generation rediscovers for itself. One recent discussion puts the matter well:

When it turns out that . . . [philosophical] principles are as plentiful as blackberries, nothing changes except the attitude of the rest of culture towards the philosophers. Since the time of Kant [but why not Thales?], it has become more and more apparent to nonphilosophers that a really professional philosopher can supply a philosophical foundation for just about anything. This is one reason why philosophers have, in the course of our century, become increasingly isolated from the rest of culture. Our proposals to guarantee this

---

29. *Rubaiyat*, trans. Fitzgerald.

# THE STRIFE OF SYSTEMS
*The Problem of Philosophical Diversity*

and to clarify that have come to strike our fellow intellectuals as merely comic.[30]

Many philosophers see the "strife of systems" as a matter of deep shame, of utter scandal—a situation of such seriousness that, if we cannot remedy it (and it seems we cannot), then we had best give up on philosophy altogether. One writer speaks quaintly of a *Philosophendämmerung*,[31] and it is a certainly true that a death wish runs like a recurrent leitmotiv throughout the history of philosophy. From the ancient Pyrrhorian Sceptics through modern empiricists (Hume), positivists (Comte and the Vienna Circle), pragmatists (Dewey and Rorty), and deconstructionists (Derrida), the dismantling or dissolution of philosophy is an ever-recurrent aspiration. Yet perhaps this is an unnecessarily pessimistic response to the situation—a natural reaction to the inevitable nonrealization of exaggerated expectations.

The theme of our discussion is the explanation of philosophical diversity, but its pivotal issue is whether philosophy survives as an enterprise of value once one recognizes that it will *never* be able to answer our questions in a way that compels communal consensus. For just below the surface runs the discomfiting fear that if we *did* acknowledge this indecisiveness, it would destroy the legitimacy of the discipline. After all, if diversity and disagreement are not transitory accidents but permanent and inescapable qualities, does this not annihilate the value of the enterprise? This, indeed, is the central problem of this book—is it possible at one and the same time to acknowledge the inability to achieve consensus as an ineliminable feature of philosophy and yet maintain its validity as an intellectual endeavor?

It is unquestionably tempting to dismiss the whole project as fraud and delusion—to respond in fox-and-grapes fashion to the disappointment of unrealized hopes! And yet, as will be argued, this is entirely the wrong reaction. The aim of this book is at once to explain the inevitable existence of philosophical diversity and to show that such diversity neither discredits the enterprise nor undermines its usefulness and validity. To see why this is so, and to come to terms with the idea that finding a definitive and universally compelling solution to its problems is simply *inappropriate* for philosophy, is to come to understand something deep and significant about this discipline—something that sets it apart from other domains of inquiry.

---

30. Richard Rorty, *Consequences of Pragmatism: Essays 1972–1980* (Minneapolis, 1982), p. 169. One defect of this account is that it portrays a permanent feature as a recent development. Also, it is a bit puzzling why we philosophers should care all that much about being taken seriously by "our fellow-intellectuals," considering our own profession's tendency to view *their* labors with some mixture of doubt and derision.

31. Kröner, *Die Anarchie*, p. 2.

# 2

# Philosophy and Paradox: The Pivotal Role of Aporetic Clusters

*1. The Task of Philosophy*

Philosophy has no *distinctive* subject matter. For *everything* is relevant to its concerns, its task being to provide a sort of *expositio mundi*, a traveler's guidebook to reality at large. The mission of philosophy is to ask, and to answer in a rational and disciplined way, all those great questions about life in this world that people wonder about in their reflective moments. In the first book of the *Metaphysics*, Aristotle tells us that "it is through wonder that men now begin and originally began to philosophize, wondering in the first place at obvious perplexities, and then by gradual progression raising questions about the greater matters too, e.g., about the origin of the universe" (982b10). Philosophy thus strives after that systematic integration of knowledge that the sciences initially promised but have never managed to deliver because of their increasing division of labor and never-ending pursuit of specialized detail. Dealing with being and value in general—with possibility, actuality, and worth—the concerns of philosophy are universal and all embracing; philosophy is too inclusive and all encompassing to have a delimited range of concern. Nor has it a *distinctive* method, for its procedures of inquiry and reasoning are too varied and diversified to give it an exclusive identity. What characterizes philosophy is its mission of grappling with the "big questions" regarding man, the world, and his place within its scheme of things, making use in this endeavor of whatever means come to hand.

Neither individually nor collectively do we humans begin our cognitive quest empty handed or with a *tabula rasa*. Be it as single individuals or as entire generations, we *always* begin with a diversified cognitive heritage, falling heir to that great mass of information and misinformation that is the "accumulated wisdom" of our predecessors—or those among them to whom we choose to listen.

But just what sort of things constitute "the data" of philosophy? They include:

(1) Common-sense beliefs, common knowledge, and what have been "the ordinary convictions of the plain man" since time immemorial;
(2) The facts (or purported facts) afforded by the science of the day; the views of well-informed "experts" and "authorities";
(3) The lessons we derive from our dealings with the world in everyday life;
(4) The received opinions that constitute the worldview of the day; views that accord with the "spirit of the times" and the ambient convictions of one's cultural context;
(5) Tradition, inherited lore, and ancestral wisdom (including religious tradition);
(6) The "teachings of history" as best we can discern them.

No plausible source of information about how matters stand in the world fails to bring grist to philosophy's mill. The whole range of the (purportedly) established "facts of experience" furnishes the extra-philosophical inputs for our philosophizing—the materials, as it were, for our philosophical reflections.

The "commonplaces" (*endoxa*) that lie at the root of philosophizing may well of course also include certain parochial commitments that represent not (purported) facts, but what is explicitly acknowledged as mere beliefs of the group—what "we Americans" or "we liberals" believe. These parochial commitments can be put aside for present purposes. It is not that they are unimportant—quite the reverse. But it lies deep in the nature of the philosophical enterprise that it should *endeavor* (at any rate) to "proceed with the limits of reason alone"—to try and to purport to address the issues by universally available means.

We neet not, of course, accept all these "givens" as certified facts that must be endorsed wholly and unqualifiedly. Every datum is defeasible—anything might in the final analysis have to be abandoned, whatever its source: science, common sense, common knowledge, the whole lot. Nothing is immune to criticism and possible rejection; everything is potentially at risk. One recent theorist writes: "No philosophical, or any other, theory can provide a view which violates common sense and remain logically consistent. For the truth of common sense is assumed by all theories. . . . This necessity to conform to common sense establishes a constraint upon the interpretations philosophical theories can offer."[1] Stuff and nonsense. The philosophical landscape is littered with theories that tread common sense underfoot. There are no sacred cows in philosophy—common sense least of all. As philosophy goes about its work of rendering our beliefs coherent, something to which we are deeply attached will have to give, and we can never say at the outset where the blow will or will not fall. Systemic considerations may in the end lead to difficulties at any point.

All the data should, however, be treated with consideration. They are all "plausible," exerting some degree of cognitive pressure and having some claim upon us. They may not constitute irrefutably established knowledge, but nevertheless they do have some degree of epistemic merit, and given our cognitive situation, it would be very convenient if they turned out to be true. The philosopher cannot simply turn his back on these data without further ado.

Still, these data are by no means unproblematic. The constraint they put upon us is not peremptory and absolute—they do not represent certainties to which we must cling at all costs. What we owe these data, in the final analysis, is *respect,* not *acceptance.* Even the plainest of "plain facts" can be questioned, as indeed some of them must be. For these data constitute a plethora of fact (or purported fact) so ample as to threaten to sink any ship that carries so heavy a cargo. The difficulty is—and always has been—that the data of philosophy afford an embarrassment of riches. They engender a situation of cognitive overcommitment within which inconsistencies arise. They are not only manifold and diversified but invariably yield discordant results. Taken altogether in their grand totality, the data are inconsistent.

The rigoristic standards of science mean that the data will always *underdetermine* theories in this domain. But in philosophy the matter is different. The relaxed standards of philosophical datahood mean that the data will *overdetermine* theories. The data with regard to philosophical issues are generally inconsistent; the plausible contentions that constitute "accumulated knowledge" contain such a diversity of claims and assertions that they become incompatible. As we set out to answer our questions about the world, we begin in a condition of cognitive dissonance in which the claims that call upon our allegiance are inconsistent with one another. Our initial belief inclinations engender cognitive overcommitment: the answers we deem it convenient and promising to give to some questions in some contexts conflict with those we embrace in others.

Just here lies the crux. Two injunctions regarding the mission of rational inquiry set the stage for philosophy:

1. John Kekes, *The Nature of Philosophy* (Totowa, 1980), p. 196.

# THE STRIFE OF SYSTEMS
*The Pivotal Role of Aporetic Clusters*

(1) Answer the questions! Say enough to satisfy your curiosity about things.
(2) Keep your commitments consistent! Don't say so much that some parts are in conflict with others.

There is a tension between these two imperatives—between the factors of commitment and consistency. We find ourselves in the discomfiting situation of cognitive conflict, with different tendencies of thought pulling in divergent directions. The task is to make sense of our discordant cognitive commitments and to impart coherence and unity to them insofar as possible.

Philosophizing always moves through two stages. At first there is a "presystemic" stage, where we confront a group of tentative commitments, all viewed as more or less acceptable, but which are collectively untenable because of their incompatibility. Subsequently there comes a "systematizing" phase of facing up to the inconsistency of the raw material represented by the "data." And this becomes a matter of eliminative pruning and tidying up where our commitments have been curtailed to the point where consistency has been restored.

Philosophy roots in contradiction—in conflicting beliefs. Philosophical problems arise in a cognitive setting, not wholly of our making, that is rationally intolerable; the overall set of contentions we deem plausible lead us into logical inconsistencies. The cognitive situation is always deeply problematic in its initial and presystemic state. The impetus to philosophizing arises when we step back to look critically at what we know (or think we know) about the world and try to make sense of it. We want an account that can optimally accommodate the data—recognizing that it cannot, in the end, accept them all at face value. Philosophy does not furnish us with new ground-level facts; it endeavors to systematize and coordinate the old into coherent structures by whose means we can meaningfully address our larger questions. The prime mover to philosophizing is the urge to systemic adequacy—to bringing consistency, coherence, and rational order into the framework of what we accept. Its work is a matter of the *disciplining* of our cognitive commitments in order to make overall sense of them. And so the demands of rational consistency come to the forefront.[2]

The key task of philosophy is thus to impart systemic order into the domain of relevant data; to render them coherent and, above all, consistent. One might, in fact, define philosophy as the rational systematization of our thoughts on basic issues—of the "first principles" of our understanding of the world and our place within it. We become in-

---

2. This view of philosophy accords closely with the spirit of Aristotle's description of the enterprise in the opening section of book beta of the *Metaphysics,* with its stress on the centrality of apories.

volved in philosophy in our endeavor to make systemic sense of the extraphilosophical "facts"—when we try to answer those big questions by systematizing what we think we know about the world, pushing our "knowledge" to its ultimate conclusions and combining items usually kept in convenient separation. Philosophy is the policeman of thought, as it were, the agent for maintaining law and order in our cognitive endeavors.

The question "Should we philosophize?" accordingly obtains a straightforward answer. The impetus to philosophy lies in our very nature as rational inquirers: as beings who have questions, demand answers, and want these answers to be cogent ones. Cognitive problems arise when matters fail to meet our expectations, and the expectation of rational order is the most fundamental of them all. The fact is simply that we *must* philosophize; it is a situational imperative for a rational creature.

## 2. Antinomies and Cognitive Overcommitment

An *aporetic cluster* is a family of philosophically relevant contentions of such a sort that:

(1) as far as the known facts go, there is good reason for accepting them all; the available evidence speaks well for each and every one of them, but
(2) taken together, they are mutually incompatible; the entire family is inconsistent.

Such a cluster is a set of otherwise cogenial propositions that, unfortunately, happen to be mutually inconsistent. They cannot all be *right*—their mutual inconsistency precludes that prospect; but they are all *plausible,* all seemingly acceptable and to some extent appealing.

In such a situation, we cannot simply appeal to "the evidence" to settle matters. The evidence has already spoken and has done pretty well all it can do at the time the difficulty arises. And so, while we know (thanks to the inconsistency) *that* something is wrong, we cannot say *what* has gone amiss.

We could, in theory, simply suspend judgment in such a case and abandon the entire cluster rather than try to localize the difficulty in order "to save what we can." But this is too great a price to pay. By taking this course of wholesale abandonment we lose too much by forgoing answers to too many questions. We would curtail our information not only beyond necessity but beyond comfort as well, seeing that we have some degree of commitment to all members of the cluster and do not want to abandon more of them than we have to.

Consider, for example, the following group of contentions, all of which were viewed favorably by Presocratic philosophers:

# THE STRIFE OF SYSTEMS
## *The Pivotal Role of Aporetic Clusters*

(1) Reality is one: real existence is homogeneous.
(2) Matter is real (self-subsistent).
(3) Form is real (self-subsistent).
(4) Matter and form are distinct (heterogeneous).

Here (2)–(4) insist that reality is heterogeneous, thereby contradicting (1). The whole of the group (1)–(4) accordingly represents an aporetic cluster that reflects a cognitive overcommitment. And this situation is typical: the problem context of philosophical issues standardly arises from a clash among individually tempting but collectively incompatible overcommitments. Philosophical issues standardly center about an aporetic cluster of this sort—a family of plausible theses that is assertorically *overdeterminative* in claiming so much as to lead into inconsistency.

In such cases, something obviously has to go. Whatever favorable disposition there may be toward these plausible theses, they cannot be maintained in the aggregate. We are confronted by a (many-sided) cognitive dilemma and must find one way out or another. In particular, we can proceed:

—To reason from (2)–(4) to the denial of (1),
—To reason from (1), (3), (4) to the denial of (2),
—To reason from (1), (2), (4) to the denial of (3),
—To reason from (1)–(3) to the denial of (4).

An apory gives rise to a group of valid arguments leading to mutually contradictory conclusions, yet each having only plausible theses as premises. It is clear in such cases *that* something has gone amiss, though it may well be quite unclear just where the source of difficulty lies.[3]

The resolution of such an aporetic situation obviously calls for abandoning one (or more) of the theses that generate the contradiction. Unexceptionable as these theses may seem, one or another of them has to be jettisoned. The restoration of consistency is an imperative. And the problem is that there are always alternative ways of doing this. Thus the ancient Greek philosophers confronted the following range of possibilities:

(1)–denial: Pluralism (Anaxagoras) or form/matter dualism (Aristotle)
(2)–denial: Idealism (the Eleatics, Plato)

---

3. This linkage of a philosophical thesis to an aporetic cluster in which it stands in correlative apposition to its rivals makes it plausible to hold the paradoxical-sounding view that "the argument for [and against] a philosophical statement is always a part of its meaning" (Henry W. Johnstone, Jr., *Philosophy and Argument* [State College, Pa., 1959], p. 32). For the position at issue only comes to be defined as such in the context of the counterpositions it proposes to exclude; in philosophy, Spinoza's dictum holds good: *omnis determinatio est negatio*.

(3)–denial: Materialism (atomism)
(4)–denial: Dual-aspect theory (Pythagoreanism)

We are plunged into such dilemmas by cognitive overcommitment. Too many jostling contentions strive for our approbation and acceptance. And this state of affairs is standard in philosophy—indeed the standard impetus to philosophical reflection.

Just here lay the basic methodological insight of Plato's Socrates. His almost invariable procedure is a process of "Socratic Questioning" to elicit a presystemic apory that sets the stage for philosophical reflection. Thus in the *Republic*, Thrasymachus was drawn into acknowledging the aporetic triad:

(1) What men call *justice* is simply what is decreed by the authorities as being in their own interest.
(2) It is right and proper (obligatory, in fact) that men should do what is just.
(3) Men have no obligation to do what is in the interest of the authorities—particularly since those authorities may well themselves be mistaken about what these interests really are.

The task of philosophy, as Socrates clearly saw, is to work our way out of the thicket of inconsistency in which we are entangled by our presystemic beliefs.

Again, consider the following trio, which affords a clear illustration of an aporetic cluster:

(1) Taking a human life is morally wrong.
(2) The fetal organism living in its mother's womb embodies a human life.
(3) Abortion (i.e., taking the life of a fetal organism living in the mother's womb) is not morally wrong.

These three theses clearly form an incompatible group. The demands of consistency call for sacrificing something. Three alternatives present themselves:

Deny (1): Regard human life as expendable in certain circumstances; abandon the idea that it is sacred.
Deny (2): Gerrymander the idea of human life so as to exclude fetuses (perhaps only those that have not yet attained a certain state of development).
Deny (3): Condemn abortion as morally wrong.

There just is no easy way out here. The issue is always one of a choice among alternatives where no matter how we turn, we find ourselves having to abandon something that seems to be plausible—some contention that, circumstances permitting, we would want to maintain and whose abandonment makes a great deal of difference.

Empiricists thus find themselves boxed into difficulty by the following quartet:

# THE STRIFE OF SYSTEMS
*The Pivotal Role of Aporetic Clusters*

(1) All knowledge is grounded in observation (the key thesis of empiricism).
(2) We can only observe matters of empirical fact.
(3) From empirical facts we cannot infer values; ergo, value claims cannot be grounded in observation (the fact/value divide).
(4) Knowledge about values is possible (value cognitivism).

There are four ways out of this box:

(1)–rejection: There is also nonobservational, namely, intuitive or instinctive, knowledge—specifically of matters of value (intuitionism; moral-sense theories).
(2)–rejection: Observation is not only sensory but also affective (sympathetic, empathetic). It thus can yield not only factual information but value information as well (value sensibility theories).
(3)–rejection: While we cannot *deduce* values from empirical facts, we can certainly *infer* them from the facts, by various sorts of plausible reasoning, such as "inference to the best explanation" (values-as-fact theories).
(4)–rejection: Knowledge about values is impossible (positivism, value scepticism).

Committed to (1), empiricist thinkers thus see themselves driven to choose between the three last alternatives in developing their positions in the theory of value.

Given an aporetic cluster, there is on the one hand substantial reason to maintain all of these collectively incompatible theses, because each "has much to be said for it." On the other hand, the bare demand of logical consistency requires the *elimination* of some of these theses. The whole of the cluster is too much—something has to give way.

And this is exactly where philosophy starts: not only in curiosity but also in wonder and confusion—in puzzlement and paradox engendered by the inconsistency of our cognitive inclinations.[4] Curiosity enters in because we have questions about the world to which we seek answers. But confusion also enters because the answers we incline to give are never totally compelling—nor even, as they stand, fully compatible with each other. In answering our various questions about the world and our place within it, we come to undertake commitments that engender overcommitment, so that we find ourselves plunged into perplexity.

Philosophical problems arise when discrepancies crop up as we conduct our cognitive business because there is discord and disharmony among the answers we give to relevant questions. Philosophical

---

4. Kant wrote: "Now *wonder* is a shock of the moral sense, arising from the incompatibility of a representation . . . with the principles already lying at its basis, which provokes a doubt as to whether we have rightly seen or rightly judged" (*Critique of Judgment*, sec. 62; trans. J. H. Bernard [London, 1892], p. 211). Our present construction of the term generalizes this overly narrow construction to include a conflict of "beliefs" as well as one of "representations."

problems root in conflict, dissonance, incoherence, incongruity. A prime mission of the enterprise is to smooth matters out. Philosophy tries to do for our cognitive landscape what the Roman road builders did for the physical landscape of their world: to develop smooth, straight ways that make it possible to get about more easily, with fewer checks and frustrations.

## 3. *How Apory Engenders a Diversity of Resolutions*

Whenever we are confronted with an aporetic cluster, a plurality of resolutions is always available. The contradiction that arises from over-commitment can be resolved by abandoning any of several contentions, so that alternative ways of averting inconsistency can always be found.

The theory of morality developed in Greek ethical thought affords a good example of such an aporetic situation. Greek moral thinking inclined to the view that the distinction between right and wrong:

(1) Does matter
(2) Is based on custom (*nomos*)
(3) Can only matter if grounded in the objective nature of things (*phusei*) rather than in mere custom

And so a cognitive dilemma arises. The inconsistency of these contentions led to the following resolutions:

Deny (1): Issues of right and wrong just don't matter—they are a mere question of power, of who gets to "lay down the law" (Thrasymachus).
Deny (2): The difference between right and wrong is not a matter of custom but resides in the nature of things (the Stoics).
Deny (3): The difference between right and wrong is only customary (*nomōi*) but does really matter all the same (Heraclitus).

We have here a paradigmatic example of an antinomy: a *theme* provided by an aporetic cluster of propositions, with *variations* set by the various ways of resolving this inconsistency. The problem of the philosopher is not one of inductive amplation but of systemic reduction—of a restoration of consistency. And philosophers fail to reach a uniform result because this objective can always be accomplished in very different ways.

The Greek theory of virtue affords another example:

(1) If virtue does not produce happiness/ pleasure, then it is pointless.
(2) Virtue is not pointless—indeed it is extremely important.
(3) Virtue does not always yield happiness.

Three ways of averting inconsistency are available here:

Deny (1): Maintain that virtue is worthwhile entirely in itself, even if it does not produce happiness/pleasure (Stoics, Epictetus, Marcus Aurelius).

Deny (2): Maintain that virtue is ultimately pointless and can be dismissed as a folly of the weak (nihilistic sophists, e.g., Plato's Thrasymachus).
Deny (3): Maintain that virtue is automatically bound to produce happiness (of itself always yields *real* pleasure)—so that the two are inseparably interconnected (Plato, the Epicureans).

Any and every resolution of a philosophical antinomy represents a distinct position, an intellectual abode that someone caught up in the underlying apory may choose to inhabit—though sometimes no one does so.

This line of consideration accounts for what is, on first view, a puzzling aspect of the field, namely, the prominence in the philosophical literature of counterargumentation and refutatory discussions. In mathematics no one troubles to argue that fourteen or thirty-two is *not* a satisfactory solution to a certain problem. This would be pointless because the number of incorrect answers is endless. But when there is only a limited number of viable alternative candidates in the running, negative and eliminative argumentation will obviously come to play a much more substantial part.

Another interesting instance of aporetic antinomy is afforded by the traditional "problem of evil," the stage for which was set by the following aporetic cluster:

(1) The world is created by God.
(2) The world contains evil.
(3) A creator is responsible for whatever defects his creation may contain.
(4) God is not responsible for the evils of the world.

As usual, there are various ways out, and the seventeenth-century thinkers who were exercised by this problem tried them all:

Deny (1): A strict naturalism (Hobbes).
Deny (2): Optimism (Leibniz) or a rejection of good/evil as an illusion based on imperfect understanding (Spinoza).
Deny (3): A theory that disconnects the chain of God's responsibility—e.g., via man's free will (Descartes).
Deny (4): Not an available option at the time.

As this example shows, aporetic clusters can establish connections between seemingly disparate theories—between, say, the reality of evil, per (2), and the origination of the world, per (1). They can reflect the linkage between distances with very different concerns. That is why systematization is so important in philosophy—because the way we *do* answer some questions will have limiting repercussions for the way we *can* answer others.

Again, consider the following aporetic cluster, which sets the stage for controversy about freedom of the will:

(1) All human acts are causally determined.
(2) Men can and do make free acts of choice.
(3) A genuinely free act cannot be causally determined (for if it is so determined then the act is not free by virtue of this very fact).

These three theses represent an inconsistent triad in which consistency can be restored by any of three distinct approaches:

Deny (1): "Voluntarism"—the exemption of free acts of the will from causal determination (Descartes).
Deny (2): "Determinism" of the will by causal constraints (Spinoza).
Deny (3): "Compatibilism" of free action and causal determination—for example, via a theory that distinguishes between inner and outer causal determination and sees the former sort of determination as compatible with freedom (Leibniz).

As such examples show, any particular way out of an aporetic cluster is bound to be simply *one way among others*. The single most crucial fact about an aporetic cluster is that there will always be a variety of distinct ways of averting the inconsistency into which it plunges us.

Aporetic difficulties sometimes vanish. If we drop our allegiance to the contentions of the cluster, they simply evaporate. Changes in science, in culture, or simply in fashion, for example, engender changes in those extraphilosophical beliefs in which philosophical problems take root. (Those domestic difficulties of Presocratic element theory no longer agitate us today.) But no matter where we take our stand and regardless of just what our overall commitments are, the pressures that cause conflict through cognitive overcommitment are inexorable in philosophy. Those philosophical issues that probe deeply into the extraphilosophical bases of philosophical concern always yield an unfailing harvest of problems.

The difficulty arises from a set of conflicting commitments that nevertheless seem "inescapable"—whose rejection seems at first sight not to be a real option at all. As an example, the theory of knowledge of the ancient Greeks revolved about the following quartet of collectively incompatible contentions:

(1) We do have some knowledge about the world.
(2) Whatever knowledge we have about the world must come via the senses (i.e., ultimately roots in what the senses deliver).
(3) There is no genuine knowledge (*episteme*) without certainty.
(4) The senses do not yield certainty.

A positive inclination toward these theses—a tendency to see them each as plausible and (presumptively) acceptable—sets the stage for philosophical conflict. A (limited) variety of exits from the inconsistency is available:

Deny (1): Maintain that we cannot have authentic knowledge about the world (the Pyrrhonian Sceptics).
Deny (2): Maintain that genuine knowledge about the world can come from reason alone (Pythagoreans, Plato).
Deny (3): Maintain that adequate knowledge need not be based on the certain but can be based on the plausible—*to pithanon* (the Academic Sceptics).
Deny (4): Maintain that the senses do yield certainty in some cases—those that result in the so-called "cataleptic" perceptions (the Stoics).

Faced with that aporetic cluster, we must make up our minds to decide between these alternatives.

Again, consider the following inconsistent quartet:

(1) We do have some knowledge about the world.
(2) Whatever knowledge we have about the world must come via the senses.
(3) Sensory experience only informs us as to how things appear, not about their (extraexperiential) reality.
(4) Genuine knowledge must relate to the (extraexperiential) reality of things.

Note here that if we reject either (1) or (2), we not only break out of the present apory but resolve the preceding one as well. Where apories are interlocked, we can resolve them systematically, *en bloc*, by suitably arranging our rejections.

If we have firm confidence in our reasonings, then it follows by the inferential principle of *modus tollens* that whenever a belief is rejected, one must also call into question some of the various (collectively compelling) reasons on whose basis this belief had been adopted. For example, if one rejects free will, then one must also reject one of the following (presumptive) intial reasons for espousing freedom of the will: "People are usually responsible for their acts," "People are only morally responsible for those acts that are done freely." The rejection of an accepted thesis at once turns the family of reasons for its adoption into an aporetic cluster. Apory, once present, tends to spread like wildfire through any rational system.

## 4. Antinomies Structure the Issues

It lies in the logical nature of things that there are always several distinct exits from inconsistency. Whenever we confront an antinomy, no matter which particular resolution we ourselves may favor, and no matter how firmly we persuade ourselves of its merits, the fact remains that there will also be other ways of dealing with the inconsistency. As far as abstract rationality is concerned, distinct alternative resolutions always remain open—resolutions leading to contrary and inconsistent results. An aporetic cluster is thus an invitation to conflict: its resolution always yields one or another of a coordinated group of mutually discordant doctrines (positions, teachings, *doxa*). The cluster accordingly sets the stage for divergent "schools of thought" and provides the bone of contention for an ongoing controversy among them. A family of inconsistent theses spans a "doctrinal space" that encompasses a variety of interrelated albeit incompatible positions.

An interesting illustration from the domain of epistemology is afforded by the so-called "Münchhausen trilemma," based on the following aporetic cluster:[5]

(1) We do sometimes have rational beliefs.
(2) To have a rational belief we must have good reasons that warrant its acceptance.
(3) A good reason for a rationally held belief must itself be (pre)warranted—it cannot afford a good reason for something if we do not have in hand a good reason for accepting it itself.
(4) A good reason for a belief must be less problematic than the belief itself.
(5) We do not obtain a good reason if the regress of warranting reasons is nonterminating—that is, goes on *ad infinitum*.

Overall we have an inconsistent group here. Theses (1)–(4) leave open only the prospect of an infinite (nonterminating) regress, which (5) rules out; while (1)–(3) plus (5) leave open only the prospect of a cyclic regress, which (4) rules out.

As long as we both reject scepticism by adopting (1) and reject irrationalism by adopting (2), it follows that there are only three exits from this aporetic inconsistency:

(3)–rejection: It is not necessary for a good reason to be prewarranted, because certain beliefs can be postwarranted; warrant can be reciprocal and cyclic (coherentism).
(4)–rejection: A belief need not be granted to something *less* problematic, for some beliefs can be self-granted; they can be self-evidentiated, so that this regress of reasons can terminate in a self-evident basis (foundationalism).
(5)–rejection: We simply accept the prospect of a infinite regress, insisting that this does not block justification since it need never be completed; it is simply a matter of going on as long as one needs to (regress-acceptance).

An interesting web of epistemological theories can be spun out through the relatively simple exercise of working one's way out of the aporetic inconsistency of the preceding cluster.

Their grounding in aporetic situations endows philosophical controversies with a certain definitiveness of structure. The various ways of resolving a cognitive dilemma present a finitely diversified structure of interrelated situations—a manageably modest inventory of possibili-

---

5. On this trilemma see Hans Albert, *Traktat über Kritische Vernunft* (Tübingen, 1968),

ties. Though positions on an issue will differ, they will neither vary without limit nor run off into rationally unmanageable variety. The issues are such that the alternative positions group themselves into a natural structure that endows the problem area with an organic unity. They map out a family of (finitely few) alternatives that span the entire spectrum of possibilities for exiting from inconsistency. Any possible position on the issue is thus bound to be a variant of one or another of a manageable (indeed generally very small) list of alternatives.[6] And the history of philosophy is generally sufficiently fertile and diversified that all the alternatives—all possible permutations and combinations for problem resolution—are in fact tried out somewhere along the line.

Philosophical positions are not discrete and separate units that stand in splendid isolation. They are articulated and developed in reciprocal interaction. But their natural mode of interaction is *not* by way of mutual supportiveness. (How could it be, given the mutual exclusiveness of conflicting doctrines?) Rather, competition and controversy prevail.

It follows that the prospect of pluralism is a necessary feature of philosophy—rooted deep in the aporetic nature of the discipline. Insofar as philosophical doctrines resolve aporetic difficulties, every position must of necessity have its rivals that disagree with it in fundamental respects. Aporetic situations just do not allow for the idea of a "common denominator" thesis that is retained by *all* of the rival theories. There are simply no "basis-invariant" positions in philosophy—doctrines that hold good no matter which approach we may choose to adopt. Any aporetic thesis can be sacrificed in the interests of achieving consistency—and in general it eventuates that all possibilities are actually tried. All of the permutations and combinations for resolving inconsistency find their adherents: all changes are rung—all of the variable elements get varied. The search of the ancient Stoics and Epicureans (Hippias) for a "natural" belief system based on what is common to different groups (espousing different doctrines, customs, moralities, religions) is of no avail because no single element remains unaffected as one moves across the range of variation. Given that rival "schools" resolve an aporetic cluster in different ways, the area of agreement between them, though always there, is bound to be too narrow to prevent conflict. The problem structure arises from the cognitive *overdetermination* of inconsistency, but whatever resolution is arrived at is simply *underdetermined* by the shared, mutually agreed commitments.

---

6. This general position that philosophical problems involve antinomic situations from which there are only finitely many exits (which, in general, the historical course of philosophical development actually indicates) is foreshadowed in the deliberations of Wilhelm Dilthey. See *Gesammelte Schriften*, vol. VIII (Stuttgart and Göttingen, 1960), p. 138.

From time to time philosophers propose a revived variant of the old Stoic program of ethics as they search for points of universal agreement among the moral codes of different cultures and societies.[7] But the decisive shortcoming of such an approach is that in philosophy there just are no such universal invariants. By the time philosophers have come and gone, everything that can be varied has been varied; by and large, there are no invariant points of universal consensus.

## 5. Can Different Schools Debate the Same Issues?

The gregarious nature of philosophizing deserves comment. In antiquity we have Aristotelians and Platonists, Stoics and Epicureans; in the middle ages, Thomists and Augustinians and Scotists; in modern times rationalists and empiricists, and so on. That philosophers fall into such doctrinal brotherhoods as "schools of thought" and "traditions" is readily accounted for by the present theory. Since philosophical doctrines issue from the untying of aporetic knots, only a limited number of solutions can be available. Philosophers thus fall into groupings that are united by an affinity of doctrinal fundamentals. It seems a fact of life that there are always different schools of thought on "the same" issues—different approaches to resolving "the same" problems.

This view meets opposition from several quarters.

Some theorists have argued that conflicting philosophical doctrines represent positions that are *incommensurable*. The various positions simply cannot be compared in point of agreement or contradiction: no common measure of comparison can be established between them. Along such lines, Henry Johnstone has maintained that no philosopher can even "imagine what it would be like for his opponent's position to be true" because each is deeply committed to the view that his *own* position "includes all the relevant evidence and therefore no statement adducing evidence against it is possible."[8] Accordingly, philosophical counterargumentation can do no more than proceed *ad hominem* with a view to internal self-consistency, limiting its attention to strictly domestic conflicts by showing that one of a philosopher's affirmations does not accord with some other. But there are no external relations at all: X just *cannot* come into contact with Y's position. A philosopher does not even address (let alone refute) the substantive position of a rival system: there simply is no way of establishing a meaningful relation between different philosophical doctrines.

Philosophers, it is maintained, share no issues in common. They hold incomparable views; they cannot disagree and cannot agree

---

7. Cf. Hector-Neri Castaneda, *On Philosophical Method* (Bloomington, Ind., 1980), p. 20, and "Thinking and the Structure of the World," *Philosophia,* 4 (1974): 3–40.

8. Johnstone, *Philosophy and Argument,* p. 1.

either. Different doctrinal positions are totally disconnected; different theories are incommensurable—they cannot be expressed in common units of thought. Philosophical theses arise (only) in context and cannot be lifted out of their contexts without a vitiating distortion. There are and can be no universal, all-inclusive contexts: all contexts are situation specific. Each thinker must be understood on his own ground, in his own terms—there is no question of thinkers *sharing* theses or theories, no position-detached basis for a comparison or contrast. There is no prospect of disagreement (or even agreement) across the divide of different theory commitments, because there is no real communication at all across these borders.

Philosophical positions thus occupy separate and disconnected thought worlds. Adherents of different theories literally "talk a different language," so that when one makes an assertion and the other a denial it is not the same thing that is at issue. In the English-language orbit, the prime spokesman for such a view was R. G. Collingwood:

> If there were a permanent problem P, we could ask "What did Kant, or Leibniz, or Berkeley, think about P?" and if that question could be answered, we could then go on to ask "was Kant, or Leibniz, or Berkeley, right in what he thought about P?" But what is thought to be a permanent problem P is really a number of transitory problems, $P_1, P_2, P_3, \ldots$ whose individual peculiarities are blurred by the historical myopia of the person who lumps them together under the name P.[9]

A cognate line of attack is favored not so much by philosophers as by intellectual historians. They sometimes maintain that every thinker stands wholly by himself, that every teaching is ultimately distinctive, every thesis so impregnated with the characteristic thought style of its proponent that no two thinkers ever discuss "the same" proposition. As one writer puts it:

> As soon as we see that there *is* no determinate idea to which various writers contributed, but only a variety of statements made with the [same] words by a variety of different agents with a variety of intentions, then what we are seeing is equally that there *is* no history of the idea [as such] to be written, but only a history necessarily focused on the various agents who used the idea, and/or their varying situations and intentions of using it.[10]

Conditions of context of place, time, education, interest, and so on, separate thinkers from one another by insuperable barriers. J. H. Randall, Jr., has formulated this view with stark directness:

---

9. R. G. Collingwood, *An Autobiography* (Oxford, 1939), p. 69.
10. Quentin Skinner, "Meaning and Understanding in the History of Ideas," *History and Theory* 8 (1969): 3–53 (see p. 38).

The problems of one age are ultimately irrelevant to those of another.... What bond is there between the aims and problems of an Athenian poet, like Plato; a Roman senator, like Cicero; a medieval monk, like Thomas Aquinas; a seventeenth-century scientific pioneer, like Descartes; a German professor, like Kant.... The philosophical problems of one age, like the cultural conflicts out of which they arise, are irrelevant to those of another.[11]

There are thus no "schools of thought" that share commitments and no "perennial issues" treated by successive generations of thinkers. Different thinkers occupy different thought worlds. The thought of every thinker stands apart in splendid isolation—discordant philosophers can never be said to contribute to the same ongoing issues: "There are simply no perennial problems in philosophy: there are only individual answers to individual questions, with as many different answers as there are questions, and as many different questions as there are questioners."[12] Philosophers of different persuasions are separated from each other by one unbridgeable gulf.

But this position exaggerates mutual incomprehension to the point of absurdity. Of course, incomprehension *can* and sometimes *does* occur across reaches of time or space when major conceptual dissimilarities are involved. But this is not generally the case.

Philosophy is a matter of publicly accessible inquiry. If he did not view his doctrines and their supporting arguments as public objects—communally available and appraisable—a thinker would be doing something very different from *philosophizing*. To lock each philosopher into the cell of some purported thought world of his own is to lose sight of the very point of the venture as a cognitive enterprise.

Philosophical positions evolve dialectically, in mutual interaction. Some are *designed* to substantiate others—or, more commonly, to disagree with them. Aristotle is deliberately seeking to criticize and replace Plato's theory of ideas; Kant is explicitly endeavoring to refute Hume's theory of causality. Different philosophies do not spring up in aseptic isolation; they evolve as rival solutions to shared problems. In general, philosophers fail to agree not because they do not *understand* each other's views but because they *reject* them.

Determinists and indeterminists do not disagree about what causality is, but about its pervasiveness. Sceptics and cognitivists need not disagree about the idea of knowledge, but about its availability. Statists and libertarians do not clash about what desires individuals have, but about the weight these should carry in public policy deliberations. All such controversies flow from agreement about the range or jurisdiction

---

11. John H. Randall, Jr., *The Career of Philosophy*, vol. I (New York, 1962), p. 7.
12. Ibid., p. 50.

or desirability of certain factors with respect to whose *nature* there is little or no disagreement.

Two polarities, the public (generally shared) and the domestic (idiosyncratic), characterize the work of every philosophical thinker. The *philosophical* historian tends to be interested more in the public side—the person-transcending issues that facilitate relationships. The *intellectual* historian dwells on the person-characteristic commitments that define uniqueness. Both sides are there to be reckoned with. But the former is crucial because our prime interest is in those philosophical issues as such. These always lie in the public domain.

## 6. Consequences of Incommensurability

Rigid adherence to the incommensurability line simply destroys the subject at one blow. If the views of philosophers cannot be brought into touch—if they are indeed incommensurable, with each theory enclosed in a world of its own—then they become altogether inaccessible. We all become windowless Leibnizian monads, but bereft of the benefit of a preestablished harmony.

A dogmatic insistence on mutual incomprehension is unprofitable and self-defeating. Contact of some sort is essential. If we cannot in principle relate the thought of distinct philosophers by way of identity and similarity, if we cannot say that here they are discussing the same (or similar) questions and that there they are maintaining the same (or similar) answers, then we shall be in bad straits indeed. For if we cannot relate $X$'s thought to $Y$'s, we cannot relate it to *ours* either.

Without the prospect of shared problems and theses considered in common by diverse thinkers, all hope of interpretation and comprehension is lost. Every thinker—indeed each one of us—would be locked within the impenetrable walls of his own thought world. If $X$ and $Y$ cannot in principle maintain the same (or similar) things, then any prospect of communication is destroyed. If one philosophical mind cannot connect with another, then *we* ourselves cannot connect with anyone either. In the absence of relatability to other times and places, the historian himself would be faced with issues that he is incapable of dealing with. If Kant cannot address Hume's problems, neither can Collingwood. If philosophers cannot speak to one another, they cannot speak to us. Any prospect of communal discussion of shared issues is at once destroyed. Deprived of the life-sustaining element of communication, the subject dies a swift death.

Philosophical positions make sense only insofar as they *deny* something: *omnis affirmatio est negatio*. They claim truth by denying falsity; they assert saving insight by attacking dangerous error. To this end there must be contrasts. If one denies the very existence of rival positions and views them as literally *inconceivable*, there can be nothing substantial to one's own view. Where there is no enemy to attack, there is no position to defend. To see rival positions as incomprehensible is to demean and devalue one's own; if opposing positions were conceptually ungraspable in their very natures, there would be little use in taking a stance that precludes them. Where no possible rival position has the least plausibility, advocacy as the solely "available" position becomes rather pointless.

To deny the possibility of philosophical disagreement by claiming incommensurability is from the very outset to abandon the enterprise as a meaningful cognitive project. Only if disagreement is possible does the enterprise make sense.

To be sure, we can never flatly say without the further ado of closer scrutiny that X and Y mean the same thing by the same words or even by the same sentences. What they mean and what they maintain may well need careful examination and analysis. It should be recognized that when we maintain relations of similarity and difference between the assertions of X and Y, we are bound to do so on the basis of comparisons made *within the framework of our own constructions and interpretations of their positions*. Our own thought about their thought is (and in the very nature of things has to be) the *tertium quid* that affords the vehicle of relation. Relations of doctrinal sameness or similarity are not transparent facts but represent *theories of ours* that must emerge from our studies and analyses. But there is—and can be—no reason of principle that we cannot cogently maintain that here and there X and Y are discussing substantially the same issue and maintaining dis- or concordant positions regarding substantially the same questions. In sum, the prospects of accord and discord cannot be dismissed on the basis of general principles.

Philosophers concern themselves with ongoing problems—problems that agitate not only their contemporaries but often as not their predecessors and successors as well.[13] And the basic problems with which philosophers deal are public property, so that the inquiries have

---

13. John Kekes has put the salient point well:

[To understand him properly, we must] go to the heart of a philosopher's concern: to the problem he wanted to solve. Plato, Hobbes, Locke, and Popper are all concerned with the nature and justification of political authority. The stoics, Spinoza, Kant, and Sartre, all have the analysis and understanding of individual freedom at the core of their ethical thought. Aristotle, John Stuart Mill, Frege, and Quine share the problem of logical necessity. Their motivation, vocabulary, rhetoric, and situations differ. But the problems are the same. . . . In sum, historical understanding makes it possible to see the point of a philosopher's work by acquainting us with the problem the philosopher was trying to solve. Without this understanding one cannot judge the work, because one cannot judge whether the problem he was trying to solve has been solved. (*The Nature of Philosophy*, p. 171)

to be conducted in the public domain by means of generally available resources.

One recent writer tells us that we should "understand philosophy not as a set of problems but as a set of texts."[14] One thus functions as a philosopher not by virtue of the problems one considers, but by virtue of those to whom one looks for inspiration, support, or opposition in the course of one's discussions. But this purported innovation sounds more radical than it is. For the question of *why one addresses those particular texts* at once arises. If one does so because of considerations of style or of historical source material, then one isn't doing philosophy. But if one does so in order to appraise the ideas and critically examine issues, questions, contentions, then one is indeed being a philosopher. But then, of course, one's concern is not with the texts as such, but with the problems being considered in those texts. The relevance of the texts becomes established through their substantive preoccupations, and so the problems become central again.

Philosophers are would-be problem solvers, and at some level of generality they always share their problems with others. The issue now before us itself affords a clear illustration of this circumstance. Our central problem—the persistence of philosophical conflict and diversity—has been on the agenda of philosophy since the time of the Sceptics of classical antiquity and is a perennial problem that has agitated philosophical thinkers in every age.

A further argument against the prospect of real disagreements also deserves consideration: the thesis that adequate understanding requires actual agreement. If this were indeed so, then no thesis or contention could be common property of thinkers who do not have common views. For to disagree meaningfully with someone's contention, we would first have to grasp it adequately—and such grasp, since by hypothesis it requires agreement, automatically precludes disagreement. No clash regarding "the same" theses is possible, because disagreement of its very nature carries meaning differences in its wake.

If understanding presupposes agreement, then the "Principle of Charity" that people by and large use their language appropriately—a harmless idea we must espouse if we are ever to understand the users of a different language—would at once commit us to a "Principle of Truth." To understand and interpret the views of another philosopher we would now have to suppose that he is by and large correct. To understand Plotinus we would have to accept his whole system in

---

14. Stanley Cavell, *The Claim of Reason* (Oxford, 1979), p. 3–4.

matters of theory and doctrine—hypostheses, emanations, categorical machinery, and all—lock, stock, and barrel. Only if we were prepared to grant the fundamental correctness of his position would we be able to understand a philosopher.

But this is clearly a far-fetched and untenable idea. The understanding-requires-agreement doctrine presents a Hobson's choice between unacceptable alternatives. For it confronts us with the unpleasant dilemma that, as regards the declarations of Parmenides or Berkeley or any philosopher whose views we may deem unpalatable, we have the choice between acceptance as essentially correct on the one hand and dismissal as wholly unintelligible on the other. Dissent from (for example) the Eleatic denial of the reality of change would mean that our view of this theoretical stance *must be* that it is at bottom incomprehensible gibberish and *cannot be* that it is simply wrong. Fortunately, however, this is not how the matter actually stands.

The doctrine that understanding requires agreement is gravely defective in giving insufficient weight to the crucial distinction between what we take to be true *on our own account* and what we take to be *their* view of the truth. The latter can, of course, differ radically from the former. And it can do so without becoming unintelligible as long as we are able to adopt a "suspension of disbelief" and form some view of how others transact their cognitive business in ways suppositionally different from our own.

Hypothetical reasoning and belief-contravening assumptions are the key here. There is indeed a link between intelligibility and truth, but "the truth" at issue has to be neither the *real* truth nor what one inclines to accept as such, but a merely *putative* truth to which one can perfectly well have recourse in the hypothetical mode of supposition, assumption, or conjecture. One can unproblematically address the question of what the situation would be if certain of one's beliefs were wrong. Hence one can come to understand the position of someone who maintains that this is so. Understanding does *not* presuppose agreement.

Accordingly, there is no good reason to think that bilaterally contemplated theses never provide bones of contention across doctrinal divides—that different schools of thinkers cannot disagree about mutually controverted issues. And this is most fortunate. The ultimate consequence of the incommensurability doctrine would be to block any prospect of that dialetical development which is in fact the lifeblood of philosophy. For the philosopher is impelled to his labors precisely because he is aware that tempting and plausible alternatives beckon that might lead the unwary into error.

## 7. Why Not Simply "Live with Inconsistency"? The Imperative of Cognitive Rationality

The maintenance of consistency is philosophy's key task. But is consistency itself not simply a mere ornament—a dispensable luxury? Rousseau wrote to one of his correspondents that he did not wish to be shackled by narrow-minded consistency—he proposed to write whatever seemed sensible at the time. In a writer of *belles lettres*, this sort of flexibility may seem refreshingly open minded. But such an approach is not available to a philosopher. Philosophy in its very nature is a venture of systematization and rationalization—of rendering matters intelligible and accessible to rational thought. Its concern is for the rational order and systemic coherence of our commitments. The commitment to rational coherence is a part of what makes philosophy the enterprise it is.

But why not embrace contradiction in a spirit of openness rather than flee from it?[15] The answer is that rejecting inconsistencies is the only road to comprehension and understanding. To the extent that we do not resolve an issue in one definite way to the exclusion of others, we do not resolve it at all. Only a coherent, alternative-excluding resolution is a resolution at all.

Philosophy, after all, is a matter of inquiry. It roots in human curiosity—in the "fact of life" that we have questions and want rationally satisfying answers to them. We are not content with information about which answers people would like to have (psychologism) nor with information about what sort of answers are available (possibility mongering). What we want is rational guidance to which answers to *adopt*—to which contentions are correct or at any rate plausible.

The presence of an inconsistency in the formulation of a position is self-destructive. To respond "yes *and* no" is in effect to offer no response at all; answers that don't *exclude* manage to achieve no useful *inclusions* either. Only where some possibilities are denied is anything asserted: "All determination is negation" (*omnis affirmatio est negatio*). A logically inconsistent theory of something is thereby self-defeating—not just because it "affirms an impossibility" but because it provides no information on the matter at issue. An inconsistent "position" is no position at all. Keeping on good terms with *all* the possibilities requires that we embrace none. But the point of having a position at all is to have some answer to some question or other. If we fail to resolve the problem in favor of one possibility or another, we do not have an

---

15. Paul K. Feyerabend embraces the concurrent use of mutually inconsistent scientific theories within a "theoretical pluralism." See his essay "Problems of Empiricism" in *Beyond the Edge of Certainty*, ed. R. G. Colodny (Englewood Cliffs, N. J., 1965), pp. 145–260 (see esp. pp. 164–68).

answer. To whatever extent we fail to resolve the issue in favor of one alternative or another, we also fail to arrive at some answer to the question. Ubiquitous yea-saying is socially accommodating but informatively unhelpful. (Compare Aristotle's defense of the law of noncontradiction in Book Gamma of the *Metaphysics*.) As long as and to the extent that inconsistencies remain, our goal of securing information on achieving understanding is defeated.

To Alice's insistence that "one can't believe impossible things," the White Queen replied: "I daresay you haven't had much practice. When I was your age, I always did it for half-an-hour a day. Why, sometimes I've believed as many as six impossible things before breakfast." But even with practice, the task is uncomfortable and unsatisfying. A profound commitment to the demands of rationality is a thread that runs through the whole fabric of our philosophizing; the dedication to consistency is the most fundamental imperative of reason. "Keep your commitments consistent" is philosophy's ruling injunction. We don't want just answers, but reasoned answers, defensible answers that square with what we are going to say in other contexts and on other occasions. And this means that we must go back and clean out the Augean stable of our cognitive inclinations.

To endorse a discordant diversity of claims is in the end not to enrich one's position through a particularly generous policy of acceptance, but to impoverish it. To refuse to discriminate is to go empty handed, without answers to our questions. It is not a particularly elevated way of doing philosophy—but a way of not doing philosophy at all, of evading the problems of the field, of abandoning the traditional project of philosophy as rational problem solving. We are compelled to systematize our knowledge into a coherent whole by regimenting what we accept in the light of principles of rationality. Philosophizing is a work of reason; we want our problem resolutions to be backed by good reasons—reasons whose bearing will doubtless not be absolute and definitive but will, at any rate, be as compelling as is possible in the circumstances. Reasoning and argumentation are thus the lifeblood of philosophy.

But why pursue rationalizing philosophy at all—why accept this discipline as an arena of appropriate human endeavor? The answer is that it is an integral and indispensable component of the wider project of rational inquiry regarding humanly important issues.

This, to be sure, simply pushes the question back: Why pursue reasoned inquiry? And this question splits into two components.

The first component is: Why pursue *inquiry*? The answer is twofold: (1) knowledge is its own reward, and (2) knowledge is the indispensable instrument for the more efficient and effective realization of other goals. We pursue philosophical inquiry because we must; because those great intellectual issues of man and his place in the world's scheme, of the true and the beautiful and the good, of right and wrong, freedom and necessity, causality and determinism, and so on, matter greatly to us—to all of us some of the time and to some of us all of the time. We pursue philosophical inquiry because it is important.

The second component is: Why *reasoned* inquiry? The answer is that man is the *rational* animal. We do not want just answers, but answers that can satisfy. And reason affords our standard of satisfactoriness in this regard. Philosophizing is not *just* a matter of being consistent; nihilism would enable us to achieve this end—if we affirm nothing our affirmations cannot be inconsistent. What we want is not consistency alone but consistent answers to our questions, answers that we can in good conscience regard as appropriate—as tenable and defensible. The "big questions" of philosophy—of man's place in nature, of free will, of duty and obligation, knowledge and ignorance, and so on—concern us too closely to permit us to feel comfortable about their being totally ignored. To be sure, here as elsewhere there is room for division of labor. They may be ignored by all people some of the time and by some people all of the time. But it is not fitting and indeed not possible that they should be ignored by all people all of the time. Even when we do not address them ourselves, we can and do take rational comfort in the realization that they are being addressed by somebody—that some people care enough about these issues to make a valiant struggle to get to the bottom of things. In sum, "we"—the community of rational beings—want to be able to claim knowledge, or at any rate "warranted assertibility," with respect to our contentions regarding the nature of things. Philosophy is an inquiry that seeks to resolve problems arising from the incoherence of our extraphilosophical commitments; to abandon philosophy is to rest content with incoherence. One can, of course, cease to do philosophy (and this is what sceptics of all persuasions have always wanted). But if one is going to philosophize at all, one has no alternative but to proceed by means of arguments and reasoning, by recourse to the traditional vehicles of human rationality.

Yet is consistency itself something altogether fixed and definite? What of the fact that there are different systems of logic? Does this not open up the prospect that one man's inconsistency is another's compatibility? Perhaps so. But at this point we must be maximally strict. If even the most fastidious logician discerns problems, we must undertake to worry. In the interests of philosophical adequacy, the propositions we juxtapose must, like Caesar's wife, be above suspicion; if there is *any* plausible basis for charges of incompatability in *any* viable sytem of logic, then adjustments are in order.

The case might be different if philosophy were a strictly practical endeavor instead of a theoretical one. In engineering, for example, or even science, concurrent use of inconsistent theories might be justified on pragmatic grounds—it might effectively guide our interactions with nature.[16] In philosophy this consolation is denied us. The aims of the enterprise are fundamentally cognitive, not practical, and from the cognitive standpoint, if we do not have a coherent doctrine, we have nothing.

As this line of thought indicates, two basic goals set the scene for philosophical inquiry: (1) the urge to know, to have answers to questions, to enhance our cognitive resources, to enlarge our information, to extend the range of accepted theses, to fill up an intellectual vacuum. But this in the nature of the case—given the character of its "data"—inexorably leads to overcommitment, to informational overcrowding, to inconsistency. And now comes (2), the urge to rationality: to have a coherent theory, to keep our commitments consistent. The first impetus is expansive and ampliative, the second contractive and eliminative. Having surveyed the terrain, we want to create an orderly map of it. We want to be able to find our way about by means of the instrumentality of critical intelligence.

But is not the impetus to knowledge (or at any rate to reasonable answers) simply a pointless exercise—an irrational fetish? May not our quest for "information" prove to be something we cannot ultimately justify?

For one thing, even if the "quest for knowledge" were mere fetishism, it still remains irrevocably ours; it is something to which we, being the sort of creatures we are, stand immovably committed. We are so constituted that we cannot be fully content where we do not feel "at home," and we cannot comfortably feel at home in a world we do not understand.

The need for understanding itself has a deeper rationale. For there is good reason indeed why we humans pursue knowledge—it is our evolutionary destiny. We are neither numerous and prolific (like the ant and the termite), nor tough and aggressive (like the shark). Weak and vulnerable creatures, we are constrained to make our evolutionary way in the world by the use of brainpower. It is by knowledge and not by hard shells or sharp claws or keen teeth that we have carved out our niche in evolution's scheme of things. In situations of cognitive frustration and bafflement we cannot function effectively as the sort of crea-

---

16. To be sure, this reflects a particular cognitive-value orientation. The matter would stand differently if, adopting Karl Marx's *Theses on Feuerbach* (1845), one took the line: "Philosophers have only *interpreted* the world in various ways, but the real task is to *change* it."

# THE STRIFE OF SYSTEMS
*The Pivotal Role of Aporetic Clusters*

ture nature has compelled us to become. Confusion and ignorance—even in such "remote" and "abstruse" matters as those with which philosophy deals—yield dismay and discomfort. The old saying is perfectly true: philosophy bakes no bread. But it is no less true that man does not live by bread alone. The physical side of his nature that requires man to eat, drink, and be merry is just one side of his nature. Man is also *homo quaerens:* he needs nourishment for his mind as urgently as he needs nourishment for his body. We seek knowledge not only because we wish but because we must.

Philosophy is a venture in cognitive orientation and rationalization. It tries to bring rational order, system, and intelligibility to the complex diversity of our cognitive affairs. Reason and argument are the philosopher's organizing instruments; relations of implication and incompatibility provide the contours of his cognitive way. He strives for orderly arrangements in the cognitive sphere that will enable him to find his way about effectively and efficiently. Philosophy is indeed a venture in theorizing, but one whose rationale is eminently practical. A rational animal that has to make its evolutionary way in the world by its wits has a deep, practical need for speculative reason.

To be sure, although we ever strive to *improve* our knowledge, we never manage to *perfect* it. The stage for our present deliberations is itself set by the aporetic cluster represented by the inconsistent triad:

(1) Reality is cognizable. Rational inquiry can in principle depict reality adequately in a coherent system of true propositions. (Thought can characterize reality in a way that achieves *adequatio ad rem*—not fully, to be sure, but at any rate in essentials.)
(2) Reality is consistent; it constitutes a logically "coherent whole."
(3) Our thought about reality eventually runs into inconsistency as we work out its ramifications and implications more fully.

Denial of (3) is a problematic option here; to all appearances, it represents a "fact of life" regarding the situation in philosophy. And (2)–denial also has its problems. Perhaps it is conceivable (just barely) that reality will, whenever offered a choice of alternatives, decide to "have it both ways"—a prospect envisaged by thinkers from the days of Nicholas of Cusa to contemporary neo-Hegelians. This is a theory that we might, in the end, feel compelled to adopt, but clearly only as a last resort, "at the end of the day"—and thus effectively never. In philosophy we want to make sense of things. A theory that says they can't be made sense of coherently and consistently may well have various merits, but it is decisively flawed. Its defect is not just a lack of rationality but one of utility as well. For an inconsistent theory fails to realize the aim of the enterprise—it provides no information.

And so, (1)–denial is the most readily available option. We must concede that philosophical thought can at best make a rough approximation of adequacy—that reality refuses cognitive domestication, so that our best cognitive efforts represent a valiant but never totally satisfactory attempt to "get it right." Such a position is not a radical scepticism that denies the availability of any and all useful information about reality, but a mitigated scepticism that insists that thought at best affords rough information about reality—not by way of definitive and indefeasible *episteme*, but by way of a "rational belief" that is inevitably imperfect and defective (its rationality notwithstanding). An element of tentativeness should always attach to our philosophical theories—we can never rest assured that they will not need to be revamped and shored up by our successors (quite to the contrary, we can count on it!).

It must be emphasized that the impetus to rationality does not in any way prejudge the *outcome* of our theorizing. It may well turn out in the end that the "principle of noncontradiction" does not hold of the world. Reality as best we can discern it may possibly turn out to be inconsistent. But what is presently at issue is not reality as such, but our *account* of it. Regardless of the world's consistency, our *theory* of it must be consistent if it is to merit serious consideration. And here it is important to recognize that thought need not necessarily share the features of its object. A sober study of inebriation is perfectly possible, as is a coherent account of the opinions of an incoherent thinker. Insistence on consistency in our own theoretical commitments does not prejudge the nature of the *objects* of our theorizing. A coherent theory of an inconsistent reality can perfectly well be contemplated.[17] A methodological insistence on consistency does not prejudge the ontological nature of the real; what is at issue is simply the consistency and coherence of our own deliberations. We might in the end be driven by rational considerations to accept the conclusion that reality is inconsistent, but this is no reason for not striving for consistency in our theory of reality.

In philosophizing we thus become entrapped in a dilemma. On the one hand we seek comprehensiveness—answers to all our questions, doctrines capable of providing for the rational accommodation of all our beliefs. On the other we stand committed to coherence in all its

---

17. But can there indeed be a consistent theory about an inconsistent reality—can one prevent the inconsistency of an object of discussion from spilling over into an inconsistency in our assertions about it? The answer is affirmative, but its details must be wrapped in the intricacies of semantical theory. See Nicholas Rescher and Robert Brandom, *The Logic of Inconsistency* (Oxford, 1979).

guises (consistency, compatibility, and proper rational order). Yet problems and difficulties arise from the clash between these two desiderata. We want to have our cake and eat it too—and, naturally enough, find it difficult to bring this off. The long and short of it is that philosophy is inextricably linked to paradox and antinomy because we inhabit a difficult and complex world, not of our making, that simply is not capable of total cognitive domestication. The dark shadow on inconsistency always obscures some parts of the scene that our philosophical inquiries seek to illuminate. The successes of the enterprise will never eliminate this shadow; at best, they manage to push it further into the background.[18]

---

18. What justifies speaking not just of *apory* but of *antinomy* as well? It lies in the logical nature of things that any aporetic cluster $C$ can be partitioned (in several ways) into two components $C_1$ and $C_2$ in such a way that there is a proposition $P$ such that $C_1$ entails $P$ and $C_2$ entails not-$P$. Aporetic clusters always engender associated antinomies.

# 3
# Why Antinomies Pervade Philosophy

## 1. Philosophical Concepts Are Fact Coordinated

Philosophy is a purposive enterprise; we pursue it in order to understand the world we live in and our place within it. Yet its task is not only to resolve our questions regarding "the big issues" of man and his works in the natural and social context, but to accomplish this in a rationally satisfactory way that enables us to extricate ourselves from the puzzlement of inconsistency which surrounds us on every side in this domain. Let us consider why this inconsistency prevails.

The central concepts of philosophy ("mind," "matter," "causality," "nature," "reality," "truth," "knowledge," "personhood," "good," "right," "justice," etc.) are, in the first instance, at any rate, borrowed from elsewhere; they are importations from everyday life and from science that function in the cognitive manipulation of experience. This is clear from even a superficial look at the various subdivisions or branches of philosophy, all of which have for their objects of consideration various domains of extraphilosophical concern—metaphilosophy alone excepted. The concerns of "human experience," in all of the manifold senses of this conception, constitute the prephilosophical basis of our philosophizing. The complex spiders' webs spun in philosophical theorizing are always attached to "the real world" of everyday life and its scientific refinements. The second-order discipline of metaphilosophy aside, the issues of philosophy revolve about extraphilosophical concerns. Philosophy addresses itself to problems that arise out of our attempts to make sense of the world as our experience presents it to us.

Accordingly, the basic concepts in whose terms we transact our experiential business are in general infused by our understanding of the world's facts. These concepts are not designed for use in "every possible world" but for use in *this* world. Their purport and their applicability relate to how matters *do* stand and not to how they *might* stand. In consequence, they rest on a basis of empirical fact or supposition. They are concerned with our understanding of the world's actual arrangements. And so their component elements are related by contingent rather than necessary linkages.

Consider an example. The philosopher's idea of *personal identity*, as ethics and philosophy of mind and philosophical anthropology deal with it, represents a conception of the sameness of persons that is a fusion of *bodily continuity* (tracking someone physically through space and time) on the one hand, and on the other *continuity of personality* (stability of memory, habits, tastes, dispositions, skills, etc.). *Persons* are to be construed as coordinated joinings of *mind* and *body*; the very concept envisages a coordination of mental and bodily activities. And so our conception of personal identity is both multicriterial and fact coordinated: it is *multicriterial* because a plurality of in-principle separable components enters in (bodily continuity and continuity of personality) and it is *fact coordinated* because these theoretically separable but conceptually joined criterial factors are held together in an integrative fusion by facts or purported facts (i.e., by a view as to how the world actually works). We find that bodily continuity and continuity of personality generally and standardly *go together*, and we proceed to build this finding into the defining conditions of the concept.

Or again, consider the epistemologically pivotal conception of *belief*. Note that two theoretically separable factors are once more at issue: verbalizations and overt behavior. Both talk and action must come together before it is unproblematically appropriate to speak of "believing." Data about his verbalizations alone cannot suffice to establish that X believes a bomb is to go off in the room shortly if his every overt action belies this (under suitable circumstances—e.g., he has no wish to commit suicide). But behavioral data alone won't clinch the matter either; evasion behavior is no more than puzzling if there is sufficient evidence that X's every statement and verbal response indicates that he is nowise under the impression that a bomb is present. All of the appropriate facts, verbal and behavioral alike, must be suitably supportive before we can unproblematically speak of X's belief. Otherwise we could not appropriately say purely and simply that X believes that P is the case but would have to use some suitably complex circumlocution: "X, while not accepting that P is the case, acts as though it were," or "X, though insisting that P is the case, certainly does not behave in an accordant fashion," or the like. The fact is that, ordinarily and standardly, actions and espousals go together, and our conception of "belief" is based on the presupposition that they do so. At the base of this concept there again lies *an empirically underwritten coordination* that places the various critical factors in a symbiotic, mutually supportive relationship. Such concepts represent the fusion of ideas whose integrity as a viable unit is underwritten by the world's facts. And if one separates what is in principle separable, the concepts disintegrate, leaving us faced with a variety of discordant analogies—some pulling this way and some that.

Philosophically germane concepts such as "personal identity" or "belief" are fact-coordinated in that they involve the coming together of theoretically separate factors in a union that is the product not of conceptual necessity but of empirical fact. They represent composites of elements whose concurrence rests on a strictly empirical foundation. They are thus based on factual presuppositions that reflect a view of how things go in the world, effectively conjoining factors that are in principle separable from one another. These factual presuppositions spare us from having to decide which of the several factors involved is ultimately determinative or decisive.[1] The body of fact $F$ prevents the concept $C$ from splitting into $C_1$ and $C_2$, averting any need for making up our minds whether it is $C_1$ or $C_2$ whose claims on $C$ have priority, and thus enabling C to function as it actually does.

And this situation obtains with respect to all of those fundamental concepts that philosophy takes from ordinary life and from science. They are, one and all, fact coordinated: they rest on an empirical foundation and turn on facts, or *putative* facts, about the workings of things. They are devised to handle the data of our experience within this world—their viability and applicability rest on presupposing certain actual or purported facts about how matters stand in the world. If things went differently in these respects, it is not just that the concept would not find application (as with the concept of a *unicorn* in this world). Rather, it is that the concept would collapse as a viable unit because a presupposition or precondition of its applicability would be destroyed. If people popped up by spontaneous generation, the existing concept of a *parent* would not just become inapplicable but would simply fall apart as a conceptual instrument—though we could perhaps still salvage something from the wreckage by defining a "parent" as someone who takes responsibility for raising an infant (in which case it could turn out that a child has different parents at different junctures).

Unfortunately, our experiential concepts—both those of everyday

---

1. The key fact is not that nature takes a benign view of our *a priori* preconceptions, but that our concepts develop within the processes of nature in ways shaped by processes of rational (rather than Darwinian) selection.

life and those of science—do not unproblematically allow the inner theoretical precision that philosophizing requires. This is clear enough with respect to the ordinary language of everyday life. As one recent writer puts it: "Ordinary language simply has not got the 'hardness,' the logical solidity, to cut axioms in it. It needs something like a metallic substance to carve a conceptually rigorous deductive system out of it such as Euclid's. But common speech? If you begin to draw inferences, it soon begins to go 'soft' and fluffs up somewhere. You might as well carve cameos on a cheese soufflé."[2]

The language of science serves philosophy no better. For though it is vastly harder and more precise, it gains that precision by impregnating its terms with substantive suppositions regarding the ways of the world. Throughout, our experiental concepts (quotidian and scientific alike) are fact reflecting. They fit the world as they do, not because of *their* character alone, but because of *the world's* character as well (be it actual or supposed). To explicate their meanings we must enter ever more deeply into material assumptions about the world's ways. As philosophical sceptics have always stressed, our terms and concepts are the products of man-made definitions and conventions and are attuned only imperfectly to the world's realities because they are based on ideas about the nature of things that are themselves unfinished, incomplete, and subject to change. Even as truth outdoes fiction, so nature outdoes thought; the complex details of its phenomena are always too varied and diverse to fit our concepts neatly. Those concepts are bound to them, but never quite tightly enough.

The indissoluble linkage between philosophically germane concepts and the world's facts has profound implications. It means that the issues of philosophy grow out of and revolve about concepts that are developed for purposes *alien* to the philosopher's own technical and theoretical concerns—concepts that deeply reflect the practical concerns of everyday life and of the natural science that enhances its resources of prediction and control over nature. The conceptions about which our philosophical deliberations center—concepts like mind, matter, causality, knowledge, truth, personhood, justice, and so on—generally have a practical and factual basis. Taken from the language of common life and/or science, they are part of the coinage we use to transact the business of our experienced world and reflect our ideas about its operations.

In our dealings with experience, our use of language never reaches the plane of theoretical perfection. We do all that is necessary by way

---

2. Waismann, "How I See Philosophy," rpt. in A. J. Ayer, ed., *Logical Positivism* (Glencoe, 1959), pp. 345–80 (see p. 366).

of exactness and precision to reach our interlocutors—but only what is necessary. Much essential work is done by the context, by the informal ground rules of understanding, by recourse to "the things everybody knows." When we say of a student that he is intelligent or of a regime that it is just, we don't mean that the one is *all that* intelligent or that the other is *all that* just—that they embody these qualities unqualifiedly, which is to say perfectly—but that the student is intelligent as students go and the regime just as regimes go. Someone who does not know how matters generally go is not going to understand us aright.

Just here is where difficulties arise. For any concept that emerges from practical concerns is bound to be blurred, indefinite, inchoate—at least in some degree. This is simply a fact of rational economy of evolutionary processes—be they biological or cognitive. Our practical resources are subject to practical limitations; they are in general no more exact, accurate, precise, general, and so on, than the situation requires. By their very nature, such concepts never achieve—never even aspire to achieve—more sharpness and determinateness than necessary for the limited purposes at hand. They are perfectly content to rest on a factual basis—to let practical and contingent effectiveness stand in place of theoretical precision and abstract adequacy. They never attain more precision than is needed "to get by" and are thus inherently resistant to that all-out precision that philosophizing demands.[3]

## 2. Clarificatory Pressures and Antinomy

The philosopher has scientific aspirations. From antiquity on, it has been a key mission of philosophy to elucidate and systematize such concepts as knowledge and justice. While the run-of-the-mill cases pose no problems, puzzle-cases will always arise here. Take some examples from Plato: How can *life* give way to *death* (*Phaedo*)? How can an inferior sector of mind—passion—frequently prevail against a superior—reason (*Republic*, bk. IV)? For theoretical adequacy we need the definitions and explications and explanations that alone can enable us to understand clearly various philosophically central conceptions. The philosopher is engaged in the Socratic quest for absolute universality and precision in the delineation of concepts. His aim is to articulate what is so always and everywhere, flatly and unqualifiedly, absolutely and unconditionally. He must of necessity push matters beyond the

---

3. In an interesting recent book, Peter Unger sees the indecisiveness of (some) philosophical disputes to root in a "semantical indeterminacy" arising because terms like "know" or "can" are equivocal in admitting of construction in line with different standards (*Philosophical Relativity* [Minneapolis, 1984], see esp. p. 15). But he neither analyzes why this phenomenon arises nor inquires into how far it extends. "No doubt, there will be relativity in more than the four areas we explored [above]" (p. 115).

level of contingent efficacy to that of theoretical adequacy. Unfortunately, the experience-geared concepts that lie ready-made at our disposal—and in whose terms the issues arise—are not fitted for this work. The conceptual scheme we devise for the handling of experience inevitably proves too crude and imprecise for our cognitive requirements. Our world-bound concepts underdetermine the specifications of theory to a point where our theorizing—once freed from practical constraints—wanders off into inconsistency.

Paradox lurks in the process of trying to impart *abstractly theoretical* clarity to concepts that are based upon *concretely factual* presuppositions. To "clarify" and "systematize" such concepts with theoretical precision is to press them beyond the cohesive capacity of those mere (but very real and crucial) facts that, by uniting their logico-semantically disparate elements into a cohesive unit, make them viable as the concepts they are. Unhappy consequences ensue if we actually persist in exerting such pressure.

Consider *personal identity* once more. As noted above, this concept unites a plurality of factors, among which bodily continuity and sameness of personality are the outstanding members. These factors are held together in a harmonious symbiosis by *factual* considerations. Suppose that, in the interests of theoretical tidyness, we decide to put our eggs into one basket and take one of these factors as essential, the other as accidental—adopting (say) bodily continuity as essential and relegating continuity of personality to the background. Immediately some clever doubter will propose a counterexample that cannot but make us uncomfortable with this choice. By concocting some fiendish electronic rewiring of their brain circuitry, he will have Messrs. A and B exchange personality characteristics: knowledge and memory, performatory capabilities, talents, inclinations, dispositions, and so on. Nothing is to remain the same except the lumps of material stuff. And now our objector protests: "According to your thesis that bodily continuity is the determining criterion, we should have no hesitancy in the case I have sketched about saying that we are dealing with the same person both before and after the personality exchange. But we unquestionably do feel a very considerable hesitancy. So this analysis that sees bodily continuity as decisive cannot be right." There is much justification in this complaint. So let us try the opposite resolution, taking sameness of personality as determinative and bodily continuity as incidental. At once, another objector comes along with a different counterexample. He has one person so changed that all of his personality characteristics become altered over the course of a month or two, while someone else's personality becomes virtually indistinguishable from what his used to be. And then he protests: "According to your thesis that similarity of personality is the key criterion of personal identity, we should not hesitate in such a case to say that the personality-altered individual is no longer the same person; it would become plausible to claim that the subject individual has metamorphosed into his simulacrum. But we would actually hesitate very much about saying this sort of thing. So bodily continuity is in fact the decisive criterion."

The implications of the two cases are diametrically opposed. Our endeavor to "clarify" the issues by determining the priorities has been checkmated. We are clearly reluctant to live with the consequences of either resolution, because a ruling in favor of the primacy of any one of the fact-coordinated plurality of criteria does violence to our intuitive assessment of those cases in which the other criteria come into prominence. Plausible arguments can be constructed for and against each resolution. Alternatives spread out before us—each plausible and inviting, yet mutually exclusive. In short, we fall into an antinomy.

A precisely analogous situation obtains with respect to the other concepts we have had in view. Take belief: if behavior is to be pivotal we hypothesize someone whose thoughts point in the wrong direction; if the mentalistic aspect is to be crucial we hypothesize someone whose actions—including verbal actions—go systematically in the counter-indicated way.

Again, consider moral credit. Ordinarily, consequences and intentions go hand in hand. But that, of course, is to some extent a piece of contingent good fortune. The impetus of theoretical adequacy demands clarification. But if *consequences* are to be determinative, we hypothesize someone whose intentions are evil but always frustrated; if *intentions* are to be pivotal, we hypothesize someone whose good intentions systematically engender utter havoc. Trouble ensues either way.

The general pattern is by now clear enough. We begin with a unitary concept $C$ that functions as it does because a body of fact $F$ fuses its theoretically disparate components $C_1$ and $C_2$ into a viable unit. The clarificatory pressures that lead us to "purify" this concept by freeing it from its dependence on $F$ lead the concept to fission into $C_1$ and $C_2$. Now certain $C$-invoking truths will hold for $C_1$ and fail for $C_2$, while others will be in the reverse condition. Where we began with truth $T_1(C)$ & $-T_2(C)$ we now face the aporetic cluster:

$$T_1(C) \ \& \ -T_2(C)$$
$$C = C_1$$
$$C = C_2$$
$$T_2(C_1)$$
$$-T_1(C_2)$$

And so no matter which way we turn in the explication of C—be it to $C_1$ or to $C_2$—we are unable to salvage something we want to maintain with respect to C.

All of our standard fact-coordinated concepts exhibit an inner tension due to the plurality of their constituent components. They function in relation to a plurality of potentially discordant paradigms, each bearing differentially on "the meaning" of the concept, but with the divergences rendered harmless by a benign alignment of the world's facts. In clarifying such concepts, philosophical theorists endeavor to set tidy fences around their boundaries of application—to fix their operations not just generally and normally, but in a "theoretically adequate" way. Philosophy chafes against the restrictions of the real—it sees its domain as that of the possible in contradistinction to the empirical sciences' narrower concerns with the merely actual.[4] Philosophy thus strives to eliminate the element of contingency and to free our concepts from their usual dependence on "mere facts." The goal is "rational understanding"—and this goal cannot be introduced until theoretical exactitude is achieved. But when we abstract from the facts in the interest of theoretical precision, trouble inevitably follows.[5]

## 3. Fact-Coordinated Concepts Resist Purely Theoretical Clarification

Throughout the realm of the fact-coordinated concepts in whose terms we accommodate our experience, it is not the abstract logic of things but the facts (or purported facts) of the world that set the standards of application. The viability of our concepts hinges critically upon (a particular view of) the facts. If we abolish this factual framework by supposition in order to clarify the issues, we thereby destroy the undergirding basis of our concepts. Our experientially based concepts are inherently geared to the contingent structure of things—saved as viably integrated units only by the factual arrangements of the world in which they evolved. They lack that abstract integrity of purely conceptual coherence that alone could enable them to survive in the harsh light of theoretical precision.

When the very meaning of a concept presupposes certain facts, its explication and analysis clearly cannot—in the nature of the case—proceed entirely on the purely theoretical level, proceeding in aseptic abstraction from all empirical matters of fact. The clarification of such issues cannot be pressed beyond the cohesive force of the factual considerations that hold the operative concepts together and underwrite their applicability.

---

4. *Philosophia est scientia possibilium, quatenus esse possunt,* Christian Wolff aptly wrote (*Philosophia rationalis sive logica* [Frankfurt, 1728; 2nd ed., 1732], p. 13 [sec. 29]).

5. These themes were elaborated in my *Hypothetical Reasoning* (Amsterdam, 1964).

Our contentions in everyday discourse and in science are always *provisoed* assertions. They are always made subject to implicit qualifications and reservations that relate to what happens *usually* or *ordinarily* or *standardly* or *other things being equal* (*ceteris paribus*) or *under suitable circumstances* or *in ideal conditions*, and so on. We say things like "men can reason" or "birds can fly," realizing full well that the claim as it stands is inaccurate and imprecise, which is to say incorrect—that qualifications will be needed that our interlocutors will (in principle) recognize. In ordinary life we get by with saying how things run *normally* or *as a rule*. In science we state how they go *ideally*, in *standard* conditions. In both cases we are prepared to abstract from murky complexities or problematic possibilities to inject the element of saving artificiality, of a conceptual gerrymandering of troublesome detail. In neither case can what we say be taken rigorously and unrestrictedly, without any "benefit of qualification."

Attuned in the first instance to the requirements of practical purpose and the needs of efficient communication, our philosophically basic concepts are geared to factual presuppositions—above all, factual assumptions as to how things normally and ordinarily run in the world. We have it (say) that *normally P*, and that *normally P → Q*. These contentions are perfectly warranted in the ordinary course of things. And so Q clearly also obtains in the normal and ordinary course of things. But *theoretically* it might happen (in *extra*ordinary cases) that not-Q, despite these conditions. When we assume that this extraordinary circumstance obtains, then we at once have an aporetic cluster on our hands (viz., P, P → Q, and not-Q). Something has gone seriously wrong, and we are driven to a choice between theses to which we are profoundly attached (seeing that they represent how things in fact standardly go).

The philosopher's quest for generality and precision has the inevitable consequence that he will sooner or later drive our concepts against the scalpel's edge of hypothetical cases that require sharp-edged and clearly articulated resolutions to bring their contentual anatomy to view.[6] This methodological recourse to puzzle-cases is readily illustrated by the example of those extravagant hypotheses that give a kind of science fiction aspect to much of the philosophizing of this tradition. In the writings of philosophers one meets intelligent robots and strikingly gifted men from outer space, dream/waking interchanges, brain transplants and personality transmigrations, amnesia

---

6. Thus Bertrand Russell wrote: "A logical or philosophical theory may be tested by its capacity for dealing with puzzles, and it is a wholesome plan . . . to stock the mind with as many puzzles as possible, since these serve much the same purpose as is served by experiments in physical science" ("On Denoting," *Mind*, 14 [1905]: 484–85).

victims with perfect recall of other people's pasts, uncannily accurate precognition, and the like. We are asked to contemplate personality exchanges between people (which one is the "same person"?) and robots whose communicative behavior is remarkably anthropoidal (are they "conscious" or not?). The idea is that such extraordinary cases are conducive to precision and that the workings of our concepts are most clearly illuminated by seeing how they comport themselves in the context of extravagant suppositions.

In the interests of theoretical clarity and generality and precision (that is to say, in the interests of his systematizing concerns), the philosopher presses against the restraints imposed by the fact-coordinated nature of the concepts he draws from science and from ordinary life—concepts with which his deliberations always ultimately deal. He seeks to separate in theory what mere contingency has joined together, to free himself of reliance on the restrictions of the real.[7] In striving for the theoretical tidiness of a generality that liberates us from commitment to contingent facts, the philosopher introduces "clarifications" and hypotheses that ultimately burst these bonds and thereby destroy the very concept being elucidated. The inner stress among logically divergent factors in our fact-coordinated concepts is (generally) resolved only by the favorable cooperation of empirical circumstance; the tension is unproblematic because the facts (as we see them) are duly cooperative. But once we tidy up our reliance on these facts in the interests of theoretical neatness, the tension breaks out. The philosopher's "clarifications" engender pressures that burst the bonds that hold our concepts together. When we set the facts aside in hypotheses and tinker with reality, difficulties crowd in upon us. Abrogation of the facts engenders paradox. The tragic destiny of philosophy is to be constrained to pursue the interests of abstract rationality by means of concepts designed to accommodate the facts of experience, to have to probe the merely possible with tools designed to handle the concretely actual, to be constrained to address the necessary in the language of the contingent.[8] Ironically, it is the very urge to clarify which lies at the root of philosophy that also engenders the intellectual tension and cognitive dissonance in which philosophical conflicts take root.

---

7. "Philosopher, c'est donner la raison des choses, ou du moins la chercher; car en tant qu'on se borne à voir et à rapporter ce qu'on voit, on n'est que historien" (Art. "Philosophie" of the great *Encyclopédie*).

8. "Contradiction occurs when the syntactic and semantical indeterminacy of the 'natural,' pretechnical, pretheoretical viewpoint surfaces in discourse. In a sense, the occurrence of contradiction can be taken as the sign of a technical discourse's having been invaded by a foreign viewpoint" (Diego Marconi, *La Formalizzazione della dialettica* [Turin, 1979], p. 73).

The philosopher's interests are theoretical, and so his standards of precision, generality, exactness, and the like, are higher than those of the practical man dealing with life's everyday affairs. Accordingly, the philosopher sees everyday language as imperfect and inadequate—in need of tidying up and supplementation. But the everyday concepts do not admit of this improvement without revision, and thus without modification—they are made for everyday use and cannot survive unaltered in the more stressful atmosphere of theoretical concerns. To clarify them, the philosopher must also distort them.

Clarification is *resolution*—the reduction of an unruly and inchoate scheme of alternative possibilities into a domesticated actuality. The clarificatory impetus of philosophical theorizing would insist on having us "make up our minds" as to which of its factually conjoined elements is theoretically decisive—or if neither is so, then as to which is to enjoy primacy and priority within that complex mixture in which they must both be co-present. But it is not difficult to see that we just cannot do this. We cannot make a neat, theoretically tidy ruling as to the relative contribution of conceptual weight to be carried by each one of the several factors linked together in one of our common concepts. For the crucial point is that a concept may be so constructed as to presuppose relationships that obtain as a matter of contingent fact. When "clarificatory" hypotheses are introduced that have the effect of abrogating these underlying facts, then difficulties are bound to ensue. When the philosopher detaches these concepts from their context and seeks to render them context invariant or context free, he actually destabilizes them. Their inner tensions burst forth and we are led into inconsistency.[9]

Theoretical systematizing leads the philosopher inexorably into distinctions and generalizations that lead outside the comfortable use of our established concepts. In subjecting our concepts to unbearable pressures—in forcing them beyond their tensile strength—he assures that his deliberations will run off into antinomy, from which they can only be rescued by distinctions that seem "forced" from the standpoint of the natural course of things. The existence of aporetic clusters is the sign of this inner tension that the pursuit of theoretical clarity and precision inevitably produces in philosophy. In the pursuit of its aims, the discipline strives toward a theoretical precision and generality that our experience-accommodating concepts are bound to resist. The mark of this resistance is our falling into aporetic perplexity.

9. There is nothing new in the fundamental idea that is at issue here. As J. N. Findlay has observed, both Hegel and Wittgenstein share "the view that it is our desire to develop thought and language in one-sided ways, to exaggerate and to fix tendencies implicit in current usage, which gives rise to philosophical puzzles and contradictions" (*Hegel: A Re-Examination* [New York, 1962], p. 23).

# THE STRIFE OF SYSTEMS
## Why Antinomies Pervade Philosophy

The philosopher's pursuit of generality and precision leads straightaway into difficulties of a special and characteristic type, because all such "clarificatory" hypotheses call for the severing of things that standardly, normally, or ideally go together. All these fact-coordinated concepts are predicated upon a certain background of standardness, and when this background is abandoned through suppositions that are intended to serve the interests of precision, the result is in fact mere confusion.

Philosophical deliberations ultimately pivot on rough-edged concepts attuned to our practical dealings in a complex world where some degree of oversimplification is always necessary in the interests of manageability.[10] In philosophy we are constantly constrained to make rough-approximation statements—"All promise breakings are morally wrong acts," for example—that eventually need further qualification and amendment, since what is claimed is not strictly and unexceptionably so (e.g., in certain cases of incapacity or of conflicts of duty) but represents how matters stand in the normal course of things. That is, we are constantly driven into aporetic clusters of this sort:

—Promise breaking is morally wrong.
—It is never morally wrong to do what we cannot possibly help doing.
—In some circumstances one cannot help breaking a promise.

Or again:

—We are only morally responsible for free (causally unconstrained) acts.
—All human actions are causally determined.
—We are in many instances morally responsible for our actions.

The role in philosophical deliberations of *counterexamples* to proposed theses is particularly noteworthy in this connection, for they lead at once into aporetic clusters along the following lines:

—In cases of type X we want to maintain that P.
—The case at hand [Produce it!] is one of type X.
—But in *this* case we are not prepared to maintain that P.

Confronted by an antinomy, we recognize that something must give way. We would prefer to ignore the difficulties, concealing them in a comfortable ambiguity rendered harmless by benign fact. But the

---

10. Language embodies "the inherited experience and acumen of many generations of men. But then, that acumen has been concentrated primarily upon the practical business of life. If a distinction works well for practical purposes in ordinary life (no mean feat, for even ordinary life is full of hard cases), then there is sure to be something in it, it will not mark nothing: yet this is likely enough not to be the best way of arranging things if our interests are more extensive or intellectual than the ordinary" (J. L. Austin, *Philosophical Papers* [Oxford, 1961], p. 133).

urge to understanding does not allow us to rest satisfied in convenient ignorance. In all such cases, we are driven to make choices. We cannot maintain everything as it stands. We must come to terms with such inconsistencies by modifying, indeed by complexifying, something we would prefer to maintain in a simple and straightforward way.

Philosophical clarifications thus come to introduce distinctions that sunder what the contingent arrangements of this world (as we see them) have *de facto* conjoined. Clarification accordingly produces not only insight but problems. We endeavor to regiment our philosophical concepts in the direction of clarity (generality and precision), but in so doing we do not merely illuminate them but inevitably distort them.[11] What is intended merely as an elucidation that makes a presystematic concept more precise actually results in a paradox-generating clash with the initial concept as it actually works, based as it was upon a unification in which the other, now-relegated factors are no less prominent. For when we set facts aside, the concept at issue itself disintegrates in a destructive fission. This disintegration manifests itself through an aporetic conflict of opposing arguments—all seemingly equally good, but all in the final analysis equally unsatisfying.

## 4. *Philosophy Cannot Abandon the Concepts of Presystemic Experience*

Philosophy arises because our ordinary ways of talking and thinking will not do—are simply not good enough to serve the interests of theoretical exactness. Given that fact-bound concepts cannot answer the needs of the situation, why not simply abandon the concepts of experience altogether in philosophy? The answer is that we cannot do so, because these concepts provide raw materials for philosophizing. The issues from which our philosophizing starts out, and in the interests of whose understanding and elucidation it carries on its work, are taken in the first instance from the realm of experience in ordinary life and in science. Experience is the stuff of life—and thus ultimately the stuff of philosophy as well. The issues the philosopher seeks to elucidate are not—in the first analysis—technical issues domestic to the field itself. They are issues that arise in the conditions of "experience"

---

11. W. V. O. Quine takes an altogether sensible stand when he objects: "In Schoemaker's discussion of Wiggins on personal identity the reasoning veers off in familiar fashion into speculation on what we might say in absurd situations of cloning and transplanting. The method of science fiction has its uses in philosophy, but at points in the Schoemaker-Wiggins exchange and elsewhere I wonder whether the limits of the method are properly heeded. To seek what is 'logically required' for sameness of person under unprecedented conditions is to suggest that words have some logical force beyond what our past needs have invested them with" (review of M. K. Munitz, ed., *Identity and Individuation*, in *The Journal of Philosophy* 69 [1972]: 490).

in everyday life and in the sciences; questions not, to be sure, *within* but rather *about* these domains of experience. Without the will and the capacity to deal with them, philosophy would lose its point, its reason for being. For it is the filiation of questions generating further questions—all of them *ultimately* grounded in our concepts for dealing with the experienced world—that keeps philosophy tied to those presystemic concepts of the experiential realm. The technical issues of philosophy are always a means toward extraphilosophical ends. We address philosophical issues to resolve issues that enable us to resolve issues, and so on, until ultimately we arrive back at questions that can be posed in the prephilosophical *lingua franca* of experience. Its connectability to the presystemic issues of our experiential world, questions about which give rise to and point to our philosophical concerns, is what makes philosophy the enterprise it is.

The aims of philosophical theorizing are "scientific" (in the broader sense of *Wissenschaft*); its assertions are intended to be altogether exact and general. But the concepts that figure centrally in philosophical discussions are always borrowed from everyday life (existence, reality, knowledge, truth, justice, virtue, etc.) or from science (matter, space, time, etc.). The discussions of philosophy always maintain some connection to these pre- or extraphilosophical notions; they can never wholly abandon them. The philosopher cannot continue to use language in quite the usual way, because just that is what led into difficulty in the first place. But he cannot simply abandon those standard conceptions. The philosopher's "knowledge" and "ignorance," his "right" and his "wrong" must be those of ordinary people. His "space" and "time" and "matter" must be those of the natural scientist. If he abandons the concepts of our prephilosophical concerns in favor of creations of his own, he thereby also abandons the problems that constitute his enterprise's very reason for being. To talk *wholly* in terms of technical concepts that differ from the ordinary ones as radically as the physicist's "work" differs from the plain man's is in effect to change the subject. The philosopher cannot at one and the same time practice his craft and forsake the everyday and scientific conceptions that provide the stage setting of his discipline. The philosopher is caught between a rock and a hard place; he cannot live with our extraphilosophical conceptions, but he cannot live without them, either, because his problems are exactly those to which they give rise.[12]

The issues and questions of experience provide the basis on which the issues and questions of philosophy secure their point in the intellec-

---

12. On these issues see the section on "Ideal Language Philosophy versus Ordinary Language Philosophy" in Rorty, *The Linguistic Turn*, Introduction.

tual scheme of things. Philosophy no more *abolishes* that ultimate level of experiential issues than scientific medicine *abolishes* those prescientific symptoms and disabilities toward whose management its efforts are in the final analysis directed. We need recourse to the terminology of experience in everyday life and in science because this provides the ultimate terms of reference for our philosophical deliberations. Connection to these presystemic issues (and thereby to the conceptual framework in whose terms they are articulated) is essential to the project of providing a basis for "understanding the world we live in." To connect with these experience-oriented questions of science and quotidian life, we must keep in contact with the concepts in whose terms they are posed.

In its explanatory purport, philosophy is thus continuous with the empirical domain of life's experience, from which its issues all ultimately emerge. To be sure, its commitment to precision and informativeness and systemic generality soon shifts philosophy onto a path of its own, where the conceptual resources of experiential description no longer avail. But the quest for the ultimate starting point of its investigations always leads back to the issues that arise at the level of prephilosophical concerns. The relevance of philosophy as a source of insight into the world we live in hinges crucially on this connection with the familiar world of our experience, this realistic intent to deal in the final analysis with the issues we ordinarily encounter in experience.

As its work gets well under way, philosophy, of course, distances itself from the concepts in whose terms we discuss our prephilosophical experience of things and only talks about matters needed to talk about matters needed to talk about things. At the level of doctrine—of contentions and answers—there is increasing remoteness and thus little if any overlap between the discourse of technical philosophy and that of life's experiences. But at the level of question-resolving concern, some thread of substantive linkage, some filiation of relevancy, will always be present.

If the deliberations of philosophy were not connectable to those of human experience through a process of developmental emergence, then they would become *pointless*. The philosopher's claim to address the problems that arise with our prephilosophical conceptions would ring hollow if the results he achieves had no discernible relationship to them. To have no bearing whatever upon the issues that can be posed in the presystemic *lingua franca* of human experience would be to become *irrelevant*. To cease to ask about the value of the world, about man's place in the scheme of things, and about our interrelations with our fellows is to give up the very project at issue. To abandon the big questions that arise in the context of our empirical interaction with the world is to abandon philosophy itself.

## 5. Philosophy and the "Limits of Experience"

In philosophy we begin with *questions* about how things stand in the world. As we address these questions via the overly ample "data" at our disposal, we are ultimately impelled in divergent directions because the inner tension of our fact-coordinated concepts pulls us in different directions. It lies in the very nature of philosophical issues that plausible arguments can be built up for each member of an inconsistent family of theses. The presystemic raw materials with which philosophy works are inherently contradictory, and these inner tensions, repressed temporarily but never wholly eliminated, inevitably break out once more within our philosophical systematizations. (The contradictory nature of proverbial wisdom also illustrates this: "Haste makes waste," "A stitch in time saves nine.")[13] Philosophy thus begins in wonder but soon plunges into paradox.

In philosophy, we need the language and the concepts of everyday deliberation because it is from these that the issues arise. Yet we cannot stay there, because the resolutions of these problems demand further clarification. And yet as we move away we sow the seeds of conflict, because when we leave these we are always pulled in different directions.

Since philosophy's fundamental conceptions are fact coordinated, antinomies are pervasive throughout. Antinomies do not represent sporadic episodes that occur in isolated and remote regions; they are central and omnipresent. They pervade philosophy—*every* philosophical issue is party to aporetic situations. Every philosophically basic concept has its penumbra of inarticulate schematism and thus carries antinomy in its wake.

Let us consider this position from a Kantian perspective. Kant's basic thesis is that we cannot legitimately apply our concepts outside the limits of *possible experience*, and that when we do so we fall into antinomies. For Kant, the applicability of our concepts is validated through a categorical synthesis that renders them viable only when deployed *within* the sphere of *possible* experience. The present position is closely analogous although critically different. It departs drastically from Kant in replacing what he sees as an *a priori* synthesis inherent in the structure of the human mind with a far less ambitious but nevertheless far-reaching *empirical* synthesis that is built into a worldview

---

13. One of the appeals of fiction lies in its being less ambiguous than life: fiction is less messy than fact and it is clearer who are the good guys and who the bad. Thus E. H. Gombrich remarks on "the willingness of the public to accept the grotesque and simplified in caricature because its lack of elaboration guarantees the absence of contradictory clues" (*Art and Illusion* [New York, 1960], p. 336).

or some sector thereof. While certain philosophically critical concepts are also held to be usable only within "the limits of possible experience," *possible experience* now means *empirically* possible experience relative to the empirical actualities of how things work in the world. Thus "possible" now means *actually* possible, and not as with Kant *transcendentally* possible. Philosophy, Kant tells us, is knowledge obtained by reason in scrutinizing the relationships among concepts.[14] But given their experiential grounding, the salient concepts of philosophy are never entirely "pure"—Kant to the contrary notwithstanding. They are not wholly disjoint from the domain of contingent fact. They are experientially "contaminated." Thus our position, though Kantian in its fundamental structure, replaces his conceptual necessity with a more modest factual counterpart.

Such a view stands in ironic contrast with that of Plato, that greatest of philosophers. As he saw it, *sensation* yields contradictory results and leads to belief (*pistis*), whose "object can be said both to be and not to be" (*Republic*, bk. V, 478). (Think of the sceptics' favorite example of the two hands, one held in hot water and the other in cold water, and then both plunged into lukewarm water.) Sensory beliefs must be corrected by *dianoia*—by reason. As Plato saw it, the philosopher's theorizing is the saving resource capable of effecting a reconciliation between conflicting sensations.

But the cruel fact is that theorizing itself yields contradictory results. In moving from empirical observation to philosophical theorizing, we do not leave contradiction behind—it continues to dog our footsteps. And just as reason must correct sensation, so more refined reason is always needed as a corrective for less refined reason. The source of contradiction is not just in the domain of sensation but in that of reasoned reflection as well. We are not just led into philosophy by the urge to consistency, we are *kept* at it by this same urge.

The following objection looms:

If the conceptions on which traditional philosophy turns involve *ineradicable* ambiguities and confusions; if the endeavor to elucidate these issues *inevitably* results in contradiction and antinomy; if philosophical controversies *invariably* turn on conceptual confusions; if all this be so, then why should we take the enterprise seriously? Surely the whole project then collapses into futility. Philosophy is then nonsense, "a meaningless game with words," a "systematic bewitchment by language." Philosophical problems should be dismissed as pseudoproblems and their solutions as pseudosolutions. Philosophical problems should be *dissolved* rather than *resolved*.

14. "Vernunfterkenntnis aus [or also *nach*] Begriffen" (*CPuR*, B741, 760).

# THE STRIFE OF SYSTEMS
*Why Antinomies Pervade Philosophy*

Such an objection grants the essentials of the present deliberations but exploits them to argue differently: "If that is actually how philosophical problems arise—if they root in the inherent inability of the concepts of extraphilosophical discourse to admit of theoretical precision—then why not simply abandon the philosophical project of striving for precision? Why embark on the quest for the grail of theoretical perfection (generality, exactness, etc.) when we realize that this quest is foredoomed to failure?" This objection represents a tempting but profoundly mistaken line of thought.

Its flaw lies in the consideration that we proceed in this way because we are rational creatures and want rationally defensible answers to our questions—particularly when we are dealing with issues that really matter to us. The questions are important and we have a real stake in them—a profound intellectual stake in understanding the world. We pursue philosophical systematicity for the same reason we pursue cognitive consistency (see pp. 38–44). They are two sides of the same quest for comprehension. We cannot abandon the quest without defaulting on our cardinal ambitions. Admittedly, we can never arrive at perfected and definitive solutions here—any more than we can in science or in religion or anywhere else in the intellectual or moral life. But all this is no reason for failing to make the effort and do the best we can. We can always make useful improvements on our performance. Even though we can never reach perfection, we can manage to attain higher levels of achievement.

A typical move of philosophical controversy is to remark that the concept C plays a critical role in the theory in question and to complain that "no one has ever given a fully satisfactory account (or analysis or explanation) of the concept C." The trouble is that the criticism is *always* apposite.[15]

In philosophizing we confront the operation of "intellectual barrier" even as in contexts of engineering we find the operation of "physical barrier." One cannot build a perfectly efficient engine, but one can build engines that are relatively more efficient than those we already have. We are impelled forward by the opportunity not, to be sure, to reach perfection, but to reduce imperfection—to do better than we have heretofore been able to do. Even as we can never contrive the

---

15. That a philosophical concept can never be rendered precise in the manner of scientific concepts follows from what R. G. Collingwood calls "the overlap of classes" in philosophy. (See *An Essay on Philosophical Method* [Oxford, 1933].) Our present analysis has many parts of kinship with Collingwood's theory of the "indefinability" of philosophical concepts, though the conclusions he draws from his principles, and his vision of systematic philosophy as "a scale of philosophies," differs from our own, more pluralistic position.

perfect machine, so we can never realize the perfect system. Some element of inefficiency will always be present in the former, some element of aporetic inconsistency in the latter. Philosophical problems arise in confusion and conflict, never attaining a perfect resolution. But this provides no reason to give up the project and no excuse for failing to grapple with it as best we can. Here, as elsewhere, we have to acknowledge the need to do the imperfect best we can. This is simply a matter of facing the realities, which is a part of man's struggle against darkness, of recognizing that nothing we can create in this world is perfect and that nothing we bring to realization will last for all time.

A summary of the somewhat complex argumentation of this chapter is in order. Addressing the question of the role of antinomies in philosophy, the chapter has developed the following line of response:

1. The pivotal concepts of philosophy all root in the experiential realities as we confront them in ordinary life and in science. They are thus always fact coordinated. They rest on contingent factual suppositions as to how things stand (or, rather, are *thought* to stand) in the world.

2. Philosophy has "scientific" aspirations. It aims at achieving a systematic precision and generality in its attempts to formulate principles of theoretical understanding.

3. Philosophy thus seeks to extrude the element of factual contingency from its key concepts—to "clarify" them by theoretical systematization to a point where factual presuppositions are no longer needed.

4. In forcing its concepts toward this clarity, philosophy presses them beyond their tensile strength; it ultimately bursts the factual bonds that hold them together as practically effective units of thought.

5. As the factual bonds are burst asunder, antinomies result. We are driven into making choices that can in principle be resolved in alternative ways. And considerations of abstract general principle (with which alone the philosopher can really content himself) are by themselves unable to effect any satisfactory resolution of the choice that these alternatives present. The role of antinomy in philosophy is thus central and pervasive.

If the deliberations of this chapter are anything like correct, it becomes clear why paradoxes pervade the philosophical terrain. For it is bound to happen that, whenever we set down the aggregate of "natural" theses that expound what makes intuitive good sense in any area of consideration, the results prove to be inconsistent. The semantical paradoxes, Goodman's and Hempel's paradoxes of induction, Arrow's paradox of rational preference, etc., do not reflect anomalous but altogether paradigmatic situations.

# 4

# Escaping Inconsistency via Distinctions

## 1. Removing Inconsistency Through Curtailments

Confronted with an aporetic cluster of collectively incompatible commitments, we naturally want to eliminate the inconsistency in which we have become enmeshed. Consistency is the most elemental demand of philosophical rationality—its lack would compromise the entire project as a cognitive endeavor.

But how can one eliminate inconsistency? In essentials, the answer is simple. One can always restore consistency among incompatible commitments by abandoning some of the beliefs that engender the difficulty. Inconsistency results from overcommitment, and we can avoid it by curtailing our commitments.

Consider, for example, that sector of seventeenth-century metaphysics that revolved about the following aporetic cluster:

(1) Extension is substantial (in constituting material *res extensa*).
(2) Thought is substantial (in constituting immaterial *res cogitans*).
(3) Thought and extension are coordinate items that have the same standing and status.
(4) Substance as such is uniform: at bottom it has but one type and is a genus of one single species.

Clearly, these contentions are mutually incompatible. The inconsistency can, of course, be removed by deletions, and this is obviously the way to go. But as always, the weeding-out needed to restore consistency can be accomplished in different ways. The following alternatives are open:

Abandon (1) and (3): Idealism of a type that regards extended matter as merely phenomenal (Leibniz and Berkeley).

Abandon (2) and (3): Materialism in the form of a theory that sees thought as the causal product of the operations of matter (Gassendi and Hobbes).

Abandon (1) and (2): Metaphysical aspectivalism and, in particular, a theory that takes both thought and material extension to be mere attributes of a single, all-encompassing substance (Spinoza).

Abandon (4): Thought/matter dualism (Descartes).

All of these exits from inconsistency were available, and all were in fact used by one or another thinker of the period.

Consider another example. Presocratic philosophizing was involved in coming to terms with the following family of mutually incompatible beliefs:

(1) There is such a thing as physical change.
(2) Something persists unaffected throughout physical change.
(3) Matter does not persist unaffected through physical change.
(4) Matter (in its various guises) is all there is.

There are four ways out of the inconsistency generated by these theses:

Deny (1): Change is a mere illusion (Zeno and Parmenides).
Deny (2): Nothing whatever persists unaffected through physical change (Heraclitus—*panta rhei*).
Deny (3): Matter does indeed persist unaffected throughout physical change, albeit only *in the small*—in its "atoms" (the atomists).
Deny (4): Matter is not all there is. There is also *"mathematical form,"* with physical change being at bottom a matter of alteration in geometric structure (Pythagoras) or in arithmetical proportion (Anaxagoras).

To free ourselves from the grasp of aporetic inconsistency, we must jettison some of the theses that have enmeshed us in difficulty. There will always be different alternatives here, so that a choice among them is possible—and necessary.

## 2. *The Role of Distinctions*

Faced with an inconsistent group of beliefs, it clearly becomes necessary to abandon one (or more) of them. In general, however, philosophers do not achieve this end wholly by way of rejection. Rather, they have recourse to *modification,* replacing the abandoned beliefs with something roughly similar yet consistency maintaining. Trying to salvage as much as one can from the shipwreck of inconsistency, one introduces distinctions. Since each thesis of an aporetic cluster is individually attractive, simple rejection lets the case for the rejected thesis go unacknowledged. Only by modifying (rather than rejecting) the thesis can we hope to give proper recognition to the full range of considerations that initially led us into the aporetic cluster.

# THE STRIFE OF SYSTEMS
*Escaping Inconsistency via Distinctions*

Distinctions enable the philosopher to remove inconsistency not just by the brute negativism of thesis *rejection* but by the more subtle and constructive device of thesis *qualification*. The crux of a distinction is not mere negation or denial, but the amendment of an untenable thesis into something positive that does the job better.

By way of example, consider the following aporetic cluster:

(1) All events are caused.
(2) If an action issues from free choice, then it is causally unconstrained.
(3) Free will exists—people can and do make and act upon free choices.

Clearly one way to force an exit from inconsistency is to drop thesis (2). We might well, however, do this not by way of outright abandonment but rather by speaking of the "causally unconstrained" only in Spinoza's manner of an *externally* originating causality. For consider the result of deploying a distinction that divides the second premise into two parts:

(2.1) Actions based on free choice are unconstrained by *external* causes.
(2.2) Actions based on free choice are unconstrained by *internal* causes.

Once (2) is so divided, the initial inconsistent triad (1)–(3) gives way to the quartet (1), (2.1), (2.2), (3). But we can resolve *this* aporetic cluster by rejecting (2.2) while yet retaining (2.1)—thus in effect *replacing* (2) by a weakened version. Such recourse to a distinction—here that between internal and external causes—makes it possible to forge an exit from inconsistency.

Consider the inconsistent triad:

—All $A$'s are $B$'s.
—All $B$'s are $C$'s.
—Some $A$'s are not $C$'s.

Note that these are incompatible only if the connecting terms that link these theses together, $A$, $B$, $C$, are used in precisely the same sense in each occurrence. If careful scrutiny manifests the least deviation—if, say, the $A$ of one of those theses is $A_1$ and that of the other is $A_2$,—then the inconsistency is removed and the problem abolished. Distinctions are thus a crucial tool for philosophical problem solving; they are the natural means for eliminating inconsistency.

Let us examine the workings of this process more closely.

Consider an aporetic cluster that set the stage for various theories of early Greek philosophy:

(1) Reality is one (homogeneous).
(2) Matter is real.
(3) Form is real.
(4) Matter and form are distinct sorts of things (heterogeneous).

By way of resolution, one might consider rejecting (2). This could be done, however, not by simply *abandoning* it, but rather by *replacing* it—on the idealistic precedent of Zeno and Plato—with something along the following lines:

(2') Matter is not real as an independent mode of existence; rather it is merely quasi-real, a mere *phenomenon*, an appearance somehow grounded in immaterial reality.

The new quartet (1), (2'), (3), (4) is cotenable.

In adopting this resolution, one again resorts to a *distinction*, namely that between

(i) strict reality as self-sufficiently independent existence

and

(ii) derivative or attenuated reality as a (merely phenomenal) product of the operation of the unqualifiedly real.

Use of such a distinction enables us to resolve an aporetic cluster—yet not by simply *abandoning* one of those paradox-engendering theses but rather by *qualifying* it. (Note, however, that once we follow Zeno and Plato in replacing (2) by (2')—and accordingly reinterpret matter as representing a "mere phenomenon"—the substance of thesis (4) is profoundly altered; the old contention can still be maintained, but it now gains a new significance in the light of new distinctions.)

Alternatively, one might abandon thesis (3). However, one would then presumably not simply adopt "form is not real" but rather would go over to the qualified contention that "form is not *independently* real; it is no more than a transitory (changeable) state of matter." And this can be looked at the other way around, as saying "form *is* (in a way) real, although only insofar as it is taken to be no more than a transitory state of matter." This, in effect, would be the position of the atomists.

Antinomies can always be resolved in this way; we can always "save the phenomena," that is, retain the crucial core of our various beliefs in the face of apparent inconsistency by introducing suitable distinctions and qualifications. Once apory breaks out, we can salvage our philosophical commitments by complicating them, by revising them in the light of appropriate distinctions rather than abandoning them altogether. For the effect of imposing a distinction $d$ on a concept $C$ is to divide $C$ into $C_1$ and $C_2$. And when this happens, a thesis in which $C$ figures, $T = T(C)$, is split into two distinct contentions:

$$d + T(C) \text{ yields } T(C_1) \text{ and } T(C_2)$$

At this point we might abandon $T(C_1)$, and with it the *overall* thesis $T(C)$, while yet retaining $T(C_2)$, and with it a substantial *part* of $T(C)$.

# THE STRIFE OF SYSTEMS
*Escaping Inconsistency via Distinctions*

And so, when this thesis figures in an aporetic inconsistency, we may well break the chain of inconsistency by replacing it with one of its distinction-modified congeners.

To be sure, distinctions are not needed if *all* that concerns us is averting inconsistency; simple thesis abandonment, mere refusal to assert, will suffice to that end. But distinctions are necessary if we are to maintain informative positions and provide answers to our questions. We can guard against inconsistency by keeping from commitment. But that leaves us empty handed. Distinctions are the instruments we use in the (never-ending) work of rescuing our assertoric commitments from inconsistency while yet salvaging what we can.

Accordingly, one generally does not respond to cogent counterarguments by abandoning one's position in philosophy but by making it more sophisticated. One can never entrap any philosophical doctrine in a finally and decisively destructive inconsistency, because a sufficiently clever exponent can always escape from difficulty by means of distinctions.

Consider, for example, the following aporetic cluster:

(1) Only real things can produce real effects (only real causes are really causes).
(2) Delusions and illusions can produce real effects.
(3) Delusions and illusions are not real.

One easy out is to reject (3) via a distinction that insists that delusions and illusions are indeed real *as such* (viz., as subjective mental episodes of a certain sort); it's just that their *objects* aren't real. So if Jones recoils in horror before an imaginary snake, the subjective side of this process (the illusory snake *imagining*) is real enough and so acts as a real cause; it's just that the (*ex hypothesi* nonexistent) snake is—being nonexistent—impotent to produce any effect. The snake itself does not really exist. It is only a figment of the imagination—though as such (viz., as an illusory *idea*) it is indeed real and can thus produce real effects, even as (1) would have it.

The history of philosophy is shot through with distinctions introduced to avert aporetic difficulties. Already in the dialogues of Plato, the first systematic writings in philosophy, we enounter distinctions at every turn. In Book I of the *Republic*, for example, Socrates' interlocutor quickly falls into the following apory:

(1) Rational people always pursue their own interests.
(2) Nothing that is in a person's interest can be disadvantageous to him.
(3) Even rational people sometimes do things that prove disadvantageous.

Here, inconsistency is averted by distinguishing between two senses of the "interests" of a person—namely what is *really* advantageous to him and what he merely *thinks* to be so; between *real* and *seeming* interests. Again, in the discussion of "nonbeing" in the *Sophist*, the Eleatic stranger entraps Socrates in an inconsistency from which he endeavors to extricate himself by distinguishing between "nonbeing" in the sense of not existing *at all* and in the sense of not existing *in a certain mode*. For the most part, the Platonic dialogues present a dramatic unfolding of one distinction after another.

## 3. Dialectical Development

Distinctions enable us to implement the idea that a satisfactory resolution of aporetic clusters must somehow make room for all parties to the contradiction. The introduction of distinctions thus represents a Hegelian ascent—rising above the level of antagonistic positions to that of a "higher" conception, in which the opposites are reconciled. In introducing the qualifying distinction, we abandon the initial thesis and move toward its counterthesis, but we do so only by way of a duly hedged synthesis. In this regard, distinction is a "dialectical" process. This role of distinctions is also connected with the thesis often designated as "Ramsey's Maxim." With regard to disputes about fundamental questions that do not seem capable of a decisive settlement, Frank Plumpton Ramsey wrote: "In such cases it is a heuristic maxim that the truth lies not in one of the two disputed views but in some third possibility which has not yet been thought of, which we can only discover by rejecting something assumed as obvious by both the disputants."[1] On this view, too, distinctions provide for a higher synthesis of opposing views. They prevent thesis abandonment from being an *entirely* negative process, affording us a way of salvaging something, of "giving credit where credit is due" even to those theses we ultimately reject. They make it possible to remove inconsistency not just by the brute force of thesis rejection, but by the more subtle and constructive device of thesis qualification.

A distinction reflects a *concession*, an acknowledgement of some element of acceptability in the thesis that is being rejected. However, distinctions always bring a new concept on the stage of consideration and thus put a new topic on the agenda. They accordingly always afford invitations to carrying the discussion further, opening up new issues that were heretofore inaccessible. Distinctions are the doors through which philosophy passes into new topics and problems.

Philosophical distinctions are thus creative innovations. They do not elaborate preexistent ideas but introduce new ones. They not only provide a basis for understanding better something heretofore grasped

---

1. Frank P. Ramsey, *The Foundations of Mathematics*, ed. R. B. Braithwaite (London, 1931), pp. 115–16.

less rigorously, they shift the discussion to a new level of sophistication and complexity. Thus to some extent they "change the subject." (In this regard they are like the conceptual innovations of science, that revise rather than explain prior ideas.) New concepts and new theses come constantly to the fore.

The continual introduction of new concepts via new distinctions means that the ground of philosophy is always shifting beneath our feet. New distinctions for our concepts and new contexts for our theses alter the very substance of the old theses. The development is dialectical—an exchange of objection and response that constantly moves the discussion onto new ground. The resolution of antinomies through new distinctions is a matter of creative innovation whose outcome cannot be foreseen.

## 4. A Historical Illustration

The unfolding of distinctions has important ramifications in philosophical inquiry. As new concepts crop up in the wake of distinctions, new questions arise regarding their bearing on the issues. In the course of securing answers to our old questions we open up further questions, questions that could not even be asked before.

Let us consider the inherent dynamic of this dialectic. The speculations of the early Ionian philosophers revolved about four theses:

(1) There is one single material substrate (*archē*) of all things.
(2) The material substrate must be capable of transforming into anything and everything (and thus specifically into each of the various elements).
(3) The only extant materials are the four material elements: earth (solid), water (liquid), air (gaseous), and fire (volatile)
(4) The four elements are independent—none gives rise to the rest.

Different thinkers found different ways out of this aporie:

—Thales rejected (4) and opted for water as the *archē*.
—Anaximines rejected (4) and opted for air as the *archē*.
—Heraclitus rejected (4) and opted for fire as the *archē*.
—The atomists rejected (4) and opted for earth as the *archē*.
—Anaximander rejected (3) and postulated an indeterminate *apeiron*.
—Empedocles rejected (1), and thus also (2), holding that everything consists in *mixtures* of the four elements.

Thus all the available exits from inconsistency were actually used.

As the Presocratics worked their way through the relevant ideas, the following conceptions came to figure prominently on the agenda:

(I) {
(1) Whatever is ultimately real persists through change.
(2) The four elements—earth (solid), water (liquid), air (gaseous), and fire (volatile)—do not persist through change as such.
(3) The four elements encompass all there is by way of extant reality.
}

Three basic positions are now available:

(1)–abandonment: Nothing persists through change—*panta rhei*, all is in flux (Heraclitus).
(2)–abandonment: One single element persists through change—it alone is the *archē* of all things; all else is simply some altered form of it. This uniquely unchanging element is: earth (atomists), water (Thales), air (Anaximines). Or again, *all* the elements persist through change, which is only a matter of a variation in mix and proportion (Empedocles).
(3)–abandonment: Matter itself is not all there is—there is also its inherent geometrical structure (Pythagoras) or its external arrangement in an environing void (atomists). Or again, there is also an immaterial motive force that endows matter with motion—to wit, "mind" (*nous*) (Anaxagoras).

Let us follow along in the track of atomism by abandoning (3). The first cycle of dialectical development is now completed. In pursuing this line of thought, the following aporetic impasse arose:

(II) { (1) Change really occurs.
      (2) Matter (solid material substance) does not change.
      (3) Matter is all there is.

As always, there are different ways out of the contradiction:

(1)–abandonment: Change is an illusion (Parmenides, Zeno, Eleatics).
(2)–abandonment: Matter (indeed *everything*) changes (Heraclitus).
(3)–abandonment: Matter is not all there is; there is also the void—and the changing configurations of matter within it (atomism).

Taking up the third course, let us continue to follow the atomistic route. Note that this does not *just* call for abandoning (3), but also calls for sophisticating (2) to

(2') Matter as such is *not* changeable—it only changes in point of its variable rearrangements.

This line of development has recourse to a "saving distinction" by introducing the new topic of variable arrangements (as contrasted with such necessary and invariable states as the shapes of the atoms themselves).

To be sure, matters do not end here. A new cycle of inconsistency looms ahead. For this new topic paves the way for the following apory:

(III) { (1) All possibilities of variation are actually realized.
       (2) Various different world arrangements are possible.
       (3) Only one world is real.

Different resolutions are obviously available here:

(1)–rejection: A theory of real chance (*tuchē*) or contingency that sees various possibilities as going unrealized (Empedocles).

(2)–rejection: A doctrine of universal necessitation (the "block universe" of Parmenides).

(3)–rejection: A theory of many worlds (Democritus and atomism in general).

As the atomistic resolution represented by the second course is developed, apory breaks out again:

(IV) 
- (1) Matter as such never changes—the only change it admits of are its rearrangements.
- (2) The nature of matter is indifferent to change. Its rearrangements are contingent and potentially variable.
- (3) Its changes of condition are inherent in the (unchanging) nature of matter—they are necessary, not contingent.

Here the orthodox atomistic solution would lie in abandoning (3) and replacing it with

(3′) Its changes of condition are not necessitated by the nature of matter. They are indeed quasi-necessitated by being law determined, but law is something independent of the nature of matter.

This resolution introduces a new theme, viz. *law determination* (as introduced by the Stoics).

Yet when one seeks to apply this idea it seems plausible to add:

(V) (4) Certain material changes (concomitant with free human actions) are not law determined.

Apory now breaks out once more; the need for an exit from inconsistency again arises. And such an exit was afforded by (4)-abandonment, as with the law abrogation envisaged in the notorious "swerve" of Epicurus, or by (3′)-abandonment, as with the more rigoristic atomism of Lucretius.

The developmental sequence from (I) through (V) represents an evolution through successive layers of aporetic inconsistency, duly separated from one another by successive distinctions, that led from the Ionian theorists to the more sophisticated doctrines of late atomism.

## 5. Intimations of Imperfection

At every stage the philosopher's resolutions of the aporetic difficulties he confronts leave a legacy of new problems. The successors of Plato, for example, faced the following inconsistency:

(1) Whatever has features that endure through time has a share in the universal and participates in it.

(2) Transient particulars have enduring features that constitute their essence and accordingly exemplify and reflect universals (ideas).

(3) Universals are "separated" (*choristos*); they are set apart and wholly disjoint from transient particulars.

These theses clearly constitute an inconsistent triad. For (1) and (2) together engender the conclusion that "transient particulars share (or participate) in the universal" and thus are incompatible with (3). Three resolutions are theoretically available.

(1)–rejection: Not a live option within the Greek tradition.
(2)–rejection: A denial of permanent essences in particular things (the nominalism of the atomist school).
(3)–rejection: Denial that universals are "separate"—they are actually present *in rebus* (Aristotle) or at any rate are taken to be present in them (the conceptualism of the Stoics).

Each of these several resolutions led to important directions of doctrinal development.

Throughout such a course of development, inconsistency becomes resolved by dropping one of the aporetic theses at issue, replacing it with a duly revised version on the basis of a suitable distinction. The procedure is one of subjecting an apory-engendering thesis $T$ to an apory-dissolving distinction $d$ with the result that: $T + d$ yields $T_1$ and $T_2$, where $T_1$ is seen as tenable, but $T_2$ is not. The "dialectical" nature of such a process is manifest in the pattern:

thesis: $T$
antithesis: not -$T$ (since $T_2$ is untenable)
synthesis: $T_1$

The synthesis may be seen as doing justice to both the "element of truth" in the aporetic thesis $T$ and to the antithetical recognition that $T$ is not tenable as such.

All the classical distinctions of early Greek philosophy were in fact arrived at through just this process:

—elemental/derivative
—permanent/changing
—being/becoming
—structure/quantity
—form/matter
—one/many
—natural/artificial
—chance/necessity
—free/constrained

All these concepts are signposts of the natural evolution of Greek thought toward the great synthetic systems of Democritus, Pythagoras, Plato, and Aristotle—systems where coordinated apories are resolved *en masse* by a handful of duly adjusted distinctions.

# THE STRIFE OF SYSTEMS
*Escaping Inconsistency via Distinctions*

The history of philosophy is a chronicle of distinctions introduced to resolve aporetic problems but yet not quite able to bring off the trick. All such philosophical dichotomies as

> objective/subjective
> sense/nonsense
> real/ideal
> analytic/synthetic
> meaningful/meaningless

represent distinctions we find useful yet ultimately wanting. In the fulness of time such distinctions "go soft" on us and call for yet further qualifications and limitations to remain operable.[2]

Such a course of development, however, never manages to achieve a total stability and finality. Recourse to a distinction always places a new categorical topic on the agenda of explanation. And as we explore the ramifications of the new concept, aporie breaks out again.

Distinctions not only resolve problems but also engender further ones. It is helpful to distinguish fish from mammals. But what of whales? Their physiology is mammalian, their lifestyle is fishlike. Are we to assimilate them to the one group or to the other? Which factors are to qualify as paramount here will depend on where our interest lies—which factors of analogy we deem *important*. Distinctions always lead to further difficulties; once we have them, we will always encounter problems regarding their application. In philosophy, our victories in conflict resolution are never permanent, because all of the root concepts of philosophy reflect fact-coordinative and thus apory-generating conceptions whose inner ramifications inevitably lead to theoretical tensions. As we proceed to refine our concepts by introducing needed distinctions and setting out the yet-further theses to which they lead, aporie will break out once more, sooner or later. The resolutions we provide for philosophical apories invariably lead to further difficulties in other sectors of the terrain. In philosophical deliberation, distinctions keep the wolf of inconsistency from the door—but, alas, always only for a limited time. As the dialectical tradition insists throughout, any formulation of a philosophical thesis eventually gives rise to difficulties that compel its revision.

Our victories over inconsistency are only local, never global. The inconsistency that distinctions avert at one point always break out again at another. The fact-laden character of our concepts means that

---

2. See, for example, the interesting account in C. G. Hempel's "Problems and Changes in the Empiricist Criterion of Meaning," *Revue International de Philosophie*,11 (1950): 41–63, rpt. in A. J. Ayer, ed., *Logical Positivism* (Glencoe, 1959), pp. 108–29.

all philosophical distinctions are imperfect; they will never work out quite the way we would ideally want. Exceptions must always be made and difficulties accommodated. Finality lies beyond our grasp so decidedly as to make a mockery of the Leibnizian ideal of instilling clarity and precision into philosophy to a point where it becomes possible to resolve disputed questions by mere calculation.

In "solving" the problems of philosophy, as in solving the problems of life, the victories we gain are never permanent—and never total. As we deploy our distinctions we simply deflect difficulties from one point to another. A sort of entropy principle is at issue: the dissonance or conceptual friction we remove at one point is increased at another. All of the experiential concepts deployed in philosophy contain an element of the factually surd that we can never quite remove. Even as thermodynamic situations generally do not admit of processes that increase the overall amount of available energy, so philosophical situations generally do not admit of processes that increase the overall amount of conceptual clarity. The distinctions that reduce aporetic frictions at some points engender new ones at others. No system can provide a perfectly efficient engine for our thought about these philosophical issues. Systemic perfection lies beyond our grasp in this domain.[3]

The fact-coordinated concepts in which philosophical deliberations root can never be fully domesticated to the philosopher's requirements for theoretical tidiness. It is the tragic destiny of philosophers that we are fated to carry out our constructive efforts with defective materials—that we must address the issues by means of distinctions that never quite work. Whatever we say is only a rough approximation in need of qualification and amendment. (The seeming self-contradiction of this statement illustrates rather than refutes the point at issue.)

## 6. Some Important Forms of Philosophical Inventiveness

Such a picture of the developmental dialectics of philosophy indicates that there are various significantly different forms of philosophical inventiveness:

(1) Identifying fruitful issues: proposing philosophically interesting ideas and topics.
(2) Posing new questions: discerning contradictions and finding aporetic

---

3. As Friedrich Schlegel stressed, following Kant, philosophy is rather a striving after scientific knowledge than itself a science (mehr ein Streben nach Wissenschaft, als selbst eine Wissenschaft). Quoted in Braun, *L'Histoire de l'histoire de la philosophie*, pp. 278–79. Where the old-school metaphysicians (Wolff, Baumgarten) saw an evolving science actually unfolding bit by bit under our very eyes, their post-Kantian successors saw simply the emergence of a blueprint for a possible future science (ibid., p. 228).

clusters. Discerning how the commitments we have come to undertake encounter difficulties and run into internal contradiction. Discovering paradoxes, antinomies, apories. Spotting further worthwhile problems and issues arising from the new refinements introduced to grapple with old problems. (Note that novelty is a matter of degree here—there must always be some connections with the preexisting issues.)
(3) Devising plausible answers: maintaining new theses—building new theories to answer the new questions that have come to figure on the agenda.
(4) Substantiating solutions: devising arguments to support the theses we propose to accept as elements of our position.
(5) Drawing distinctions: introducing discriminations that enable us to make our way out of aporetic situations by appropriate theory refinements.
(6) Projecting new conceptions: entertaining new possibilities and elucidating their relations and implications.
(7) System building: consolidating each of our commitments with reference to others, assuring the coherence and consonance of the current answers with those we incline to give to other questions on other occasions. Systematization enables us to coordinate issues and, in particular, to address diverse aporetic clusters and conjointly provide resolutions for them *en bloc*.

The complexity of philosophizing thus accounts for there being room for very different contributions—ranging from the detail work of refining distinctions and polishing arguments to the grander level of the new theses and theories devised by the master innovators.

The last item on the preceding list deserves particular comment. Aporetic clusters come "not single spies but in battalions" (as Shakespeare put it). For in abandoning a thesis and adopting its denial, we at once render conjointly problematic the whole family of theses that constitutes the grounds on which the abandoned thesis was based. Moreover, two aporetic clusters might well share a certain thesis $T$ in common, so that by dropping $T$ we can "kill two birds with one stone," thereby achieving a useful cognitive economy, in that a single distinction can effect a resolution of several apories. In philosophy, as in other intellectual endeavors, economy of means in problem resolution is a paramount consideration. (Distinctions and complications, like entities, are not to be multiplied beyond necessity.) Note, however, that in such cases the thesis we reject will not necessarily be the individually weakest link in the aporetic clusters at issue. Systemic considerations may lead us to depart from the indications of considerations of individualized acceptability (plausibility) and drop those theses whose abandonment yields the optimal outcome on an overall basis.

This line of thought explains why systematization is so important in philosophy. A sort of cost-benefit analysis is at issue in the various ways of removing inconsistency—a reckoning of the gains and losses produced by the deletions and retentions involved in finding an exit from inconsistency. But this has to be carried out *globally*, not *locally*. Systematization is the indispensable means for achieving an overall economy of means in the accomplishment of our cognitive objectives. It is a source of great strength—but of weakness as well. For it is also the process through which the inevitable inconsistency of the ultimate implications of our philosophical commitments is brought to light.

# 5

# Developmental Dialectics

### 1. The Convergence of Traditions

Consider the problem of restoring consistency to an inconsistent group of theses: $A$, $B$, $C$. By abandoning (say) $C$ and replacing it with $C'$ through recourse to a distinction, $B$ will obviously also become implicated if the distinction-affected term is operative in it as well. Thus $A$, $B$, $C$ will change to $A$, $B'$, $C'$. Similarly, had we decided at the outset to abandon $B$ and replace it with a distinction-resultant $B^*$, we would also be led to alter $C$ to $C^*$. Now if it should happen that $B' = B^*$ and $C' = C^*$, then these two seemingly different approaches will actually converge to one selfsame result. This sort of convergence does sometimes occur in philosophy.

For example, consider the following apory that underlay the development of the theory of knowledge in the post-Aristotelian period of classical antiquity:

(1) We can secure knowledge (*epistēmē*) in factual matters.
(2) Knowledge must be certain.
(3) Perception is our only source of factual knowledge.
(4) Perception does not yield certainty.

The Stoics began by abandoning (4) as it stands but qualifying it by a distinction. Perception, they held, can and actually does yield certainty in some particular cases (those of so-called "cataleptic perceptions"). Accordingly, they proceeded to maintain:

(1)   We do have factual knowledge.
(2.1) Knowledge must be (sufficiently) certain.
(3)   Perception is our only source of factual knowledge.
(4.1) Perception does yield sufficient certainty for knowledge.

The Sceptics of the Middle Academy, on the other hand, began by giving up (1) but once again had recourse to a distinction. In experiential matters we do not, they held, secure actual *knowledge* (*epistēmē*) but merely plausible *quasi knowledge* (*to pithanon*). Accordingly they went on to maintain:

(1.2) We do not have authentic factual knowledge but only mere quasi knowledge.
(2) Authentic knowledge must be absolutely certain though quasi knowledge can get by with a *mitigated* certainty.
(3) Perception is our only source of factual knowledge (of *any* description).
(4.2) Perception does not yield absolute certainty but only the mitigated certainty sufficient for quasi knowledge.

Something very interesting has occurred here. If one is prepared to identify the *sufficiently* certain "factual knowledge" of the Stoics with the "quasi knowledge" of the Academic Sceptics, then these two groups of propositions become effectively equivalent. Despite their different points of departure, the two theories coalesce into substantial agreement.

The example shows that in resolving an apory, it *can* happen that the strategy of rejecting a thesis and yet saving it by imposing a distinction (with a correlative rereading of the other pertinent theses) may possibly yield a convergence of "rival" traditions. The phenomenon of consilience, of reaching a common destination from remote initial starting points, can occur—particularly under the pressure of close interaction when each party reacts with some degree of accommodation to the theses of its nominal "opponents."

Some philosophers are enchanted by this idea of convergence. They take as their model the doctrine of "the coincidence of opposites" (*coincidentia oppositorum*) of Nicholas of Cusa. All philosophical opposition, they say, is only seeming disagreement and is destined in the final analysis to give way to doctrinal consonance. The overall course of philosophy is an evolutionary development in which all of the conflicts of the inadequate present will, in the end, inevitably harmonize into one grand coherent synthesis.

Now this, of course, is a genuine possibility. But there is no sign that it is actual and no reason to think that it will ever be. All historical indications go clean against this universalization of convergence. The partisans of ultimate consilience are misled by the charm of this prospect into taking convergence as the standard case—into seeing something that *can* happen as something that *must* happen. Actually, however, converging lines of development of this sort are extremely rare in the history of philosophy—very much the exception rather than the rule. In general, the resolution of inconsistency provides for an ever more nuanced diversity of doctrine.

## 2. The Growth of Complexity and Its Dialectical Ramifications

When conflicts of aporetic inconsistency among our beliefs arise, we would ideally like a resolution that extricates us without engendering further difficulties of its own. But this desideratum is unattainable in philosophy. No matter how elaborately qualified with distinctions, our fact-coordinated experiential concepts can never achieve theoretical perfection; the impurity of surd fact can never be fully eliminated.

In philosophy we constantly confront the painful fact that rules have their exceptions. A substantive thesis of the form "All $A$'s are $B$'s" is always problematic—never totally and unexceptionally true. Inevitably the situation is that $A$'s are only qualifiedly $B$'s—standardly, predominantly, typically, and normally. And the search for conceptual distinctions to implement the needed qualifications is never ending. William James wrote: "Things are 'with' one another in many ways, but nothing includes everything or dominates over everything. The word 'and' trails along after every sentence. Something always escapes."[1] James does not go far enough. In philosophy, "and" may trail along after every sentence, yet "but" trails along after every paragraph. The job of elaboration is never quite finished. The difficulties we resolve at one point through seemingly helpful "clarifications" burst out again at another. No formulation of a position can dispel all the problems, answer all the questions, resolve all the difficulties.

Ramsey shrewdly observed that while we can make many things clearer, we cannot make anything altogether clear in philosophy. The "noise" of cognitive dissonance can never be fully eliminated. For the distinctions we draw in philosophy do not remove the element of fact involvement of the concepts at issue but only cushion its impact on one particular point. As we continue to press our concepts harder in the direction of theoretical clarity they will fission once more and antinomy will set in again. As a philosophical position develops, as it expands in intellectual space through the extension and refinement of its thematic concepts, inconsistency breaks out within it. Fundamental revisions with different and more elaborate distinctions, further complications and sophistications are always called for. There are no "final answers" in philosophy, no definitive resolutions.

In philosophy there is an ever-renewed need for further refinements and extensions. We arrive at the fundamental law of philosophical development: *Any given philosophical position, at any particular stage in its development, will, if developed further, encounter inconsistencies.* No formulation of a philosophical position can ever be fully adequate—definitive finality is destined always to elude us.

---

1. William James, *A Pluralistic Universe* (New York, 1909), p. 321.

As the thought of a philosopher becomes fully elaborated—as its conceptual mechanisms are refined and extended and clarified by himself, by his followers, or by his "school" and his tradition—inner tensions will come to light within the overall set of its commitments. Trouble breaks out within the fundamental commitments of the system in the form of aporetic inconsistency; further difficulties always arise; additional qualifications and refinements are always needed.

The development of a philosophical position is thus a never-ending task that takes on the form of a dialectical cycle of the kind depicted in figure 1. In philosophy, we can never manage to reach a natural stopping point at which *everything* that needs to be said has been said. No doubt the situation is worst at first. It is an objection standardly cast against a new philosophical contention that it is "unclear"—and so it is bound to be until its implications and ramifications get worked out. But to some extent the setting out of a philosophical position *always* remains programmatic. At any and every stage we have no more than a rough, imperfectly developed project on which further work needs to be done by way of overcoming difficulties and removing inexactnesses. Our efforts at philosophical system building can never succeed in achieving both total comprehensiveness and total coherence.

Finality is unattainable in philosophy. There is not a paragraph of a philosophical text on which a duly sagacious thinker cannot write a volume of massive commentary. And what is true of the initial paragraph holds for every paragraph of that commentary as well. (C.D. Broad's massive commentary on McTaggart's *The Nature of Existence* affords a good illustration.) Every attempt to articulate a systemic position embodies that instability of inner contradiction that paves the way for its further development and modification. There is always more to

*Figure 1*
THE DIALECTICAL CYCLE OF PHILOSOPHICAL INQUIRY

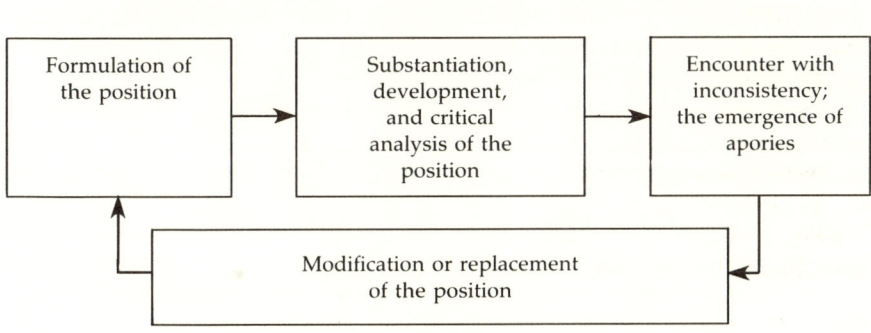

be said. As Schlegel rightly maintained, even the most elaborate system is but a mere fragment.[2]

And so the development of a philosophical position moves from a level of relative accessibility (elementality, fundamentality) to one of increasing technicality (elaborateness, sophistication). The system becomes rearticulated and reformulated in a way that is ever more ramified and complex. Philosophizing is, as it were, a dialectical game that can be played at different levels of difficulty.

When one examines the historical development of a philosophical position, one can always discern the unfolding of its inner perplexities—those crisis junctures at which it slips into inconsistency. It is this ultimate encounter with inconsistency within "established" philosophical positions that makes for inherent instability and provides the dynamical impetus to the continual alteration or replacement of philosophical systems.

Our philosophical questions are always answered incompletely, in ways that inevitably leave further crucial detail to be supplied. Philosophy moves inexorably toward becoming an inquiry into issues of increasing technicality and sophistication. And this makes interested bystanders impatient. They cry, "Will philosophy ever again address the heavens? Will it contribute anything to man's vision, rather than merely clarifying it?"[3] But this sort of complaint overlooks the filiation of means and ends in question resolution that links the technical issues of philosophy to the fundamental presystemic questions from which they arise. We are driven to those technical microissues by the inexorable necessity of addressing them in order to secure rationally adequate resolutions of the presystemic macroissues afforded by "eternal problems" of philosophy.

The answers we give to philosophical questions are always only rough and approximate. Our solutions to philosophical problems engender further problems. They are always open to challenges that require additional elaboration and refinement. In philosophy we are always impelled toward greater sophistication—our problem solving distinctions always bring yet further distinctions. We are led to compound wheels upon wheels—adding further epicycles of complexity to the theories we are seeking to render acceptable. But inconsistency-averting elaboration at one point only engenders further difficulties at another. No articulation of a philosophical system is free from problems.

---

2. For a compact account of his views see Braun, *Histoire de l'histoire de la philosophie*, pp. 278–85 (see esp. p. 283).

3. "TIME Essay: What (If Anything) to Expect from Today's Philosophers," *Time*, January 7, 1966, p. 25.

*Figure 2*
THE PROBLEM-DIALECTIC OF PHILOSOPHY

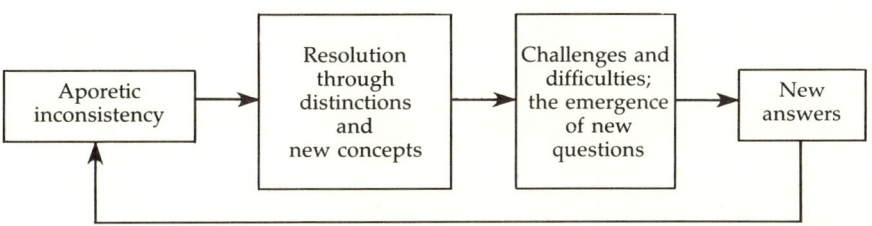

There is a process of ongoing dialectical oscillation between systematization and cognitive dissonance along the lines depicted in figure 2. Aporetic cycle succeeds aporetic cycle. We are faced with the fundamental law of dialectics: the prospect of a system that is finished and "perfected" is an illusion—no final (absolute, definitive) formulation of a philosophical position is possible.

In our dealings with aporetic clusters and antinomies in philosophy, consistency, once reestablished, will not remain forever. For in resolving our problems we begin with the simplest viable solutions. But trouble invariably lurks around as yet unturned corners. The fact-coordinated character of philosophical concepts precludes the prospect of a global (universal, all-purpose) context in which their inner tensions can be resolved once and for all. As we elaborate our philosophical positions by following the standard and natural, indeed *inevitable*, policy of giving the most straightforward and "plausible" answers to different questions in different contexts, we find ourselves plunged into inconsistency; solutions adequate in one context are inadequate in another.

To be sure, one need never grant that a philosophical doctrine as such is inadequate, but only that its specific *formulation* in a particular "state of the art" is. The doctrine as a whole should be seen as a diachronic organism, something that develops and grows and changes over time, maintaining its identity not in its specific content but in its general orientation and, above all, in its genealogy—its exfoliative linkage to the core commitments from which it arose. A doctrinal position as such (i.e., in contrast to its specific formulation) is schematic, maintaining its identity through successive systemic formulations by its overall programmatic tendency rather than through its substantive detail.[4]

---

4. This point was stressed particularly in the theory of philosophical systems articulated in Kröner's *Die Anarchie der philosophischen Systeme*. He wrote, "Weil das betreffende Problem in jedem dieser aufeinander folgenden Systeme eine gewisse Phase oder Stellung, Behandlung oder Lösung mitmacht, kann man kurz von der *Phasenreihe* eines Problems (Problemphasenriehe) sprechen" (ibid., 82, n. 1).

## 3. A Glance Backward: Hegel and Herbart

The ongoing dialectic of objections and replies, of continual refinement in the light of new approaches, means that the work of philosophy can never be completed. It is not feasible that anyone should ever be in a position to "have the last word" on these issues. Philosophical formulations are driven by an inner conceptual dynamic toward their own replacement. In philosophy as in science (but not in art!), someone's making a certain contribution to the tradition may be of permanent value, but that contributon itself is never permanent. This both explains and is confirmed by the peculiar nature of "progress" in philosophy. For such progress is generally made by going back to some essentially identical earlier position and reworking it, articulating it with greater sophistication and defending it with greater ingenuity against counter-arguments—themselves increasingly refined in the ongoing course of critical interchange—that exploit the residual difficulties that can never be altogether extruded from a philosophical position.

A dialectical process of Hegelian proportions is at work. According to Hegel, it is the essential character of human reason to involve itself in contradictions—conflicts of commitment that it first posits but then overcomes through an eventual reconciliation at a higher level. However, the philosopher who analyzed this aspect of the history of the subject most clearly was Johann Friedrich Herbart. He proposed that the history of philosophy should be recast in issue-oriented form and should in fact be written in terms of the development of doctrines devised to resolve successively encountered antinomies. The history of philosophy, he held, should be written as a history of *problems* (and thus in a genre of which, even today, we have but a few fragmentary samples).

Herbart maintained that the experiential concepts in whose terms we represent and process our cognitive experiences in science and ordinary life always involve internal conflicts. An experiential concept $A$ unites two disparate elements $M$ and $N$ that do not stand in a logico-conceptual union but are united by a strictly factual bond. There is a tension or contradiction here. We can neither (on theoretical grounds) maintain that there is, a fusion of $M$ and $N$ in $A$, nor yet (on factual grounds) can we deny this connection outright. Logic rejects the conceptual fusing of $M$ and $N$, experience rejects their separation. All we can do is suppose that there is some new element, some distinction that splits $M$ into $M_1$ and $M_2$, one of which is rigidly joined to $N$, the other strictly distinct from it. At best, then, we can see $A$ as an unstable compound, oscillating between $A_1$ (where $M_1$ is problematically conjoined with $N$) and $A_2$ (where $M_2$ is unproblematically disjoined from $N$). Accordingly, every experiential concept is the ground from which some suitable "supplementary concept" must emerge to yield a distinction capable of restoring consistency.

Herbart saw the prime task of philosophy as the reworking of our experiential concepts so as to restore consistency—to effect an integration that relegates these inner contradictions to the realm of mere appearance. Philosophy strives to overcome the internal inconsistency of our presystemic concepts. Throughout our philosophizing, those experiential concepts will inevitably come to be transcended by successors who seek to resolve the tensions of their presystemic predecessors. This process, Herbart's "method of relations" (*Methode der Beziehungen*), is the counterpart in his system of the Hegelian dialectic. As Dilthey put it:

> Herbart was the first who regressed analytically from the course of philosophical development to the particular problems that were the prime mover in the minds of individual thinkers. For him, philosophy was "the systematic study (*Wissenschaft*) of philosophical questions and problems." And so he responded to the question of the nature of philosophizing with the reply that it is "the endeavor to solve problems." In the first redaction of his *Introduction to Philosophy*, he places the motive force to philosophizing in the puzzles and contradictions regarding the nature of things. Our trying to put the pieces together, to see the world whole, occasions our initial discovery of philosophical problems.[5]

## 4. The Structure of Philosophical History

Herbert Spencer's law of development from indefinite homogeneity to more definite heterogeneity may not hold for biological development, but it certainly does hold for philosophical evolution. There is an ongoing exfoliation of more complex and internally diversified theories—an unfolding on whose course the aporetic theses at issue become increasingly refined and nuanced by means of successive distinctions.

In philosophy, old doctrines never die, they just take on new guises. They become increasingly complex and sophisticated to meet the demands of new conditions and circumstances. In the course of the dialectical progress of philosophical development, more complex questions, more refined concepts, and more subtle distinctions are constantly introduced. There is not only increasing sophistication in conceptual machinery but also an ongoing expansion of the problem horizon of the particular doctrine at issue as new theories are introduced to resolve the aporetic inconsistencies of prior commitments.

To overcome the inconsistencies that arise at any given level of philosophical development, we must push on to the next, introducing more distinctions, more refinements, more detail and sophistication. We encounter here a key aspect of the developmental dynamics of

---

5. Wilhelm Dilthey, *Gesammelte Schriften*, vol. VIII (Stuttgart and Göttingen, 1960), p. 134.

*Figure 3*
THE STRUCTURE OF PHILOSOPHICAL DEVELOPMENT

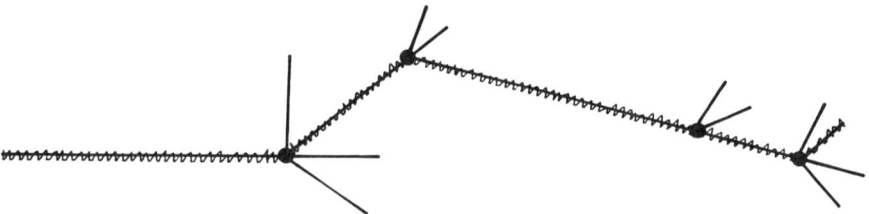

The nodes of the "tree" represent aporetic situations, and the paths that issue from these represent the diverse "positions" that afford an exit from inconsistency.

philosophy: the impetus to the ever-continuing development and refinement of our philosophical positions. We are impelled to move ever further from the simpler presystemic issues that afford the starting point of our philosophical deliberations. (That is why philosophers nowadays are always much more comfortable in talking with colleagues about technical problems than in explaining to the plain man how these technical discussions bear on the big issues.) The history of philosophy consists largely in an ongoing confrontation between competing positions standing perpetually in conflict, though changing in detail through increasing sophistication and complexification.

In the general course of things, the dialectical unfolding of philosophical history presents a unified picture of treelike proportions. The tradition that develops a philosophical position lurches from one apory to the next in the manner depicted in figure 3. At any given node, a theorist is in principle able to go back to a prior node and move forward along another path (*reçuler pour mieux sauter*, as Leibniz liked to say). Moreover, one can also use "the wisdom of hindsight" to go back and introduce (as it were, *ex post facto*) new nodes at earlier junctures. Revisionism always affords an alternative to simple development. New and previously overlooked distinctions and refinements can be introduced at any stage.

This is why major philosophers are always driven back to making a fresh start. They have a penchant for "going back to square one" to create new paths out of (or *around*) old problems, and accordingly view the inconclusiveness of earlier work with relish rather than dismay. Kant is typical in this regard when he writes in the *Prolegomena to Any Future Metaphysics* that "my purpose is to persuade all those who think metaphysics worth studying that it is absolutely necessary to pause a moment . . . regarding all that has been done as undone."[6] The pros-

---

6. Immanuel Kant, *Prolegomena to Any Future Metaphysics*, trans. L. W. Beck (New York, 1950), p. 3.

pect of picking up the threads of earlier stages is ever present in philosophy—which explains why the history of the subject plays such an important role in its own development.

We arrive at a model of philosophical development that is essentially exfoliative. Every philosophical position is linked to and developmentally derived from a prior doctrine that contains its root idea. (In the realm of philosophical thought as in physical nature we have *ex nihilo nihil*.) This exfoliative process involves a super engrafting of new distinctions upon old, with new topics and issues continually emerging from our efforts to resolve prior problems. There is an unending process of introducing further elaborative refinement into the setting of old, preestablished views, which sees an ungoing emergence of new positions to implement old doctrines. Thus, every philosophical concept and position always has a genealogy (an "archeology," in currently fashionable terminology) that can trace back its origins programmatically through a means-end chain of problem solving. Every position and distinction has its natural place in the developmental tree.

No one has stressed this aspect of philosophy more emphatically and eloquently than Dilthey: "Wholly in vain do various thinkers try to cast the whole past away in an endeavor to make a fresh start freed from all prejudgments. They cannot shake off what has been. The gods of the past come back uninvited to haunt them. The melody of our lives is inevitably sung to the accompanying voices of the past."[7] Nothing that belongs to the subject is wholly isolated or disconnected; the new is always part of an old, preestablished program. (Even Berkeleyian immaterialism has its neo-Platonic precursors.) And there is no reason of principle why the exfoliative process should ever stop.

The natural evolution of a philosophical school of thought is such that one always retains (some of) the old doctrines, adheres to the old credos and formulas while constantly pouring new wine into the old bottles. The school is the "same" school because its key theses (though increasingly seen as extremely rough approximations) are still retained—its doctrinal allegiances (as opposed to its explanations) continue the same. It fights under the same old banners and celebrates the same old heroes. But the actual substance of its deliberations constantly changes through ongoing "refinement." (Often, indeed, the discussion wanders off into mere technicalities, with philosophers addressing issues that have evolved from issues that have evolved from issues, and so on, losing all sight of that crucial guiding thread of relevance needed to preserve a connection with the fundamental questions that gave the whole process its start.)

7. Dilthey, vol. VIII, p. 226.

In philosophy we are thus faced with persisting schools of thought—ongoing traditions of doctrinal commitment in a continual state of inner development and mutual conflict. Such schools are united by agreement on first principles, but they are continually fragmented into subschools and sub-subschools through differentiation in matters of (increasingly subtle) detail. The process is one of a biological and evolutionary format with the development of genera, species, and ever more differentiated varieties. Things get increasingly complicated. Philosophizing is always a mixture of conservation and innovation—of preserving some element of a tradition while yet transforming it. Like it or not, even the most radical innovator in this field has some claim to the proud title of *conservator*, once applied honorifically to Jupiter and the Roman emperors. But this coin also has its other side.

## 5. Sic Transit

In the long run, any given contribution to the dialectic of philosophical development will eventually become obsolete in the light of subsequent criticism and refinement. Its value, however great, will ultimately become "merely historical" in that it will no longer count as a useful component of the *current* stage in the discussion of the issues.

Every state-of-the-art configuration of a philosophical doctrine is inherently unstable.

Moreover, new conflicts constantly recur intrasystemically. New apories arise as we develop systems further and make divergent resolutions. Inconsistency breaks out again and again as we refine our answers for the $n$th level of approximation to the $(n + 1)$st. There is bound to be an ongoing succession of "family quarrels" within the various schools of thought.

Throughout the process envisaged by the aporetic model of philosophical development, the old diversities persist. The different programs created by different resolutions to *old* questions remain in place. All philosophers work within one or another long-established tradition; they cannot sever the links that bind them to the past of the subject. Old conflicts regarding fundamentals never die—they just take on a new and more sohisticated garb. The old alternatives remain intact in essentials, defined by the fundamental aporetic theses that later developments refine. The lines of resolution initially embarked upon need never hit a dead end—they can simply continue on their separate paths.

We can now see more clearly why the study of the history of philosophy is an integral part of the study of the subject itself. One can only understand the character of current positions—can only grasp their need for all those distinctions—by retracing the steps that have brought matters to their present pass. Philosophical genealogy is crucial to comprehending the bearing of a philosophical concept, thesis, or argument. Only by following through the dialectical "family tree" of distinctions can we come to see the root issues out of which a philosophical doctrine arose and from which it draws its relevance to human concerns—and thus its significance.

The dialectical format for schematizing the developmental process in philosophy also opens up interesting prospects for analysis. For example, it makes it possible to raise certain historical questions that would otherwise seem wild and senseless. In considering how an antinomy defines a spectrum of competing positions, one can now pose the essentially negative question of why a certain theoretically available position was not actually taken—why a certain "ecological niche" in philosophy was allowed to stand empty at a certain juncture. One can ask in a perfectly meaningful way why certain philosophical positions were *not* taken at a particular stage in the development of the subject—and expect to receive an informative and illuminating response, perhaps in terms of the intellectual presuppositions or preconceptions of the day.

The dialectical model of philosophical development carries significant implications for philosophical historiography. For it indicates the desirability and explanatory utility of describing at least the major outlines of the course of philosophical history in terms of such an explicitly dialectical format. In highlighting points of similarity and difference, such a process serves to clarify the philosophical concepts and distinctions and theses at issue in the articulation of various philosophical positions. (The ancient Greek doxographers provide a pioneering if somewhat crude model in this respect.) An account in these terms is a most useful way to recast our perceptions of philosophical history.

We return once more to the promise that has been made again and again of a sketch of the history of philosophy (or some of its departments) on dialetical principles. Such an account would present, at least in outline, the succession of aporetic difficulties and apory-removing distinctions through which various philosophical schools of thought have evolved in interactive rivalry. As yet we have little more than illustrations of this programmatic prospect. But even this is enough to suggest that a fuller realization of the program would provide a most illuminating and valuable resource, affording a clearer and more cogent idea of the development of philosophy as a process with a coherent developmental structure that endows it with a fundamental historical unity and integrity. It would enable us to supplement the purely biographical and chronological approach with a systematic account of the development of lines of thought rather than a disjoint-seeming series of ever-changing views of particular thinkers.

## 6. The Burden of History

Hegel saw the history of philosophy as a succession of systems, each system naturally giving rise to the next and each characteristic of the historical era in which it was developed—the whole process inexorably leading toward Hegel's own philosophy. But the idea that every age has its characteristic philosophy is profoundly wrong. Not only are alternatives always open, but at some level of approximation the same old alternatives continue to be open.[8] Unlike creative activity in music or fine arts, philosophizing is not a matter of transiently all-embracing styles but of ever-recurrent doctrines. Dilthey was right in stressing, against Hegel, that the development of philosophy is not a sequential succession of all-dominant systems but an ongoing parallelism of conflicting systems that assume different historically conditioned configurations.[9] Our interest in the history of philosophy should never be *merely* historical, for it is by understanding the twists and turns by which our position has attained its present configuration in the forging flavors of ongoing controversy that we can best understand exactly what that position amounts to.

Overall, what we have in philosophy is not the evolution of consensus but continuing controversy. The quarrel between idealists and realists, determinists and free-willers, sceptics and cognitivists, deontologists and consequentialists, and so on, all represent branchings in a river that flows on and on.

Dilthey was among the first to stress this and to make the enduring strife of systems a central plank of his theoretical platform:

The contest among rival world-views cannot be brought to a decision at any significant point. The course of history effects a selection among them, but their main types stand forth alongside each other self-sufficiently, impassable yet indestructible. Owing their existence to no decisive demonstration, they can be destroyed by none. The individual styles and the particular formulations of each type come to be "refuted," but their rooting in human life persists and fortifies and continually produces new forms.[10]

Philosophical history since classical antiquity unfolds as an ongoing refinement of preexisting doctrines, a development in whose course ever-

---

8. To say this is not, of course, to deny that philosophers of a given age usually share a great many assumptions.
9. Dilthey, vol. VIII, pp. 131, 134.
10. Dilthey, vol. VIII, pp. 86–87.

more sophisticatedly divergent doctrines emerge from the fundamental discords of old, established programs. It is marked by the persistence of the conflict between the schools, an ongoing rivalry of systems.

Philosophical problems root in apories, and there are always different alternative exits from aporetic inconsistency. No strictly abstract argumentation, no "proof" predicated on general principles alone can constrain one of those to the exclusion of others. No philosophical arguments are without presuppositions—none is free from any and all precommitments; each presupposes some preferential or eliminative mechanism. And there will always be alternative options here. The door of rational tenability can never be shut on the prospect of solutions different from those we ourselves favor.

Primarily perennial in *philosophia perennis* are not only its questions but also the doctrines and thus (alas) the *disagreements* of the discipline.[11] Convergence is a coincidence in the other sense of the term as well—an improbable accident. Different systems of philosophy reflect different approaches, different perspectives, different worldviews. And these are permanent theses and unconquerable, representing perennially recurrent leitmotivs within the human condition.

The spectrum of major doctrinal alternatives was mapped out by the community a long time ago. The battles of the present are fought in new theaters of conflict, but the combatants fight (like it or not!) in the same wars. As Dilthey saw, "The multiplicity of philosophical systems spreads about us and surrounds us on all sides; throughout the span of their existence they have denied and contested one another."[12] The philosopher cannot accept the precept of the theologian Henry Venn: "Never on any account dispute: Debate is the work of the flesh (i.e., the devil)." In philosophy, controversy is the lifeblood of the enterprise. Philosophical disagreement is perennial—and inevitable.

Surely philosophical issues do die off? "Nobody could now win credence who asserted that to be is to be a quantity of water, however plausible that doctrine might have looked to Thales."[13] But matters are never that simple. The notion that everything in the world is composed of one uniform type of stuff that is highly changeable and "fluid"—that

---

11. The root idea of the perennial in philosophy was devised by Renaissance humanists to confirm the continuity of Greek and Christian philosophizing (see esp. *De perenni philosophia* [Venice, 1540] by the papal librarian Augustinus Steuchus [1497–1548]). Leibniz revived this ideal and projected it into modern philosophy (see Saturnio Alvarez Turienzo, "Révélation, Raison et 'Philosophia Perennis,' " in *Révue des sciences philosophiques et théologiques* 64 [1980]: 333–48). My only criticism of this tradition is that it sees a singular where I see a plural: *philosophiae perennes*. The permanent lies not in a common core of various systems, but in the distinctive root ideas of the systems themselves.
12. Dilthey, vol. VIII, p. 25, and cp. p. 152.
13. John Passmore, *Philosophical Reasoning* (New York, 1961), p. 39.

to be is to be a form of substance of which water is a useful paradigm—can certainly not be written off. Yet surely no philosopher is concerned about the mental processes of angels! True enough! Yet philosophers have not ceased to contemplate the nature of superhuman intelligence—though they are nowadays more likely to discuss them in the setting of computers or extraterrestrial aliens than in that of angels. The point is that philosophical issues do not die out in essentials—they simply alter their form to accommodate themselves to new circumstances. We cannot issue death certificates in philosophy.

The question "Is the natural world the product of the creative agency of an underlying intelligence?" has been debated by philosophers since antiquity. One tradition (stretching from Anaximander to Democritus to Hobbes and beyond) responds negatively. A second tradition (from Anaxagoras to Plato to Berkeley and beyond) takes an affirmative line. A third tradition (from Pyrrho to Kant to Carnap) wants to dismiss the question as inappropriate. There is no good reason to think that a metaphysical issue like this will ever be settled; the only reasonable stance is to expect an ongoing rivalry between these three competing schools of thought.

Sometimes, to be sure, philosophical problems do indeed vanish. When an aporetic cluster is simply abandoned—its members no longer seen as plausible (as with those examples from Presocratic matter theory)—then we do indeed resolve, or rather *dissolve*, the philosophical problems that the apory otherwise engenders. Such problems aren't *solved*, they just fade away. But in general this happens only with more or less technical problems of nth order detail. The basic problems always remain in place, firmly rooted in some fundamental element of the human condition.

In philosophy, the root problems and the manifold of their fundamentally discordant resolutions are always "available." Doctrinal disagreements may lie fallow for a time. But they are always still there potentially, dormant like the princess of the fairy tale, awaiting the kiss of dedication that brings them back to life.

What most working philosophers would dearly love to have is what Descartes promised them—a liberation from the history of their subject, a justification for laying aside the burden of the past. From Sextus Empiricus to Comte and beyond, we find an ever-recurrent series of illustrations of the fact that no philosopher who offers this will go unappreciated—those who experience the sense of liberation from the dead hand of their over-ambitious predecessors will deluge him with gratitude. And yet no promise is more empty.

Philosophy cannot separate itself from its past without ceasing to be what it is. No promise is more beguiling and yet more futile than that now, at last, we have for the very first time grasped things as they really are. Every creative philosopher yearns to build from the ground up—to put all earlier labors aside, turn to a fresh page, and "consider as undone all that has been done."[14] Yet it cannot be. In philosophy the shadow of the past dogs our every leap into a brave new future. The dream of independence from the past is vain—turn where we will, we travel along paths already marked out, however roughly and imperfectly, by our predecessors. The destiny of philosophy in this regard is portrayed by the precept *Plus ça change, plus c'est la même chose*. Method, style, concept can be new. But doctrine is destined to be familiar—caught within the boundaries of long-fixed possibilities. Leibniz wrote to Bossuet that he did not so much wish to refute or destroy as to make discoveries and construct something on foundations that have already been laid.[15] This represents a sensible and realistic view; we are *all* destined to build on foundations that are already laid. The ways of exiting from the toils of inconsistency are limited. Any position is destined to be yet another variant of this or that old, fundamental doctrine.

Let us turn briefly from the past to a consideration of the future.

The dialectical model sketched in this discussion affords a schema for describing the *form or structure* of philosophical development, but emphatically not one for predicting its *substance*. The model is devoid of predictive utility at the substantive level, for this whole account relates to the *form* of philosophical history and not to its substantive *content*. We can never say in advance what new subjects can be introduced by means of "saving" distinctions.

Philosophical development is a matter of ongoing conceptual innovation. This has important consequences. For while we can roughly predict in advance what the underlying issues on the agenda of future philosophy will be—they will be, in essentials, those that have always been there, the problems of man's knowledge of the world and his place within it—we cannot foresee details of what solutions to these problems will be offered and what sorts of standards will be deployed to judge the adequacy of knowledge, justice, and duty will not go away—in some form or other they will always be there (though there will always be some Pyrrhonists who would have us jettison the lot). But by what conceptual contrivances these views will be argued is something regarding which we must, in the very nature of things, remain profoundly ignorant. Philosophizing is a creative process; there

---

14. Kant, *Prolegomena*, sec. 3.
15. "Je n'aime pas tant à refuter et à détruir qu'à découvrir quelque chose et à bastir sur les fondemens déjà posés" (Akad. I, 8, p. 123 [3/13 July 1692]).

is and can be no inner law of philosophical development with regard to matters of substantive detail.

The basic issues that define the discipline are stable, however. Philosophical doctrines lead a charmed life. They need never die on the field of battle. The power of distinctions means that a way of healing wounds is always at their disposal. Philosophical doctrines hold aloft banners that may be deserted but can never be destroyed. However thorough their defeat in battle may seem, they can always rise, phoenixlike, from the conflagration to continue the war on another day.

# 6

# Cognitive Values and Antinomy Resolution

## 1. The Problem of Evaluative Selection

Confronted by an aporetic group of collectively inconsistent yet individually attractive theses, the philosopher must sacrifice some of these individually appealing components on the altar of consistency. But abstract reason and logic tell us only *that* we must resolve the inconsistency and not *how* to do so. Some of our allegiances must give way to others—but which to which? Abstract rationality does not help us here; when it has said and done all it can, it can only impose the discipline of consistency; the problem of choosing between alternatives remains.

It cannot be overemphasized that the conflict between alternative philosophical positions cannot be resolved by logic and rigorous reasoning alone. General principles alone do not speak for one resolution *vis-à-vis* another. Nor does strictly evidential reasoning mend matters. By hypothesis, all of the parties to an aporetic inconsistency are plausible and evidentially well spoken for; it is not until after the evidence has said all it can that apory has taken firm hold. This process of constraining a rational resolution to aporetic conflict requires a resource over and above what can be straightforwardly evidentiated. There simply are no incontrovertible "hard facts" that can establish a philosophical thesis, because by the time a philosophical issue arises, those "hard facts" have *already* done all they can. To say this is not to deny that those "self-evident truths" near and dear to the hearts of commonsense philosophers exist, but rather to deny that philosophical positions can be established by their means.

Invariably, every proposed "resolution" of an antinomy involves a particular combination of retentions and rejections. Each choice represents a distinctive balance of costs and benefits, enabling us to retain some things we would like to have at the price of giving up others. Each has its own characteristic balance of advantages and disadvantages. And it is these that must be our guide. To exit from the inconsistency we must have some measure of value; we must deploy some standard for evaluating the attractions of the theses at issue. Our finding all those aporetic theses plausible is what got us into trouble in the first place; we now face the problem of *weighing just how plausible* they are.

Every way of averting inconsistency in aporetic situations realizes its benefits at the cost of departing from some of our presystemic views. Resolving the paradox thus turns on determining the relative acceptability of the various theses that are a party to the conflict. An eliminative pruning based on evaluatively preferential selection becomes indispensable.

To work our way out of apory, we must thus proceed on a *quasi-economic* basis. We face the harsh realities of the human condition—few of the world's desiderata come cost free. Every resolution regains consistency *at a price*, an "opportunity cost" in terms of lost desiderata. A process of cost-benefit appraisal is involved, though, to be sure, the issue is one of rational rather than material economy. To determine which resolution is optimal, which is the least costly, we must be in a position to do comparative evaluation—*cognitive* evaluation, of course, with respect to epistemic costs and benefits.

What better, more rational way of evaluating contentions can there possibly be than that of seeing how cogent we find the arguments that speak for them? But this issue has its problems. Something is always a bit suspect about proofs and demonstrations in philosophy—so much so that one recent writer maintains that "all the proofs in a good book on philosophy could be dispensed with, without its losing a whit of its 'convincingness'."[1] For the ultimate burden of philosophical substantiation is not carried in system-internal proofs and demonstrations but rather by the premises, presuppositions, and precommitments that underlie them. At this stage, however, we are thrown back on rudimentary, extrasystemic considerations.

In philosophy, the acceptability of the overall argumentation turns pivotally upon the conclusions to which it leads. The standard way of assessing a philosophical doctrine is not only on the acceptability of its basis (the principles that constitute the *terminus a quo* of its argumentation), but no less importantly on the acceptability of its outcome (the

---

1. Waismann, "How I See Philosophy," p. 282.

consequences that afford its *terminus ad quem*).² For one cannot evaluate the strength of a philosophical argument *independently* of assessing the overall plausibility of the consequences that it yields. But this fact means that we *already* need to be in a position to assess the relative merits of the various theses that are a party to the controversy—that is, to carry out the very task that this process is designed to accomplish.

The fact is that this eliminative phase takes the form of what is, to all intents and purposes, a form of intellectual cost accounting, a cost-benefit analysis. Its *modus operandi* consists in the evaluation and appraisal of the various "costs" and "benefits" of the several alternatives and proceeds via a weighing of the standing of the alternatives *vis-à-vis* various parameters of merit (and demerit). These include not only formal criteria like consistency, uniformity (treating like cases alike), comprehensiveness, systemic elegance, simplicity, economy ("Ockham's razor," etc.), but also various material standards of probative process like closeness to common sense, explanatory adequacy, inherent plausibility to provide for the allocation of presumption and burden of proof. It is upon these pre- or subsystemic factors that the persuasive weight of philosophical argumentation must ultimately rest.

Accordingly, the probative situation of philosophy calls for an essentially evaluative resource within our methodology itself—a means for assessing the (strictly intellectual) costs and benefits involved in the adoption or rejection of alternative doctrinal positions, for cognitive evaluation, in short.

The lesson of these considerations is not that there are no good arguments for a philosophical position. It is just that such arguments must be developed on the basis of a cognitive-value orientation—that the evaluation of their cogency must hinge on suitable standards and criteria of merit. And such standards can differ potentially from person to person. The assessment of the reasons that alone can validate a philosophical thesis is an orientational or perspectival matter.

As Dilthey rightly insisted, one never gets to the root of a philosophical system through reasoning alone.³ No system, no position in

---

2. As Bertrand Russell put it, where philosophical issues are concerned, we have an *inductive* situation that yields "reasons rather for believing the premises because true conclusions follow from them, than for believing the consequences because they follow from the premises" (Preface to *Principia Mathematica* [Oxford, 1910]). Cf. Plato, *Republic*, bk. VII, 533.

3. "Niemals trifft man auf die Wurzel eines Systems in einem blossen Räsonnement" (Wilhelm Dilthey, *Philosophische Schriften*, vol. VIII [Stuttgart and Göttingen, 1960], p. 150).

philosophy can be validated solely through considerations of abstract rationality. We cannot resolve philosophical disputes by recourse to the philosophically unproblematic facts of extraphilosophical knowledge, because the issue of the bearing of those facts will always itself become a party to the philosophical dispute. No resolutions of the issues can be validated by reasoning from the objective facts of the matter or on the basis of abstract general principles. There will have to be some resort to essentially normative considerations based on cognitive-value determinations. In philosophical argumentation, "the facts" will never of themselves enable us to decide matters, because the issue is always in part one of the evaluative principles that determine the import of the facts.

## 2. The Pivotal Role of Analogy and the Role of Cognitive Values

Behind and beneath a philosophical system stands the question of cognitive cogency. Be a system ever so elegantly worked out, in the final analysis the question is always: Do we find it plausible, acceptable, appealing? Be its intellectual food ever so carefully prepared and processed, the cook ever so painstaking, the question remains: Do we find it palatable? On this question, the system itself can have nothing to offer—the issue is extrasystemic. About the acceptability of some of its particular theses given certain others, the system can say much. But its *overall* acceptability is an external question about which the system itself can say nothing decisive, since whatever it says immediately *internalizes* the issue.[4]

There are two ways of proceeding in philosophical deliberations: we can reason *for* our position or *from* it. The latter approach is *esoteric*: we address those who share our basic premises or principles, those who, as regards fundamentals, are "already converted"—those who are, as it were, birds of our feather. Such esoteric argumentation proceeds from the internal commitments of our system. An *exoteric* appeal, by contrast, proceeds from outside the framework of our systemic commitments. Here we cannot simply reason from the basic premises or principles of our position—they themselves are in question. Addressing those who do not share our systemic commitments, we must argue in a way that is wholly system-external. Here we can only proceed by way of promising examples and plausible analogies. Esoterically we can attempt to demonstrate or prove our contentions; exoterically we can only seek to persuade, to secure acceptance for them by looser,

---

4. Cf. J. F. Herbart, *Sämtliche Werke*, vol. II, ed. K. Kehrbach and O. Fluegel (*Aalen*, 1960), p. 288.

more rhetorical devices.[5] The one leads along the paths within, the other faces the problem of making an entry from without.

In the final analysis, the burden of philosophical argumentation is borne by exoteric rather than esoteric reasoning. A systemic approach is unavailable at the start, because the entire system itself remains in contention. When arguing *for* the fundamental commitments of our system, we cannot argue *from* them. We must look in another, system-detached direction.

When we abstract from our systemic commitments to argue for its fundamental theses and presuppositions, we are driven to argue *extra-systemically*—without the prospect of any appeal to our systemic commitments. Once the rudiments of a system are in hand, we can argue in terms of their "implications," using already consolidated theses as "givens" for inferential derivations. But system-external, root argumentation must proceed through analogy to certain seemingly unproblematic issues that lie wholly outside our systemic framework. We are driven to reach outside the system to assimilate its views to other, cognate situations that seem unproblematic. The work of exoteric root argumentation in philosophy is to lead one into accepting the basic commitments of a position without already presupposing some of them. It proceeds to establish plausibility through assimilation to something one already accepts, invoking certain clear cases to serve as models for other, more problematic ones.

At this juncture all we can do is make use of parallels and analogies to substantiate our contentions. Exoteric, extrasystemic root argumentation for a philosophical position is always a matter of arguing by analogy. Until a system has been built up sufficiently to bear further development on its own, analogy is our only substantiative recourse in philosophy. We must assimilate the problematic situations that arise in our philosophizing to the relatively unproblematic considerations of the extraphilosophical arena. That is why examples are so prominent in this domain: they invite us to draw the fundamental analogies on which a thinker relies as supports for the basic theses he wishes to maintain.[6]

---

5. This use of the distinction follows in the footsteps of Leibniz, who writes: *Est tamen inter philosophandi modos discrimen ingens, alius enim est, ut sic dicam Acroamaticus, alius Exotericus. Acroamaticus est in quo omnia demonstrantur. Exotericus in quo quaedam sine demonstratione dicuntur, confirmantur tamen congruentiis quibusdam et rationibus topicis, vel etiam demonstratoriis, sed non nisi topice propositis, illustrantur exemplis et similitudinibus* (A VI, 2, p.416). On these issues cf. Walter Tinner, "Leibniz: System und Exoterik," in *Esoterik und Exoterik in der Philosophie*, ed. H. Holzhey and W. C. Zimmerli (Basel, 1977), pp. 101–16; and K.-R. Woehrmann, "Die Unterscheidung von Exoterik und Esoterik bei Leibniz," in *Akten des III. Internationalen Leibniz-Kongresses*, vol. III (Wiesbaden, 1980), pp. 72–82.

6. Cf. Waismann, "How I See Philosophy," pp. 281–82.

Consider an illustration. Suppose that we want to argue extrasystemically for the thesis "An agent has no moral responsibility for acts done involuntarily." To substantiate the thesis at this level, we begin by noting that there are various clear cases, such as acts done under duress. Generalizing beyond this point, we then endeavor to assimilate to these clear cases various others that are less clear (e.g., psychological or other sorts of "pressure"), affiliating the relatively problematic cases with others that are not only more straightforward but also seen as archetypical. And this, of course, is a matter of argumentation by analogy—of conforming what we might say in problematic cases to what we would say in others where the situation is more clear cut.

The determinative role of analogy in root argumentation at the extrasystemic level of philosophizing means that reasoning in this context will amount to the more informal mode of argumentation discussed by Aristotle in the *Topics* in contrast with the more demonstrative modes of reasoning treated in the *Analytics*.[7] But, of course, even informal, presystemic argumentation is still argumentation—still a recourse to good reasons and the dialectic of rationality.

The "logic" of analogical reasoning accordingly becomes a paramount consideration for philosophy. Analogical arguments are never valid or invalid simply and outright, but only more or less plausible or cogent. For arguments by analogy turn on two sorts of factors:

(1) The *extent of analogy* in terms of the number of similariies in relation to the number of dissimilarities.
(2) The *degree of analogy* in terms of the relative importance (weight, significance) of the various similarities and dissimilarities.

The second of these factors is particularly important. When one argues by analogy, the issue of cognitive value (importance, significance, weight, centrality, priority) cannot be avoided. The issue becomes a matter of assessing *significant* similarities and *insignificant* differences. How heavily are the points of kinship that constitute "the positive analogy" to be counted, and to what extent are they offset by the points of discrepancy that constitute "the negative analogy"? Similarity in unimportant respects will obviously count for less or perhaps not count at all. Differences in peripheral respects can be ignored. The evaluative issue of the importance of various points of relative similar-

---

7. The idea that root argumentation for a philosophical position requires an extraphilosophical mode of reasoning—a "rhetorical logic" related in spirit to the project of Aristotle's *Topics*—was urged in Eberhard Rogge's seminal book, *Axiomatik alles möglichen Philosophierens* (Meisenheim am Glan, 1950). Henry W. Johnstone, Jr., has recently developed this idea in various publications. See his *Philosophy and Argument*, and *Validity and Rhetoric in Philosophical Argument* (University Park, Pa., 1978).

ity is inextricably present in an argument by analogy. An argument by analogy proceeds in terms of an assimilation and differentiation of respects, and it is crucial to have a standard for assessing just how *important* the various points of similarity and dissimilarity are in particular cases.[8] In such situations, the matter is not one of *yes or no*. What counts is the comparative issue of greater or lesser importance. To assess the alternatives we must be able to make a comparison between them, in particular by weighing their several points of similarity by some sort of common measure.

Suppose that the usual dictionary definition of a fact-coordinated concept C tells us that X (*inter alia*) figures among its features; for example, that silver has the highest thermal and electrical conductivity of any substance. What now if those items we characterize as C were to lack this one particular feature—assuming, say, that silver were a less agile conductor or that many other substances were more agile. Would all those "silver" objects now no longer be *silver?* No doubt we wouldn't cross this bridge unless we got to it, but how we then crossed it would depend on which analogies to the standard situation still remain in place and just how important we deem them relative to those we have to forego. The issue becomes one of "judgment" if we are assessing the relative importance (centrality and so on) of various factors. Reasoning from analogies is always a matter of judgement and interpretation in which something other than mere factual description is always involved.

Analogies are never conclusive, never decisive. But they do carry some weight—and if their impetus is to be evaded, this weight must be set aside. To do so, we must be in a position to assess this weight. When conflicting analogies or competing paradigms pull in opposite directions, we need a guiding value framework to settle the issue of priorities.

In philosophical controversy we are constantly exchanging counter-considerations, tossing the burden of argument back and forth. We need measuring scales for weighing this burden, for evaluating those crucial factors of importance and significance on which the bearing of the considerations that are adduced will inevitably depend.[9]

What considerations deserve *some* weight in point of theoretical relevancy is determinable on a basis that is impersonal and value free, but just *how much* weight in relation to others is not. This is something

---

8. On reasoning by analogy, see the classic discussion in J. M. Keynes's *A Treatise on Probability* (London, 1921), as well as the up-to-date treatment of J. F. Ross, *Portraying Analogy* (Cambridge, 1981).

9. The conceptions of presumption and burden of proof at issue here are treated at some length in my *Dialectics* (Albany, N. Y., 1977).

that hinges on our intellectual orientation: it is a matter of our *approach* to the facts, of the light in which we propose to view them. And this is a function of our "interests" in both senses of the term (what we deem significant and what we deem profitable for our own concerns). The issue now is one of priority and value.

The values we are dealing with here are *epistemic* values. They deal with the normative issue of what we *should* accept, all right, but "should" relative to the interests of inquiry itself. These cognitive values turn on epistemic parameters of the sort inventoried in table 1.

Such cognitive values provide the yardsticks by whose means we resolve issues of priority, certainty, emphasis, significance, urgency, and the like, in the exploitation of analogies. Cognitive evaluation is no doubt partly a matter of learning about the objective facts, but not entirely—and that is the crux. Considerations of fact and evidence affect issues of cognitive value but do not determine them.

One's cognitive values reflect an *intellectual predilection* regarding the cognitive serviceability of relevant data. This is a matter of one's *predisposition* to assign probative weight, to give priority or precedence to this rather than that sort of probative consideration. Matters of cognitive axiology reflect the different standards of importance (significance, priority, centrality) that we bring to the factual materials with which

*Table 1*
A SAMPLER OF COGNITIVE VALUES

|  | Utility-Analogous | Probability-Analogous |
|---|---|---|
| Individual | *Significance-Oriented*<br>important/unimportant<br>significant/insignificant<br>illuminating/unhelpful<br>informative/uninformative<br>interesting/uninteresting<br>weighty/trivial | *Plausibility-Oriented*<br>plausible/far-fetched<br>relevant/irrelevant<br>uniform/discordant<br>established/novel<br>ordinary/unusual<br>general/idiosyncratic<br>natural/unnatural<br>simple/complex<br>exact/inexact |
| Contextual | *Pragmatic*<br>central/peripheral<br>immediate/remote<br>firm/fragile<br>fundamental/surface<br>fruitful/sterile<br>deep/superficial<br>urgent/negligible<br>pressing/deferable | *Systemic*<br>coherence-consistency<br>uniformity-homogeneity<br>comprehensiveness-inclusiveness<br>completeness-self-sufficiency<br>self-supportiveness-autonomy<br>economy-efficiency<br>elegance-harmony<br>regularity-orderliness |

we deal. Mere *relevance* as such (having some weight or other) is a matter of the evidential situation of objective relations and impersonal standards. But *significance*—the issue of just how much (relative) weight pertains to one item *vis-à-vis* others is bound to be to some extent variable from person to person. Cognitive values (importance, significance, etc.) are not properties we discover to preexist in the things we investigate; they are characteristics that we impute to things and their features in the light of our own concerns.

It is important to recognize, however, that such evaluative predispositions need by no means always *prevail* in our reasoning. One will in some cases be impelled in a certain direction of credence in spite of and notwithstanding one's inclinations in another, even as one may incline to trust some source, but bitter experience may ultimately undo this initial inclination. The presumptions at issue are like most legal presumptions in being defeasible—liable to be upset or reversed by sufficiently weighty counterindications. A probative orientation exerts a certain cognitive pressure, but its force is not infinite and irresistible but can be dampened and even ultimately deflected and redirected. Accordingly, such orientations themselves are not necessarily fixed and immutable. They can change as the result of the pressure of consequences to which they themselves lead.

The fact/value distinction is once more at work. To be sure, the *fact* that X holds certain values is itself always a strictly factual matter. But the *propriety* of this position is not a factual matter. And propriety is the crucial issue. To use a factual thesis P as a premise for reasoning, one must set out from P itself and not from the fact that X believes P. Similarly in the value case, to use the value thesis V as a premise of reasoning, one must see V itself as appropriate and not rely on the fact that X values V.

But cannot our values—cognitive values included—simply be rationally inappropriate, irrational, even bizarre? Of course they can. It would be strange indeed to deem clouds more important than atoms. But strictly rational constraints only eliminate part of the spectrum, leaving much undecided. They are delimitative, not determinative or decisive, and always leave open a wide range of options. Whatever "in" and "out" they indicate always leaves a large gray area in between.

Analogy is the machine through which cognitive values relating to issues of importance and plausibility become recruited into our criteria of acceptability as well. The controlling role of analogy in launching and guiding our philosophical deliberations means that the reasoned substantiation of philosophical positions is always ultimately based on an appeal to cognitive values. As practical rationality calls on us to conjure with economic costs and benefits in deciding about actions, so epistemic rationality calls on us to conjure with these cognitive costs and benefits in resolving issues of philosophical judgment.

There are close relations between cognitive values and values in the broader sense. The cases we take as central in the realization of cognitive positions—our archetypes and paradigms—will also reflect our values at large. They serve as standards of acceptability. The Pythagorean concern for harmony with the universe, the Aristotelian emphasis on self-worth, Stoic insistence on self-sufficiency, Marxist dedication to social homogeneity, and the like, all reflect value commitments that manifest themselves in the choices of the cognitive paradigms deployed in evaluating theses. And all such value differences express and manifest themselves in our cognitive proceedings via the weight borne by analogies with various clear-cut cases.

Philosophical analogies generally operate through archetypes—archetypes for nature (as an organism, an artifact, a mechanism, a god), for man (as an animal, a mechanism, a minigod), for the state (as a family, an army, a mutual-benefit society). The philosopher's construction of probative cogency deploys these analogies as yardsticks of plausibility and acceptability.

In Plato, we have the analogy of mathematical objects as ideal models for natural objects ("ideas"). In Spinoza, we assimilate causality to reasons ("the order and connection of ideas is the same as the order and connection of things"). In Leibniz, persons are paradigm substances and personal identity the paradigm for individuation. In Hume, mathematical demonstration is the archetype for all reasoning. Every philosopher has his pet analogies on which the central ideas of his system pivot and by reference to which its key theses are motivated.[10]

But as Plato stressed, our concepts represent archetypical ideas (*paradeigma*) that are only imperfectly attuned to the recalcitrant realities of the world. Their use involves us in considerations of more or less and calls for exercising judgment in a way that involves an element of person-differential evaluation in problematic cases. This circumstance has far-reaching implications.[11]

---

10. Cf. Stephen C. Pepper on "root metaphors" in *World Hypotheses*.

11. On paradigms as cognitive values, see Thomas S. Kuhn's *Structure of Scientific Revolutions* (Chicago, 1962); and compare Gerald Doppelt, "Kuhn's Epistemological Relativism," in J. W. Meiland and M. Krausz, eds., *Relativism: Cognitive and Morals* (Notre Dame, 1982), pp. 109–46. Regardless of whether the Kuhnian analysis of paradigm-based disagreement accurately reflects the situation in natural science, the fact remains that it applies substantially to philosophy. Kuhn, by focusing too intently on the earlier, less "developed" stages of natural science, perhaps held science too closely to the paradigm of philosophy, somewhat ironically producing an inverted way of "putting philosophy on the high-road of science."

## 3. Philosophizing Hinges on Cognitive Evaluation

In addressing the questions of philosophy, we don't just want answers, we want *cogent* answers that have the backing of good reasons. Reasoned argument alone is the proper instrument of philosophy. But to secure good reasons for our views, we must be in a position to evaluate the merit of arguments by analogy, which means that we must be in possession of value-laden norms and standards. Having a cognitive-value posture is a *sine qua non* for being able to develop the only sort of argument by which a philosophical position can ultimately be defended.

The question of the ultimate bearing of analogical considerations and reasonings is always with us in philosophy. Whether certain analogies are actually *appropriate* and just how *cogently* their deployment confirms a conclusion are always germane questions. And this issue of the epistemic standards by which we assess the bearing of relevant considerations can only be addressed in the light of cognitive values.

The cogency of arguments by analogy cannot be appraised through their inputs alone; this requires some reference to their outputs as well. We cannot avoid weighing the costs of endorsing these results. A cognitive-value orientation is not an algorithm for producing solutions to philosophical problems relative to prefixed constraints but serves to define the constraints themselves, forming a part of what is needed to mark a solution as acceptable, to see that the "solution" actually is a solution. When philosophizing in line with Socrates' injunction to "follow the argument where it leads," we must also consider whether we are willing to be there.

Philosophizing is a labor of reason, of endeavoring to back contentions by cogent arguments that afford good reasons for their acceptance. But this goodness and cogency is an inherently *evaluative* matter that turns on the weight we are prepared to give various considerations in the probative scheme of things. Some thinkers see it as crucial to their acceptability that philosophical contentions be intuitive. If they agree with our intentions, well and good; if they are counterintuitive, so much the worse for them. Others see intuition as a siren song that beckons us to error and confusion. Again, some see precedent as an index of truth, others as a token of vulnerability. Some see established usage as authoritative, others as an idol of the tribe. The issue of cognitive valuation is inherently controversial.

Epistemic values do not amount to contentions or doctrines but rather to intellectual orientations or predispositions. They inhere in the contingently adopted categories and concept frameworks we bring to bear in making sense of our experience (John Dewey), in the explanatory paradigms we favor (Thomas Kuhn), in the principles of interpretation we espouse (Hans-Georg Gadamer), in the metaphors we apply as guiding hypotheses (Stephen Pepper), in the styles of argumentation or "logics" that we use in constructing arguments (Hans Leisegang[12]). They are not mere teachings or doctrines but cognitive *points of view* (orientations). After all, the cognitive values that condition our philosophizing are reflected in what we take to be our prime model of "knowledge" for this field, be it mathematics (Spinoza), science (Kant), religion (gnosis), law (Austin), art (Schelling), literature (Derrida), and so on. They are "ideological" in reflecting our attitudes rather than purely factual. The sort of orientational disagreement that, on this approach, is held to underlie doctrinal disagreement is itself ultimately evaluative.

The Goodmanian nominalist does not disprove the existence of sets as distinct from their elements—he *refuses to allow* that they can play any role in "adequate explanation." The Quinean realist does not refute the existence of possibilia—he *does not countenance* them in philosophical expositions. The explanatory recourse to such resources is viewed as a defect, a liability, a demerit. Their role is rather as a mechanism of appraisal than as an argued doctrine. With Goodman we have to "see" that abstracta are bad, with Quine that possibilia are—on the basis of considerations like simplicity, economy, elegance, and so on. At bottom, the issue pivots on matters of evaluation rather than doctrine—of ideology rather than information.[13]

These orientations regarding cognitive valuation are a crucial part of the probative machinery by which we validate (support, justify) our beliefs. In providing the instruments by which we forge the fundamental analogies for exoteric argumentation, they shape and canalize the

---

12. See this obscure philosopher's interesting work, *Denkformen* (Berlin, 1928).

13. A very different but yet structurally analogous approach to philosophical pluralism, namely the *axiomatic* approach, sees the differences in the teachings of different schools to rest ultimately in a difference regarding axioms: fundamental commitments, presuppositions, basic premises, first principles, or ultimate beliefs about the nature of the world. The root of differences is seen as residing not in methodology but in divergent fundamental thesis-commitments. (For an interesting development of this position, with its emphasis on ultimate commitments—in the very broad sense of this term—see Johnstone, *Philosophy and Argument*.) The present approach does not take this line. For I reject the conception of ultimate theses in the domain at issue. Indeed, it would be *unphilosophical* to characterize a commitment to philosophical theses in terms of ultimacy. One must reject the very idea of "ultimate commitments" in philosophy—the espousal of theses one is not prepared to defend. As Hegel quite properly stressed, there can be no axioms in philosophy. In rejecting the axiomatic approach as inappropriate in philosophy, I also reject the particular account of pluralism that accompanies it—an account that is, in its general structure, much like my own.

probative processes through which teachings and doctrines come to be accepted. His cognitive values provide the philosopher with the orienting perspective regarding "good argumentation" through which his position can be developed and consolidated.

Thus, even when exactly the same body of "evidence" is available to different philosophers, they might well evaluate it very differently. Because different backgrounds, different courses of "experience" can be operative, they may work things out in rather diverse ways. Differing as to matters of "cognitive value"—as regards relevance, significance, centrality, and so on—they come equipped with different standards of appraisal and thus carry their reasonings from common premises to very different conclusions. In philosophical contexts, there is no universal answer to the question of the weight or authority of any particular sort of probative consideration, no universal way to determine unproblematically just how good our "good reasons" are. And, obviously enough, argumentation about this issue is bound to fall within its own purview. Though no doubt important in general, cognitive values thus play an altogether decisive role in philosophy.

The "evidence" available to us in philosophy cannot resolve the problems. For one thing, those evidential data are, as it were, part of the problem rather than its solution, since they are what engenders those aporetic difficulties that lie at the root of the matter. The question becomes one of the ultimate *bearing* of the evidence. And the crucial fact is that the evidence secures its bearing only within an orienting framework of cognitive values. The evidence cannot resolve questions of system "from without" (so to speak), because, with philosophical issues, it itself gets its bearing only relative to our fundamental systemic commitments.

In philosophizing we impart rational coherence and structure to the (inconsistent) raw materials that the "data" of the field afford us. We instill systemic order into the aporetic issues that emerge from "presystemic" considerations. But we can manage to do this only on the basis of (cognitive) values.

Strictly factual demonstration is one thing, normative argumentation is another. The one is strictly objective and proceeds from unproblematic evidence alone; the other involves issues of evaluation. The analogies on which philosophical arguments ultimately rest always involve normative considerations. They are not objectively presuppositionless knock-down-drag-out demonstrations. Factual demonstration knows only of person-indifferent results and operates at the level of universally applicable general principles. It talks the language of "It is clear that . . . ," not the language of "I am clear that. . . ."[14] It is no respecter of persons; the potentially idiosyncratic positions of particular individuals lie outside its purview. This is not the basis on which we can proceed in philosophy. For the "facts of the matter" are incapable of enforcing a unique resolution. Cognitive axiology is pivotal: *the taking of a particular philosophical position involves a rational choice that depends crucially upon having an evaluative posture*. Criteria of cognitive significance are indispensable to the exploitation of arguments by analogy as standards of acceptability. The pivotal role of cognitive values in philosophizing validates, for this domain at any rate, the cogency of Hans Leisegang's thesis that there are no universal *laws* of thought but only variable *forms* of thought.[15]

Philosophical argumentation can never succeed in demonstrating its claims on a strictly factual and evidential basis. For the issue of *how much weight* to give to the facts and the evidence of the sort adduced in the argumentation will always arise to give the issue a new and more problematic turn. Different philosophical theories may well claim to take account of all of the importantly relevant facts and yet be based on wholly disjoint considerations, precisely because they assess matters of importance and bearing in very different ways.

Which resolutions are *available* in response to a philosophical problem is a matter of evidentially validated fact. But the *acceptability* of these various positions poses uneliminable issues of evaluation. Both evidence and evaluation thus have a bearing on philosophy. The exploration of alternatives, the mapping out of the space of possible positions, is a matter of evidential reason. But the adoption and substantiation of a particular position—its rational defense *vis-à-vis* alternatives—are matters not of objectively evidential but of evaluative reason, since they can only proceed from the vantage point of a particular cognitive-value orientation. The pivotal role of analogies in philosophical reasoning means that axiology is an indispensable aspect of probative methodology in this field.

One's cognitive values accordingly play a determinative role in philosophical reasonings. A philosophical argument can always be construed as having an implicitly conditional form: "Given a certain set of

---

14. Compare Kant on theoretical/logical vs. practical/moral certainty in *CPuR*, A829-B857.

15. See Leisegang, *Denkformen*, esp. p. 9. Cf.: "There is no such discipline as a philosophically neutral 'logic' which leads to pejorative judgments about philosophical theses. The 'logic' of *Language, Truth and Logic* and of *The Logical Syntax of Language* was far from presuppositionless. It appeared to be so only to those who were antecedently convinced of the results of its application, and thus were prepared to accept persuasively loaded definitions of logic, significance, and similar terms" (Rorty, *The Linguistic Turn*, p. 6).

cognitive values, such-and-such a position is appropriate." Philosophical problem solving indispensably demands as input value judgments whose character is not dictated one-sidedly by "the inquirer-independent nature of things" but requires a personal contribution by way of determining values and setting priorities in cognitive matters.

In resolving philosophical apories we must always choose to retain some theses and abandon others. And this calls for weighing the costs of abandonments against the benefits of retentions. These weighings can be carried out in different ways by different people without any lapse in *rationality*—without any deficiencies of *reason* as regards issues of logic or "common sense" or other modes of impersonal rationality predicated on incontestable general principle. The plausibility judgments that canalize these choices will, in the final analysis, turn on matters of cognitive value. Although "purely evidential reason" cannot by itself achieve solutions here, *man* nevertheless can (and does) make a choice, one that inevitably reflects man-supplied *values or standards.* Philosophizing is a matter of resolving an ultimately evaluative choice one way or another, of propounding a resolution that emerges as optimal in the light of principles of cognitive evaluation.

If this perspective is essentially correct, it follows that one cannot philosophize *in vacuo*. Theoretical considerations of pure general principle never suffice for the rational settlement of philosophical issues. Philosophical problem solving cannot proceed in the absence of value *inputs* to provide the principles of plausibility and presumption that alone can resolve an aporetic inconsistency.

Evaluatively conditioned reasoning always has individualized involvements. Its results are not universal matters of impersonal general principles of abstract rationality but embody elements of person relativity. Not just impersonally determinable facts but the particular values of individuals play a pivotal role in its deliberations. This applies also (and emphatically) to the cognitive valuations that underlie philosophical argumentation. What people deem useful, informative, significant, congenial, plausible, or the like is bound to affect their problem resolutions.

Unavoidably, one's probative-value orientation provides the "point of view" one brings to the controversy and uses to assess the "costs" and "benefits" involved in the retention and rejection of conflicting theses. Because of the fundamentality of argumentation by analogy in philosophical thought, a philosopher's doctrine is bound to reflect his cognitive values. Cognitive values not only lie in the eye of the beholder, they do so in such a way as to condition what he beholds.

Regardless of whether we agree or disagree with Protagoras' precept that "man is the measure of all things," he was right in that at any rate, man is the *measurer* of all things. In themselves, all facts are mere facts; it is only the structure of our interests and concerns that endows them with significance and importance. Cognitive evaluation goes beyond objective factuality.

In philosophy we can unproblematically agree about problems because considerations of abstract rationality afford a commitment-indifferent *lingua franca* that enables us to identify aporetically problematic situations as such. We can tell "objectively" where the apories are. But we cannot tell "objectively" how to resolve them, and thus we do not agree about answers. In philosophy, position taking is always *intra* orientational—always based on commitment to a certain set of cognitive values. Interorientational cogency detached from any such particularized commitments is simply unattainable.

The arguments through which philosophers address their problems and establish their positions are thus never altogether conclusive, never probatively conclusive on unproblematically factual grounds. For analogy is never decisive; similarity is never identity. The persuasiveness of an appeal to analogy always lies partly in the eye of the beholder. The exoteric appeal of philosophical argumentation does not constrain; other options are always open. Philosophical reasoning is inherently nonpreemptive; variant conclusions can always be reached from the same evidential basis by those who choose to see matters in a different light. We can always avoid a given resolution *if we are prepared to take a particular sort of evasive step*—if we are willing to pay the price required for the evasive maneuver.[16] David Lewis has made this point clearly and cogently:

> Whether or not it would be nice to knock disagreeing philosophers down by sheer force of argument, it cannot be done. Philosophical theories are never refuted conclusively. (Or hardly ever. Gödel and Gettier may have done it.) The theory survives its refutation—at a price. . . . what we accomplish in philosophical argument: we measure the price. Perhaps that is something we can settle more or less conclusively. But when all is said and done, and all the tricky arguments and distinctions and counterexamples have been discovered, presumably we will still face the questions which prices are worth paying, which theories are on balance credible, which are the unacceptably counterintuitive consequences and which are the acceptably counterintuitive ones. On this question we may still differ. And if all is indeed said and done, there will be no hope of discovering still further arguments to settle our differences.[17]

---

16. "In principle a philosopher can always invoke some idiosyncratic criterion for a 'satisfactory solution' to a philosophical problem (a criterion against which his opponent cannot furnish a non-circular argument)" (ibid., p. 2). Cf. Passmore, *Philosophical Reasoning*, p. 36.

17. David Lewis, *Philosophical Papers* (Oxford, 1983), p. x.

The question of how acceptable we find philosophical theses extrasystemically is bound to turn crucially on recource to such a cognitive value orientation; on how important, plausible, substantial, and so on, we deem certain points of comparison in relation to others. And importance is not something absolute and wholly objective; it always turns in part on the approaches, contexts, and perspectives that we adopt to provide a setting for the "objective facts" as we proceed to deal with them. In philosophy, abstract probative rationality (Kant's *theoretical* reason) cannot by itself constrain a position; this can be achieved only by a normatively committed rationality (Kant's *practical* reason). Some element of person-relative valuation is always present.

This evaluative dimension of the matter explains the ultimate inconclusiveness of philosophical argumentation. Philosophical argumentation is inevitably *nonpreemptive.* It can never preclude the prospect that a different position can reasonably be taken by someone who happens to hold a different stance regarding the evaluative issues.

Diverse philosophical positions obtain because different individuals and groups are implicitly committed to different cognitive priorities and preferences—committed not merely regarding the objective facts and therefore incapable of being dislodged on this basis alone. It is for this reason that, as one recent writer laments, "Attempts to substitute knowledge for opinion (in philosophy) are constantly thwarted by the fact that what *counts* as philosophical knowledge serves itself to be a matter of opinion."[18] Yet this still does not get the matter quite right. Admittedly, we do not secure in philosophy the hard knowledge of demonstrated facts, determined as such by intersubjectively cogent considerations of abstract reason alone. But then again, we do not get mere opinions, constrained only by arational factors of a psychological or social sort, factors operating in the order of causes rather than reasons. Rather, what we get are *judgments*—reasoned, albeit value-grounded, determinations in favor of particular alternatives. In philosophy all position taking is a matter of "judgment calls."

## 4. The Loss of Objectivity

Value dependence is inevitable in philosophy; recourse to cognitive values is always needed to extract a particular position from the range of competing alternatives with which philosophical antinomies confront us. Consider once more the example from seventeenth-century metaphysics already discussed above:[19]

---

18. Rorty, *The Linguistic Turn*, p. 2.
19. In sec. 1 of chap. 4, pp. 64–65.

# THE STRIFE OF SYSTEMS
*Cognitive Values and Antinomy Resolution*

(1) Extension is substantial (in constituting material *res extensa*.).
(2) Thought is substantial (in constituting immaterial *res cogitans*).
(3) Thought and extension are coordinate items that have the same standing and status.
(4) Substance as such is uniform; at bottom it has but one type and is a genus of one single species.

If, with Descartes, we put a relatively low premium on uniformity and homogeneity of substance in our judgments of plausibility—if the analogy of nature is our guide—then we are obviously going to abandon (4) and resolve this aporetic cluster in a dualistic manner. If, however, we stand with Spinoza in putting a high premium on substantive uniformity and homogeneity—if the analogy of his God is our guide—then we shall enroll in the ranks of the monists and drop (1) or (2) or both. The character of problem resolution in philosophy, the way in which we resolve aporetic inconsistency, reflects differences in cognitive values and canalizes them into doctrinal differences.

Presuppositions as to cognitive values are not *premises*. They do not enter the discussion overtly and explicitly. Like the piles that support a building in a sandy terrain, they are hidden away out of sight. But the fact that we do not see them does not mean they are not there or that the role they play is not an essential one. Our appraisals of cognitive value—of significance, importance, and centrality—crucially condition the course of our philosophical argumentation.

Claims about the true nature of philosophy are themselves philosophical. And so they too can be addressed from the vantage point of the present methodology. In particular, consider the following aporetic cluster:

(1) Philosophy is a venture in inquiry; its mission is to answer questions and solve problems by providing good reasons for accepting particular resolutions.
(2) Philosophy addresses "the big issues" of human concern regarding man's place in the world's scheme and seeks to resolve "the big questions" that arise here.
(3) The probatively cogent, rationally convincing arguments through which alone good reasons can be provided in philosophy must be modeled on the pattern of scientific discourse in point of value-free objectivity and impersonality. Philosophizing must be quasi-scientific (genuinely *wissenschaftlich*).
(4) Those "big issues" of presystemic thought do not, as such, lend themselves to objectively impersonal quasi-scientific resolution.

Here (4) is to all appearances a fact of life, built into the very nature of philosophy's problem situation. The apory thus admits of just three exits:

(1)–rejection: One abandons the view of philosophy as inquiry and either rejects the whole subject as illegitimate (per positivism) or sees it in a very different light (eg., as a matter of enlightenment, of enhancing our awareness of possibilities, per much of contemporary hermeneutics).

(2)–rejection: One abandons philosophy's traditional concern for those "big issues" and concentrates on issues of technical detail. (This stance is implicit in the practice of much of contemporary philosophizing in the analytic tradition.)

(3)–rejection: One acknowledges the infeasibility of achieving rationally convincing, probatively cogent argumentation in philosophy by means of objective, value-free, quasi-scientific reasoning. (This is the stance of our present theory, which accepts the validity of *normative* reasoning relative to a nonobjective, potentially person-variable cognitive-value orientation).

Our own approach emphatically rejects the objectivism of (3) and, retaining theses (1) and (2), maintains the traditional view of philosophy and its mission. But, as usual, it salvages some part of (3) by means of a distinction—through its acceptance of a normatively relativized, value-geared conception of cogent reasoning in this domain.

This perspective on the issue also helps to explain why a considerable sector of contemporary Continental philosophy has no use for Anglo-American analytic philosophy. For the Continentals are themselves deeply committed to (2) and take the analysts to be committed to the "scientific" model of (1) cum (3) and thus led to rejecting (2). To resolve the difficulty, the Continentals incline to reject (1). The real culprit, however, is (3).

Philosophizing thus steps outside the sphere of probatively unproblematic demonstrations from the objective facts. In philosophy, the taking of particular positions is always a matter of evaluative commitment. This is, of course, transparently clear in the "value disciplines" of ethics, politics, aesthetics, and so on, where the substantive issues themselves involve values. But it also obtains in the other branches of philosophy (theory of knowledge, metaphysics, etc.), where exoteric argumentation inexorably calls for cognitive evaluation regarding matters of importance, centrality, and so on. Philosophy joins the humanities in its status as a field in whose deliberations considerations of value are bound to play a determinative role.

If philosophical positions ultimately root in values, philosophy cannot be wholly objective, any more than can any other humanistic enterprise. We come back to the time-honored principle (as old, at any rate, as Schopenhauer's insistence that our worldview is as much a matter of will as it is of intellect) that value-free results of impersonal cogency are not generally available in the *Geisteswissenschaften*. It is an important moral of post-Kantian philosophy that one cannot resolve issues in a humanistic discipline like philosophy short of taking an evaluative stance. In the final analysis, philosophical argumentation is never fully objective but is always personalized to some degree.

But while it is true that philosophical problems are not solvable "objectively," without recourse to variable commitments regarding cognitive evaluation, it would be quite wrong to maintain that philosophical issues are undecidable and that philosophical disputes are unresolvable *as such.*

In a stimulating little book called *Sceptical Essays,* Benson Mates has recently argued that "the traditional problems of philosophy . . . are intelligible enough, but . . . absolutely unsolvable." He insists that "the reason why philosophical problems are not solved is that, like the antinomies (of logic) . . . they are unsolvable though intelligible. They are conceptual knots that cannot be undone."[20] But Mates's discussion can and should be read as indicating insolubility only in the specfically *evidential* mode of resolution, that is, solution through evidential considerations alone. In *this* regard Mates is right; one cannot possibly work one's way out of an aporetic situation in the direction of one particular resolution without deploying the appropriately evaluative resources needed to effect a choice. Philosophical problems are unresolvable *in the absence of evaluative inputs.* One cannot distance oneself from value commitments without exiling oneself from philosophy.

In science we don't expect to get answers to our questions without determining the requisite facts. Neither should we do so in philosophy, where, to be sure, some of the relevant "facts" will be of an evaluative sort. But once we take the stance of an evaluatively laden cognitive orientation—once we adopt an evaluative standpoint—then we do indeed obtain definite answers to our questions. Neither in philosophy nor anywhere else can we reasonably expect to secure unique, determinate answers to our questions independently of possessing those—here *evaluative!*—resources required to obtain them in the prevailing circumstances.

The dependence of philosophizing on values was also divined by the logical positivists, who wanted to do away with philosophy as such precisely because of their antagonism to the invocation of values in cognitive contexts. The conscientious scholar, so Otto Neurath insisted, must work in a manner that is wholly presuppositionless and

---

20. Benson Mates, *Sceptical Essays* (Chicago, 1981), p. 3, and cf. pp. ix–x, 20.

value free. Hence he must work without philosophy and confine his attention to science as such.[21]

We confront an aporetic triad:

(1) Philosophical problems are legitimate and solvable cognitive issues.
(2) The solution of philosophical problems is only achievable through recourse to (cognitive) values.
(3) Recourse to values is illegitimate in rational inquiry.

The positivists, typified by Neurath, exit from inconsistency by abandoning (1). We ourselves abandon (3). Both opposed parties rightly share acceptance of the pivotal thesis (2). The idea of a value-free philosophy is no more than a mirage.

We must take care, however, to refrain from joining the positivists in leaping to the conclusion that philosophical problems are mere pseudoproblems because they cannot be resolved objectively. We must refrain from equating rational validation and endorsing the idea that there is no rationality where objectivity is absent.[22] To take this stance is to overlook the prospect of a mode of rational justification whose basis is not entirely objective and impersonal but in some respects personal and subjective. There is no reason to think that rational validation cannot invoke person-relative standards of cognitive utility in a way that provides for relativity, all right, but a relativity that is not arbitrary and beyond the pale of rational deliberation.

To adopt this stance, however, is to accept that discussion across the divide of conflicting positions, however useful it may be in highlighting the issues, will *not* settle philosophical disputes. Different values express themselves in different cognitive priorities and thus in variant resolutions to philosophical problems. Their discordant values will impel people in different directions in theoretical as in practical affairs. At the end of the day, philosophers must still agree to disagree. And the circumstance that these disagreements ultimately root in differences regarding cognitive value means that philosophical disputes are always to some extent a matter of arguing at cross purposes—of discussing the common issues on the basis of very different approaches.

21. "Wissenschaft *ohne Weltanschauung*" should be his motto. He should strive "eine metaphysikfreie Atmosphäre . . . [zu] schaffen, und wissenschafftliche Arbeiten auf *allen* Gebieten durch logische Analyse zu fördern" (Otto Neurath, "Soziologie im Physikalismus," p. 149, trans. in his *Philosophical Papers*, ed. R. S. Cohen and M. Neurath (Dordrecht and Boston, 1982), pp. 58–90 [see p. 58]).

22. The very first sentence of Peter Unger's recent book, *Philosophical Relativity* (Minneapolis, 1984) presents the stark alternatives: either objective or arbitrary (p. 3). His discussion is predicated on the idea that there is a clear dichotomy, so that if one side fails, the other prevails: either "objectively right" or "merely arbitrary." This facile division certainly has its problems.

# 7

# Orientational Pluralism: The Inevitability of Value Diversity

## 1. Doctrinal Diversity Reflects a Diversity of Values

Generation upon generation, philosophers have dreamed of "setting philosophy on the sure road of a science" (as Kant put it). They see philosophical issues as presenting problems about which sensible, well-informed, reasonable people must eventually reach agreement, and they yearn for a key to unlock the door to those ultimately definitive solutions. Controversy and disagreement are perhaps even a possible means to this end. In just this spirit, A.O. Lovejoy urged the American Philosophical Association to organize its annual programs into structured controversies on well-defined, clearly delineated issues, anticipating that by the end of each convention a consensus would emerge as to the winning side of the debate.[1]

However attractive this prospect may be, it is doomed to disappointment. For it is based on a profound misunderstanding of the probative situation in philosophy, where the very conditions of rationality admit of rational dispute. Precisely because the issue of the appropriate standards of cogency and acceptability for characterizing *good* reasons and *good* arguments in philosophy is an inherent part of philosophy itself—and therefore a subject for controversy and debate—we are never in a position to enforce rational consensus across boundaries of doctrinal divergence. Abstract rationality cannot resolve the issues on its own, because the very norms and criteria by which we evaluate arguments—the canons of cogent argumentation—themselves reflect

---

1. A. O. Lovejoy, "On Some Conditions of Progress in Philosophical Inquiry," *The Philosophical Review* 26 (1917): 123–63. See Daniel T. Wilson, "Professionalization and Organized Discussion in the American Philosophical Association, 1900–1922," *Journal of the History of Philosophy* 17 (1979): 53–69.

our cognitive-value orientations. They are accepted by individuals (or communities) on the basis of potentially variable evaluative postures. (Think of the difference between the analytically, hermeneutically, and existentially minded thinkers among contemporary philosophers.)

The force of a philosophical argument is never absolute and objectively compelling. Considerations of strictly evidential tenability are impotent to eliminate conflict and narrow the range of alternatives to one rationally qualified result. The persuasive cogency of a position is of necessity confined to those who accept the particular principles on which it rests, principles that ultimately revolve about matters of cognitive value. Once we recognize that what is to be deemed tenable (valid, appropriate) in philosophy must turn on cognitive values, we can no longer expect to achieve consensus in philosophy through purely rational constraint on the basis of the objective "facts of the matter."

Philosophical position taking is a matter of *judgment*. Philosophizing is never a matter of determining what *is* on a strictly evidential basis, but of deciding *what is to be done*—of *taking* positions on the basis of adopted values. To accept a philosophical position is to make an *ex parte* declaration from the vantage point of a particular cognitive value posture.

The central role of *cognitive values* in philosophizing means that learning philosophy is not only a matter of mastering facts but also one of acquiring a "point of view," of forming cognitive attitudes, of acquiring affinities and allegiances in matters of exploiting "the data."

Yet can *rational* people really disagree in philosophy? Must their very rationality not engender consensus in matters of belief? Is rationality not an inexorable constraint to accord? By no means! Rational people need not agree, because:

(1) Their basis of judgment—that data and the background information available to them—may well differ.
(2) And even when their background information is the same, their cognitive values may lead them to differ in those cases where different values point toward different resolutions.

The salient fact is that, in philosophy, rational men can differ in their reactions to the data, both in regard to what they deem cognitively significant and in regard to the plausible inferences they are prepared to draw from this.

Its recourse to values means that philosophical argumentation cannot rationally *constrain* consent save intramurally among those who share the basic commitment to a particular cognitive value. The cognitive situation in philosophy is not such that one can impel the disputants to agreement on pain of forfeiting their claims to rationality.

# THE STRIFE OF SYSTEMS
*The Inevitability of Value Diversity*

Rational discussion need not produce consensus in this domain. It need go no further than to clarify the extent of the range in which they agree to disagree and to sharpen the participants' understanding of the points of disagreement at issue.

The objective facts at our disposal are inadequate to enforce coordination and consensus in philosophy. The claims of personal judgment must reign supreme. Joseph Glanvill complained in 1665 that "while men fondly doat on the *private* apprehensions, and every *conceited Opinionist* sets up an infallible claim in his own brain, nothing can be expected but eternal *tumult* and *disorder*."[2] Without accepting Glanvill's negative construction of this situation, we may yet endorse the fundamental idea that the persistence of the strife of systems (that "eternal *tumult* and *disorder*") ultimately roots in the inevitability of personal judgment (those "*private* apprehensions") as a basis for problem resolutions.

Catholic theologians have long argued against Luther that chaos and anarchy would reign in religion if everyone heeded his own conscience and followed his own best judgment. But that is exactly where the situation is in philosophy. Where neither abstract reason nor enlightening revelation can constrain consensus, private judgment must in the end prevail. If that leads to chaos and anarchy, so be it. In philosophy, a Lutheran position is the only realistic alternative. The issues admit of no categorical resolution without appeal to evaluation—without some normative recourse to "cognitive utilities" that divide the community into distinct "schools of thought." Disagreement accordingly reflects diversity in cognitive evaluation. And conflict regarding values (even merely cognitive values) is ultimately unresolvable on a presupposition-free, objective basis, because disputes about values are themselves always inherently evaluative.

A philosophical position of ours can be considered (1) "from within," from the standpoint of the value commitments of *our own* orientation, or (2) it can be considered *ab extra*, from the standpoint of some hypothetically adopted alternative arrived at by suspending disbelief and using our imaginations to adopt "for the sake of argument" a stance that is not actually our own. But a philosophical position can never be substantiated value neutrally, from no particular value orientation at all.

Given that our own cognitive values represent "where we actually stand," we have no way (short of a suspension of disbelief) to disengage ourselves from it. One enterprising theorist tells us that "there

---

2. Joseph Glanvill, *The Vanity of Dogmatizing* (London, 1665), quoted in R. H. Popkin, *The History of Scepticism from Erasmus to Spinoza* (Berkeley and Los Angeles, 1979), p. 16.

may even be ways of catapulting oneself, at least temporarily, into different philosophical perspectives. Various drugs seem to have given (people) the experience of how the world looks and feels (to others)."[3] But such a departure from our "normal" posture is always bound to seem aberrant after we return to it; like a bad (or good) dream, it is something we are bound, in the end, to deem undeserving of probative weight. We have little choice but to see matters in the light in which those experiences we deem authentic puts them. We are locked into our value posture even as we are locked into our belief system. The realization that others see matters differently is bound to leave us substantially unaffected. We can detach ourselves from where we actually stand by "making believe" (by way of supposition or hypothesis), but we cannot manage it with commitment.

The development of a philosophical position is a matter of systematization, of placing distinct facts within a network of order. But, of course, different systemic structures might well accommodate the same ground-level facts. System building is always a matter of "evaluation" of what is central and what peripheral, of what is important and what insignificant. Leibniz rightly distinguished between *eruditio*, the knowledge of merely aggregated fact, and *philosophia*, the knowledge of fact as normatively coordinated and systematized.[4] System building always reflects the significance of particular ideas through their interrelations in a wider "nomic" framework that embodies principles of cognitive value that we bring to the process of systemic organization.

Some hold that cognitive importance is not person relative because it is essentially factual in representing a second-order fact that reflects how nodally a given fact fits into the wider rational network of environing facts. But while this is largely true, it does not alter matters. For that "rational network of facts" is itself a creature of our devising that reflects our interests and concerns—our cognitive values.

One recent writer suggests that "the possibility of objective justification (in philosophy) depends on using problems of life as the external, context-independent standard with reference to which our (philosophical) theories must ultimately be justified."[5] But, of course, the issue of the terms in which we are to address these "problems of life" is itself philosophically problematic. The justificatory resources at work

---

3. Robert Nozick, *Philosophical Explanations* (Cambridge, Mass., 1981), pp. 19–20.
4. "*Philosophia ab eruditione differt, quemadmodum id quod est rationis sive juris, ab eo quod est facti.*" Leibniz to Huet, March 1679 (Akad., vol. II, p. 465; *Philosophische Schriften*, ed. C. I. Gerhardt, vol. III [Berlin, 1887], p. 14).
5. Kekes, *The Nature of Philosophy*, p. 197.

vary with place and time, person and situation, context and circumstances—in short, they are themselves value reflective and largely variable from group to group and individual to individual. The great practical universals of the human condition—food, shelter, clothing, socialization, reproduction—arise at a level of fundamentality that leaves anything as sophisticated and content laden as a philosophical position gravely underdetermined. Everyone—sceptics and cognitivists, realists and idealists, materialists and immaterialists—will agree that men must breathe, eat, sleep, and so on. The "problems of life" are to the philosopher somewhat as rocks and clouds and tables are to the physicist. In a sense they are what the discipline is all about. And yet dealing with them as such will not take the discipline very far.

In philosophy, the use of "sound logical principles" to reason from "the incontestable facts of the matter" is never able to resolve the choice between alternatives. For, confronted by rival courses of reasoning that lead to incompatible results, we cannot settle the matter of superior and inferior without begging the question of cognitive valuation. Appeals to facts and principles fail to deliver a decisive resolution, because different views of facts and principles are themselves parties to the dispute.

Discordant philosophical systems reflect differences in cognitive values—differences in normative orientation toward the data afforded by our experience of the world.[6] They are in large part conditioned by the approach or attitude with which we set about our philosophical labors. This was clearly seen by Dilthey, who wrote:

> One never gets to the root of a philosophical system with mere argumentation. This can be concluded from the fact that decision in the grand questions of philosophy by strictly logical means has heretofore totally eluded us and that there is simply no prospect, however remote, of reaching any decision. And so we must seek for the different types of *Weltanschauung* that underlie the various philosophical systems.[7]

Not that philosophy is a matter of insight or intuition or blind allegiance. It is undoubtedly a matter of rational reflection and reasoning. But the reasoning at issue rests on cognitive values. It is a reasoning based on "facts" that are not unproblematically objective and that are not matters of public property but of people's evaluative judgments.

An evaluative orientation can, of course, be criticized externally, from the vantage point of *another* evaluative position. Might it not also

---

6. Wilhelm Dilthey, *Gesammelte Schriften*, vol. VIII (Stuttgart and Göttingen, 1960), p. 150.
7. Ibid.

be subjected to an "internal critique" in the hypothetical mode—by our occupying it and finding it untenable, by our "trying it on for size" and thus finding it to have shortcomings from within?

But shortcomings by what standards? As long as the position is internally self-supporting, these cannot be its own—they must be ours that we have somehow smuggled in. When we "try it on to see how it feels," it is still a matter of how it feels *to us* on the basis of whatever value orientation we have.

And yet people do sometimes shift from one cognitive-value orientation to another. Surely there are conversions in philosophy! Of course there are! But this sort of fundamental change in values amounts to an ideological reorientation that is never a matter of being driven out of our position by the force of rational argumentation alone. Conversion in matters of philosophical fundamentals are changes of mind that are, at bottom, changes of heart, discontinuous quantum jumps to a different value outlook that can, of course, be rationalized and legitimated by reasons and arguments—but only *ex post facto* from the vantage point of the new orientation itself. Philosophical concessions are Gestalt switches that lead to rather than result from altered courses of reasoning.

One recent discussion maintains: "There are, of course, such things as philosophical conversions. They occur perhaps when one philosopher tries out another's interpretation and discovers that it fits the world better."[8] This contention is highly problematic. For how can a philosopher judge that another's interpretation "fits the world better"? It clearly cannot fit *his* world better—the world as he himself conceives of it from his accepted point of view. And certainly no external objective standard, no impersonal "God's-eye" point of view, is accessible to him. Accordingly, this idea of adopting a rival doctrine by hypothesis and "trying it on for size" just will not do.

Agreement in a *hypothetical* mode is thus relatively easy to achieve in philosophy. "If you accept such-and-such a probative basis, then it is only rational to maintain such-and-such a position." There is no problem about agreement at this merely hypothetical level. But when one shifts to the issue of the *appropriateness* of the basis and the *correctness* of the position as such, then matters change drastically. For now we are constrained to decide matters on the basis of "where we stand." Philosophers, like others, can achieve a suspension of disbelief and can thus manage to see, hypothetically yet "from within," as it were, what is involved in maintaining a contrary position. But even in assuming someone else's position by way of hypothesis, a philosopher is still saddled with his own values!

8. Dilley, "Why Do Philosophers Disagree?" p. 227.

# THE STRIFE OF SYSTEMS
*The Inevitability of Value Diversity*

Understanding of and respect for the values of others are certainly possible and appropriate in philosophy. We can come to comprehend and even in one sense to "appreciate" the positions of others. But this is not, of course, to *adopt* them. It is to deem them worthy of consideration but not of credence. To come to understand the positions of others and to grasp why they see them as correct are by no means to find those positions in any way compelling for oneself. Even as in factual matters we can sensibly deem it justifiable for somebody else, given the evidence that is at his disposal, to accept something that we ourselves reject, so in philosophical matters we can (and should) sensibly deem it justifiable for him, given the probative standards that he espouses, to accept something we ourselves reject.

By "taking somebody else's point of view" we can certainly come to *understand* his position better. But that is far from *agreeing* with it. Understanding is not acceptance! (*"Tout comprendre c'est tout accepter"* is as dubious a dictum in philosophy as in everyday life.) To say this is not, of course, to insist that a philosophical "conversion" cannot possibly happen, but rather to say that there is no earthly reason to think that it will, let alone *must*. (Rare is the student of exotic doctrines, however penetrating and assiduous, who actually adopts their teachings.)


## 2. The Import of Orientational Pluralism

Although the grounds for ongoing diversity and discord lie in the very nature of philosophical inquiry itself, very different reasons might nevertheless underlie this fact. For the basis of variability might lie (1) in the nature of the *problems* or issues of philosophy, or (2) in the nature of the *theses* propounded as solutions to them, or (3) in the nature of the *arguments* used to defend the appropriateness of these solutions. Our present theory sees the cause of diversity in a combination of all three of these factors. It takes the stance that, *owing to the schematic nature of the concepts involved, philosophical deliberations always issue in cognitive overdetermination, with every member of a group of mutually incompatible contentions supportable by justificatory arguments of substantial prima facie cogency*. Positive philosophical argumentation is accordingly *nonpreemptive*: the fact that a good case can be made out for one particular answer to a philosophical question is never a sufficient reason for denying that an "equally good case" can be produced for some other, incompatible answers to this question. In philosophy one never manages to refute someone else's position by developing a cogent case for one of its alternatives.[9] It is a characteristic feature of the field that its problems admit of alternative, mutually incompatible resolutions. In philosophy we cannot maintain a sharp line between knowledge and plausible belief.[10]

Metaphilosophical pluralism maintains that distinct and conflicting positions are always in principle available with respect to philosophical issues. A specifically *orientational* pluralism goes beyond this in holding that there are different cognitive-value schemes, diverse probative perspectives, relative to which discordant alternatives can be validated vis-à-vis their competitors. It maintains that the extraevaluative data of the problem, the objectively discernible "facts of the matter," are underdeterminative and by themselves insufficient to constrain a particular resolution, though that indeterminacy can be removed once a cognitive-value orientation is in hand. The result is the inevitable existence of "schools of thought"—the circumstance that different positions admit of rational endorsement. For where alternative standards for appropriate problem resolutions are available, alternative resolutions must be expected.

Orientational pluralism accordingly takes a systematic stance toward philosophical questions, as indicated in table 2. It sees the typical situation in regard to philosophical questions in its own characteristic terms, striving to find a safe passage between scepticism on the one hand and absolutism on the other.

In science one might say things like "Whereas people used to think that P, everyone now realizes that Q is the case." For example, "Galen's theory of the origin of disease through humor imbalance is nowadays abandoned as just plain wrong." But one cannot talk that way about philosophy. One can indeed say things like "Few people nowadays seriously espouse Plato's theory of ideas" or "There are no longer adherents to Aristotle's theory of final causes." But no careful writer would (or should!) say things like "Philosophers realize that the theory of ideas is untenable" or "We now know that the theory of final causation is just wrong."

---

9. Friederich Waismann put the point by saying that there can be no proof in philosophy because "proofs require premises. Wherever such premises have been set up in the past, even tentatively, the discussion at once challenged them and shifted to a deeper level," with the result that "no philosopher has ever proved anything." "How to See Philosophy," in *Contemporary British Philosophy: Third Series*, ed. H. D. Lewis (London, 1958), pp. 447–90; see pp. 447–48.

10. For a discussion of relevant themes see Passmore, *Philosophical Reasoning*; W. B. Gallie, *Philosophy and Historical Understanding* (London, 1964), esp. chap. 8 on essentially contested concepts; Johnstone, *Validity and Rhetoric in Philosophical Argument*; Morris Weitz, *The Opening Mind* (Chicago, 1978); and Kekes, *The Nature of Philosophy*.

# THE STRIFE OF SYSTEMS
*The Inevitability of Value Diversity*

Table 2
ALTERNATIVE STANCES TOWARD A PHILOSOPHICAL QUESTION

I. The question is improper, illegitimate, meaningless (nihilistic scepticism, positivism).

II. The question is meaningful but intractable; it has a range of possible answers, per the family $A_1, A_2, \ldots A_n$. But we cannot achieve a good and compelling reason for adopting any one of these resolutions (agnostic scepticism).

III. The question is meaningful and tractable. Its answer is $A_i$ and we can substantiate this:

   1. *Demonstratively*, by showing that this is the only rationally acceptable answer (demonstrative absolutism)

   2. *Plausibilistically*, by showing that this is the optimally tenable answer, the very best alternative relative to

      (i) uniquely appropriate standards (plausibilistic absolutism)

      (ii) orientationally relativised standards (orientational pluralism)

The diversity of positions reflects the unachievability of presuppositionless demonstrations. We are constrained to speak for ourselves, not for the subject. We must use very different tones of voice when we talk *in* philosophy (where we state our own positions) and when we talk *about* philosophy (where we purport to describe the general situation). (What is said substantively *in* philosophy can be as dogmatic as we please, but what we say descriptively *about* it must be said with caution if we are to speak responsibly.)

In philosophy certain positions and theses may be rejected as "counterintuitive," or as poorly argued, or as unpalatable to the contemporary mind. But in this discipline it is incongruous—and a sign of a braggadocio that immediately rubs any knowledgeable person the wrong way—to talk in the language of universally accepted fact and say things like "It is now known that . . . ," "It has recently been demonstrated that . . . ," "X has definitively established that . . . ," or the like. No conscientious philosopher would dismiss even such "outlandish" positions as Gassendi's occasionalism or Berkeley's immaterialism in this way. Philosophical claims can quite properly be advanced in the language of belief or even reasoned conviction. But it is a token of naiveté (or pomposity) to picture them as matters of generally received knowledge or universally acknowledged fact—to advance them in the language of impersonal demonstration rather than the more modest language of reasoned judgment.

The term *judgment* is chosen with deliberation here. For philosophy is not "a matter of mere opinion." On the contrary, responsible philosophizing is a matter of rational systematization subject to the discipline of good reasons and cogent argumentation. It is just that the provision of good reasons in philosophy always involves a recourse to cognitive values as part of the underlying standard of goodness. For the question of the standard by which a given value is properly to be judged is itself always a value-question. Once we enter the value domain we are trapped; there is no way out, no way to resolve its issues by external means.

*3. The Inevitability of "Schools of Thought" and the Unattainability of Consensus*

All that one can do in philosophy is view the issues from one or another of a variety of methodological orientations. The crucial fact is that *the very nature of a cognitive-value orientation is such that one cannot occupy several of them at once*. To be sure, in philosophy one can "shift orientations," but the transition is so rendered that when the new orientation is attained the old one is lost. The shift involves a sort of intellectual conversion experience—one cannot retain the old values alongside of the new ones. An *axiological* (rather than *logical*) incompatibility obtains: the new priorities force the old ones aside. It lies in the very nature of the case that divergent evaluations are not contenable.

With cognitive values as with all values, people can and will see matters differently; different philosophers are bound to adopt different cognitive-value orientations. We thus reach the stance of what might be called an *orientational pluralism* in philosophy, a position that maintains that philosophical positions hinge on diverse views regarding matters of cognitive value, so that philosophical disagreement becomes inevitable.

On such a view, consensus is unattainable in philosophy. Philosophical problems always admit of diverse solutions, and philosophical argumentation, being normative in nature, admits of different results. The link between rationality and consensus is broken. If philosophical adequacy hinged on finding strictly objective and presuppositionless criteria of philosophical "success" that would provide for rationally constrained agreement, then the enterprise would be foredoomed to failure.

"But when philosophers $A$ and $B$ disagree from their respective orientations $O_A$ and $O_B$, this simply means that, in order to settle the quarrel between them, we must move up to a higher $O_A{*}O_B$ from which their quarrels can be composed, their views reconsidered. The key to conflict resolution in philosophy lies in an upward ascent to more inclusive perspectives." How pleasing does this strategy sound, and how tempting has it been found by dialectial philosophers since Hegel's day! But it has the fault of most pat solutions—it doesn't work. Diverse cognitive-value orientations just don't admit of combination or compromise or "sublimation" to a higher level. In matters of evaluation we cannot have it both ways. We cannot at once give *A* priority over *B* and yet have *B* take priority over *A*. It is either-or; having one set of values preempts the prospect of having another. Philosophical issues are inherently debatable. They reflect appraisals made from inherently uncombinable evaluative standpoints that accord differential priority to different sorts of considerations.

The division of the discipline into conflicting "schools of thought" is thus inevitable in philosophy. The diversity of cognitive values points practitioners toward different resolutions of problems. There is no compromise with orientations, no way to "split the difference" in setting value priorities. In matters of action we can compromise, accommodate differences, "meet the other fellow halfway." But in doctrinal matters we cannot achieve this. (That's why it is particularly fortunate that we can achieve peaceful coexistence through accommodations in action despite differences in thought.)

It is, of course, perfectly true that we do not *choose* our values but *find* them ensconced in place. We "make" our values no more than we "make" our nature, personality, disposition, predilections, and so on. But values, even cognitive values, are nevertheless variable and person-relative. A cognitive value (importance or significance, for example) is not a wholly objective feature of things; to some extent it always lies in the eye of the beholder. The rational nature of things does not determine that the value commitments of one person must be those of another. Person-to-person variability is an ineliminable aspect of cognitive value.

Note that these deliberations do *not* take the following line: "Philosophical issues cannot be settled decisively, because they turn on evaluative matters, and about values there can be no argument." Not at all! Obviously there can be a great deal of argument about values. The point is simply that such an argument can never be settled extraevaluatively without any resort to evaluative presuppositions. There is no value-free basis of appeal on whose terms value argumentation can be resolved objectively by reason alone.

How could one possibly adjudicate between rival cognitive-value orientations? Only by looking at their consequences and appraising them—relative to some value orientation! There is no noncircular way of proceeding here, no presuppositionless basis. Values are inherently controversial in a way that facts are not. A plausible case can perhaps be made for saying that in factual matters there is only one ideally appropriate set of evidential standards. The nontheoretical (practical) aims of the enterprise—prediction and control—suffice to enforce uniformity. But this line would emphatically *not* be viable in the normative domain, where abstract rationality cannot settle matters even in principle, so that even "what would be ideally appropriate" is not something that can be resolved monolithically. Here no theory-external goals are available to settle matters. The issue hinges on values, and the question of their appropriateness is itself an evaluative issue.

The only way to impugn a rival philosophical position without presupposing some competing substantive commitments is to launch an attack on internal consistency—on bare coherence, and this is a process of very limited utility. The upshot is that refutatory argumentation is altogether indecisive in philosophy. Its weight is never absolute. In the final analysis, an unproblematically eliminative refutation of a philosophical doctrine can never be developed on a value-neutral basis. No effective critique of a philosophical position is available to us save from the vantage point of another, because the basis from which alone such a critique can be developed will itself constitute (part of) a philosophical doctrine. There is no neutral "God's-eye point of view" from which philosophical positions can be criticized or evaluated by those of us who dwell outside the Garden of Eden.

Philosophical argumentation would be wholly universal (impersonal, objective) in cogency and appeal only if it were an exercise in strictly probative rather than evaluative reason. And this it is not and cannot be, in the nature of the case. To demand strict impersonal facticity in philosophy is to demand that the field be other than it is. Philosophical issues *cannot* in their very natures be resolved on a value-free basis.

That philosophical judgments are determined through and conditioned upon cognitive values—that they are to this extent personalized—precludes any prospect of the impersonal rational enforcement of communal consensus. In philosophy, there is not and cannot be a rational closure to debate. For there is no way in which *purely* rational, totally objective and value-free considerations can constrain one particular way of resolving a philosophical problem.

To be sure, *technical* merit in philosophy—mere *system-internal cogency* as opposed to acceptability or correctness—is something else again. Technical adequacy is a matter of process, not of product, and so is relatively unproblematic. Competent workmanship can be recognized by anyone who learns enough about the issues. Everyone can agree that Plato, Aristotle, and Kant are great philosophers who have opened up new and important issues, conceptions, arguments, and systemic visions. The unproblematic character of technical as opposed to substantive merit explains why philosophers can reach consensus about the quality of each other's work as distinguished from its correctness (and why they can reach agreement in grading their students' essays.) One can perfectly well admit as well-wrought a case for a position one simply cannot accept. The question of whether a position is correct is never doctrinally unproblematic in philosophy; the question of whether it is more or less workmanlike is. Workmanship and craftsmanship are relatively objective and impersonal qualities. However, the usual diversity of views is bound to prevail regarding the *substantive adequacy* of these productions (not just whether they are interesting, influential, and so on, but whether they place the issues in a clear and cogent light or are false starts in unpromising directions).[11]

Unlike *technical* merit, however, *substantive* merit is a matter of right mindedness, of moving the discussion in "the right" direction. And this is always bound to be as nonconsensual and controversial as philosophical issues themselves. Thus, technical consensus is possible and is able to bring technical progress in its wake. But substantive consensus (solving the problems satisfactorily) and substantive progress (enlarging the domain of satisfactorily solved problems) is something else again. For this is bound to pivot on value consensus, and value consensus lies outside our grasp.

The pivotal role of cognitive values in the substantiation of philosophical positions explains why philosophers in general are notoriously impatient with one another's views. Herbert Spencer's reaction to Kant is typical:

[At age twenty-four, I came across] a copy of a translation of Kant's *Critique of Pure Reason*. . . . This I commenced reading, but did not go far. The doctrine that Time and Space are "nothing but" subjective forms,—pertain exclusively to consciousness and have nothing beyond consciousness answering to them,—I rejected at once and absolutely; and, having done so, went no further. . . . Tacitly giving an author credit for consistency, I, without thinking much about the matter, take it for granted that if the fundamental principles are wrong the rest cannot be right; and thereupon cease reading—being, I suspect, rather glad of an excuse for doing so.[12]

Even as people generally find life in an alien social environment stressful and uncomfortable, so it can be painful to enter into a thought world predicated on commitments one finds uncongenial. It is uncomfortable even to contemplate a reevaluation of one's values. (Why else should people feel so strongly antipathetic toward wholly innocuous others whose *only* offense is that they do not share their values?)

---

11. The irrelevance to traditional philosophical controversies of the fact that philosophers can agree on technical issues is maintained on the basis of interesting historical data and theoretical arguments by Rorty in the introduction to *The Linguistic Turn*.

12. Herbert Spencer, *Autobiography*, vol. I (London, 1904), p. 289.

This line of thought also clarifies the role of sympathy in philosophy and the "politics of allegiance" that characterizes its cultivation. Every philosopher, it seems, has his heroes and villains and classifies his fellows into those whom he sees as allies and those he sees as enemies. Philosophers are guided by an ideology that is at bottom not just a matter of doctrine, reflecting not just overt beliefs but underlying cognitive values as well.

What philosophers of different persuasions have in common is a shared heritage of problems and proposals for their resolutions. But from there onward they part ways, picking and choosing what to emphasize and what to downgrade, what to recognize as significant and what to deem secondary and peripheral, what to see as plausible and what as far fetched. A great deal can be inferred about a philosophical book simply by examining its index: Who are the thinkers to whom attention is paid and who is ignored? Which topics and issues are deemed important and which ones insignificant? Which problems are attended to and which are overlooked? Once we know that much about a philosophical book, we can infer a good deal about its doctrinal orientation and tendency, because we can make some pretty good guesses about the cognitive values that are at work.

Inevitably only some (at best) will receive the message that a philosophical book conveys as its author would have it. Only those with suitably oriented cognitive values will listen to it in a sufficiently favorable state of mind. Of course, a philosopher does not *intend* to address a restricted audience; he sends his message forth in the fond hope that it will reach everyone and meet with favorable reception everywhere. But this is little more than wishful thinking—the realities of the matter just don't permit things to work out like that.

## 4. Whence Cognitive Values? The Key Role of "Experience"

As we work our way out of the aporetic inconsistency of overcommitment, the possibility of conflicting doctrines is inevitable. This circumstance creates the prospect—the opportunity—for philosophical disagreement. Still, why is this possibility realized? Even if alternative positions are always available *in theory*, why should there not *in practice* simply be agreements? It is, after all, theoretically possible that despite there being room for disagreement, people should not occupy this room, that consensus and harmony should reign, notwithstanding the possibility of discord. But that's just not how things go. Yet why is this so? Why should philosophers not agree regarding cognitive values? Might there not after all be a uniformity of evaluation that embraces all practitioners? Is it not simply fortuitous that different people should have different values? Furthermore, are value orientations rationally grounded or are they little more than arbitrary and accidental attitudes? A cluster of important issues lurks here.

Hume was right in this, at any rate: values are derivable neither from matters of abstract reason nor from matters of observed fact. All values, cognitive ones included, transcend issues of information to involve an element of decision and action, of position *taking*.[13] Cognitive valuation in particular, calls for *according significance* to certain considerations, seeing certain matters as important, and taking certain cases to be archetypical. Such values involve taking a particular approach to "the objective facts," calling for a personalized response to an objective situation. Values are not matters of passive observations of impersonal facts but of an active engagement in the world's affairs. They do not issue from intersubjectively invariant considerations but emerge as products of individual human judgment based on an individual background of experience. The "facts" they represent are imbued with subjectivity. They reflect a variably personal response, recourse to which helps to explain why even rigorous rationalists often resort to phrases like "cannot persuade myself to think," or "find it difficult to accept," or "cannot bring oneself to believe." Their prominence explains philosophers' perennial complaints about being misunderstood.

Variability is built into values because *value positions are defined as such relative to one another*. To give X priority over Y is sensible only in a context where the prospect of giving Y priority over X also beckons. A value position can exist as such only in the context of rival alternatives.

Our cognitive values emerge from the operation of many different factors: our culture, the "spirit of the times," the heritage of our teachers and their opponents, our general intellectual orientation. Conditioning experiences of every kind—shaped under the pressure of nature and nurture, of personal temperament, economic and social settings, cultural exposure, and so on—will all come into it. A person's cognitive values, like his or her values in general, reflect a diversified spectrum of causal determinants. For better or worse, people have different values because the experiences on which human values hinge, cognitive values included, are substantially variable across the spectrum of the human community.

Recognizing the pivotal role of values in philosophy, F.H. Bradley

---

13. It must be stressed that this position does not call for postulating an absolute fact/value divide, taking the view that facts are entirely *irrelevant* to values. All that need be maintained is that factual considerations underdetermine value positions. If in fact $n$ people are killed there can be no denying that this is (other things being equal) something that is bad. But the question of just how bad in relation to other potential evils will remain open.

wrote that "metaphysics is the finding of bad reasons for what we believe upon instinct," yet he had the wisdom to add: "but to find these reasons is no less an instinct."[14] Still, this does not get matters quite right. For it is not *bare* instinct but *educated* instinct, an intuition shaped and informed by experience, that is at issue.

Dilthey used a Darwinian analogy to explain philosophical proliferation. Even as the profusion of nature fills every ecological niche with organisms attuned to their specific conditions, so too the profusion of the human spirit fills every ideational niche with a doctrine that realizes its specific possibilities.[15] The real explanation is perhaps less romantic but leads to much the same result. It pivots on the fact that value postures are the product of a complex interaction between nature and nurture. Both play a key role. Nature (natural inclinations, preferences, biases) makes a substantial impact. And nurture, represented by a course of experience under the conditioning impetus of cultural setting, historical context, and so on, is even more important. The values that people hold reflect the structure of their experience. And different courses of experience are incompossible realities. In consequence, the variation of cognitive values within the wider community is effectively inevitable; experience is too diversified and variegated in philosophically relevant situations to issue in a single value scheme.

Cognitive values are a matter of experientially conditioned inclinations. They involve "intuitions," all right, but largely learned rather than instinctive ones. They reflect our sense of the plausible or bizarre, natural or outlandish, normal or weird. And these inclinations are shaped by the invariably varied course of our experiences. Philosophers deploy their analogies and construct their reasonings in the light of an experientially formed sense of importance (significance and the rest). But, of course, very different experiential formations are possible.

The diversity of values is inherent in the fact that man is not a mere mechanism. Our emplacement in nature is sufficiently loose and variable to permit diverse responses to uniform situations, reflecting not the present circumstances alone but the course of past experience as well. To be a person is to be a creature that can forge his own set of values independently of others.

Cognitive values indicate what one finds cognitively significant on the basis of one's experiences. But experience bears on our cognitive values through a complex feedback process. On the one side, it itself affords a key determinant of valuation. On the other side, our cognitive values determine the weight we allot to different sorts of experi-

14. F. H. Bradley, *Appearance and Reality* (Oxford, 1893), p. xii.
15. Wilhelm Dilthey, *Gesammelte Schriften*, vol. VIII, p. 235.

ence. In particular, in interpretative systematization philosophers are bound to give very different weight to:

—observations and their scientific interpretations;
—feelings of right and wrong, duty, obligation, and so on (the "moral sentiments");
—value experiences of aesthetic or affective response;
—interpersonal "sympathy" and empathy.

Issues of priorities, of what experiences really count, and for how much, themselves provide indispensable raw material for philosophizing.

Philosophy is a fundamentally reflective enterprise. And it reflects the structure of human experience. As experience changes (as between different people or between the different temporal stages of a person's life) so do values change, and changes in cognitive values bring changes in philosophy in their wake. There is no prospect of uniformity, of consensus. The biblical story of the Tower of Babel carries a far-reaching lesson. For better or worse, the prospect of homogeneous uniformity across the human scene is unattainable. Philosophers do not and will not agree on cognitive values, because cognitive values emerge from a mixture of nature and nurture, and life inevitably equips people with different natures and different courses of experience.

Such a view of philosophizing envisages a kind of enlarged empiricism. Empiricists see our knowledge of the world as ultimately rooted in *sensory* experience. The present orientational theory sees our philosophizing as rooted in cognitive values, which in their turn reflect the course of *ideational* experience.

## 5. Are Philosophical Problems Pseudoproblems?

We are now in a position to address a question that may well have been on the reader's mind ever since chapter 3. If it is indeed the case that issues of philosophy come to the fore in antinomies that reflect the imperfections of language, does this not destroy or at any rate trivialize philosophical problems? Are they not thereby reduced to the status of mere pseudoproblems?

The response is an emphatic negative. Those linguistic tensions that underlie aporetic inconsistency are only the *symptoms* of the difficulty and not its root *cause*. Those verbal differences are in themselves not fundamental; they are the surface manifestations through which fundamental value differences can come to expression. The internal instability of our fact-coordinated concepts reflects a fundamental tension in our thought. It lies in the very nature of these problematic cases that *different* analogies can be seen as central or paradigmatic. Different cognitive priorities can be established, different values implemented in those alternative constructions of philosophically relevant terms. The issues admit of different constructions, and different resolutions, in a way that reflects different cognitive values. And these differences regarding matters of cognitive value themselves represent deep differences in cognitive ideology—and thus in worldview.

While philosophical problems arise out of the "inadequacy" of everyday language to the theoretical purposes of our "big questions," and while those philosophical disputes can indeed come to settle on the appropriate construction of words, this emphatically does not trivialize the issues. It merely provides the theater of conflict, in which deep "ideological" differences can come to overt expression. Philosophical disputes are by no means pseudoquarrels about "mere words"—the issues at stake are enormous. (What sorts of creatures are we men? What do we owe to ourselves and to others? What manner of place is the world we live in?) Accordingly, those differences among philosophers as to the right way of resolving apories are never "merely verbal." They are the vehicles that transmit a deeper difficulty, they are surface reflections of underlying judgments of importance that implement different standards of cognitive value.

In compact overview, the present account of philosophical diversity takes the following line:

1. Philosophical controversies are reflected in *verbal* problems, because to resolve philosophical problems (apories) we need to introduce distinctions to attain greater linguistic precision.
2. By the very nature of aporetic conflicts, this can always be done in several different ways. We can always develop a more "systematic" account of matters by moving in one of several different directions.
3. To support one of these resolutions *vis-à-vis* its alternatives, we need to stress different sides of the relevant analogies. We can settle on different cognitive priorities and stress different cognitive paradigms. That is, we must bring into operation cognitive values: ideas as to what the really important factors are.
4. These cognitive values can implement prejudgment of the relative importance of adverse factors from our understanding in various different ways, ways that reflect different causes of experience issuing in different appraisals of what is central, peripheral, important, coincidental, and so on.

## 6. The Persistence of Conflict

William James characterized the differences at issue as ultimately temperamental in character. In his classic essay titled "The Present Dilemma in Philosophy" he wrote:

The history of philosophy is to a great extent that of a certain clash of human temperaments. Undignified as such a treatment may seem to some of my colleagues, I shall have to take account of this clash and explain a good many of the divergencies of philosophers by it. Of whatever temperament a professional philosopher is, he tries, when philosophizing, to sink the fact of his temperament. Temperament is no conventionally recognized reason, so he urges impersonal reasons only for his conclusions. Yet his temperament really gives him a stronger bias than any of his more strictly objective premises. It loads the evidence for him one way or the other.[16]

Still, this stress on *temperament* as the root cause of philosophical disagreement does not get the matter quite right. It overemphasizes nature at the expense of nurture, whereas our philosophical value orientations are rather acquired than innate (though differences in temperament do doubtless play some role).

It is thus an illusion to think, with Dilthey, James, and others, that one could extract a philosophical typology from a survey of the characteristic types of human psychological disposition. A great deal more is involved. For while the temperamental "psychology of the individual" does indeed play some role *in his or her choice* among the alternatives, the range of those alternatives, and thus the spectrum of available philosophical positions, is fixed independently of psychological considerations by the structure of the data and problems of the field. (An individual's choice of his or her favorite season of the year is, no doubt, psychological; but the available range of alternatives is unaffected by the vagaries of human psychology.)

Nevertheless, the psychologism of Dilthey, James, Schiller, Lazerowitz, and company, is a step in the right direction in its suggestion that the ultimate basis of philosophical disagreement is extratheoretical. For probative valuation is a *methodological* resource and, and such, is "logically prior" to the reasoned adoption of whatever specifically doctrinal stance we may take on its basis.[17] Disagreement at this level cannot always ultimately be settled through rational discussion, because rational discussion inevitably proceeds on a plane where these differences are already firmly in place.

If philosophizing indeed hinges on cognitive values, then the inevitability of pluralism follows of necessity. An "ideological" position

---

16. "The Present Dilemma in Philosophy," p. 363. See chap. 1, note 14, above.

17. John Henry Newman puts the point as follows: "All reasonings beginning from premises, and these premises arising (if it so happen) in their first elements from personal characteristics, in which they are in fact in essential and irremediable variance with one another, the ratiocinative talent can do no more than point out where the difference between them lies, how far it is immaterial, when it is worthwhile continuing an argument between them, and when not" (*A Grammar of Assent* [London, 1871], chap. 8, pt. 3, sect. 10). The whole of the immediately following section of Newman's book is a magisterial analysis of how differences in approach to probative method make themselves felt in interpretative analysis.

is always one among others, defined and determined by the nature of its alternatives.

Pluralism in philosophy is thus inescapable. The central issues of human existence arise in every time and situation. As life continues, so do the problems of life and the lessons of life. The key experiences of human existence continue to flow in the same old channels. And so diverse orientations also persist, reflecting the different value emphases that emerge from different courses of experience. No unproblematic, universally conceded basis of first principles is available; subjectively differential values are bound to enter in. Only those who share a value orientation can take a specific position or adopt a particular resolution. Philosophical positions cannot make good their unconditional claims to the assent of all.[18] And so there can be no "position of philosophy" but only a plurality of positions of diverse philosophers.

As orientational pluralism sees it, the *aspiration* of philosophy is always greater than its actual *performance.* Our philosophizing aspires to produce something absolute, definitive, universal. But it succeeds only in yielding something parochial, something rationally compelling not to everyone but only to the suitably like minded, to those who share a certain cognitive-value orientation.

In his stimulating essay on philosophical disagreement, F. C. S. Schiller wrote:

The great philosophic issues themselves are not essentially obscure. . . . What is, therefore, most sorely needed in Philosophy is the institution of thorough and systematic discussion of the great questions in dispute. . . . I believe that they could clear up and clear away a majority of the questions which cast a slur on Philosophy in considerably less time, . . . five to ten years. . . . As for the few questions which, like the clash between optimism and pessimism, are perhaps too vital and cut too deep into personality to be disposed of thus, they could at least make clear the ground of difference, and agree to differ.[19]

The present deliberations indicate the inappropriateness of this view. For the differences at issue *always* reflect value differences. They are like "the clash between optimism and pessimism" in kind, even if not in degree. Those deep-cutting disagreements are the rule, not the exception. In such matters, the idea of a settlement through friendly discussion is an unattainable illusion. The injunction "Just keep talking

---

18. Are values not inherently universal? Their adherents always claim that they are. But we must distinguish between "hold universally *for* all men" and "held universally *by* all men." If I hold objectivity (for example) as a cognitive value, then I maintain, no doubt, that it is appropriate for all men—that all men *should* aspire after it. But this of course does not mean that they actually do so.

19. Schiller, "*Must* Philosophers Disagree?" p. 14.

until you reach agreement" is pointless. It is only natural to expect that the parties concerned will *never* reach this point (save through exhaustion, sociability, or some other irrelevancy). People will not reach agreement, because they resolve the issues in fundamentally discordant ways on the basis of different values engendered by different courses of experience.

Orientational pluralism enables us to have it both ways, so to speak. From the angle of the individual philosopher, it takes the stance that people are rationally entitled to work out answers to philosophical problems in ways that are rationally cogent according to their own cognitive-value orientations. Nevertheless, recognizing that other orientations are available to others, we need not thereby feel compelled to dismiss as utterly worthless and pointless the work of colleagues whose conscientious labors lead them to other solutions. We can be confident in our attachment to our own positions without falling into a parochialism that writes off as altogether pointless the work of our competitors in the field. (Their labors may be misguided, but they are not futile.)

Under the influence of transitory fashions or powerful personalities, consensus can for a time prevail on a limited scale in philosophy. A certain ecological niche in the cognitive-value spectrum may go unoccupied for a time, and various schools of thought may go unrepresented. But when this happens it is a merely contingent matter of fortuitous accident. In principle, the prospect of diversity is ever present.

Hegel's dictum that "philosophy is its time grasped in thought" does not do sufficient justice to variation, to the fact that the circumstances of a certain time do not constrain a single solution but in principle allow all the old disputes to continue in some duly adjusted form. The Zeitgeist may be unfavorable for a time, and the cognitive fashions of the day may prove unsympathetic to a particular orientation. But it will spring back to life in due course. Dilthey put the key point well:

The history of philosophy, however, is in fact a competition between opponents who are not mortal and die off with particular individuals, but rather perpetuate themselves from person to person. Every page of the history of philosophy confirms this fact. Every page belies Hegel's belief in the encapsulation of successive ages in representative figures. . . . The development of philosophy must transpire within this very strife of systems.[20]

Conflict in philosophical doctrine invariably persists because there is always room for diverse orientations, and circumstances are such that this room will sooner or later come to be occupied.

20. Wilhelm Dilthey, *Gesammelte Schriften,* vol. VIII, p. 132.

Our analysis accordingly sees philosophical disagreement as a cognitive manifestation of evaluative differences, differences, in this instance, as to specifically *cognitive* values relating to matters of epistemic utility and plausibility. Philosophers disagree because differences regarding cognitive values lead them to different standards of cogency and different criteria of acceptability. Conflict persists because the prospect of diverse value orientations is ever present within the wider community—because, having different ends in view, the philosophers of different "schools" are always to some extent arguing at cross purposes. We do not reach a stage where everybody resolves the issues in the same way, because we've *already* embarked on divergent roads. And we *continue* to keep apart because these differences are ultimately differences in values. The persistence of competing doctrines in philosophy is for all practical purposes an *inevitable* phenomenon.

## 7. A Review of the Argumentation

It is useful to review the overall structure of the present analysis of the grounds of pluralism. It has two stages: the first is an account of how it is that there is always *room* for doctrinal diversity—how it is that doctrinal disagreement is always *possible*. This account has the structure set out in the following three steps:

(1) The concepts that lie at the root of our philosophical deliberations are always fact coordinated.
(2) Clarificatory pressure upon fact-coordinated concepts always engenders antinomies.
(3) There are always diverse mutually alternative possible exits from antinomy.

The second stage of the argument moves from the possibility of doctrinal disagreement to its inevitable actualization through the subordination of doctrines to values. This part of the argument also has three steps:

(1) A problem of choice is always inherent in the aforementioned diversity.
(2) This resolution cannot proceed on purely evidential grounds but always requires a resort to considerations of cognitive utility (significance and importance), whose character is inherently evaluative.
(3) The community is virtually bound to differ in its cognitive-value evaluative commitments, since different people are bound to hold different values on the basis of different courses of experience—different modes of enmeshment in a diversified world.

This view of the matter indicates that philosophical disagreement is not the product of perversity or incompetence but lies in the nature of philosophical problems and the mechanisms available for their resolution. In philosophy, the absence of consensus is not the fortuitous and eliminable product of human failings but is inherent in the value-intensive nature of the enterprise.[21]

Philosophy thus represents an inherently humanistic project. Its deliberations hinge on the availability of evaluations. And evaluation makes for person-to-person variability. Others, or, at any rate, some among them, are always bound to take different lines. (To be sure, that's quite beside the point for us. We do, or should, have our own values; we are, or should be, prepared to follow our own drummer.) The community as a whole is bound to constitute a theater of conflict. The market is too large and complex to be cornered.

---

21. However, while the existence of conflicting positions is inevitable, their exposition by way of magisterial syntheses is not. The great systemic formulations of Plato, Aristotle, Aquinas, Leibniz, Spinoza, Kant, Hegel, were a matter of contingent good fortune. Orientational pluralism is a theory about the *form* of philosophical dialectic, not about its *content*.

# 8

# The Range of Reason

## 1. The Infeasibility of a "Neutral" Basis of Philosophical Appraisal

Philosophers take their positions in line with what counts for them as good reasons. Yet the crux of their enterprise is rational deliberation, and how can one possibly deliberate about what counts as a good reason without begging the question? To argue rationally we must proceed in line with some preestablished understanding of what a good argument is, and exactly this is the point at issue. A cognitive standard cannot effectively be defended *ex nihilo*, without presupposing the judgments of cogency it itself is to supply. There just is no *external* vantage point from which to appraise the cogency of our argumentation. The all-inclusive comprehensiveness of philosophy's purview—the discipline's autonomy—means that there simply is no "extrinsic," doctrinally neutral, presuppositionless standard for assessing philosophical doctrines.[1] To evaluate philosophical positions, or even to dismiss them all as worthless, is in fact to take a philosophical position.

In philosophical problem solving, the idea of eliminating possibilities by value-free and doctrinally uncommitted "rational criticism" will not work. For only by adopting some evaluative standard of appraisal can a philosophical position be criticized or defended. Cognitive values inevitably underlie the rational espousal of any substantive philosophical position.

There simply is no noncircular way of proceeding in philosophy; its reasonings hinge on cognitive values, and one cannot dispute about

---

1. Cf. Stephen C. Pepper, "Reply to Professor Hoekstra," *The Journal of Philosophy* 42 (1945): 101. As Pepper has cogently argued, the idea of strictly neutral evaluation of philosophical theses is simply mistaken in "expecting an unquestionable criterion of truth and factuality to be at hand" in this domain.

values from a value-free standpoint. No philosophically useful standard can be extrinsic to philosophy. There simply is no absolute, evaluatively neutral, normatively presuppositionless basis on which philosophical problems can be addressed or resolved.

The cardinal injunction of cognitive rationality is "Align your beliefs with good reasons." But this leaves a great deal of room for deliberation and debate about the underlying standards for assessing the goodness of reasons. In philosophy, this matter of the norms and standards of acceptability is not only a crucial part of the solution but an inevitable part of the problem as well. Whenever and wherever we make a start at philosophical work, we have to take some standard for granted, to presuppose a given basis of resources in point of probative methodology. And whatever we take as the working basis for our philosophizing is something that can itself be questioned and will need to be discussed and legitimated in due course; something to which we shall eventually have to return in order to assess, weigh, justify.

The question "By what criterion or standard is a philosophical doctrine, be it metaphysical or epistemological or moral, to be deemed superior to its rivals?" is itself a supremely philosophical question in which cognitive values are heavily involved. A cognitive orientation can be appraised only from the vantage point of another. There is no value-external basis for supporting (or criticizing) an evaluative position, no neutral vantage point from which such positions can be appraised. A thesis of the form "Any adequate philosophical argument must meet the condition C" is itself always indelibly philosophical. Of course we espouse our cognitive standards for good reasons and justify their adoption by good reasons (as we see them). But such reasons and such supportive arguments are always themselves value-invoking. They are not prior or external to the evaluative domain but firmly grounded within it and themselves form part and parcel of our overall framework of cognitive values.

Positivistically inclined philosophers deem values irrationalizable. They see value differences as basic and rationally intractable, reflecting an ultimately unreasoned matter of taste. As Reichenbach insists in *Experience and Prediction*, different people simply have different cognitive goals.[2] Some guide acceptance by probability and potential for truth, others adopt beliefs that diminish distress. And there are no cogent rational grounds for choosing between these or any other internally coherent cognitive-value schemes. But this line of thought misses the key point. It is patently false that there is no disputing values, cognitive values in particular. Quite to the contrary! While there may

---

2. Hans Reichenbach, *Experience and Prediction* (Chicago, 1938).

be no disputing *tastes*, the fact is that, values being what they are, there is ample room for disputes about them. We certainly can reason about values and certainly can evaluate them. It is just that we cannot do so on a basis that is not value committed; the reasoned defense of values must itself invoke values. (And the same, of course, holds for facts, so this is not something uniquely bad about values.)

The crucial thing is that argumentation about cognitive values will always itself have to be based on cognitive values. The value realm is closed; there is no entry from without. In debating values we must invoke values. (Of course this is true in the factual realm as well—to debate facts rationally one must deploy facts. Such "circularity" is not vicious; it simply means that we are operating on a grand scale, dealing with self-sufficient galaxies rather than dependent planets.)

Our standards of cognitive value condition what we accept and themselves constitute part of what we accept. No neat, logical separation is possible. Every philosophical school views the issues in the light of its own commitments. There is no value-free basis from which values can be criticized *substantively*, as distinguished from merely formal criticisms based on lapses from self-consistency. We are caught up in a situation of a cyclical feedback. In appraising a standard one must have some evaluative *locus standi*. All rational deliberations that have evaluative outputs must have evaluative inputs; one cannot enter into the value domain *ab extra*.[3]

It is obvious enough that in philosophy one's rationally adopted views are bound to hinge on one's criteria for successful argumentation. The difficulty is that the relationship is one of symbiotic reciprocity. One's criteria for successful argumentation will also in part depend upon one's substantive views. One cannot evaluate the overall adequacy of a philosophical argument independently of assessing the acceptability of its consequences. Where it takes us is always relevant; if it leads seriously *ad absurdum*, then something is amiss. But we ourselves must be the judges of what is absurd. Accordingly, reasoning from premises or assumptions, no matter how strict, can never constrain us, because if we don't like the tidings we can always kill their bearer. The question of the plausibility of their conclusions is always a relevant factor in the evaluation of philosophical arguments. We are

---

3. To be sure, one probative value-orientation can be "superior" to another in the scope of its relevancy-considerations or the liberality of its admissibility-conditions. (Compare, for example, the narrower sympathies of logical positivism with the ampler scope of Hegelianism or Cassirer's cultural neo-Kantianism.) The crux, however, is that the "loss" or "gain" at issue can only be seen as such from an existing value-orientation that is already in place.

trapped in a probative circle: the adequacy of our arguments hinges on the acceptability of their conclusions, and the acceptability of the conclusions hinges on the adequacy of our argumentation. However, this is no paradox but simply a reflection of the closed, synoptic nature of philosophical reflection.

The linkage between a philosophical position and the "good reasons" that support it is always mediated by value-invoking standards of argumentation. But these standards themselves reflect a philosophical position, so that an ascent to higher levels of substantiation is inevitable. In philosophy, the linkage between reasons and position occurs within a *framework of substantiation* that itself requires validation. In this field, no methodological issues lie beyond the pale of critical reflection, not even those that set the aims of the discipline and the standards of adequacy of their realization.

To justify holding a philosophical position (indeed any belief) is to show that there are good reasons for holding it. Implicit in the offering of reasons is the background of a *standard* in virtue of which they can qualify as good and cogent. In principle, this standard too must bear scrutiny and must itself be justified by some standard. What are we to say of the regress at issue here? We had best deny that it is infinite, since otherwise we are in grave difficulty.

Absolutism sees the regress as terminating in self-evident principles that need no validation. They stand secure and invulnerable because there are no viable rivals, no real alternatives.

Orientational pluralism sees the regress as terminating in a self-supportive set of cognitive values. These values admit of alternatives all right, but these alternatives are unavailable *to us* (though not absolutely and to everyone) because we stand precommitted to the orientation at issue.

Absolutism sees the regress as terminating *globally* in a way compelling to everyone alike. Orientational pluralism sees it as terminating *locally* in a way that's convincing to those (but only those) who hold a particular set of cognitive values. It prefers the variability of a relativity of values to the dogmatism of a rational compulsion whose basis it cannot find compelling.

In philosophy we cannot obtain a context-detached mechanism for appraising our position from a source in which our position is wholly uninvolved. Philosophical standards are necessarily position-internal. There is no neutral, evaluatively presuppositionless standard that cuts across the positional divides, no fulcrum for the Archimedean lever that weighs philosophical doctrines by some common measure. Our standards of appraisal are themselves discipline internal—part and parcel of the disputable material of philosophical deliberation. We cannot separate our probative methodology from our substantive concerns. A relationship of symbiotic feedback unites them in inextricable interlinkage. Subscription to a probative standard in philosophy is itself a matter of cognitive valuation, of forming an "ideological" allegiance.

There is no point in complaining of "investigator bias" in philosophy. Without such bias, without an investigator-supplied input of cognitive values, there can be no investigation at all. Whatever argumentation is deployed for or against a cognitive-value orientation is itself developed relative to an orientation. There is no objective, value-free basis from which philosophical issues can be resolved—the issue of philosophical methodology itself prominently included.

Perhaps we can resolve matters by turning from the recalcitrant balkanization of the actual "community" of philosophers to a hypothetical *ideal* order at a remove where clash and conflict are left behind. In an interesting recent book, John Lange contemplates judging the adequacy of philosophical views by reference to an "ideal community of inquirers" whose philosophical theories will converge on certain positions that *ipso facto* are to be deemed adequate: what makes a philosophical assertion true is that it claims what would be accepted by the ideal community.[4]

This approach to presuppositionless objectivity is foredoomed to failure in philosophy. There is no reason to think that there is but one homogeneous ideal community rather than a plurality of "ideal types." The hypothetical "ideal community"—like the Wise Man of the Stoics or the "ideal observer" of modern ethical theory—is not going to resolve matters but is bound to be part of the problem. For what condition is one to place on this idealized entity, and what assumption is one to make of its *modus operandi?* What sorts of rationality conditions is it to satisfy? What sorts of methods are we to suppose that it employs? All the old problems spring up again in the context of this new approach, once we put clothes on the mannequin and begin to say something about where the idealized community stands. To say that "the real truth" is what the consensus of the ideal community decrees is of the same order of uselessness as saying that the truth is what God believes. We have no way to get there from here. As one critic sensibly puts it, "An ideal set of adequacy criteria to which we can have no reliable access is roughly as good as none at all."[5]

---

4. John Lange, *The Cognitivity Paradox* (Princeton, 1979), p. 111. A similar device was earlier employed by Karl-Otto Apel in his book translated as *Towards a Transformation of Philosophy* (London, 1980).

5. Todd Moody, "Progress in Philosophy" (Ph.D. diss., Temple University, 1982), p. 53. I am grateful to Professor Moody for placing a copy of his dissertation at my disposal.

# THE STRIFE OF SYSTEMS
*The Range of Reason*

The issue of what a good philosophical argument is, is itself deeply problematic. Philosophical argumentation has been modeled on mathematical demonstration, scientific reasoning, legal inquiry, political debate, and so on. Accordingly, we have been told that proper philosophical reasoning should proceed by way of mathematical proof, inductive inference, juridical inquiry, rhetoric, and so on. Demonstration, probable inference, dialectic, plausible reasoning—a great profusion of models have been advocated. The very question of what is a sound probative method in philosophy is a deeply philosophical, and thus controversial, issue. The probative standards we deploy in philosophy—the criteria of good reason, cogent argument, meaningful assertion, and so on—are themselves value-laden and thus themselves parties to the dispute.

Philosophy is autonomous in that there is no extraphilosophical vantage point for assessing the acceptability of philosophical claims, claims about the proper mission of philosophy and about the appropriate conditions of adequacy for its work. Issues *about* the discipline that must be resolved within the discipline and the conditions that apply to philosophical contentions in general must apply here as well.

To be sure, someone might respond as follows: "Granted that the substantiation of a philosophical position hinges on cognitive values, still that doesn't establish pluralism. It simply shows that the absolutely correct *position* must hinge on the absolutely correct *orientation*."

But how can absolute correctness be assessed? Clearly not *ab extra:* we have no direct, reasoning-independent access to the truth and so cannot validate an orientation on the basis of its leading to appropriate philosophical theses. (The question of what theses merit acceptance is precisely what we use this orientation to resolve.) A value can only be substantiated (or criticized) from a vantage point that is itself a potentially disputable value position. But even so, cannot such orientations themselves to be (more or less) justified through rational deliberation? The answer, "yes," raises the immediate counterquestion: "But justification of what sort?" Clearly the justification must itself rest on cognitive values. We can indeed defend our cognitive-value position, but only from a vantage point that is itself value-laden. These cognitive-value doctrines are themselves philosophical, and in philosophy every argument *for* a position is an argument *from* a position.

This explains why a Kantian "transcendental argument" is unavailable as a means of establishing objective conclusions regarding philosophy. The thrust of such an argument is to reason to the conditions under which alone a given endeavor (such as mathematics or natural science) is possible. But this is impossible with respect to philosophy. For we can only reason in this way if we are in a position to set out from a determinate characterization of the aims of the enterprise—a well-secured contention that *X*, *Y*, and *Z* are its definitive goals. But any thesis about "the true nature of philosophy" is itself immediately philosophical, fraught with cognitive valuation, and deeply controversial. This circumstance blocks any prospect of realizing the neutrality requisite for objectivity in this case.

## 2. Against Indifferentism: Orientational Pluralism Does Not Make the Choice Among Positions Into "a Mere Matter of Taste"

If alternative ways of resolving philosophical issues are always available, does it not follow that it makes no real difference which way we turn and which cognitive-value orientation we adopt?

The question at once becomes: Difference to whom or what? Clearly it makes no difference to the enterprise of philosophy as such. The discipline as an aggregate whole can maintain a lofty and even-handed indifference. In its collective entirety, philosophy is inherently pluralistic, permitting alternatives without constraining unique solutions.

Yet while philosophy as a whole may remain indifferent to the conflict of positions, the question does, of course, make a great difference to individual philosophers. For they, unlike the discipline as a whole, do indeed come equipped with those normative standards and commitments that enforce unique and differentiated resolutions. In this regard, our cognitive-value orientation will make "all the difference in the world." The reasoned endorsement of positions must come at the level of *philosophers,* not at the level of *philosophy.*

Protagoras was only partly right. Each side of a philosophical dispute can defend its pro-or-con position with equal rigor and vigor. But certainly not with equal *validity*—since we can assess this matter of validity/cogency/plausibility only from a cognitive-value orientation that is bound to be doctrinally committed in a way that prejudices the issue for any given appraiser.

The individual is inherently monistic. He has, or can develop, only a single value framework and must arrive at one particular set of weights and priorities. The individual philosopher can, and naturally does, espouse a cognitive-value framework and adopt a particular position on its basis. The community, to be sure, is inherently pluralistic. There is no such thing as a communal value posture. The community has to encompass the entire spectrum of alternatives; it cannot "average out" the inherent contradictions to arrive at some monolithic yet coherent result by "splitting the difference." From the angle of the philosophical community as a whole, the shape of the discipline is bound to be that of a mosaic of discordant positions.

Does this orientational pluralism not engender indifferentism? Does it not mean that the adoption of one philosophical position rather than another is no more than "a mere matter of taste," a fortuitous and ultimately irrationalizable preference, akin to that for coffee over tea? By no means! To take this line would be to ride roughshod over the fundamental distinction between mere *tastes and preferences* on the one hand and authentic *values* on the other. For the reasoned choice of a position hinges on the adopting of certain cognitive values. And to think of values in terms of taste-dependent preferences is to have a peculiar and distorted perception of values. Values are not irrationalizable. A perfectly good rational defense of one's cognitive value system can be built up, but it will itself be value-geared and thus not without an element of probative circularity. People hold their values for perfectly good reasons—but always reasons that themselves are ultimately evaluative in nature.

This doctrine of orientational pluralism may be a form of relativism, but it is *not* one of indifferentism; it does not see the choice between alternatives as rationally indifferent, unmediated by the operation of reason and rational deliberation. The crux is simply that it is *normative* (partly value geared) rather than *evidential* (purely fact-geared) reasoning that is at issue. The undoubted fact that there are alternatives does not mean that we must view them as equally meritorious. For flesh-and-blood people do indeed come equipped with an evaluative point of view that militates toward a particular resolution of value-reflective choices. Since people are committed to a point of view, it is emphatically *not* a matter of rational indifference to them which alternative position is adopted. Given our status as creatures that have not only preferences but values, these theoretical issues will matter enormously to us. Preferences, in contrast, are irrationalizable; they are what they are, without grounds or reasons. But values are always defensible. They must be supported by reasons and arguments, grounds that, to be sure, cannot themselves in the very nature of things be value-free.

Reasoned adoption of a philosophical doctrine is ultimately a matter of taking a stance optimally conformable to one's cognitive values. When we take a philosophical position, it is of importance to us precisely because it reflects our value posture. Even the quarrels of long-dead philosophers are matters that we take to heart and on which we are bound to take sides and have sympathies.

It is only to be expected that some theorists would propose taking the following line: "Once philosophers realize that their arguments are at bottom about values, they will come to recognize that their disputes cannot be settled by rational discussion. Their debates and disagreements are bound to come to an end—petering out in a good-natured 'agreement to disagree'." But the matter is not so and cannot be so, because *values* are at issue here in a way that conditions the cognitive shaping of our view of the world and our place in it. We are thus precluded by the seriousness of the issues from seeing the matter as one that is so indifferent that we can simply agree to disagree. Values are, of course, *important* to us—that is exactly what values are all about. Where one's values are at stake, one cannot in good conscience take the matter lightly on the model of an idle preference of some sort (tea vs. coffee). The seriousness of the issues prevents us from regarding our opinions as *mere* opinions. A recognition of the pivotal role of cognitive values does not degrade philosophy but rather highlights its importance. In saying that the choice among philosophical positions is at bottom a matter of value, we certainly do not slight or degrade the issue. On the contrary, given the importance of what is at stake with values, cognitive values included, we thereby underscore its transcendent significance.

Orientational pluralism takes the following line:

The choice between alternative positions is of interest and importance. We must make every effort to assure that from our own standpoint, we have made the very best resolution that is available to us. The fact that other resolutions are possible—resolutions that might well be adopted by others who appraise the issue differently—should not faze us for a moment. We have to go on from where we are. Once we have done the best that can be done within the framework of our own values, we may rest content. The fact that others with different value commitments might resolve the matter differently is simply *irrelevant* to our own resolution of the issues.

Once a cognitive-value orientation is in hand, only one member of the range of alternatives is (in general) optimally appropriate. (An orientational *monism* is the obverse side of orientational *pluralism*.)

But does not orientational pluralism put everyone's position on a par? Does it not underwrite the view that all the alternatives ultimately lie on the same level of acceptability?

The question again is: Acceptable to whom? The discipline as a whole maintains a certain olympian indifference—a noncommittal neutrality. However, this certainly does *not* mean that my position is just as acceptable to you as to me. The fact that the discipline as a whole incorporates other positions does nothing to render a firm and fervent commitment to one's own position somehow infeasible, let alone improper.

Consider another objection:

Value espousal may *motivate* the selection of one particular position but cannot *justify* it. And this consideration critically undermines philosophy as a rational enterprise.

But of course the appeal to a value can justify if the value itself is justified. And of course we are bound to take the stance that we are justified in holding the values we do on the basis of our "experience" or "understanding of the world," and so on. To be sure, this justification of values itself involves values and is thus position-relative. It is a justification for me (or perhaps anybody in my shoes) though not, to be sure, a justification that will compel anybody and everybody regardless of the nature of their cognitive values. The fact is that my probative values can justify my resolving the issues in a certain way. Just this is the key point—that philosophical justification is locally posture-relative and not globally universal.

In *evaluating* positions we have, of course, no alternative to doing so from the perspective of our cognitive values—our own cognitive point of view. (It wouldn't *be* our point of view if we didn't use it as such.) And given its natural emergence from our own point of view, our doctrinal position is, of course, going to emerge as optimal on its own telling. (That *your* position is going to emerge as optimal on *your* orientation's telling is, of course, going to come to *me* neither as news nor yet as something intimidating.) It makes a crucial difference to everybody which position one adopts, though not in exactly the same way. We cannot view philosophical disagreement in the light of "a mere divergence of opinion." It is a serious conflict, as one would expect when something as important as one's values is at stake. Each thinker, each school, is bound to take a strongly negative stand toward its competitors: belittling their concerns, deploring their standards, downgrading their ideals, disliking their presuppositions, scorning their contentions, and so on.

A philosopher's adoption of a standard cognitive value is never arbitrary but is always guided by justifying considerations. Albeit evaluative in themselves, these grounds are utterly reasonable and compelling *for him* because they have a telling force and cogency relative to his own commitments (which, to be sure, may differ from those of others). Even as people can, quite properly, have different *personal* loyalties and allegiances, so philosophers can have different *cognitive* loyalties and allegiances.

Yet does orientational pluralism not put everyone's position on exactly the same plane? Well, yes and no. Orientational pluralism does see alternative philosophical positions as enjoying a parity of status from an *external* point of view; all responsibly developed positions are valid from a suitably favorable cognitive-value orientation and indefensible if we proceed from no orientation at all. But this externalized parity cannot be transmuted into an argument against such theories, cannot be made over into reason for not accepting them at all. For individuals do in general have a value orientation and are able to resolve issues by its means. (The fact that words are meaningless until people endow them with meaning does not entail that they continue meaningless once they have done so.)

The long and short of it is that orientation pluralism does *not* put everyone's position on a par, save from the unachievable olympian point of view of the community at large. Each individual stands fully and decidedly committed to his own orientation, so that there is no question of *indifferentism* in acknowledging the pivotal role of values. For people have values and cannot be indifferent about them, and it is people who hold philosophical positions. (Philosophy at large may be indifferent between values and the various positions they underwrite, but of course is not a doctrine available for the taking.)

It must be denied categorically and with vehemence that the orientational pluralist is an indifferentist who cannot be seriously dedicated to his own substantive position and cannot see it as espoused for good and compelling reasons. Even though philosophical issues do not admit of producing a position that is *uniquely adequate* on grounds of abstract theory, there still remains the fact of an *optimal solution for us*, that is, for someone who shares the cognitive values that determine our own probative principles—our sense of the important, significant, and so on. We should realize that if we do not prevail in general and *contra mundum* (as we indeed cannot do), we can still work out a good solution to such problems *relative to a certain basis* of orientational commitment that others can (in principle) share.

To be sure, our orientational pluralism does not insist on absolute commitment at every time and season. It is perfectly prepared to let philosophizing sometimes proceed in a hypothetical and experimental spirit, letting us construct a doctrinal edifice without outright commitment, simply to see what sort of structure can be made available. But it does insist that we must eventually return to the recognition of the cognitive values that indicate that this resolution is one to which we do not stand committed. (Either that, or else we have to make the quantum jump to a new set of values.)

Philosophical questions are not irresolvable; they can indeed be answered. But, alas, they can only be answered on the basis of value commitments and in consequence can always be answered in distinct and conflicting ways. Appropriate answers can indeed be found, only to find them we must proceed on the basis of a (potentially variable) cognitive-value orientation. To be sure, Philosophy—the sum total of philosophical positions—does not provide any determinate answers. But particular positions indeed do so, and that's exactly what is at issue in developing *our* philosophy. Orientational pluralism is unproblematically able to regard philosophy in the light of the traditional mainstream view as a matter of problem solving, of getting rationally validated answers to our questions as to these matters of first principle.

We cannot resolve our philosophical deliberations presuppositionlessly by calling upon the Recording Angel to tell us "the God's-eye view of the facts of the case." All we can do is to assess as best we can on which side the strongest case can be built and to which side the weight of good reason inclines. We cannot tell which thesis or theory deserves our credence save by assessing which are better spoken for than their rivals. And here "better" must of course mean "better by the standards and norms that we ourselves accept." (We cannot get at the *real* truth save via the epstemic mediation of *our* truth.) The fact that others may accept different standards and may thus see the matter differently is simply irrelevant *for us*. That those whose probative commitments differ from ours should arrive at different results may well annoy us but cannot properly give us pause, cannot undermine the appropriateness *for us* of our own convictions. When Luther refused to recant at the Diet of Worms of 1521, he told the assembled dignitaries:

Your Imperial Majesty and your lordships demand a simple answer. Here it is, plain and unvarnished. Unless I am convicted of error by the testimony of Scripture or . . . by manifest reasoning . . . I can not and will not recant anything. For to act against our conscience is neither safe for us, nor appropriate for us. On this I take my stand. I can do no other. God help me. Amen.[6]

Taking this sort of stance is the most, and the best, that we can do in philosophy.

But is it not defeatist to give up on the search for "the uniquely appropriate" answer in a transperspectival, orientation-invariant sense? Surely not! If the situation is indeed as we have portrayed it, pluralism is not defeatist, but simply realistic—a recognition of "the facts of life." On the view being advanced here, it follows that relativistic pluralism is inescapable given the logical structure of the situation—a situation in which the unavailability of a *uniquely tenable* solution is simply an inevitable fact. To be dissatisifed with the sort of relativism that is at issue in orientational pluralism is to embrace the illusion that "the God's-eye point of view" has a role to play in the theory of human cognition.

Orientational pluralism is based on recognizing the questions of philosophy as *meaningful*; it sees the issues as *momentous* and the in-

---

6. Cited in Henry Bettensen, ed., *Documents of the Christian Church* (New York, 1947), p. 285.

quiry as *legitimate*. The project is a serious one, and it is important that in pursuing it we do the very best we can. But this does *not* mean that we can attain communally monolithic solutions in orientation-independent ways.

## 3. Does Orientational Pluralism Support Irrationalism?

The nature of orientational pluralism is helpfully clarified by considering the following objection: "To accept philosophical pluralism is to acknowledge the infeasibility of attaining a unique and communally compelling result. It is, in effect, to concede the incapacity of reason to deal with these matters satisfactorily. In thus placing the issue beyond the powers of reason, pluralism extends an open invitation to irrationalism." Addressing this objection is essential to a just estimate of orientational pluralism's approach to philosophical diversity.

Philosophizing is not a mere matter of fortuitous taste! Reason and rationality play a crucial role. In philosophy as elsewhere, rationality is concerned with determining the best means to given ends. And throughout the present account our flag has been nailed to the mast of the rational inquiry model, which sees the task of the enterprise in terms of answering our philosophical questions in a way that is consistent, coherent, comprehensive, systematic—in sum, rationally cogent. The idea of rationality can thus be maintained. Our orientational approach to philosophical problem solving sees it as subject, from beginning to end, to a rigorous application of the orthodox decision-theoretic model of rational choice—as a matter of cost-benefit optimization (relative to an endorsed utility standard for reckoning costs and benefits).

Orientational pluralism holds that there is indeed a uniquely appropriate answer to philosophical questions relative to a particular stand on the fundamental issues of cognitive value. It depicts the process of validating this answer in terms of the classical model of rationality—as the quest for the optimum resolution relative to the *totality* of relevant materials (cognitive-value considerations included). The doctrine envisages a rigid structure of reason, of optimizing the systemic structure of one's commitments in the light of certain value subscriptions, of adopting that (uniquely) correct solution as that which all rational considerations (values included) indicate as best.

To be sure, there are difficulties. For there can be no general agreement about the yardsticks for measuring cogency (plausibility, acceptability) in the setting of philosophical argumentation, because the issue of cognitive value—of significance, cogency, plausibility, and acceptability—is itself a proper subject for philosophical dispute.

One can indeed legitimate one's values in a rational way that proves fully convincing to oneself. But one cannot necessarily thereby refute someone else's. Rational discussion thus cannot of itself constrain consensus in evaluative matters. One can develop a position that one is fully entitled to see as rationally decisive. But such a position will not necessarily satisfy another.

Yet does not abandoning the absolutism of an insistence on an "unconditionally true and correct" answer that rationally compels universal assent—settling instead for a relativized variety of "perspectivally appropriate answers"—spell the abandonment of a rational approach to problem solving?

Orientational pluralism responds with an emphatic negative. To begin with, it must be stressed that orientational pluralism incorporates a great many straightforwardly rationalistic constraints and commitments. For one thing, in its reliance on the machinery of apories and antinomies, the theory views the clash of doctrines not as chaotic and cognitively intractable but as reflecting an orderly and well-defined structure of clearly prescribed alternatives. To take a substantive position on a philosophical issue is to make a choice among alternatives whose characters are fixed entirely by the nature of the problem at hand. There is in fact not a *chaos* or *anarchy* of systems but an orderly exfoliation of them along discrete, logically delineated channels of apory-resolving alternatives. On such an analysis, the diversity of positions (at any given level of sophistication and complexity) simply *exhausts all the possibilities within* a well-defined range. These possibilities represent the spectrum of different ways of restoring consistency to the apory in which the position has (at that level of discussion) become enmeshed. Given such a limited group of tenable alternatives, it is clearly *not* the case that rational constraints are left behind. The point is simply that some of these constraints are bound to be of an evaluative nature.

Moreover, from the theory-internal standpoint of a *given* cognitive value orientation, it is (or should be) subject to cogent demonstration that there is some uniquely best resolution to a philosophical issue. A developed cognitive value system will generally admit of only one resolution to the antinomy inherent in the aporetic cluster that sets the stage for philosophical problems. That someone who holds *those* cognitive values should be led to *that* particular resolution is a perfectly objective, reason-constrained matter that admits of no idiosyncratic variation. Orientational pluralism is not committed to the laissez-faire liberalism of "everyone has a right to his own opinion." In general, only one way of working things out will be optimally consonant with a given value orientation. So here again there is an element of rational stringency. As orientational pluralism sees it, philosophizing is an altogether rational process—a matter of plausibility-maximizing relative to our cognitive values.

So what we have here is not irrationalism, but an accommodation of philosophy to the standard rationality model of utility maximization. The choice among salient philosophical positions is seen as rigidly delimited by considerations of rationality. The salient injunctions are:

(1) Restore consistency!
(2) Do this in such a way as to optimize the acceptability of the result (relative, of course, to your own standards of cognitive utility—your own scheme of cognitive values)!
(3) Carry this optimization out in the simplest, most straightforward and economical way!

On this telling, a philosophical doctrine purports to be the best solution of a problem (or, at any rate, the best that can be had in a particular state of the art) relative to certain evaluative constraints. That "the best" here involves evaluation in a way that introduces an element of relativism, resting on standards that fail to be wholly objective and shared universally, clearly does not stand in the way of rationality.

Orientational pluralism accordingly insists that a rational justification can indeed be found for a philosophical position. But it sees this justification as inherently normative. It does not, to be sure, go on to hold that "there is no (rational) disputing about values." On the contrary! It sees endless room for rational debate here. Yet it does hold that the value field is closed; that reasoning about values cannot lead outside—that values cannot be defended without values. We can *hold* values nondiscursively, but we can only *legitimate* them discursively with reference to other values. This can always be done; values are not like mere tastes and preferences, for we can always dispute about them in rational argumentation. Such dispute about (some) values, though, must appeal to (other) values. What is at issue here is not a denial of rational justification in philosophy, but a thesis about its nature, namely, that it admits of diversity of modes because of its evaluative involvements.

In sum, orientational pluralism emphatically does *not* turn its back on rationality. It does not deny that philosophical positions can be subjected to rational assessment and criticism. It merely insists that this can only be done from the vantage point of some orientational stance or other—that there is, for us, no prospect of any value-neutral, God's-eye-view vantage point wholly outside the range of evaluative postures from which a philosophical position can be appraised.

## 4. Pluralism and the Impetus of Reason

Consider the aporetic cluster represented by the following inconsistent triad:

(1) Philosophical issues cannot be resolved by reason.
(2) There is no serviceable recourse beyond reason for resolving philosophical issues.
(3) Philosophical issues can be resolved satisfactorily.

As is usual in these cases, there are alternative approaches for dealing with this aporetic conflict:

Abandon (1): Insist that these philosophical issues can indeed be resolved by reason alone (rationalism).
Abandon (2): Maintain that there is some intellectual resource for the resolution of such issues that transcends the limits of reason (transcendentalism).
Abandon (3): Deny that these philosophical issues represent problems that admit of attainable resolution. This can be done by either (1) an *agnostic scepticism* that retains the issues as meaningful but sees them as insoluble, or (2) a *nihilistic scepticism* that rejects them as meaningless or otherwise illegitimate.

Regarding the scepticism inherent in (3)–rejection we need say little at this point; it will be criticized at length in chapters 12 and 13. Let us contemplate (2)–rejection. Here one would postulate an intellectual resource transcending the limits of reason, a cognitive mode of extrarational insight in line with the following sorts of alternatives:

I. *Extrarational insight based wholly in the intellect*
   —by way of a natural intellectual capacity
   — by way of a supernatural intellectual capacity
II. *Extrarational insight based wholly in the will*
   — by way of an essentially voluntaristic capacity that is affective rather than intellectual

One would accordingly arrive at three sorts of programs for the settlement of philosophical issues:
   —gnosis, intellectual intuition, mind's-eye insight (Plato and Neoplatonism, Descartes)
   —divine inspiration, mystical vision (Heraclitus, St. Paul, Simon Magnus, Meister Eckhart)
   —will (Schopenhauer) or desire (psychologism) or faith (Pascal, Kierkegaard, William James)

Any such theory treats philosophizing as a cognitive activity that reaches beyond reason itself through the deployment of some extraordinary cognitive resource that supplements reason by an informative insight of some nondiscursive sort. (The difficulty, of course, lies in establishing the cognitive credentials of this purported resource.)

Orientational pluralism, however, denies the need for philosophy to "rise above reason" in this way. It is a strict rationalism that implicitly rejects thesis (1). Disdaining both scepticism and transcendentalism, it upholds the capacity of reason itself to come to grips meaningfully with philosophical issues.

The crux, however, is that the "reason" at issue is to be normative rather than factual reason. For the "reason" that resolves philosophical issues can only manage to do so on the basis of cognitive values. Though these values themselves are not whole and entire products of evidential cognition; they rest on a foundation that is always in part noncognitive. This, of course, does not make them nonrational (let alone irrational). We can perfectly well reason and deliberate about values—it is just that we *cannot* do this on a basis that is itself wholly probative and nonevaluative.

Still, while rejecting (1) as it stands, orientational pluralism does indeed retain a duly qualified version of this thesis, subject (as usual) to a certain distinction:

(1') Philosophical issues can indeed be resolved by reason broadly construed, namely by (evaluatively) *normative* reason, though to be sure they cannot be resolved by *theoretical* (or probative) reason alone.

Recourse is made to a distinction between the theoretical/probative mode of reason and a normative use of reason that proceeds not merely with a view to "the objectively determinable facts" alone but also involves certain crucial values. Strictly theoretical reason is taken to require supplementation by evaluative commitments before a resolution can be achieved in philosophical problem solving.

Such a position looks to the taxonomy of reason presented in table 3. On this basis, orientational pluralism views philosophy as a venture

*Table 3*
THE TAXONOMY OF REASON

*Theoretical* (Probative; Acceptance-Oriented)
　—*formal* (mathematics, logic, formal theories of structure in language, design, etc.)
　—*evidential* (factual reasoning in science and common life)

*Practical* (Pragmatic; Choice-Oriented)
　—*evaluative*
　　—*axiological* (value-oriented)
　　　—geared to cognitive values
　　　—geared to affective values
　　　—geared to moral values
　　　—and so on
　　—*prudential* (interest-oriented)
　—*instrumental* ("value-free" means-ends reasoning in technical decision making)

in discursive reasoning based on cognitive norms and values—a project of evaluative/normative reason rather than one of strictly evidential/factual reason. In this way, orientational pluralism takes a strictly rationalistic stance, although it is rationalism of a particular, qualified sort—one that allows values to figure within the precincts of reason. It sees the resolution of philosophical questions as a matter not beyond the capacity of reason as such but merely beyond the capacity of strictly factual reasoning.

In all ages, sceptics have told us that "no single position in philosophy is categorically acceptable because the claims of each are invalidated by the existence of the rest." This sort of statement sounds wise but fails to be so. It is predicated on the view that only what is rationally acceptable to *everybody* can qualify as acceptable to *anybody*. Accordingly it overlooks the deep difference between purely "theoretical" reason that hinges on the probative force of purely objective considerations, and "normative" reason that calls for some element of evaluative (and thus potentially person-differential) input.

To be sure, a cognitive value would not be a value for me if I did not *purport* its absoluteness. But that itself does not make the value absolute. And this decisively affects the status of our philosophical doctrines. As we ourselves see it, that which we accept should be endorsed by everybody else as well. But relativity remains. The claims of reason are universal claims; as I myself am bound to see it, what I accept as correct should be accepted by everybody. But even though the *claims* I make are absolute, and though I take myself to be fully *entitled* to make them, I cannot thereby validate my truth claims in an absolute way. Claims to universality need not themselves be shared universally. In philosophizing we indeed *claim* universality and absolutism. But that does not offset the relativity of our claims themselves.

## 5. The Rational Imperative

But what of those theorists who want to set reason and rationality aside, who propose to cease all commerce with reasoning and argumentation and turn philosophy from the pursuit of rational belief to some fundamentally noncognitive enterprise? Whatever sort of "enlightenment" they are pursuing, it is not problem solving. And herein lies the flaw. We are led to philosophize because we want not just *answers* but *reasoned answers*—doctrines, positions, worldviews AND rational grounding for their espousal. All of these elements are essential components of one integral whole. In philosophy, answers without reasoning are useless and reasoning without answers are unavailing.

It would leave a philosopher totally frustrated and dissatisfied to play the yes-or-no game of Twenty Questions with the Recording Angel. For we want not only answers, but *explanations* (clarifications of the concepts involved) and *reasons* (indications of *why* those answers are more adequate than their competing alternatives). Both arguments and imaginative ideas are needed. Ideas without arguments are fruitless, arguments without ideas sterile.

To be sure, philosophy has two sectors. One, based on *the model of valuation*, approaches philosophizing as a matter of developing sensibility. The enterprise is one of intellectual orientation, consciousness expansion, value cultivation. The other sector, based on *the model of inquiry*, sees philosophy as a matter of question answering, problem solving, and theory building. Philosophers sometimes lose sight of the fact that both sectors are crucial—that unexamined values are rootless and unguided inquiries are unavailing. In philosophy, the dimension of valuation and the dimension of theorizing both desperately need one another; theory is hamstrung without appraisal and appraisal is impotent without theory. The two undertakings stand in a symbiosis of reciprocal dependence.

In consequence, the cultivation of evaluative sensibilities is not enough by itself. What militates toward the orthodox view of philosophy in terms of problem solving is that we have questions and want answers—that man is the cognitive animal (*homo sapiens; homo quaerens*) But, as usual, we can usefully deploy a distinction; namely, the distinction between "establishing" and "providing good reasons for" a certain contention. In the present case, however, these good reasons are not purely evidential but normatively conditioned. (But, of course, normative reason is still a sector of reason as such.) Accordingly, the orientational pluralist rejects the sceptical view and insists that reason can indeed resolve philosophical questions, though, to be sure, the "reason" at issue is not purely theoretical reason but *normative* reason.

It may perhaps be possible in some domains to validate views without recourse to discursive reasoning about the issues, by proceeding through the guidance of some sort of insight or intuition. But whatever result this sort of sensibility may yield, it is not philosophy. For philosophy is not just a quest for answers to questions and solutions to problems; it is a quest for defensible answers and tenable solutions. And the defensibility and tenability at issue are matters to be adjudicated in the court of reason. That philosophy is inherently a labor of reason is itself a philosophical thesis—perhaps the most fundamental and reasonable one of all.

If a rational choice between conflicting philosophical positions and doctrines were impossible, the situation would be incalculably tragic. Because the human condition being what it is, we must make a choice.

We are emplaced *in medias res* in a difficult world, and to get about satisfactorily within it must orient ourselves cognitively. We have no alternative but to choose, arbitrarily if need be. (As Pascal put it: "You must play. It is not optional. You are embarked."[7]) But if we could not *rationalize* our choice in the best sense of this term, if we could not articulate a satisfactory rationale for it, then we could not satisfy the deepest demands of our nature as "the rational animal."

To be sure, we cannot say *a priori* that the real is rational, that our quest for rational understanding is bound to prove successful. We must simply hope for the best and do our utmost to realize it. Trust in reason may in the end prove unavailing. But we will never know short of reaching that end—and so effectively never. All we know is that we won't get there if we don't try. We have nothing to lose. And so the rational course is to proceed in hope.

The upshot of these deliberations is clear. Orientational pluralism is deeply committed to reason and rationality. It is emphatically not a version of irrationalism. While it does indeed insist that philosophizing requires a resource beyond *theoretical* or *probative* reason as such, it still finds this resource within the broad framework of reason, namely in the *evaluative* or *normative* sector of this domain. It is predicated on the conviction that rationality is a resource that is strong enough to survive the shift from absolutism to a value-oriented relativism.

---

7. Blaise Pascal, *Pensées*, sec. 343 (Lafuma) = 233 (Brunschvicg).

# 9

# What Orientational Pluralism Means for Philosophy

## 1. *The Individual and the Community*

The difference between "my philosophy" and "the enterprise of philosophy at large" is crucial. The nature of philosophical work makes it natural and proper for the stance of the individual to be monistic. The individual philosopher can—and should—"take a position" for articulation, elaboration, and advocacy. Yet the stance of the community is pluralistic—it is not feasible, and perhaps not even desirable, that any one particular position should prevail across the board.

In philosophy, the way of the community at large is not an available option for the single individual. For the community need not (and will not) "make up its mind" among conflicting alternatives, as an individual must. The weight of rationality—of consistency and coordination—bears down upon the individual in a way that the community in its aggregate totality can and does simply ignore.

One cannot reproach the individual philosopher for being "parochial." His allegiance to particular values is not a failing but the inevitable requirement of substantive work in the field. The individual philosopher is bound, and entitled, to take an evaluative stance toward the spectrum of alternative probative orientations themselves. But in philosophy there is no theory-neutral starting point, no fulcrum for an Archimedean lever. The appraisal of a philosophical argument can thus only be carried out "from within," so to speak; that is, from the vantage point of a prior probative position from which the theses and inferences at issue can be assessed. As long as we wish to take positions on the substantive issues, we cannot avoid potentially controversial cognitive-value commitments.

In philosophy, the community and the individual are thus very differently situated. The individual must "take his stand"—must define, substantiate, and develop his *own* position from his own evaluative point of view, which reflects his own assessment of matters of cognitive significance and importance. But he can never hope for consensus, for dominance, for ultimate victory over the rest. He cannot expect to carry the whole community with him through the force of mere reasoning and argumentation.

From the standpoint of the individual—internal to his probative orientation and his own cognitive values—the perspectival approach takes much the same position as the unique reality view. The philosopher sees his own position as right and proper; everyone else's as just wrong. But there is also the standpoint of the community as a whole, in the full richness of its orientational diversity. Here the openly relativistic stance of a variegated pluralism applies. *De omnibus disputandum est* is the motto of philosophy, but not of the philosopher. The position of the individual is monistic and absolute while that of the community as a whole is pluralistic and multi-perspectival. Depending on the point of view one takes, the present account can be characterized equally well as an orientational monism or an orientational pluralism.

## 2. In Philosophy We Cannot "Rise Above the Battle"

Philosophical argumentation is inherently value laden; there simply is no neutral vantage point from which the cogency of philosophical positions can be determined objectively, in the absence of any and all person-variable evaluative inputs. In philosophy we thus cannot rise above the battle of the schools. The proliferation of points of view is inherent in the enterprise. We cannot attain a "position of reason" outside the arena of controversy. To stand above the controversy is to cease doing philosophy; we can only do the work of the discipline—can only provide answers to its questions—by *taking a stance* on inherently controversial matters of cognitive value. We have to choose between leaving the battlefield altogether (thus simply abandoning the project) and continuing the fight. Philosophy is inevitably an arena of conflict.

In philosophy there is no orientation-detached court of appeals. We can only proceed from our own particular vantage point. Whoever is not satisfied with deliberations tinged with limitations of person-relative contexts cannot deliberate at all in this domain. There is no "higher standpoint," no nondoctrinal basis, for the appraisal of doctrines. Whatever is produced is simply another product of the philosophical mill, simply another doctrine to be set alongside others as an object of analysis and controversy and refinement. We cannot at once remain in philosophy and transcend its limitations.

If we persist in cultivating the discipline, there are two things we must realize. First, we shall not win, if winning a victory means establishing consensus by inflicting an incontestably decisive defeat upon our opponents in rational disputation, converting and/or confuting them once and for all. And second, we shall not have clear sailing—difficulties will break out in our own camp; our own position will not be free from problems as it is further developed. The battle is bound to continue; we shall have to slay the dragons as they come forth, realizing full well that even while we struggle yet others will appear further down the road.

Attainment of a God's-eye view independent of our parochial value posture is simply not feasible in philosophy. This is another aspect of the story of "the fall of man" in *Genesis*. Expelled from the Garden of Eden, we have no choice but to see matters *sub specie humanitatis*. Yearning for absolutes, we face the discordant ambiguities of the human condition and must come to terms with pluralities. The story of the Tower of Babel is deeply symbolic. In this epistemic dispensation we have to live with diversity and discord. The unavailability of absolutes makes it unrealistic to expect consensus. We just have to do the best we can with the resources at our disposal, recognizing that they are incapable of constraining the rational resolution of communal debate. The epistemological situation of philosophy cries out to be characterized in theological terms.

## 3. Is Philosophy a Guide to Life?

Philosophers traditionally view the task of the discipline as providing rational guidance to thought and action. But can philosophy do this job? The motto of Phi Beta Kappa, America's oldest academic confraternity, is the proud dictum "Philosophy is the guide of life" (*philosophia biou kubernetes*). Is this claim defensible? Does philosophy indeed provide a satisfactory guide to decision and action in the practical affairs of life?

It is all too clear that philosophy at large affords no useful guidance for the governance of our affairs. Philosophy is a domain of clashing contentions without consolidated results; it has no theses, lessons, teachings—only possible problems and conflicting solutions. No one bears more eloquent testimony to this than the philosophers themselves. Philosophy, as Benedetto Croce maintained, "gives rise to those inconclusive and interminable arguments which are so frequent with professional philosophers that they seem to have become a natural element in their lives, where they come and go . . . in vain, always agitated here and there and everywhere, but always at the same stage of development."[1] Philosophers have often cast envious sidelong

---

1. Benedetto Croce, *History as the Story of Liberty*, trans. S. Sprigge (Chicago, 1970), pp. 147–48.

glances at the sciences, with their demonstrated capacity to solve the problems and settle the controversies of the field and yield a continually increasing number of established findings that reflect a general consensus.

Philosophy as such—the enterprise as a whole, in the richly discordant diversity of its intramural conflicts and disagreements—obviously does not provide a guide to life. At this level of comprehensive generality, our questions get not one answer but a babel of conflicting answers from which no useful guidance can be extracted. If we are to *apply* philosophy we must have a particular philosophy to apply. But there is no body of established and agreed theory in philosophy that one can "apply" in the way we can in, say, physics or biochemistry. Just what are the implications of this?

*Applied philosophy* (as it has come to be called) has to do with the implementation of philosophical ideas, methods, and beliefs in resolving the cognitive, normative, and practical issues we face in everyday situations in "the real world."

There are different ways of applying philosophy, however. In particular, there are *personal* applications to one's own concerns and in the specific context of one's own life, and there are also *public* applications to the governance of society's affairs. The former is relatively straightforward. Once one *has* a philosophy and has taken one's personal position on philosophical issues, one can usefully put it to work in making one's decisions and conducting one's affairs. But the issue of applying philosophy in the public domain raises more substantial difficulties.

For only insofar as we have an agreed-upon and shared "public philosophy" can we make use of philosophy as a basis for problem solving in the public forum. It is at just this point that we encounter a decisive roadblock. Living in a pluralistic, diversified, and ideologically balkanized society, we lack that doctrinal consensus that alone could give us a philosophy that we could apply unproblematically in the arena of public policy.

At the outset of his *Meditations,* Descartes expressed the intention that, until his own philosophy was fully formed, he would continue to guide his conduct of life's affairs by the "extraphilosophical" resources of common sense and established custom. This is surely a sensible course. As Descartes clearly saw, an individual's guidance must await the development of *one's own* philosophy. Until we have formed our own framework of values and have thought through its implications, we had best cling to the security of the tried and tested and let ourselves be guided by custom's familiar and established ways. Until one's own philosophical position is available, one can expect no useful guidance from philosophy as such.

Not the discipline as a whole but only the products of one's own particular mode of practicing it can possibly afford helpful direction and informative answers. Only at this particularistic level can we achieve a definite position regarding the right and the good, the beautiful and the sublime, the significant and the important. Only from one's own philosophy, and not from philosophy *per se*, can guidance for thought and action be extracted. Questions we can indeed get from the enterprise of philosophy at large. But if it is *answers* that we want (and it surely ought to be), then we can only obtain them from *our own* philosophy. To secure answers to our questions we must work them out on some basis with which we ourselves can come to terms. If we want to put philosophy to work we must first develop a philosophy to apply. Thereafter there is no problem; once we have a philosophy in place, we can draw upon it for counsel.

But what of philosophy *per se* in its full and impersonal generality? Philosophy *per se* only provides a catalogue of possibilities, a collection of blueprints. But a blueprint does not afford us a habitation; to have a dwelling we must have some particular structure. Philosophy-in-general cannot answer our questions, only whatever particular philosophy we ourselves accept can do so.

Given that the enterprise as a whole cannot achieve universally acceptable resolutions of the substantive issues, can we obtain any useful lessons from it? We can indeed. From philosophy at large we can learn about the questions of the field and their presuppositions, the range of possible answers, the ramifications of various positions, and so on. Even the position-detached study of philosophy as a whole can provide a powerful stimulus to thoughtful reflection and a great aid to us in working out our own positions. The study of philosophy is "consciousness raising"—it makes us aware of problems and issues and sensitizes us to the bearing of various sorts of considerations. Its utility, however, is not as a solver of life's problems but as an intellectual stimulus toward cultivating those resources of reason and thoughtful reflection by which an intelligent person can tackle the problems he or she faces. The lessons of philosophy at large relate to possibilities, not actualities—to what might be said rather than to what any one particular thinker is prepared to say. And this, of course, stops well short of yielding substantive answers to philosophical questions.

Strictly speaking, then, there is but one way in which to full-bloodedly "apply" philosophy—namely, by first developing a philosophical position of one's own and thereafter proceeding to put it to work in resolving issues. And this is difficult in the public domain because we lack a public philosophy.

However, there remains that other, less committed way of "applying" philosophy where what is at issue is not the particular *substance* (results, findings) of philosophical inquiry but its general *structure*. We delineate the issues, clarify the problems, pinpoint what questions must be decided, and examine what sorts of considerations must be taken into account. This generalized mode of applied philosophizing has the merit of not presupposing that the substantive issues have been settled in an incontestable way. But for this very reason it is a resource of somewhat limited utility. For such "applications" do not resolve the issues but merely assure that whatever solutions we ultimately adopt will be of high quality in point of technical articulation. They serve to assure that the deliberations at issue are sensibly managed, that they are adequately developed and achieve *technical* merit but not that they must assert themselves in any particular *substantive* direction.[2] What is at issue with *this* methodological mode of applied philosophy is not *problem resolution* but merely that crucial preliminary of *problem clarification*.

Such a procedure can indeed enable us to achieve technical adequacy in our deliberations. It can ensure that we pay due attention to such matters as defining the issues, bringing to explicit recognition things that must be taken into account, pinpointing relevant considerations, avoiding confusions, identifying factors that must be distinguished, clarifying connections between seemingly disjoint considerations, drawing attention to ramifications and complexities that must not be lost sight of, and so on. All the analytical and synthetic tools of philosophizing can be brought to bear, leading us to pay heed to the various pieces of the puzzle and to coordinate them in their holistic unity. But all this methodological care only means that we have followed our route carefully; it does *not* mean that we arrive at the proper destination. These essentially probative resources only assure that whatever solution we can secure through use of other (substantive) resources is well worked out and cogently presented. They cannot determine the *nature* of our answers but only that they are competently substantiated. Accordingly, their utility, though real, is limited. Precisely because they are not substantive they do not enable us to resolve the real issues themselves, which are almost always of substantive bearing. (Care of process and procedure does not guarantee adequacy

---

2. But does not the choice of a philosophical method reflect cognitive values and thus itself step back into substantive philosophy? The answer is, in a word, yes. When the applied philosopher writing in the public domain makes use of philosophical methods, he does or should do so not in the spirit of using "the (normatively) *right* method" but in that of using "a (factually) *widely used* method"—one that philosophers generally recognized as competent make use of.

of result. Great pains and efforts can be expended in building up a house of cards.)

This merely procedural sort of "applied philosophy" is a mode of cognitive accounting, as it were. It insists on methodological rigor in keeping the books—on clarity, consistency, and coherent integration. But when all is said and done, this does not take us very far. Accountants as such do not deal in substantive determinations. They do not make decisions; they assure that those who do make decisions are able to see exactly what the upshot is in terms of the assets and liabilities they engender. Substance must come *ab extra*—not from probative process but from substantive commitment.

## 4. Are Orientationally Bound Positions Worth Having?

Given the stance of orientational pluralism that a particular position in philosophy can only be maintained against other rival alternatives from the vantage point of an evaluative stance—specifically, a cognitive-value orientation—can the appropriateness of the enterprise be defended? Can a discipline be deemed rationally legitimate in which one takes positions that ultimately rest, not on matters writ large in the impersonal and objective scheme of things, but upon one's own particular evaluative orientation?

Surely there is a perfectly good point to the enterprise of finding what are (given our own orientation) demonstably appropriate solutions to the philosophical problems to which we address ourselves. It makes good sense to set about the work of finding answers that afford us the satisfactions of rational cogency, even if they may well leave somebody else dissatisfied. As long as its potential inappropriateness from *someone else's probative orientation* nowise invalidates or undermines the appropriateness and cogency of a given position *from mine*, why should this mere lack of universality occasion discontent?

There is something foolish in reacting in petulant disappointment against a discipline that fails to deliver wholly incontestable truths into our hands. Why should we not accept with good grace the fact that justification in this domain is evaluatively conditioned and thus inherently controversial? Whoever promised us that philosophy would do more than this—and what could we blame for our counting on such promises save our own folly? After all, what is the history of science but the graveyard of rejected theories? Yet who abandons natural science upon learning that the "established knowledge" of one generation is the error of another? In science we are perfectly prepared to rest satisifed with the best we can do with the resources at our disposal, realizing that others (specifically, our successors) may well think differently on these subjects. How can we demand more in philosophy?

# THE STRIFE OF SYSTEMS
*What Orientational Pluralism Means for Philosophy*

Does orientational pluralism not entail that philosophy is pointless? Is it not vain to seek the solution of a problem if one cannot arrive at a thoroughly objective (absolutely and intersubjectively valid) answer but only at one that is appropriate relative to the standpoint of a certain cognitive-value orientation? If *that* is how the matter stands—on such a footing of orientational pluralism—then why not abandon the whole enterprise? Can philosophy survive as a legitimate rational enterprise once the fact of pluralism is acknowledged—once it is conceded that different people properly and legitimately disagree regarding the correct solutions of its problems?

What our philosophizing does is strive to give us, with maximal cogency and coherence, a systematic formulation (not of God's hallowed truth but) of our own position—a set of answers to our philosophical questions that represents the duly systematized ramifications of our own cognitively evaluative posture. To be sure, our position might not suit somebody else who stands elsewhere in regard to orientational fundamentals. But, so we must suppose, it does suit the lay of the land on which we ourselves stand. It is (by hypothesis) the very best result that it is possible for us to realize, given our probative/methodological commitments. How can any reasonable person ask for more? Given that these commitments suit our own position, who are we to be dissatisfied with them? If indeed they are the best that can be done relative to our own orientational commitments, what ground is there *for us* to be dissatisfied with them because they do not suit the judgment of somebody who sees the issues in a very different light? What entitles us to the hubris of insisting, "Only what can convince *everyone* is good enough for me"?[3] Who promised us the comfort of the companionship of all rational minds in this world? (Surely not the deity who exiled us hither from the garden.)

To abandon the idea of finding a solution to a philosophical problem that is acceptable *to everyone* is emphatically not to despair of finding a solution satisfactory *to oneself*. This consequence would follow only if it were seen as a precondition of having an answer satisfactory to oneself that this answer will (in principle) have to satisfy everybody else as well. But this sort of generalization would only be appropriate if we were not here dealing in the *normative* domain. It would only be appropriate if the situation of philosophy were very different from what it is and, in the nature of the case, must inevitably be. Philosophy is a matter of rational problem solving—albeit one that proceeds in the domain of normative rather than theoretical reason.

---

3. To be sure, we believe that what convinces us *should* convince everyone, but that's something else again.

There is no point in complaining of what cannot be helped. Depreciating the value-boundedness of philosophical positions would only make sense relative to the supposition that it might be possible to resolve such issues in a manner that makes no appeal to values. But if, as our deliberations indicate, one must reject this supposition as mistaken, then it is surely irrational to deplore as unworthy something that is acknowledged as the best that can be had in the circumstances. It is, after all, quintessentially rational to refrain from asking for something that cannot in the nature of things be had. And this clearly is the case with respect to presuppositionlessly absolute demonstrations of philosophical correctness. The course of rationality is surely to accept the enterprise as rational inquiry shows it to be.

Someone might perhaps argue as follows:

Conflicting philosophical positions simply annihilate one another. Communal diversity betokens the infeasibility of any satisfactory resolution. The plurality of positions entails that none is tenable.

But this position is gravely flawed. It is predicated on the mistaken idea that rational credence cannot rest on a person-differential basis—that with regard to rational belief, one is entitled to believe only what *everybody* is entitled to believe. But this will not do. The everybody must be "everybody who stands where I do." One's position is indeed universalizable, but only *limitedly*, with respect to a relativized cognitive-value orientation.

In philosophy, our own position simply will not stand uncontested and unrivaled. But unless we are exceedingly naive and starry eyed, this fact should not distress us. There are indeed other "available" positions, but they are available only to those who see matters in a different light. That those who have different perspectives on things—who occupy an orientational posture different from our own—should come to think differently about philosophical issues does not and should not in the least countervail against the sense of legitimacy that underpins *our* holding the position we ourselves deem it appropriate to adopt. Once we have found what we have good reason to see as "the better way," why need it daunt us that others see the matter differently, especially when we do not regard their reason for thinking so particularly persuasive?

It would be profoundly mistaken to abandon philosophy in sceptical disillusionment because purely rational constraint is not realizable in this doamin. Philosophy is not a zero-sum game where one loses because one is unable to *win over* the rest of the field (in both senses of this expression). Why should we ask for more than to answer philosophical questions to our own satisfaction? Why should it daunt us that others see matters differently?

We are not put off from our social theories, our political opinions, or our religious beliefs by the unavoidable fact that alternatives to our own positions exist and that others adopt them. Why then should this circumstance undermine us in our philosophical convictions? Someone who thinks that value-bound resolutions aren't worth having has lamentably little confidence in his values. To take the stance that a value-dependent position isn't worth having is simply foolish; it takes a strangely detached and deprecatory view of our own values. But, of course, however attached we are to these values, and however fervently we believe that others *should* share them, we cannot but recognize that they *will* not.

## 5. Does the Relativity of Philosophical Claims Undermine the Worth of the Enterprise?

Orientational pluralism does *not* plunge us into the feckless subjectivity of arbitrary taste. To reemphasize: relativity is not tantamount to subjectivity. The cognitive values we hold are *not* arbitrary and unrationalizable—subject only to psychological or sociological explanation and incapable of rationally articulated grounding. They can be fitted out with a perfectly viable rational defense. It is just that this grounding is never itself free from some element of self-evidencing evaluativeness. (This circumstance would be a basis for appropriate objection, though, only if the situation could possibly be otherwise—which it cannot.)

Let us examine more closely this charge that philosophy is not worth bothering about if it cannot deliever something absolute and altogether objective, something that is valid *semper et ubique et pro omnes*, without any recourse to person-relative evaluative commitments.

The first point to be made here is simply that, the factually empty relationships of pure mathematics arguably apart, *nothing* in the domain of human "knowledge" satisfies this requirement. Even natural science does not yield absolutes; it is a commonplace that the "scientific fact" of one day easily becomes the error of later eras. In philosophy, at any rate, we have little alternative but to accept orientation-relatively warranted truth claims as the best we can get. And there is no reason to be dissatisfied with them—after all, we do (*ex hypothesi*) actually hold whatever value orientation lies at the basis of our views. The very name of the game in philosophical inquiry is problem solving—getting answers to our questions and resolving the antinomies that confront us. What other possible *rational* standard could we use apart from rational optimization relative to the data and the probative methods that enable us to exploit them? If it is indeed inevitable that the basis of resolution must be value conditioned, then we have no alternative but to make the best of this.

To be sure, we must consider if there is anything improper (illegitimate) about letting our (cognitive) values play a role in taking a position. But the answer here is simple. It emerges from two considerations. (1) Some recourse to value guidance is indispensable—there is no going on without it. And (2) this being so, the quest then becomes: Whose values *should* we use? If we've got to use some, it is obviously rational to use our own. There is no basis for a charge of impropriety here.

A simple sorites argument emerges:

—We need and want to resolve philosophical problems.
—We can only get a resolution on the basis of some recourse to (cognitive) values.
*Therefore:* We are justified (that is, *practically* justified) in having recourse to values.
—It would be dissonant (foolish and "inconsistent") to rely on values different from those we actually hold.
*Therefore:* We are justified (that is, *practically* justified) in having recourse to our own (cognitive) values.

The justification of philosophizing on the basis of our value commitments is a practical justification of the standard means-ends sort. But it is a practical justification of a theoretical endeavor.

It might be suggested that once doctrinal antagonists recognize the nature of their dispute—once they realize that the controversy ultimately arises from differences in cognitive values—they should (so it might seem) simply agree to differ. They will then come to recognize that their differences cannot be settled by rational controversy, and debate would cease. But, of course, that's not how it is. All disputing and endeavors at confutation would not come to an end. Philosophers do not cease to quarrel, because they realize that the basis of their debate is ideological. (Who does?)

If we take our cognitive values seriously, if they indeed *are* our values and thereby mean enough to us that we are prepared to let them count for something in our approach to matters of choice and decision, then it seems oddly diffident that we should not allow them to count. After all, there is no good reason that we should be diffident about our values. Man is not only the *rational* animal but also the *normative* animal. He alone among the earth's inhabitants sets rules, laws, norms, standards, evaluations for himself. Such normative commitment is an essential feature of our *modus operandi* in the world.

Evaluation is an indispensable guide in our cognitive as in our practical affairs. It makes no sense to fail to accept the ramifications of this fundamental fact.

But must we not regret that philosophers cannot agree, that rationally enforced consensus is unattainable in the discipline? That will depend on what, exactly, one's cognitive values are, as so much else does. If consensus is seen a precondition for *rational* credence, then of course regret is very much in order. But if one is prepared to recognize that (1) this is an *inevitable* feature of philosophy, which nevertheless nowise precludes (2), that it is perfectly appropriate for the individual practitioner to arrive at his own (rationally defensible) results, then one is entitled to doubt that regret is called for.[4]

Why, after all, should one be dissatisfied with a *relatively* appropriate answer to a philosophical issue, one that can be shown by cogent argumentation to be appropriate "from where one stands," given that the relativization is to a probative orientation that one does in fact hold? If we can work out a resolution that is authorized by our own perspective, then why should we not be perfectly content? Given that we indeed hold the values at issue, why should we hesitate to follow their lead?

Orientational pluralism is thus no impediment to doctrinal commitment on philosophical issues. There is no reason that the mere existence of different positions should leave us immobilized like the ass of Buridan between the alternatives. Nor are we left with the gray emptiness of equalitarianism that looks to all sides with neutral and uncommitted indifference. A rational choice among the alternatives can indeed be made, albeit one that hinges on having a certain standpoint as to the cognitive values at issue. This is, to be sure, a form of relativism, but it is one that relativizes the outcome on a basis that we do indeed adopt, a value perspective that we do indeed occupy. Such a relativism does *not* underwrite indifferentism.

## 6. The Values Underlying the Present Account Itself

The present account of philosophy and philosophizing stands committed to two contentions: (1) that the reasoned defense of any philosophical position requires recourse to a family of cognitive values, and (2) that any contention about the aims and methods and true nature of philosophy—any claim about what philosophy is really like or how philosophizing is properly to be done—is necessarily itself (part of) a philosophical position. The reasoned defense of our own position of

---

4. Some might even welcome diversity of opinion for its own sake. But this is probably not sensible and certainly not necessary.

orientational pluralism will thus itself have to invoke cognitive values. But which ones? Just what is the cognitive-value orientation that underlies the present account itself?

All of the materials needed to answer this question are already in hand, since the preceding discussion has been very explicit about the matter:

(1) Philosophy addresses "the big issues" of man's place in the world's scheme of things. It is thus a process of inquiry that confronts questions and endeavors to provide answers to them.
(2) Philosophy is committed to reason. In philosophizing we seek to provide good reasons for adopting particular answers to our questions.
(3) In answering its questions, philosophy exploits our extraphilosophical commitments and endeavors to make sense of them—in particular to render them coherent. Philosophy tries to instill consistency and coherence; it cannot rest indifferent in the face of aporetic situations.
(4) Philosophy is a venture in rational systematization. "Maximize information by securing the optimal balance of answering questions relative to avoiding incoherencies." Philosophical rationality is a matter of optimization in problem solving.

Fundamental to the present account is thus the view that responsible philosophizing is a matter of rational systematization subject to the discipline of good reasons and cogent argumentation. We thus obtain a view that puts the key values of cognitive rationality—information, good reasons, coherence, system—at center stage. We stand committed to the view that philosophy is a *cognitive* endeavor and that, however difficult this may prove, philosophy should endeavor to keep its feet on the high road of science (of *Wissenschaft* or *scientia*). The analogy of science is the pivot of the value orientation on which the present account of philosophy takes its stand.

Much of the hesitation to accept a cognitively determinative role for values doubtless stems from the complaint that it is a matter of "wishful thinking" to allow our values to play a guiding role in relation to the theses we espouse. But this complaint overlooks the sort of values at issue. The values that enter in are specifically *cognitive* values—matters of appraising significance, centrality, and cognitive priority. They relate to what we deem *important*, not to what we deem *appealing*. They no doubt reflect the character of our experience, but our experience as it actually is, not as we would like it to be. They are emphatically not a matter of *congeniality*, of what we would like to have so.

We confront an aporetic situation:

# THE STRIFE OF SYSTEMS
*What Orientational Pluralism Means for Philosophy*

(1) There are no universally agreed and incontestable standards in philosophy.
(2) A cognitive venture that lacks agreed communal standards to which all reputable productions must conform is pointless.
(3) Philosophizing is an appropriate endeavor; it is not pointless.

The sceptic abandons (3), the absolutist (1). Orientational pluralism, by contrast, abandons (2). In countenancing as valid and legitimate standards whose operations involve cognitive values, it can continue to see philosophical inquiry as meaningful and appropriate. It steadfastly refuses to concede that the unavailability in philosophy of an incontestable value scheme that provides objective standards for enforcing rational conviction on a communitywide basis destroys the validity of the enterprise. It regards valuation, notwithstanding its variability, not as a contaminant but as a source of dignity.

It is totally inappropriate to think it somehow threatening or demeaning that philosophy is based on values. After all, so is life. There is surely something bizarre about thinking that philosophy is not of value because it is based on values!

# 10

## Truth and Reality: Ramifications of Relativism

*1. Views Regarding Our Cognitive Access to Reality*

Differences in philosophy's approach to the truth about reality can be accounted for in terms of various distinct models.

(1) The Multifaceted Reality View sees the matter as follows. In philosophizing we address a vast, complex, internally diversified reality that our feeble intelligence cannot manage to grasp whole. In dealing with this vast manifold, we tend to overemphasize what falls within the scope of our limited experience. The situation is akin to that depicted in the splendid poem "The Blind Men and the Elephant" by John Godfrey Saxe, which tells the story of the blind sages, those

> six men of Indostan,
> To learning much inclined,
> Who went to see the elephant,
> (Though all of them were blind).

One sage touched the elephant's "broad and sturdy side" and declared the beast to be "very like a wall." The second, who had felt its tusk, announced the elephant to resemble a spear. The third, who took the elephant's squirming trunk in his hands, compared it to a snake; while the fourth, who put his arms around the elephant's knee, was sure that the animal resembled a tree. A flapping ear convinced another that the elephant had the form of a fan; while the sixth blind man thought that it had the form of a rope, since he had taken hold of the tail.

> And so these men of Indostan,
> Disputed loud and long;
> Each in his own opinion
> Exceeding stiff and strong:

# THE STRIFE OF SYSTEMS
*Ramifications of Relativism*

> Though each was partly in the right,
> And all were in the wrong.

Different accounts—seemingly discordant philosophical doctrines—all quite correctly characterize the truths of different realms of one, all-embracing reality. Reality is complex and internally diversified, presenting different facets of itself to inquirers who approach it from different points of departure.

On such an approach, diverse philosophical systems are seen as describing reality variably because they describe it in different aspects or regards. *Everybody is right*—but only over a limited range. Every philosophical doctrine is true *more suo*—in its own way. In principle, the various accounts can all be superimposed or superadded. Apparently diverse positions are viewed as so many facets of one all-embracing doctrine; they can all be conjoined by "but also." An overarching complex reality embraces them all; every finite inquirer has merely got "a piece of the action."

The Multifaceted Reality View thus *combines* the several apparently discordant alternatives in a way that gives to each a subordinate part in one overarching whole. Reconciliation between diverse doctrines can thus be effected *additively* through the formula "but furthermore in *this* regard," even as the elephant is spearlike in respect to his tusks and ropelike in respect to his tail. William James's pluralism was of just this sort:

> There is nothing improbable in the supposition than an analysis of the world may yield a number of formulae, all consistent with the facts. In physical science different formulae may explain the phenomena equally well—the one-fluid and the two-fluid theories of electricity, for example. Why may it not be so with the world? Why may there not be different points of view for surveying it, within each of which all data harmonize, and which the observer may therefore either choose between, or simply cumulate one upon another? A Beethoven string-quartet is truly, as some one has said, a scraping of horses' tails on cats' bowels, and may be exhaustively described in such terms; but the application of this description in no way precludes the simultaneous applicability of an entirely different description.[1]

Clearly, when there are different aspects that we propose to combine and conjoin—to "cumulate one upon another"—then we have an aspectival and mere-part-of-a-whole conception of the relationship between our systematizing and its object. Nelson Goodman's theory is of much the same kind. For him, the question is not "What is the way the world is?" but rather "What are the ways the world is?" and the

---

1. William James, "The Sentiment of Rationality," in *Writings*, p. 325.

answer is not a clear clarion response but a many-voiced chatter.² Goodman presents this approach in the following way:

> If I were asked what is *the food* for men, I should have to answer "none." For there are many foods. And if I am asked what is the way the world is, I must likewise answer, "none." For the world is many ways. . . . For me, there is no way that is the way the world is; and so of course no description can capture it (however complex and self-contradictory it might be!). But there are many ways the world is, and every true description captures one of them.³

This rejection of "*the* way the world is" is not a denial that there is a fact of the matter but simply an insistence that it is complex and many-sided. Such a theory has it that *every* party to the conflict is right, each in its own incomplete way. All the variant positions are viewed as constituent components of one complex truth. Each is perfectly correct "in its own place" or "in its own way"; each gives the truth, yet none gives the whole truth.

In line with such a view, Dilthey maintained that any metaphysical doctrine does no more than present one particular aspect of the world within the particular horizons of our thought: "Each is thus far correct. But each is one-sided. The possibility of embracing all these aspects together is denied to us. The pure light of Truth can only be glimpsed by us in variably refracted light rays."⁴ Nietzsche, too, inclined to this line of thought. He endorsed a "perspectivism" based on the idea that "the more eyes, different eyes, we can use to observe a thing, the more complete will our 'concept' of this thing, our 'objectivity,' be."⁵

(2) The No-Reality View holds that in philosophical systematizing we are dealing with an illusion. It maintains that theorists do not agree with one another because there is nothing to agree about—they are all chasing a chimera. No "ultimate reality" exists for our philosophizing to characterize, or at any rate none that is accessible to human inquiry. There is no truth or reality in these matters, no IS, but only a variety of unverifiable opinions, of mere appearances, of what only SEEMS. *Everybody is wrong*. The whole enterprise is based on the erroneous presupposition that the so-called "problems" of philosophy are suffi-

---

2. Nelson Goodman, "The Way the World Is," in *Ways of Worldmaking* (Indianapolis, 1978), esp. p. 31.

3. Ibid.

4. Wilhelm Dilthey, *Gesammelte Schriften*, vol. VIII (Stuttgart and Göttingen, 1960), p. 229.

5. Friederich Nietzsche, *On the Genealogy of Morals,* trans. Walter Kaufmann (New York, 1969), p. 119. Cf. John Atwell's commentary: "So 'objectivity' rightly understood, is an ideal: it is a construct consisting of every creature's comprehension of what a thing 'is.' For any individual, 'objectivity' is an unattainable goal, though by adopting numerous perspectives, the individual can attain more and more 'objectivity' " ("Nietzsche's Perspectivism," *Southern Journal of Philosophy*, vol. 19 (1981): 157–70 (see p. 164). On such a view, subjectivity is simply *partiality,* inherent in finitude and limitation.

ciently meaningful to admit of such a thing as "a correct solution." The "problems" of philosophy are pseudoproblems. All the competing positions on philosophical issues are just so much rubbish, which, following Hume's advice, we would do well to "commit to the flames."

We are thus led to a deeply sceptical view of philosophy; its deliberations are seen as totally disconnected from any bearing on truth and reality. Both the positivist's dismissal of metaphysics as empty verbiage and Kant's insistence that classical philosophizing was altogether pointless (because significant discourse about reality must restrict itself to the confines of experience alone) are instances of this sort of view.

(3) The Unique Reality View maintains that philosophy deals with sensible and solvable problems, problems to which one solution is correct and all the alternatives wrong. *Only one priviledged party to a dispute is right;* everybody else is barking up the wrong tree. Philosophical issues are meaningful and have unique and definite solutions that sufficiently careful and subtle inquiry can bring to light. It's all a matter of having the right approach (or method or axioms or whatever).

Most classical metaphysicians inclined to this absolutistic view. William James derided their position as follows:

If we look at the history of opinions, we see that the empiricist tendency has largely prevailed in science, while in philosophy the absolutist tendency has had everything its own way. The characteristic sort of happiness, indeed, which philosophies yield has mainly consisted in the conviction felt by each successive school or system that by it bottom-certitude had been attained. "Other philosophies are collections of opinions, mostly false; *my* philosophy gives standing-ground forever,"—who does not recognize in this the key-note of every system worthy of the name?[6]

On this model, exactly one position among competing alternatives is uniquely correct. The "real truth of the matter" is seen as a perfectly well-defined and workable idea.

(4) The Perspectival Reality View takes the following stance. *One and only one position is appropriate from a given perspective of consideration; but there is a variety of perspectives.* No one doctrine is itself inherently "the right one," none can make good an absolutistic claim to being uniquely correct. We have no *direct* access to the philosophical truth save via the conditioning mechanisms of a cognitive perspective. And regarded from different perspectives of consideration, philosophical issues demand different and discordant resolutions. Reality may or may not be multifaceted, but our view of it is bound to be so. And so, no party to a philosophical dispute is right *simpliciter* and unquali-

---

6. William James, "The Will to Believe," sec. 5, in *Writings*, pp. 723–24.

fiedly, because "right *simpliciter*" is an ultimately *inapplicable* conception in this context. Everybody (who is sufficiently careful and workmanlike) is right in the light of his own mode of approach, but no one can make good the totalitarian claim to be so unqualifiedly and absolutely.

Each of these different views of how diverse philosophies relate to reality has its own characteristic reaction to philosophical conflict and contradiction:

(1) The multifaceted reality theorist says: "Yes, that's just what one should expect. The prevalence of controversy in philosophy merely shows that we are dealing with a complex reality that presents conflicting appearances."
(2) The no-reality theorist says: "Yes, that's just what one should expect. In meddling with these meaningless issues we would of course run into contradiction and conflict."
(3) The unique reality theorist says: "Yes, that's just what one should expect. Most philosophers are chasing after false gods. They have the wrong starting point (premises, methods). Having got off to the wrong start they will of course wander off into various sorts of error."
(4) The perspectival theorists says: "Yes, that's just what one should expect. Different theorists have different perspectives (orientations, angles of approach). So of course they will come up with conflicting results."

Each of the various theories about the roots of disagreement and diversity thus has its own characteristic diagnosis of the prominence of disagreement and discord in philosophy. And each theory offers its own prescription:

Different positions are seemingly available,
—so embrace them all (syncretism);
—so reject the whole lot of them (scepticism);
—but that's an illusion—only one is "really" available (absolutism);
—so seek out the (normatively) best one—the one that accords optimally with your own cognitive value posture (orientationalism; axiological relativism).

These alternatives call for closer examination and assessment.

## 2. Where Orientational Pluralism Stands

There can be no question about where our present theory stands on the matter; its inclination toward the perspectival view is marked. Nevertheless, true to its own nature, orientational pluralism sees the situation as one of a choice between alternatives that is guided by particular cognitive values.

It should be stressed, accordingly, that this stance represents a particular position regarding the *methodology* of philosophy. At the level of substantive *ontology*, where what concerns us is the nature of the things rather than the nature of philosophy, orientational pluralism as such is altogether neutral. On the question of ontological monism or dualism or pluralism, of idealism vs. materialism vs. monism, and so on, orientational pluralism as such has nothing to say. It is a theory about the nature of philosophy and not about the nature of the world.

Orientational pluralism adopts a Perspectival Reality View in its approach to *philosophy in general*. It takes the stance that the community as a whole will inevitably take various distinct and discordant positions. However, with respect to *the concrete labors of the individual practitioner* involved in the actual pursuit of philosophy, orientational pluralism takes a different line. Here it inclines to the absolutistic stance of the Unique Reality View: from the probative vantage point of a particular cognitive-value orientation, one particular resolution is, in general, going to prove optimally acceptable.

When working out one's own position one is bound to develop a particular doctrinal resolution of the controverted issues. In actually doing *philosophy* we must address the issues, and this is best done by answering the questions and taking a substantive stand. Here the Unique Reality View prevails; we can take the view that there is only one truth in philosophy though there are many mistaken ideas about it.

In *metaphilosophy*, however, where our own commitments are put into suspension (or *bracketed*, in Husserl's terminology), the pluralist position of the perspectivalist model is the natural one. But of course at this point, the point where our own evaluative position is bracketed out and where we adopt a deliberate suspension of disbelief, we are no longer doing philosophy as such but viewing philosophy from afar, so to speak.

The salient difference between the Multifaceted Reality View (which orientational pluralism disdains) and the Perspectival Reality View (which it endorses *at the global level of philosophy in general*) is that facets, unlike perspectives, can be combined. With different parts or facets we can conjoin the several part-stories into one coherent overall characterization of the whole. But an aspectival approach rules out the possibility of such a conjunction. We can combine "honest-to-his-friends" and "unscrupulous-to-his-business-associates," but we cannot combine the "honest-through-and-through" that his friends claim for him with the very different *overall* verdict at which his business associates arrive. With the Perspectival Reality View, what is judged from each perspective is *the whole* of reality and not just some *part* of reality. Precisely because perspectivally effected judgments are on-the-whole judgments we cannot combine them.[7] If we have it that

Seen from $O$: $P$ is true
Seen from $O'$: $P$ is not true

Then the notion of a new superpositional perspective $O * O'$ from which $P$ is (or is not) *really* true is eminently problematic. The crucial difference is that the many-facets approach points the way to a single, all-inclusive position, the perspectival approach to an irreducible plurality of positions.

Distributively, for any particular individual there is, no doubt, a uniquely "right and proper" perspective—namely his own. But collectively there is none. Reality no doubt *embraces* individual divergences, but it cannot *fuse* them. A plurality of perspectives cannot be made over into one plurality-embracing perspective.

## 3. Against Absolutism

A sensible stance toward objectivistic absolutism in philosophy is bound to be ambivalent. Every seriously developed philosophical position undoubtedly sees itself as uniquely correct. But, of course, the internal purport of such claims is one thing and their external status is something else. The paradoxical fact is that from a subjective (individual-oriented) point of view, the claims of a philosopher are absolute, while from an absolute (communally oriented) point of view, they are subjective.

Absolutism is the metaphilosophical position that philosophical theses can be established categorically by rationally compelling argumentation from entirely objective grounds, without presuppositional relativization to some orienting perspective of probative norms—that is, without reliance on any cognitive-value orientation. It is maintained, contrary to orientational relativism, that philosophical arguments can be adequately, nay, *compellingly* cogent without reliance on "subjective," potentially variable cognitive values. What we have here is a flat-out insistence that philosophical contentions can be validated by the presuppositionlessly context-free machinations of pure reason. The rationalists, Kant, and logical positivists of the stamp of Ayer and Reichenbach exemplify these stances.

Its insistence that metaphilosophical theses as to how philosophy is

---

7. The issue is clearly treated by Jack Meiland in "Perspectivism and Concepts," in *Praxis and Reason*, ed. Robert Almeder (Washington, 1982), pp. 91–105 (see esp. pp. 100–01). See also the critiques of perspectivism in Kröner, *Anarchie*, pp. 16–17.

properly conducted are themselves philosophical constrains orientational pluralism to view this absolutist position with respect. It too is a "tenable" position that can be espoused from an available cognitive-value perspective. Can orientational pluralism survive this recognition that the nose of the enemy's camel has entered its tent? Can it reject absolutism without being untrue to itself?

Of course it can. Admittedly, absolutism is a perfectly intelligible doctrine and one that is perfectly self-consistent, too, since it will see itself as the absolute truth. But, of course, we who are not precommitted to it need not see it in that light. Absolutism is not itself a formulation of God's own truth; it is no more than the claim of a particular, and highly problematic, probative orientation.

Having conceded that absolutism is a *possible* posture, orientational pluralism is still entitled to ask if it is *acceptable*.

To be sure, if it were to propose an *absolute* refutation of absolutism, orientational relativism would be untrue to itself. If absolute refutations of substantive philosophical positions could be given (and absolutism *is* a substantive philosophical position), then orientationalism would be incorrect. So the orientationalist must proceed in his own characteristic way by weighing up costs and benefits, evaluating the bearing of pro- and-con considerations. And just this is what has been going on through the deliberations of this book. In briefest summary, the considerations that tell most weightily against absolutism are:

1. Presumably, if categorically compelling demonstrations of substantive philosophical doctrines were possible, we would be in a position at this stage in the history of the subject to give some cogent examples. But this is not so (cf. chapter 1).
2. Philosophical issues arise in aporetic contexts, and no value-free resolution on compelling grounds of abstract rationality is available. This makes disagreement and diversity inevitable (cf. chapters 2 through 7).
3. The issue of what constitutes sound reasons and adequate demonstrations in philosophy is itself a normative one that is inherently controversial and admits of (perfectly appropriate) debate (cf. chapters 8 and 9).

The fact that he views a position as tenable from *some* perspective does not oblige the pluralist to see it as acceptable from his own. And so we can reject absolutism without inconsistency. This rejection is not a tacit acceptance of absolutism because it need not itself be seen as absolute.

## 4. Does Its Relativism Undercut Orientational Pluralism Itself?

Does its very lack of absoluteness—its axiological relativism—not impair the cogency of orientational pluralism? Even if such a pluralism is not actually self-inconsistent, is it not self-defeating?

To facilitate rigorous reasoning, a bit of symbolism will be helpful. Let us adopt the following notation:

$V{:}P$ for "relative to the cognitive-value orientation $V$, one is rationally entitled to maintain the substantive philosophical position or thesis that $P$" or, more briefly, "$V$ endorses $P$."

Such a contention to the effect that some doctrinal position holds for a certain cognitive-value orientation is itself an absolute (factual, aperspectival) thesis. And so,

$$V{:}P$$

will always be philosophically unproblematic. Unlike the thesis $P$ itself, the conditionalized proposition that a certain cognitive-value orientation endorses it is simply *not* a substantive philosophical contention; it is a strictly factual claim that, as such, is straightforwardly true or false.

But, of course, what we need for substantive philosophical deliberations is to maintain theses of the type of $P$, rather than theses that, being of the form $V{:}P$, are devoid of philosophical substance. And the move from $V{:}P$ to $P$ calls for actually assuming the stance of a cognitive value orientation (viz., $V$). The operative inferential scheme takes the form:

$V{:}P$
$V$ merits adoption
___

Therefore, $P$

Orientational pluralism holds that one is never in a position to claim a substantive philosophical thesis $P$ without going the route of this scheme, that is, without adopting a cognitive-value orientation. A claim to the effect that a philosophical thesis obtains is never justified categorically (absolutely) but only via the adoption of a suitably favorable value orientation.

Orientational pluralism ($Z$) certainly does not assert that philosophical theses cannot be maintained as true. We do *not* have $Z{:}{-}(\exists P)P$. This would be foolish, for then this doctrine itself would be impotent to maintain anything. What orientational pluralism does assert is that whenever a philosophical thesis $P$ is maintained, then there is in the background an (accepted) cognitive-value orientation $V$ such that $V{:}P$.

But what about this claim itself? It too is clearly philosophical. And so it too holds only for some value orientations (e.g., that of pluralism), while its negation is also maintained on some value orientations (e.g., that of absolutism). Where one stands regarding the thesis will thus depend on one's own orientation. Does this not leave the matter in a parlous condition?

Abstractly considered, orientational pluralism is itself in the same boat as other substantive philosophical positions, being valid on some orientations (e.g., itself) and invalid on others (e.g., according to absolutistic objectivism, $A$). At this level of deliberation we only get the (factual) theses: $Z{:}Z$ $Z{:}{-}A$, $A{:}A$, $A{:}{-}Z$. We can only say in the one case what we can say in the other.

As orientational pluralism sees it, this is all we can do without taking any orientational or doctrinal stance. Only by taking an orientational stance can we cut the Gordian knot and maintain something substantive in philosophy. And this holds true for the thesis of orientational pluralism itself.

Does this not leave orientational pluralism in a disadvantaged state *vis-à-vis* its absolutistic rival?

To be sure, it is indeed *claimed* by objectivist absolutism ($A$) that the truth of a substantive philosophical thesis is demonstrable objectively and absolutely; that if $P$ is true relative to the (purportedly) "correct" objectivistically absolute cognitive-value orientation $A$, then $P$ is true, period.

(1) $(\forall P)\ (A{:}P \to P)$

But of course this claim itself is not absolute and orientation indifferent; it only holds relative to the preferred cognitive-value posture adopted by objectivism itself. What we *actually* have in an unproblematic way is not (1) as such, but merely:

(1.1) $A{:}\ (\forall P)\ (A{:}P \to P)$

But in conceding that absolutistic objectivism is *available* as a tenable position, does orientational pluralism not sow the seeds of its own destruction? By no means.

Philosophers of absolutist inclinations sometimes argue that orientational pluralism has no alternative but to take absolutism at face value. They propose to reason as follows:

(1) If something is true according to the value scheme of $A$, then it is (absolutely) true:
$(\forall P)\ (A{:}P \to P)$
(2) Absolutistic objectivism itself is true by its own value scheme:
$A{:}A$
(3) It follows from (1) and (2) that absolutistic objectivism is the (absolutely) true doctrine: $A$ itself is true.

The flaw of this argument arises from the inappropriateness of (1). For (1) does not hold as such and absolutely, but only conditionally, relative to *A* itself, per (1.1) above. It is only an instance of the harmless and universal schema:

($\forall V$) ($V$: ($\forall P$) ($V$:$P \to P$))

After all, any (viable) orientation sees itself as delivering "the real truth." But, of course, we need not regard *A* in the light in which it sees itself. To accept (1) is to acknowledge absolutism as "the real thing" (rather than just another orientation). While the absolutist himself may see the matter in this light, there is no reason why the rest of us should.

Orientational pluralism is predicated on two propositions:
1. Only from the vantage point of a cognitive-value orientation can a philosophical position be validated.
2. The contention that a particular orientation merits adoption is itself a philosophical position.

On this basis, it follows that there is no justifying an orientation without having an orientation, without taking the stance of a commitment to cognitive values.

Of course, no vitiating infinite regress need arise. We can simply adopt an orientational position and then proceed to justify it on its own telling. The justification of a value orientation can and indeed must be essentially circular; it is always, in a way, question begging.

But to acknowledge this fact of life is not to offer a telling objection to orientational pluralism. It is merely to reassert this position. As orientational pluralism sees it, that's just the way it is. Objectively, all cognitive values *are* in the same boat, with all of us standing on shore with no way to get there from here short of "taking the plunge." There is no "objective" nonorientational justification; the price of entry into the justificatory sector of the normative sphere consists in adopting an orientational stance.

The stance of orientational pluralism is thus as follows:

Different solutions to philosophical problems and different doctrinal positions are *possible*. Which one we can sensibly endorse will depend on our cognitive-value orientation, and different orientations are *available*. Which position we can see as *correct* or as *acceptable* thus depends on the particular cognitive-value orientation we take. And this also goes for the doctrinal elements of a value orientation itself: what orientational theses are appropriate will also depend on which value orientation we take. But there is no "uniquely valid" orientation. Which one seems valid or reasonable to us is a function of the course of our experience. Thus, a variety of philosophical positions is always *tenable*—can always be maintained from the vantage point of some possible value orientation. (Though we ourselves, equipped with a particular cognitive-value orientation, are bound to see a particular position as correct.)

Admittedly, the approach to philosophy envisioned by orientational pluralism is itself merely one alternative position among others, with such rivals as scepticism and absolutism also contesting the field. Does such a relativistic position not simply annihilate itself through its recognition that rival positions exist and are, in principle, just as available? Does not its recognition of alternatives ultimately undermine orientational pluralism? Someone might well object as follows:

> Just as you yourself hold a given doctrinal position regarding philosophy (viz., orientational pluralism) to be substantively correct, so the rival sceptic, absolutist, and so on, will hold his. And even as you defend yours on the basis of your values, so does he by his. Since you cannot defend your values by absolute value-free criteria, you must grant that, objectively speaking, these rival positions are every bit as good as yours.

Can one not once again employ the classic objection to Protagorean relativism—that it saws off its own supports?

Not really. For the crucial fact is that orientational pluralism, while indeed seeing itself as one position among others, is *not* committed to regarding them all as having equal merit. It does not see its rivals, such as objectivistic absolutism, as *correct*, but merely as *tenable*—that is, as arguable from some "available" orientation. Thus one cannot secure the refutation:

$$Z:A$$
$$A \rightarrow -Z$$

Therefore, $Z: -Z$

The first premise clearly fails. For orientational pluralism does not endorse the *acceptability* of $A$, but only its *tenability*, only that there is some "available" cognitive-value orientation $V$ such that $V:A$. (And note that "$V:A$" is a factual thesis, which, in the particular case of "$Z:A$," is simply false, though in that of "$A:A$" is doubtless true.)

Some writers have argued that orientational pluralism is self-refuting in a more sophisticated way. According to one critic, the objectivist-absolutist can argue as follows against the orientational relativist:

> The orientational relativist can't have any nonrelativistic argument against me, and must indeed accept the equal relativistic truth of my position. But accordingly to my position, relativism is objectively false and unacceptable. Hence relativism is objectively false and unacceptable if relativism is self-consistent.[8]

---

8. This quotation is taken from a paper by an anonymous colleague, "Against Orientational Pluralism in Metaphilosophy," for which I served as a blind referee for the journal, *Metaphilosophy*.

In detail, this argument against relativistic pluralism has the following structure:

(1) Z: tenable A     Supposition about Z
(2) tenable $A \to (\forall P)(A{:}P \to P)$     Supposition about A
(3) Z: $\forall P\ (A{:}P \to P)$     From (1) & (2)
(4) A: – tenable Z     Supposition about A
(5) Z: – tenable Z     From (3) & (4)

But this argument fails. Premise (2) is simply incorrect. To assert the tenability A is not to concede the truth of whatever A claims. This last is no more than a contention of A's, and in conceding the tenability of A we do not concede this claim itself, but only *its tenability* (not its acceptability but only its maintainability). And on this basis, we do not obtain (2), but only

(2') tenable $A \to$ tenable $(\forall P)\ (A{:}P \to P)$.

And when this replacement is made in the argument, we do not get (3) but only the innocuous

(3') Z: tenable $(\forall P)\ (A{:}P \to P)$.

And so we do not get (5) but only

(5') Z: tenable (– tenable Z).

And this result is quite harmless. It says simply that P generously countenances as defensible positions that do not reciprocate.

Against the relativism of Protagoras, Socrates argued along the following lines: "If every contention is simply a matter of mere personal opinion, devoid of objective justification, then so is this position of yours, that everything is a matter of mere personal opinion. And so the position undercuts itself, leading to the result that it lacks any basis of proper justification." This sort of objection would indeed be serious. But it would be misdirected if aimed at the relativism of an orientational pluralism, because this doctrine rejects the contention that the only *proper* justification is *objective* justification. Recourse to a normative justification based on cognitive values enables us to maintain the distinction between "justified conviction" and "mere opinion" while yet abandoning the view that justification cannot be relative.

We can concede to Protagoras that everything is debatable in philosophy—even unto this very thesis itself—and yet maintain that some things fare better in debate than others. The fact that such doctrines are available (to those who are differently oriented from us) does not mean that we ourselves need see them as correct—or even as reasonably plausible.

And so all these various arguments against orientational pluralism on grounds of its being self-defeating are flawed. None survives the critical light of close scrutiny.

We must be prepared to come to terms with the following aporetic cluster:

(1) Philosophical positions can (and should) be established through cogent reasoning; they can (only) be sensibly adverted on the basis of good reasons.
(2) Cogent reasoning must be strictly objective; only those reasons can qualify as good that exert their rational compulsion on everyone alike.
(3) Objectivity is unattainable in philosophical matters; we can only avail ourselves of reasons whose cogency varies in various cognitive perspectives.

Three routes to averting inconsistency are open to us here:

(1)–rejection: A view that denies that philosophical position-taking can be warranted (scepticism).
(2)–rejection: A view that insists that cogent reasoning is possible in philosophical matters on the basis of orientationally variable considerations (Orientational pluralism).
(3)–rejection: A view that insists that objectivity is attainable in philosophy; that philosophical considerations can be established on the basis of abstract general principles alone (objectivistic absolutism).

Its recognition of this antinomy as a genuinely aporetic cluster—conceding that (2) is plausible to that limited extent—is as far as orientational pluralism need go toward recognizing the impetus to objectivity. But such recognition of a rival objectivism need nowise undermine its self-confident view of itself as providing the best available option.

## 5. The Pursuit of Truth

The following apory confronts us:

(1) Problems are adequately dealt with only if solved by absolute, communally compelling standards.
(2) Philosophy can solve its problems; it can in principle provide answers to "the big questions."
(3) There are no absolute communally compelling standards in philosophy.

Three alternatives present themselves here:

(1)–rejection: We can abandon the gearing of adequacy to universality and go over to a relativistic position.
(2)–rejection: We can abandon philosophy as a matter of problem solving, jettisoning it as a cognitive enterprise of question resolution.
(3)–rejection: We can adopt an absolutist stance and take the "true believer" position that there actually are absolute standards (presumably our own).

Orientational pluralism opts for the first alternative and takes the relativistic line.

Such a view has it that a philosophical thesis can be argued for only relative to a particular probative orientation. Justification *simpliciter* would have to amount to "justification from *the right orientation*"—from the only ultimately correct and appropriate one. And this idea cannot be implemented, because there is no such thing as "the uniquely appropriate orientation" here. It is of course tempting to ask, "But what position is *actually* correct—absolutely and perspective independently?" But this tempting question is problematic. It is not that we can't get an answer to it but that whatever answer we secure is simply our own answer. (We are always disinclined to regard our own perspective as just that; perspectives are diaphanous, and one tends not to see them as such.) In philosophy there just is no way of judging the actualities of the matter independently of our probative perspectives—our cognitive-value orientations. If someone insists on pressing the question "But which perspective is really correct—which is the right one?", the proper response would be an outright dismissal. For while "the right one as seen by A" or "as seen by B" makes sense, "the right one *simpliciter* and absolutely" does not. In philosophy, the judgment of adequacy cannot be decoupled from our probative perspectives.

But what does all this axiological relativism imply for the question of "the truth of the matter"?

In philosophy we do indeed embark on the search for the truth. Our putative truth is indeed *the truth* as we see it and not just "what we would like to have as the truth" in some wishful-thinking sense. To say, "T is true from the probative perspective X" comes to saying that from the vantage point of X, "T is indeed true." The fact that our search is bound to issue in *our* truth does not prevent its being a search for *the* truth. Nothing prevents our seeing *our* truth as *the* truth; on the contrary, everything conspires to this end. Indeed, it would not be *our* truth if we did not see it as *the* truth. (Of course, this does not prevent us from realizing that it may well have its imperfections—indeed, that we ourselves might, on further thought and inquiry, come to change our minds about it.) All we are ever able to bring home at the end of a day of inquiry is *our* version of the truth. That we *take* this to be *the truth* is an inevitable fact that betokens our unavoidable parochialism. Orientation pluralism does not abrogate the idea of "the real truth of the matter" in philosophy; it simply recognizes that every practitioner is bound to form his own view of it—that nobody has a direct line to the Recording Angel.

The truth we get hold of in philosophy is bound to be the truth as our cognitive-value perspective reveals it to us. We have nowhere else to go, no way of "getting outside." The perspective of our rivals is *alien* to us; their cognitive priorities are not ours. Nor can we manage to transcend our position and achieve a "God's-eye view." At the level of substantive philosophical issues, there is no "position of reason" that is above the chatter of the diversified positions of various practitioners. To say this, however, is not to abandon the search for the truth but only to recognize its nature. Philosophical doctrines are justified, not absolutely, but from the variable positions of different individuals. We simply have to do the best we can in the epistemic circumstances in which we find ourselves. The saving grace is that an "exclusion principle" is operative that precludes any one of us (the working philosophical practitioners) from assuming more than one such vantage point at a time.

Does orientational pluralism not have the consequence that reality is unknowable? Or is it perhaps a schizophrenic theory that holds that there are as many realities as there are schools of thought; that whatever some perspective (or group) maintains as true *is* true—that there are as many realities as there are theories on the subject?

By no means! Orientational pluralism as a metaphilosophical stance neither denies nor fragments reality. To repeat, it is not an *ontological* position; it is wholly compatible with the view that there is such a thing as reality and that there can, in the final analysis, be but one correct theory about it. We do not have an "anything goes" theory here. Orientational pluralism does not hold that whatever people think to be true is true; it does not identify *truth* with mere *belief*. And it does not hold that it ultimately doesn't matter what people think about reality because there is no reality. It is deeply committed to the classical position that there is a reality at whose characterization our inquiries aim. Its pluralism is not ontological but *epistemological*. Its stance is that while there no doubt is only one reality, there are bound to be many theories about it, because one can only substantiate philosophical contentions from the vantage point of a cognitive-value orientation. Its view of philosophizing—of actually engaging in philosophical inquiry—is a perfectly orthodox view of "the truth of the matter." Orientational pluralism is, to be sure, a pluralism that fragments matters. But what it fragments is not reality or truth, but justification. Orientational pluralism is a doctrine about the epistemology of philosophy, not a theory about the ontological nature of the real; its pluralism inheres in epistemological rather than ontological considerations. It does not fragment reality but only (and harmlessly) people's ideas about it; it envisages a pluralism of *views* regarding the truth, not a pluralism of *truths*. The plurality that orientational pluralism asserts is located in the domain of doctrine and not in that of reality itself. It is not the world as such that it takes to be fragmented, but the world of thought. (To be sure, it recognizes that our sole cognitive access to reality itself proceeds through the mediation of our ideas about it.)

A theory that sees truth claims as perspectivally relative is emphatically not a theory of relative truth. With orientational pluralism we do not have to do with a distinctive (and multiply variable) *mode* of truth; rather, we have to do with distinctive (and variable) convictions about the one and only truth. What is variable is not the truth itself, but people's *ideas* about it. The crux is not that there are two distinct kinds of truth, the factually and the normatively based, but that there are two distinct sorts of *access* to truth, two different sets of bases for truth claims.

An epistemologically qualified view of the truth clearly does not lead to multiplicity of diverse "modes of truth." Suppose that:

(1) Seen from perspective $O$: $P$ is true.

This is certainly *not* to be construed as:

(2) Absolutely and unconditionally: $P$ is true-from-$O$.

Nothing useful is to be gained by fragmenting a monolithic "is true" (potentially warrantable from various perspectives $O$) into a multiplicity of relativized "is $O$-true." In fragmenting truth in this way, we would drastically alter the character of truth claims. To take this step is to invite all sorts of difficulties. For example, if $P$ emerges as true from my perspective ($O$), while from yours ($O'$) it eventuates that not-$P$ does, then we will clearly disagree. But of course "$P$ is $O$-true" and "$P$ is $O'$-false" are unproblematically compatible. With *explicitly* relativized truth claims, the prospect of agreement and disagreement is aborted, since they are recognized as factual rather than philosophical contentions.

Of course, once we ourselves *accept* the perspective $O$, the move from $O$-truth to truth *simpliciter* is automatic. As we ourselves see the matter, having the cognitive values we actually do have, one particular philosophical position is uniquely true. All the same, this path to truth is not absolute and unconditional; that matter of "having the cognitive-value orientation we actually do" plays a pivotal role. What is relative here is not *truth* at all (how could "the truth" be relative?), but rational belief about, or, if you prefer, rationally purported *knowledge* of, the truth.

In philosophy we cannot say that "the real truth" is what holds as justified from *every* orientational perspective. Nothing does. We cannot say that "the real truth" is what holds as justified from the *canonical* perspective—the universally *correct* one, the one at issue in the philosopher's penchant for the myth of the God's-eye view. For only God knows what this is; there is no way for us to come to it. (Even if He were to tell us, the questions of whether it is indeed He who is actually doing the telling and whether we had heard Him right would at once become a focus of philosophical controversy.) Moreover, we cannot say that the real truth is what holds as justified from *some* perspective or other—from at least one perspective in the diversified spectrum of available perspectives. For it is rationally incongruous to opt concurrently for incompatible alternatives. The best we can do on behalf of our own solutions to philosophical issues is to claim that they afford "the truth *as we see it*," yielding a position that is bound to be accepted as correct by those who share our basic commitment to a particular probative-value orientation. The "canonical" will be only what is so *for us*.

The claims staked by a philosopher are inherently absolute and universal. For example, he may, sharing C. S. Peirce's cognitive optimism, say (from the vantage point of this orientation): "Inquiry is destined to lead us eventually to the truth." Well and good; this is a philosophical thesis with which we can agree or disagree, and for or against which we might be minded to argue. But of course if he were to say, "We cognitive optimists hold that inquiry is destined to lead to the truth," then he is no longer speaking as a philosopher; he is only the spokesman for a group. In saying, "I think that *P*" or "We *X*'s think that *P*" he is giving us a mere *report* and not as yet advancing a thesis. This sort of thing, which stops well short of outright assertion, is not philosophy. The *justification* a philosopher advances may be orientationally limited in its appeal; but his claims as such are unrestricted and universal. (A philosopher's claims are not themselves rendered contentually parochial through the fact that his reasons for advancing them are.)

Philosophical claims are thus categorical; seen "from within"—internal to an accepted position—philosophical theses are purportedly of eternal and unqualified validity, context free and absolute. But when we consider our position "from without," suspending for the moment our own commitment to it, we see that it competes with other no less peremptory claims. We can surely recognize our philosophical truth claims as being no more than claims. Every claim to truth is a claim to absolute and eternal truth—that's just the sort of thing truth is. But this does not mean that every such claim is absolute and eternal.

Philosophical inquiry is such that, while each (sufficiently diligent) worker will indeed arrive at *his or her own* solution to problems, no one solution can rationally constrain the adhesion of all rational minds, regardless of the "mental set" of their cognitive values. In these circumstances, we must acknowledge the difference between: (1) a *globally* valid resolution that is demonstrably right in itself, by its very nature (and is thus correct from *every* valid point of view, so to speak), and (2) a *locally* optimal (or acceptable) resolution that is cogent for those committed to a certain orientation.

It follows that such "demonstrations" as there are in philosophy do not have an absolute but only a relative force. In effect they can be put in the form: IF you are prepared to make certain methodological commitments (i.e., to adopt a certain particular probative-value orientation), THEN you will arrive at a certain particular solution to the problem. A rational constraint is clearly at issue here, but it is relative to an orientation rather than absolute. In philosophy we have no alternative but to follow the guidance of our cognitive values. And it is this very fact that divides the community into distinct and discordant "schools of thought."

## 6. Relativism and the Problem of Protagoras

Does orientational pluralism not collapse into an all-vitiating subjectivity that sees every rival position as equally valid? Does its relativism not engender an indifferentism that sees everyone's claims as equally acceptable—or unacceptable?

Consider the famous *homo mensura* doctrine of Protagoras: "Man is the measure of all things, of what is, that it is, of what is not, that it is not."[9] Cicero took this to say "that that which appears to each man is true for him."[10] Now there are many ways of interpreting such a relativism. One is the harmless and innocuous thesis "What is *seen* as true will depend on the seer." Another is the far more problematic "There is no such thing as the truth at all, but only what different people *think* to be true—so there can be no knowledge but only opinion." This last sort of radical relativism is emphatically *not* supported by our orientational pluralism. As it sees the matter, we have every right to take our own seriously reflective judgments to represent items of knowledge as authentic as anything else we can obtain.

Nothing whatever prevents the orientational relativist from having a position and giving short shrift to its rivals. After all, one should not be dismayed if other solutions than one's own are accepted by people whose criteria of acceptability for solutions differ from one's own.

---

9. Sextus, *Adv. Math*, bk. VII, 60; cf. *Pyr. Hyp.*, bk. I, 216.
10. *Iudicium Protagorae est . . . id cuique verum esse quod cuique videatur* (Cicero, *Academica* [*pr.*], bk. II, 46, line 142).

From where we ourselves stand, this can do nothing to undermine the adequacy—nay, *inevitability*—of those solutions endorsed by the standards to which we ourselves are committed. Nothing in relativism prevents the relativist from having a position of his own. ("But he cannot *justify* it!" Of course he can—by his own standards, the only ones that can carry any weight with him.)

When we speak *in propria persona* from the angle of our own orientational perspective, then (as with any other individual's perspective) there is going to be only one "correct" answer. Relativism is only viable when it takes on epistemological form; *ontological* relativism is ultimately incoherent. It makes no sense to say that what anybody *thinks* to be true *is* true (though this is perfectly acceptable if we add the saving—and trivializing—rider "according to him"). We must not pluralize the truth as such but only people's ideas about it, recognizing that the only cognitive access we have to what *is* true is via what our own orienting perspective sees as true.

But, of course, the fact that there is only one reality and only one true theory about it does not help. We have no way of telling what it is *independently* of the triangulations of our imperfect inquiry. No telephone line connects us with the Recording Angel. The best and most we can do is exert our cognitive efforts as best we can according to our own lights. More than that (more than doing the best we can) we obviously cannot do.

Such a theory does not see the truth as unknowable; indeed, it urges us to do our best to catch glimpses of it. Nor does it see reality as multiple and regard every theory of it as equally acceptable; on the contrary, we are enjoined and entitled to see our own theory as correct. All we are called on to do is to acknowledge that *relative to their own orientations* (which we, of course, see as misguided), others are equally entitled to see their versions of the truth as equally warranted. We are certainly not called on to see other orientations as equal to our own. Our orientation would not be *our* orientation if we did see them in this light. Our view of the *truth* would not be what it is if we did not see our purported truth as *the* truth.

It is by no means the case that philosophical reasonings and arguments are unqualifiedly "subjective." For what is at issue with objectivity is something that "must" be accepted, as a matter of general principle, at some level of generality

—by all rational intelligences,
—by rational intelligences of a specifically human configuration,
—by those who adopt a certain cognitive method,
—by those who accept certain theses or methods or presuppositions.

Objectivity is a matter of degree rather than an absolute.[11] Viewed in this light, philosophical reasonings are not strictly subjective but hold objectively for all who share a certain cognitive-value orientation. Rational cogency and stringency remain, though on a relativized basis. Above all, cognitive values are *not* subjective in the way tastes are (with the result that *de gustibus non est disputandum*). We can always argue about value with rational cogency. The crux, as we have seen, is simply that when we argue about values, our arguments themselves always involve values. It is not *rationality* that is unavailable in this sphere, but absoluteness—the capacity to resolve issues in the absence of any and all potentially person-differential value inputs.

Any adequate philosophical cognitive-value orientation should be self-supportive in viewing the claims it itself endorses as (genuinely) true. It should see its truths as a real truths. Deliberation on these issues pivots about an aporetic cluster:

(1) Any philosophy that is worthy of the name stakes absolute claims to truth.
(2) Philosophies are manifold and variable.
(3) Any teaching that is variably one among many cannot make good absolute claims to truth.

Three ways out are in theory available here:

Deny (1): Reject the idea that philosophy makes categorical (absolute) truth claims.
Deny (2): Hold that there is only one "real" philosophy and that the rest are sham, merely *seeming* philosophies (pseudophilosophies).
Deny (3): Maintain the epistemic thesis that a perfectly appropriate claim to categorical (absolute) truth can be made on a basis that is relative and orientationally variable.

The first alternative flies in the face of the facts. The second represents an unappealing absolutism that is highly problematic in the light of the historical realities. Only the third appears to be viable. And this, in fact, is the approach taken by orientational pluralism.

The relativism at issue is sometimes objected to as follows:

If I hold that truth is subjectivity, what status am I to give to the denial of the proposition that truth is subjectivity? If I produce arguments to refute this denial I appear committed to the view that there are criteria by appeal to which the truth about truth can be vindicated. If I refuse to produce arguments, on the grounds that there can be neither argument nor criteria in such a case, then I appear committed to the view that any view embraced with sufficient subjec-

---

11. For a useful discussion of this point see Thomas Nagel, *Mortal Questions* (Cambridge, 1979), pp. 206–09.

tive passion is as warranted as any other in respect of truth, including the view that truth is not subjectivity.[12]

But this argument does not tell against our present analysis, which draws a clear line between a *subjectivity* that bases positions on feeling not argument, and a *relativity* that can provide for reasoned justification, albeit from a person-relative basis of reasoning.

Relativism, like other philosophical doctrines, itself roots in an aporetic cluster—namely, that of the contentions that, given a plurality of conflicting positions (doctrines):

(1) Validity lies somewhere within the conflict of doctrines; *at least one* position is acceptable.
(2) Among conflicting positions, *at most one* can reasonably be accepted.
(3) All the conflicting positions stand on the same footing; all have an equal status—including an equal acceptability status.

Here (1)–(2) yield that exactly one position is acceptable and the rest not. This conflicts squarely with (3). We thus have three options:

(1)–rejection: No position is acceptable; all are alike without merit. There is no real truth in these matters, only what people think to be true (scepticism).
(2)–rejection: Several of those conflicting positions are equally acceptable. They stand on the same footing; it is a matter of rational indifference which one is adopted—or perhaps one should take the heroic step of conjoining them all (indifferentism or syncretism).
(3)–rejection: The positions are of radically different merit and status. One alone is acceptable; the rest represent various forms of error (doctrinalism, dogmatism).

Orientational pluralism draws a distinction here. From the angle of the individual (and thus relative to a particular set of cognitive values) it espouses doctrinalism; from the angle of the community it embraces the indifferentist stance.

But the relativism at issue is robust (i.e., discriminatory) rather than weak-kneed (i.e., indifferentist). It reflects the stance: "Certainly, these philosophical positions are held relative to a basis, and different people have different bases. But I have great confidence in mine. Given that I stand where I do, I hold that only one position qualifies as correct."

We must, moreover, distinguish between versions of relativism—and in particular, must distinguish a relativity of *truth* as such from a relativity of *truth-claims*. On the one hand, there is *epistemological* relativism (relativism with respect to perspectival or *purported* truth—truth from the vantage point of a particular orientation)—where (2) goes by the board but (3) is retained. On the other hand, there is *ontological*

---

12. Alasdair MacIntyre, "Existentialism," in D. J. O'Conner, ed., *A Critical History of Western Philosophy* (New York, 1964), p. 512.

relativism with respect to "the real truth"—where (2) is retained and (3) is abandoned. Our relativism is only of the epistemological sort. Orientational pluralism is not a no-reality view but merely holds that in philosophical matters there is no epistemic access to reality without an orientational commitment. It is not that a rational choice among competing alternatives is impossible as such, but only that it is not possible in the absence of a cognitive-value orientation.

To reemphasize: the salient point is that the relativism of orientational pluralism is epistemic, not ontological. It is a relativism of *acceptability*, not a relativism of *truth*. No doubt the truth in these matters (whatever *that* might be) is, like all truth, absolute. But it is not, of course, this absolute with which we have to deal. Our dealings are with truth as best we can discern it—with warranted assertability (to use John Dewey's useful expression). In philosophy (as in science) we cannot deal in truths as such, direct and unmediated, but only in *claims* to truth—claims based on a differential and shifting probative basis.[13]

Ontological truth-relativism is the doctrine that truth as such is relative in being context dependent or person dependent. Something that is true for you is false for me; something that is true in this context is false in that. It is a doctrine tied to the multifaceted reality view, a doctrine that holds that reality can somehow accommodate discordant truths. It must be emphasized that this is *not* a doctrine to which our orientational pluralism stands committed. For there is a great difference between truth-relativism and justification-relativism. The epistemological aspect is pivotal. It makes no sense to speak of "what *is* true from a point of view" in *contradistinction* to "what *is held to be* true from a point of view." For what is correlative to a point of view is not real but merely apparent truth—not the truth as such but only the truth as it is seen to be. When I (or you) say, from our respective points of view, that *P* is true, we do not say it is so from our points of view, but say flatly that it is so. (That's why we *disagree* if you say *P* and I say not-*P*.) What is point-of-view correlative is not *actual* (real) truth but *apparent* truth, or, better yet, not *truth* as such

---

13. In recent years, Peter Winch and his supporters have argued for a relativism of the standards of rationality, holding that beliefs and actions can only be regarded as rational within a framework of standards and criteria of rationality appropriate to the cultural setting in which those beliefs and actions arise. The *rationality* of cognition and praxis is always a framework-internal issue in the sense of Rudolf Carnap's well-known distinction between internal and external questions. See Peter Winch, *The Ideal of a Social Science* (London, 1958); and "Understanding a Primitive Society," *American Philosophical Quarterly* 1 (1964): 307–25; and for a survey of the resulting controversy see Joseph L. Esposito, "Science and Conceptual Relativism," *Philosophical Studies* 31 (1977): 269–77. The presently envisaged relativity of the value-standards of philosophical argumentation espouses at the level of the probative standards of different *philosophical* "schools" a position roughly comparable to this sort of *cultural* relativity of the cogency-standards of rational deliberation.

but only the *justification* of truth claims. The truth is no doubt one, but that does not prevent our beliefs from being (and quite appropriately being) many. We frail humans have no route to ontological certainty save via forking paths of epistemological certitudes.

Such a relativism is not subjectivistic. What makes the difference is not the mere difference of person but the difference of situation. Warrant as such is something impersonal; if it holds for X, it holds for anyone in X's situation as well. There is indeed universality, but only in conditionalized form. And so one can be rationally justified in holding one's position in one's own case or situation without thereby aspiring to that level of universality that would enable one to persuade another rational person who is differently situated to adopt it as well.

There is no question that orientational pluralism represents a form of relativism. But its relativism is one of justification rather than truth, of adequacy rather than correctness. Truth relativism claims the existence of a conflict within the range of *true* beliefs. Justification relativism only contemplates a conflict in the range of *justified* beliefs. It represents the relatively innocuous doctrine that justification is context dependent or person dependent. It holds that it may be perfectly justified and appropriate for you to believe one thing and for me to believe another, given the differences in the respective backgrounds of experience on which we base our judgments. It is not involved in claiming that the truth as such is variable, but only that the basis on which we judge the truth can vary (and vary not only with regard to evidence but with regard to the standards by which that evidence is utilized and deployed). The doctrines held to be true from a given cognitive orientation are held to be true in the fullest sense, absolutely true. But this is only what they are *held* to be. To be true from an orientation is not to be *true*, period, but *conditionally* true—to be something that might be held from a particular vantage point that one may or may not be inclined to adopt oneself.

Justification relativism is accordingly not committed to the *ontological* theses that the truth as such is variable and situation dependent. It simply maintains the epistemological theses that (1) nothing can be *determined* as true without a standpoint (as regards evidence, standards, and so on) and (2) that different people can and quite properly do have different standpoints.

## 7. Does Orientational Pluralism Mean We Must Abandon the Pursuit of Truth?

Consider the following thesis:

The fact that philosophers always have and always will disagree shows that their discipline is unable to yield *knowledge*—to provide us with cognitive access to authentic truth.

This contention is altogether mistaken. Nothing in orientational pluralism suggests that "the pursuit of the truth" is an inappropriate or unrealistic goal of the enterprise. Of course, we will not be able to portray whatever position we arrive at as representing more than *our own perception* of the truth. In the circumstances, it hardly makes sense to characterize our solution to a philosophical question in absolutistic terms as affording that solely appropriate answer that can and should be seen as uniquely correct by everyone alike. The best one can do in the very nature of the case is to establish one alternative as optimally tenable in the light of the standards of significance and plausibility that constitute a certain probative-value orientation, and so to establish the truth as best we ourselves can come to see it.

To be sure, the idea of "the truth" is of small interest to many philosophers nowadays. Heidegger, for one, regarded those so-called absolute truths as no more than "remnants of Christian theology in the problem-field of philosophy."[14] Of themselves, truth and falsity, correctness and incorrectness, adequacy and inadequacy, sense and nonsense approached as issues of semantic theory or epistemological explication simply do not interest the hermeneuticist. He wants to know what role the *ideas* about these issues have in the sphere of authentic human experience; he does not ask about what these ideas *mean* but about what people *do* with them. Truth as such is something he is eager to abandon.

And not he alone. In stressing the pluralism of philosophizing, William James wrote:

*The* Truth: what a perfect idol of the rationalistic mind! I read in an old letter—from a gifted friend who died too young—these words: "In everything, in science, art, morals, and religion, there *must* be one system that is right and *every* other wrong." How characteristic of the enthusiasm of a certain stage of young! At twenty-one we rise to such a challenge and expect to find the system. It never occurs to most of us even later that the question "What is *the* Truth?" is no real question (being irrelative to all conditions) and that the whole notion of *the* truth is an abstraction from the fact of truths in the plural.[15]

Inspired by James, pragmatists are quite prepared to abandon concern for truth.

But this reaction is gravely misguided. Epistemological relativism has no ontological consequences for the nature of truth as such. The fact that "our truth"—the truth as we see it—is not necessarily that of others, that it is no more than the best *estimate* of the real truth that we

---

14. "Reste von christlicher Theologie innerhalb der philosophischen Problematik" (Martin Heidegger, *Sein and Zeit* [Leipzig, 1923], p. 230).
15. William James, "Pragmatism and Humanism," in *Writings,* p. 450.

ourselves are able to make, should not disillusion us about it and should not discourage us. Young or old, we are well advised to pursue the truth as best we can and to stick by what we find until such time as something comes along that we ourselves can honestly deem better.

Recognizing that others see the matter differently need not daunt us in attachment to our own views of the matter. There is clearly no conflict between our commitment to the truth as we see it and a recognition that the adoption of a variant probative perspective leads others to see the truth differently. Given that we ourselves occupy our perspective, we are bound to see *our* truth as *the* truth. But we nevertheless can and do recognize that others see the matter in a different light. The circumstance that different people see something differently does not destroy or degrade the thing as such.

As long as we are *serious* about philosophical inquiry we must actually have a perspective of consideration and take an evaluative position by assuming a cognitive-value orientation. And here—"internally" from our own point of orientation—we ourselves cannot consider other positions as genuinely on a par with our own. As long as we have "the courage of our convictions," as long as we stand committed to the cognitive values that undergird our philosophical position, only one resolution of a philosophical problem is optimal, only one particular answer acceptable. Once a probative orientation is seriously adopted, only one "correct" answer is ever available. If we are to take our philosophizing seriously we must ourselves approach it from the angle of the Unique Reality View. When we are pursuing our philosophical inquiries this is a stance we are certainly able—and perfectly entitled—to take.

It is not only possible but sensible to work out the appropriate answer to a philosophical problem as best we can determine it "from where we stand," relative to our own evaluation-laden plausibility commitments, and nevertheless to recognize that other theoretically viable solutions are available and need to be reckoned with. Accordingly, one should regard the task of the individual inquirer in a very different light from that of the enterprise at large in its historical and communal aspect.

We can say unproblematically that "our philosophy has it that *P*" but never that "philosophy has it that *P*." A philosopher can tell us what *his* philosophy says, but never what *philosophy* says. Orientational pluralism is a mode of relativism in that it sees the acceptability of philosophical positions as predicated on commitment to particular cognitive-value orientations that can, quite appropriately, differ from person to person.

At the substantive level of actual philosophizing, our own "cognitive stance" is determinative—and determinative of what we unhesitatingly maintain as the truth. We assert it seriously, and all serious assertion is assertion *as true.* Life being what it is, the existence of contrary views need never prevent the rational man from articulating with confidence and assured conviction those philosophical views that represent how matters stand "to the best of our knowledge and belief." To say, "As best I can possibly determine it, *P* is the truth, but of course I cannot really endorse *P* unless it secures the backing of others" is surely to take an unduly diffident view of our powers. In philosophy we should neither expect our position to be the focus of a consensus nor be discouraged when it fails to be so.

To say, "What everybody else sees as true should presumably count as such for me as well" is perfectly proper in science and common life but ultimately useless in philosophy, where there is and can be nothing that *everybody* must see as true. If we are prepared to accept only what everyone does, we must go empty-handed. And to say the converse, "What I see to be the truth should count as such for everybody," is simply megalomania. In philosophy we have to face up to the truism that what is good enough for us is good enough for us—that we would do well to rest satisfied with the only view of the truth we can possibly obtain, namely our own. There is something petulant about saying, "I want answers to my questions, but only answers that will convince everyone else as well."

The "relativistic" stance that philosophical positions can only be maintained relative to a certain approach (perspective, orientation, or the like) emphatically does not prevent one from taking a dogmatically committed view of the real truth, provided one is ready to hold (as philosophers generally are) that one's own approach is the uniquely appropriate one. There is nothing about orientational pluralism that constrains it to be at odds with philosophical commitment.

In philosophy we have no choice but to pursue *the* truth by way of cultivating *our* truth; we have no direct access to truth unmediated by the epistemological resources of rational inquiry. And, given the ground rules of philosophical inquiry, this means that our view of the truth is bound to be value linked and thus standpoint correlated. To say that this is not good enough and to give up on our truth—to declare petulently that if we can't have *the* absolute, capital-T Truth that of its very nature constrains everyone's allegiance, then we won't accept anything at all—is automatically to get nothing and to abandon the pursuit of truth as such. It is foolishness to say that an orientation-bound position is not worth having in a domain where a position is only to be had on this basis. Once we see that a contention whose justification is orientation bound is *the most we can in principle hope to validate* in philosophy, we are well en route to recognizing why this is the most we should ever ask for. It is rationally inappropriate to demand something that cannot be had.

Orientational pluralism accordingly does not deny that the pursuit of truth remains the pivotal aim of philosophizing. It merely stresses that we can carry this pursuit on only according to our own lights. In philosophy as in all human inquiry we *aim* at the absolute and definitive capital-T Truth. But all we can ever attain is our (potentially erroneous and problematic) view of the truth. And this is good enough. Defining "where I stand"—determining my own position in light of alternatives—is the main mission. (And it is difficult enough.)

Orientational pluralism is thus also describable as orientational monism. It is not simply compatible with but demands an individual philosopher's dedication to a particular present position. To be sure, such dedication need not be dogmatic. One need not see one's position as final and definitive, as graven changelessly on stone tablets. As with our beliefs in matters of scientific theory, we can see our position as the best that can be done at the existing time of day and as subject to adjustment and emendation in the light of future developments, as correct "in essentials" though perhaps not "in detail." (To *this* extent, the distinction between *our* truth and *the* truth can be maintained in this as in other matters.)

The orientational pluralist is not concerned to deny that there *is* such a thing as a reality that affords the "facts of the matter" and that adequacy to this reality is what determines the truth. He is concerned with noting that we've all got our own particular ideas about reality, and that none of us has access to it in a way so direct and total that the claims of others are annihilated. The fact that truth and reality "are somehow out there" in a thought-independent realm of their own is—even if conceded—simply beside the point; there is nothing that *we* can do with it.

There is no earthly reason not to recognize that what we get in philosophy, like what we get in any other area of inquiry, is not the truth itself in its definitive authenticity, but only what we take to be the truth. Our access to truth is always epistemically mediated—we secure the truth not as such but only "as best we can tell." The prospect of a God's-eye view obtained *sub specie aeternitatis* lies beyond our reach. We have no choice but to rest content with what we can actually get.

Nothing in orientational pluralism compels us to see our philosophical doctrines as *mere opinions.* They are indeed opinions of sorts, but there is nothing "mere" about them. They are *judgments*—matters of reasoned conviction for whose acceptance we (warrantedly) take ourselves to have good reasons. The fact that these "good reasons" can only count as good from the perspective of a given cognitive-value orientation nowise precludes them from being good reasons. (That's just what good reasons are and have to be in this domain.)

The key lesson is that one must take a stand. One must "choose sides" in the debate: "Never mind about the others; they may follow a different drummer. Our job is to follow ours." In the very nature of the case, we have no alternative to proceeding on this basis. If we give up on the pursuit of *our truth*, we give up on the pursuit of *the truth* itself. The epistemic condition of man is that we can get at the latter only via the former! Certainly, to claim more than this in philosophy—to portray what *we* find to be the truth as "the agreed truth of the discipline as a whole"—would be to falsify facts. It makes sense to ask where a particular philosophy stands but not where philosophy stands. When *P* is a thesis of philosophical generality and interest, then anyone who makes statements of the form "Philosophy teaches that *P*" or "Philosophers have established that *P*" is bound to be talking nonsense.

The orientational pluralist does *not* propose to abandon the pursuit of truth in philosophy. He simply enjoins us to recognize that, short of adopting a probative value posture, there is no way of conducting inquiry in this domain and that such a posture is never a community-wide universal. And, of course, *since we ourselves do have such a posture*, one that we presumably deem as uniquely right and proper, we need not and should not be intimidated by the fact that others—poor benighted souls!—would work matters out differently. Axiological relativism does not entail indifferentism. In philosophy—as in morals or politics—the fact that one must inevitably defend one's position on the basis of one's values certainly does not impede our taking the stance that our position is right.[16]

16. It is a characteristic feature of an axiological relativism in contrast to an evidential one that we are not in a position to concede that someone else's basis of judgment may be superior to our own. I can, quite sensibly, grant that your *information* may be superior to mine, but not that your *values* are.

# 11

## Is There Progress in Philosophy? The Problem of Unattainable Consensus

*1. The Complexity of the Question in the Absence of Consensus*

The issue of philosophical progress is difficult. It pivots on just exactly how we are to assess progressiveness in this domain, and this question is far from straightforward.

Progress in an intellectual enterprise is a matter of an increasingly more adequate (or at any rate less inadequate) fulfillment of its mission. But just exactly what this mission is can be problematic and debatable.

Moreover, there will clearly be as many ways of making progress in a given domain as there are elements of the goal structure of the enterprise, since improved performance with respect to any one of these elements will have to count. Accordingly, progress will split into modes and regards. When there is no single goal but a variety of interconnected objectives, the issue will become equivocal, raising questions of priority to which no straightforward answer may be available. In the case of philosophy, the situation would seem to be one of just exactly this internally complex sort, because very different goals might plausibly be taken to be at issue (solving problems, giving direction to life, broadening our intellectual horizons, and so on). This very issue of privacy and priority among the goals of philosophy is itself an inherently philosophical question that is bound to be problematic and debatable. The question of progress in philosophy is thus a real hornet's nest.[1]

We certainly do make progress in philosophy in the sense of coming to address more and diverse questions. Even a cursory survey of

---

1. Some interesting deliberations on the topic are provided in Moody, "Progress in Philosophy."

the journal literature would suffice to show that most of the issues debated today were not even raised a generation ago. There is no doubt that progress is made in philosophy in terms of providing more (putative) answers to a wider variety of contemplated questions. Yet do philosophers not just *raise* questions and propose answers but manage to *resolve* the issues to everyone's satisfaction? Do they achieve an ever-growing and deepening agreement on the issues? Seemingly not. If progress is measured by consensus, by settling the problems to everyone's satisfaction, philosophy certainly does not progress. The issues get more complex and their elaboration more sophisticated, but consensus remains as elusive as ever.

The evolution of philosophy is a matter of the concurrent development of discordant traditions and points of view in ongoing and increasingly sophisticated rivalry. Philosophy is the battlefield of a perpetual struggle between divergent approaches developing in continual opposition and apposition, destined never to subside in the comfortable harmony of general agreement. The Humean "noise and clamor" of disagreement in philosophy is a formative component of its fate. Thought on philosophical problems develops through an exfoliating complexity that leaves its practitioners just as far apart as ever on the basic issues. The existence of diverse probative orientations prevents the realization of agreement within each successive era and thus blocks any prospect of achieving a stable state of philosophical opinion that remains constant from one historical era to another. In philosophy, rival "schools" are (or could be) at work at every historical juncture. As the details become more refined, the disagreements become more intricate and diversified. There is no prospect of philosophical consensus because we are here concerned with the ongoing development of discordant programs. If growing consensus in resolving issues is to be the criterion of progress, then philosophy does not progress at all.[2]

## 2. The Balance Sheet: Technical vs. Doctrinal Progress

But, of course, this is not the end of the story. The work of philosophizing involves principally the following characteristic tasks (cf. pp. 75–76 above).

(1) Issue identification: pinpointing philosophically interesting ideas and topics. Identifying potentially fruitful philosophical themes.
(2) Problem posing: discerning philosophical problems and questions. Finding what sorts of inner strains and stresses exist within our cognitive inclinations and commitments on philosophically relevant issues.

---

2. The first philosopher to hold, in essentials, the view of this paragraph was the erudite German historian of philosophy, Dietrich Tidedmann (1748–1803). For a compact account of his views see Braun, *Histoire de l'histoire de la philosophie*, pp. 184–87.

(3) Problem solving: providing answers to philosophical questions. Unraveling the aporetic difficulties that arise in this context and discerning appropriate ways out of difficulties.
(4) Thesis substantiation: devising arguments that substantiate the theses we propose to adopt as problem solutions. Placing our position on a more amply elaborated basis of argument.
(5) Concept enhancement: analyzing our concepts. Projecting new and useful concepts by introducing distinctions, classifications, and so on.
(6) Horizon enlargement: entertaining new possibilities for theorizing and relating them to our prior concerns.
(7) Systematization: seeing more fully and exactly what commitments our positions presuppose and implications they have. Tracing out more fully the lines of thought at issue in our positions. Putting our questions and answers into a structure or framework that resolves issues with maximum overall rational effectiveness and economy.

The *technical* merits of philosophical work (breadth of concern, refinement of distinctions, suitability of question posing, rigor of argumentation) are objective matters open for all to see. The issue here is on the one hand a matter of more detailed analysis, more subtly wrought distinctions, and on the other of more comprehensive synthesis, more ably contrived combinations of elements. As in architecture, care for details is to be combined with a care for integrative comprehensiveness. Its technical quality as an intellectual performance (as opposed to its acceptability) is something that all careful students of a philosophical position should be able to discern, regardless of their assessment of its correctness. Technical merit is a matter of hypothetical merit relative to a simply *assumed* framework, not of categorical merit relative to an *established* framework. Philosophers of the most diverse commitments need encounter no difficulty in coming to agreement regarding the matter of technical quality and competence of workmanship as an instance of its type (*sui genesis* merit). (That is why doctrinally diversified examiners can usually reach easy agreement in evaluating the work of their students.)

However, the issue of the *substantive* merit of a philosophical position—its acceptability or correctness—does not simply hinge on the merit of its technical articulation; it is categorical rather than hypothetical, substantive rather than procedural. The conditional status of a solution as a solution from a certain postulated perspective of consideration is open for all to see. But whether that perspective itself is appropriate is something else again. This issue is not just technical but essentially evaluative, and the solution to it must, in significant measure, lie in the eye of the beholder.

There is little room for doubt that philosophy can and does make progress on the technical side—that later efforts can provide for more refined concepts, subtle distinctions, elaborate arguments, and so on. Over the years, philosophers have made substantial methodological advances, acquiring increasingly more delicate analytical tools and more powerful methods of synthesis. Moreover, new sorts of data can be forthcoming—innovations in the natural sciences or in the formal sciences (logic, theory of evidence, theory of language)—that bear significantly on our handling of philosophical issues. Again, more sophisticated machinery of argumentation can be devised—probatively useful innovations in logic, dialectics, inferential reasoning (e.g., probability), and so on. New ways of looking at the issues and instruments for reasoning about them are constantly being devised, and new modes of supportive argumentation are constantly coming upon the scene. Philosophy clearly makes progress in enhanced sophistication in the technical machinery by which philosophical positions are articulated. In particular, philosophical inquiry expands ever more luxuriantly into new issues. There is an ongoing diversification of concern with the opening up of new problem areas. The historic course of philosophy is marked by more thorough exploration of an ever widening problem space.

But this development in the technical resources of philosophy does not lead toward consensus on matters of substance. It does not move us toward a decisive resolution of those core issues from which philosophical deliberations exfoliate. If the standard of progress is to be the attainment of consensus with respect to the acceptability of doctrines—establishing one philosophical position as definitively "correct" *vis-à-vis* its rival alternatives in a way that rationally compels the assent of all dispassionate minds—then there is no progress in philosophy.

As the dialectic of controversy proceeds, the issues of philosophy become sharpened and clarified through the elaboration of the implicit complexities and the introduction of new distinctions and more sophisticated reasonings. There is a progressive development in regard to subtlety and complexity. We come to recognize in greater and more elaborate detail just where our commitments are bound ultimately to lead. But in the course of this process we only see more and more clearly just where and how we disagree.

In philosophy, as in other value-geared enterprises, innovations and sophistications in methodology do not result in settling the issues—they just raise the quality of the debate in which the ongoing disagreements manifest themselves. The history of philosophy is akin to an intellectual arms race where all sides escalate the technical bases for their positions. As realists sophisticate their side of the argument, idealists sophisticate their counterarguments; as materialists become more subtle, so do phenomenalists, and so on. At the level of basics, the same old positions continue to contest the field—albeit that evermore powerful weapons are used to defend increasingly sophisticated positions.

The issue of philosophical progress will accordingly depend crucially on exactly how we construe the mission of the enterprise. The goal structure of philosophizing prominently includes such items as the following:

—To identify issues that must be discussed
—To detail the questions that must be addressed; to provide a detailed and fully elaborated account of the problems of the field
—To elaborate the possibilities for answering questions; to map out the space of alternative lines of response to the issues that determine, in essentials, the various *positions* that can be held on philosophical questions
—To provide and defend specific answers to an ever-widening range of questions; to develop more elaborate arguments for substantiating one's claims about them
—To devise more powerful and sophisticated conceptual tools for dealing with the issues
—To explore more fully the implications and ramifications of the issues and provide for an ever-more ample range of consideration
—To devise increasingly comprehensive systemic frameworks for organizing and coordinating our answers to philosophical questions
—To establish consensus; to resolve the substantive issues in such a way as to secure general approbation and assent.

The issue of progress will hinge critically on the place that we assign to these various objectives in the overall scheme of things. It is a question of cognitive values; of goals to be emphasized and relative priorities among them. What makes the issue of progress in philosophy especially problematic is not just that there are various goals—*any* complex enterprise has a plurality of goals. Rather, it is that one cannot unproblematically establish any priority ranking among these goals—that the significance and centrality of these various goals are themselves philosophically controversial. The question of progress in philosophy is thus itself a quintessentially philosophical issue—one that critically turns on cognitive values.

In confronting this issue, the salient fact is that *by every criterion save the last alone,* philosophy does indeed progress. Constant innovations provide new vistas of consideration, new issues and problems, new and deeper arguments, more subtle distinctions, more adequately elaborated systems, and so on. In every sector of doctrine-internal development—in philosophical technology, so to speak—there is substantial improvement. But all this sort of domestic progress in the quality of the technical articulation of positions provides no adjudication between contending doctrines and so does nothing to produce consensus regarding the question of acceptability. Consensus with regard to the *technical* matters of merit relative to hypothetically *given* standards does not underwrite consensus as regards acceptability as such, where the issue of the appropriateness of the standards is itself in question. If by "consensus" one means agreement about acceptability (as seems to be the usual construction), then philosophy affords little prospect for a progress geared to the ongoing development of consensus.

We face the following aporetic situation:

(1) In any legitimate cognitive discipline there must be the prospect of progress.
(2) Progress in any legitimate cognitive discipline must consist in resolving problems by communally agreed standards.
(3) Philosophy is a legitimate cognitive descriptive.
(4) Philosophy cannot manage to resolve its problems by communally agreed standards (since there are none).

Here (4) represents a fact of life. So, if we adhere to the progressive ideal represented by (1), then we can either jettison (3) and join with sceptics and positivists in dismissing philosophy as a legitimate cognitive discipline, or we must reject the progress/consensus linkage represented by (2).

Orientational pluralism unhesitatingly opts for the latter course. It is prepared to construe progress in an essentially technical perspective—as a matter of added sophistication in the interests of remedying project-internal deficiencies. But that this view of progress should engender a consensus is something it neither expects nor requires.

## 3. Abandoning Consensus as a Prime Desideratum

The issue of priorities among its goals accordingly emerges as the key to the question of progress in philosophy. The central consideration is that of the relative importance among its cognitive aims of communal consensus on the substantive issues as compared with the other, more substantively oriented desiderata of philosophizing.

Obviously, this question of goal priority is itself a quintessentially philosophical one, heavily imbued with a commitment to cognitive values. And here, as elsewhere, philosophers will of course disagree. Some do indeed take agreement and consensus as the salient goal of the enterprise—Karl-Otto Apel, for example.[3] Expanding Peirce's doctrine regarding the role of consensus in relation to specifically *scientific* inquiry, he regards communal consensus as a "transcendental presupposition" of *all* inquiry and insists that for there to be progress in philosophy there must be a *convergence* of opinion among philosophers. The prime imperative for philosophers is that implicit in the Kant-reminiscent transcendental question: "What theoretical line would (best) make convergence in the unlimited community (beginning with but not limited to the philosophical community) possible?"[4] Philosophers should accordingly seek guidance for their conception of progress "in the idea of the realization of that unlimited community of interpretation which is presupposed by everyone who takes part in critical discussion (that is, by everyone who thinks!) as an ideal controlling standard."[5] But this conception of a transcendental "unlimited community" is not so much an ideal as a mirage—an "ideal" only in the wistful sense of "it might be nice if." For there is no reason of principle why the unlimited community should be any less diverse in its philosophical conceptions than the real community is and ever has been. With regard to such philosophical issues as (for example) the parameters of progress in the field, the community, be it wide or narrow, is effectively bound—given the evaluative aspect of the matter—to see the issues in differently refracted colors.

Yet what is one to make of the fact that philosophers cannot reach a meeting of minds—that philosophy cannot attain consensus? Consider the following aporetic cluster:

(1) Philosophy provides knowledge.
(2) Knowledge requires that consensus be attainable in principle.
(3) Philosophy does not afford consensus.

Here (3) is simply a fact of life. We are thus forced to choose between (1) and (2)—between a sceptical abandonment of the cognitive claims of philosophy and a recognition that consensus is infeasible in some cognitive domains. Orientational pluralism unhesitatingly rejects (2) and is prepared to recognize a normative mode of cognitive validation. It takes the stance that we are entitled to make confident cognitive claims for *our* position, notwithstanding the existence of rivals over whom we cannot prevail by rational suasion alone. And so it abandons consensus as a prime desideratum for philosophy and as a requisite for progress in this domain. For rationally enforced consensus is some-

---

3. See esp. his *Towards a Transformation of Philosophy*.
4. Ibid., p. 104.
5. Ibid., p. 123.

thing one cannot hope to achieve. One can develop a perfectly sound supporting case to legitimate my holding of a certain position, but this need not be of a sort that will persuade someone else. I can validate my own commitment to my position without having the means to compel my adversaries to give up their side of the controversy. For I can have a perfectly good rational basis for holding my position, albeit an evaluative one—taking my stance on the basis of the cognitive values I do indeed hold. In philosophy, one can secure rational conviction for oneself without being able to achieve rational predominance over others, simply because the basis of that rational conviction can (and must) be in some degree personal.

This question of cognitive priorities is itself a matter of value that poses a quintessentially philosophical problem that revolves about the following inconsistent triad:

(1) Philosophy makes progress in the matters that really count.
(2) Philosophy does not progress in point of communal consensus.
(3) The achievement of consensus is a key goal of philosophical inquiry.

Three resolutions are available here:

Abandon (1): Deny that philosophy makes progress (thereby effectively negating its claim as a valid cognitive discipline).
Abandon (2): Adopt a "True Believer Aproach," insisting that there indeed is a growing consensus, but only within the community of *real* philosophers, thus in effect excommunicating most of the community (namely, those who don't see things our way).
Abandon (3): Reject communal consensus as a pivotal desideratum in philosophy.

This last alternative is, of course, the position of orientational pluralism, which disqualifies consensus as an appropriate requirement or desideratum, seeing its realization as precluded on general principles whose operation lies deep in the very nature of the enterprise. In philosophy we just aren't going to get consensus, and the search for it is a quixotic quest.

Inability to achieve *consensus* is very different from an inability to achieve *answers*. The latter would be something far more serious. Absence of consensus simply means that not everyone will accept the answers we ourselves arrive at, and this need not necessarily dismay us—provided that we can find answers whose credentials we ourselves deem satisfactory. The nature of the enterprise and the conceptual make-up of its problems are such that it is unreasonable to expect consensus and inappropriate to lament its absence. And so, inability to achieve consensus in philosophy is not a proper subject for regret.

But does rationality not demand consensus? We confront the following aporetic cluster:

(1) Reason demands consensus.
(2) Philosophy is committed to meeting the demands of reason.
(3) Philosophy is a viable project; it can in principle discharge its mandate and honor its commitments.
(4) Philosophy does not and cannot achieve consensus.

As ever, there are various exits from the aporetic inconsistency:

(1)–denial: It is *not* irrational to abandon the requirement of universal consensus (relativism).
(2)–denial: Philosophy can dispense with the demands of rationality (irrationalism).
(3)–denial: Philosophy is not a feasible project. It is simply a fraud and delusion (scepticism, positivism).
(4)–denial: Philosophy can achieve consensus; the day must come at last when all rational thinkers, regardless of their evaluative or ideological allegiances, reach agreement on philosophical issues (absolutism, objectivism).

Orientational pluralism stands committed to the first of these alternatives. It sees rational credence in philosophy as relative to a normative basis of cognitive values. And since it acknowledges that this basis is (at least in part) appropriately person-differential, it does not accept consensus as a legitimate requirement of rationality in the philosophical domain.

Accordingly, we are able to respond to the question "Is there progress in philosophy?" with an emphatic affirmative. But this progress takes the form of a development *within* the various competing philosophical positions, and not by way of dissolving the disagreements between them. It is a matter of intradoctrinal progress in improving the development of positions rather than extradoctrinal progress in settling the conflict between them to everyone's satisfaction.

Once we abandon consensus as an inappropriate desideratum for philosophy, we are left with the result that by every *appropriate* standard, the discipline is indeed progressive, at least in principle. And this abandonment of consensus is no defect. For, given the very nature of the philosophical enterprise, this putative desideratum does not constitute an appropriate goal. It makes no sense to ask for that whose attainment is *in principle* infeasible.

## 4. The Contrast of Scientific Consensus

Faced with pervasive conflicts, a strategy common to philosophers of the most different persuasions is to resort to pragmatism. Thinkers of otherwise profoundly different views—the voluntarist William James, the neo-Kantian C.I. Lewis, the positivist Rudolf Carnap—all agree that conflict-resolution in philosophy should proceed by finding that approach which best conduces to satisfying our practical purposes. As James was wont to put it, "ideas become true just insofar as they help us to get into satisfactory relation with other parts of our experience."[6] And so the idea arises of using *satisfaction* as an arbiter among conflicting doctrines.

But there are good reasons to think that this strategy will not work. For one thing, many or most philosophical debates relate to issues that are relatively remote from practical affairs. Bishop Berkeley would be the first to deny that an immaterialist is committed to principles of bridge building that would serve to differentiate him from an atomist. More significantly, however, what counts as "working out" satisfactorily for philosopher No. 1 may not qualify as such for philosopher No. 2. This is a topic on which there is once again the most profound disagreement. Finally, even if pragmatic considerations *did* militate for one doctrine over against another, the adherents of the latter will presumably disdain to give them weight, loftily maintaining that the object of philosophical inquiry is to grasp the truth, not to feather our nests. The force of pragmatic efficacy (benign practical implications) as a governing desideratum itself is an issue of controversy. Recourse to praxis reflects a deeply evaluative posture—the probative efficacy of praxis is a party to the dispute rather than a neutral arbiter capable of settling it.

Pragmatism accordingly does not qualify as a destroyer of relativistic pluralism in philosophy.[7] Because the issues addressed are so different, this powerful constraint to *scientific* uniformity is denied us in philosophy. In philosophy, unlike science, the very bearing of praxis is itself a matter that belongs in the agenda of debate. The long and short of it is that there is no uncontested, value-external way of resolving this value-laden issue of probative methodology in philosophy.

Someone might put a pejorative gloss on all this: "In science we get real knowledge; in philosophy mere conjecture. In science we get at the real truth of things; in philosophy merely at people's variable ideas about the truth. In science we 'learn' and 'come to know', in philosophy we 'think' and have 'opinions'." But this invidious comparison does not really stand up. Even in science, where consensus is a realistic

---

6. William James, *Pragmatism* (New York, 1907), p. 58.
7. In the domain of *scientific* knowledge, however, the situation is crucially different in this regard. See the author's *Methodological Pragmatism* (Oxford, 1977).

# THE STRIFE OF SYSTEMS
*The Problem of Unattainable Consensus*

prospect, absoluteness does not seem to be within our reach. After all, drastic changeability reigns in science. The theoretical truths of science are, often as not, *filiae temporis:* the "scientific truth" of one generation is the "gross error" and "roughest guesswork" of the next. Where are the "scientific truths" of one hundred years ago? Where will *our* "scientific truths" be a thousand years hence? We certainly do not have the least assurance that our distant successors will deem our best efforts any more correct or definitive than we ourselves think those of our predecessors.

The fact that interpersonal objectivity is an index of warrant in natural science reflects the character of science rather than the character of warrant as such. The prizing of contemporaneous consensus needs—and *in science* obtains—the backing of a suitable rationale. Here there is a cogent epistemologico-metaphysical account of why consensus matters to validity, and it is not based merely on conformity, fashion, group pressure, or some other sort of flawed thinking. We demand consensus in science because we are entitled to expect to have it on the basis of pragmatic considerations inherent in the enterprise. The controls we impose via the ground rules of observation, experiment, and theoretical triangulation are such that our claims are accessible always, everywhere, and (in principle) to everyone. The very nature of the discipline in point of its data, its issues, and its methods is such that we would expect its claims to be the focus of intersubjective agreement.

But the pragmatic considerations crucial for science simply do not apply in philosophy. For here they are part of the problem rather than the solution. The issue of the nature and objectives of philosophy as a discipline is itself one of its controversial topics. The crucial difference between science and philosophy lies in the consideration that consensus *within* a discipline is only a sensible and appropriate requirement where there is consensus *about* the discipline. The circumstances that render the quest for consensus in science not only desirable but effectively necessary are altogether missing in philosophy.

Peirce never tired of insisting that if there is a truth of the matter at all, all serious inquirers will ultimately come to agreement about it. If this is indeed so, then all the indications are that there indeed is no "truth of the matter" in philosophy. But it is not quite so. For in philosophy (unlike science) there is no reason to think that all serious inquiry must ultimately lead to the same conclusion.

In the strictly factual inquiries of science, the justificatory regress of standards ends in a situation of agreed fixity. He who does not simply *accept* certain particular aims (description, explanation, prediction, control) is just not doing science. He excommunicates himself from the community of practitioners by taking into hand a different practice. (Even here there are *some* borderline issues: parapsychology and creation science, for example.) But the boundaries are by and large fixed. Now, while there is indeed an inside and outside to philosophy, a difference between philosophy and nonphilosophy (between philosophy and geography, say), the boundaries that separate them are so murky that we have little alternative to accepting as a philosopher anyone who claims to be doing philosophy and whose discourse has some connection with the traditional issues of this field. (Whether or not he is a *good* philosopher according to our own evaluative lights is of course a very different issue.)

In science, we have a situation where the community agrees in essentials because that agreement *defines* the community. Those who opt out of the consensus effectively opt out of the discipline as well. But in philosophy the matter stands on a very different footing. To be sure, what distinguishes philosophy from science is not that cognitive values have no role in science (they surely do!), but that their role there is comparatively noncontroversial—largely fixed by the very nature of the discipline as a cognitive enterprise. The definitive goals of science—description, explanation, prediction, and control—engender pragmatic constraints which are strong enough to enforce consensus regarding the range of operative values. Intersubjectivity, repeatability, observer-independence, and so forth, are elements of the value structure of science because they are demanded by the goals that define this project as a characteristic venture. But this sort of situation does not obtain in philosophy.

There is thus a deep difference between science and philosophy. For in science there are purely factual and objective monitors of adequacy—namely the pragmatic issues of observation and experiment, prediction and control. No such factual monitors are available to us in philosophy. And this has important consequences. It means that by studying how science *is* done we can (reasonably expect to) learn how science *ought to be* done. But this is not so in philosophy, where no theory-external monitors of adequacy are available.

Its prominence as an intellectual paradigm since the seventeenth century notwithstanding, science is simply the wrong model for philosophical inquiry. Its demands for consensus—for repeatable observations, reproducible experiments, interpersonally universal data, and objective conclusions—are simply inapplicable in a field where value espousal must exert its differential pressure. In value-oriented disciplines we must be prepared for diversity because (*ex hypothesi*) our only avenue to warrant is via the potentially differentiated normative route. Intersubjective consensus is a *sine qua non* of warrant only in those fields (like science) where there is good reason to expect a linkage between objectivity and warrant, and certainly not in those fields where we have every reason to think that such a link cannot possibly exist.

The salient difference between science and philosophy is not that scientific argumentation is value-free and that of philosophy value-laden, but that the standards one uses in scientific reasoning (at a given state of the art) are seen as mandatory; to reject them then and there is to reject science. And so one's reasons for rejecting them cannot be scientific; to abandon the prevailing standards is to abandon science and do something else—to withdraw for the community. (An absolutism of sorts is thus perfectly appropriate in science.) But in philosophy the matter is altogether different. To propose abandoning the prevailing standards is not to withdraw from philosophy but to practice it—at any rate as long as the abandonment is supported by reasons. Unlike the situation in science, there is no point in philosophy at which further value disagreement carries one outside the boundaries of the field. Philosophy's all-encompassing nature means that deliberations regarding its standards are themselves philosophical arguments. All arguments for rejecting the enterprise are, to philosophy, philosophical arguments. The most the sceptic can do is give up the enterprise—without reason. And the absolutist is left without an essential prop for his position—a natural stopping point for the regress of justification.

In contradistinction to philosophy, science is an inherently consensus-governed endeavor. The very nature of the discipline enforces a uniformity of cognitive values; there are communally agreed standards as to what counts as a significant question, what counts as having an answer to it, and what counts as a good argument for or against that answer. All this is governed by the theory-external aims of the enterprise in terms of prediction and control over nature.[8] Because of this uniformity, inherent in the nature of an enterprise where observation rather than evaluation is pivotal, scientists are able to achieve a substantial measure of consensus on the substantive issues.

In natural science we thus aim at consensus not so much because we prize it in its own right but because the character of the discipline makes it an index of adequacy. We think of "nature" in such a way that if something isn't objective and interpersonal, it can't be part of natural science. The repeatability of experiments is prized in science

---

8. On these issues, cf. my *Methodological Pragmatism*.

because it represents a crucial index for whether or not we've got things right. In philosophy, however, there is no objective and uncontroversially value-free standard.[9] One man's "success" is another man's "failure."

If we contrast a "purely objective," factually consensus-geared *scientific* enterprise with the "subjective" and value-intensive family of *humanistic* enterprises, then philosophy is squarely on the latter side. Its deliberations and findings are substantially conditioned by the value perspectives of its practitioners. And cognitive values are matters of allegiance rather than observation. (This, of course, is not *criticism* of the humanities but a recognition of their essential difference from natural science. Whether being "value free" is itself of value is one of the evaluative "ideological" issues that pose quintessentially philosophical questions.)

When we articulate a position in philosophy, we create a structure that is limited in its scope. It will never be able to accommodate everybody. Only those who share our cognitive values (or can somehow be persuaded to do so) can be brought under its roof. But if the structure is built well upon a solid foundation it can (in principle) last forever. Whatever shocks it may sustain, it will always be possible in principle to do the necessary work of renovation and shoring up. And if it affords a sufficiently attractive habitation, there may well one day be some members of the community tempted to occupy it and carry out the necessary work. Philosophical theories are not temporary and transient in the manner of scientific ones. Being more loose and flexible they are also incomparably more durable. That is why "progress" in philosophy and progress in science are very different sorts of things. Science, too, aims at something absolute and definitive, but it yields no more than the best that can be done in this particular stage of an evolving state of the art. Our successors of generations hence will think our present science no more correct than we ourselves deem the science of generations past. The difference, however, is that while science cannot establish a consensus *across* generations (though it does pretty well at intragenerational consensus), philosophy cannot establish a consensus *within* generations (though it can attain broad intragenerational consensus within the framework of ongoing traditions).

Science has the advantage in point of extensiveness. Occasional matters of current controversy at the cutting edge of the frontier apart,

---

9. Already in the early 1680s, Leibniz wrote that the reason why we progress better in scientific rather than philosophical matters is that in the *mathematica*, unlike the *metaphysica*, we can monitor adequacy through experimentation. See G. W. Leibniz, *Textes inédits*, ed. G. Grua, vol. I (Paris, 1948), p. 31.

it is able to realize communal consensus to the point of virtual unanimity. But it pays for this on the side of duration. Scientific doctrines live a mothlike existence—they have their brief flutter in the light before being consumed in the flames of innovation and progress. When in the course of innovation the communal consensus wanders off elsewhere, the old position is abandoned on the scrapheap of obsolete, no longer relevant doctrines whose interest is "only historical." Precisely because the scientific community operates more or less *en bloc*, there is no fragmentation into splinter groups to carry on the work of pouring new wine into old bottles.

Following the siren-call of science is bound to erode the sense of legitimacy for the value-bound humanist, the philosopher included. It engenders the attitude that if claims are not objectively substantiable they are not worth having. Such an attitude engenders a lack of confidence in one's own project: a failure of nerve, confidence, and commitment.

The prominent place of science in modern life makes such an attitude toward philosophy enormously tempting. Yet the philosopher, with his dedication to theoretical clarity, should be the last to succumb to this temptation. The "facts" to which science addresses itself arise from intersubjectively available observation rather than from a value-sensibility that is potentially different from person to person. The phenomena that science takes as data for its theory-projection and theory-testing are publicly accessible to man *qua* man, rather than those which are in some degree subjective and personal—emerging from a particular background of experiential conditioning. Accordingly, science strives to be "value free" in minimizing further recourse to values once it has fixed upon those fundamental cognitive values that characterize it as the cognitive enterprise it is (viz., description, explanation, prediction, and control). Value-appreciation—how things strike people against the informational setting of their personal (idiosyncratic) experiences or their sociocultural background—is something science deliberately leaves aside to concentrate on the impersonally measurable features of things. The value-dimension of experience—our recognition as such of those features of things in virtue of which we deem them significant or interesting or worthwhile—remains outside the range of science's concerns. But in philosophy we cannot put them aside through the very nature of the case. Where different enterprises are at issue, different ground-rules must obtain.

The philosopher should thus be the first to question the validity of natural science as a model for cognition in general and to deny the appropriateness of the analogy between science and philosophy as cognitive disciplines. If his field is indeed a member of the value-intensive humanities, and if the cognitive situation in philosophy is accordingly profoundly unlike that of science, then why on earth should its failure to answer to the scientific paradigm be taken to indicate a lack of legitimacy?

## 5. Progress in the Absence of Consensus

We face the situation of the following apory:

(1) There is progress in philosophy.
(2) Philosophy is a mode of rational inquiry.
(3) Progress in rational inquiry is contingent on and measurable through movement toward consensus.
(4) There is no movement toward consensus in philosophy.

Since (4) may be taken as a given, three alternatives confront us:

(1)–abandonment: Seeing philosophizing as an enterprise of inquiry that is doomed to stagnation—a possible but futile endeavor. Philosophy is a vessel hopelessly becalmed at the very outset of its ambitious voyage.
(2)–abandonment: Abandonment of philosophy as a venture in rational inquiry, either seeing it as a delusion (scepticism) or as a venture in enlightenment or spiritual uplift or some other sort of noncognitive project.
(3)–abandonment: Severing the supposed linkage between progressiveness and success in cultivating the discipline on the one hand and the evolution of a rationally enforced consensus of the other.

The stance of orientational pluralism is an unhesitating endorsement of this last alternative; it is prepared to disconnect progressiveness from consensus.

In philosophy, progress is confined to the technical side in a way that leaves the substantive issues unsettled for the community as a whole. Philosophers do not make *interdoctrinal* progress in settling the rivalry of alternative positions to arrive at an achieved consensus. But they do (or *can*) make *intradoctrinal* progress. With the passage of time and effort the exposition of any given position does (or can and should be) continually more subtle, nuanced, sophisticated—better armed at various points and better prepared to meet objections and attacks. It can afford an increasingly secure and comfortable home *for us*, even though we recognize that others prefer a very different sort of habitation.

The account of the development of any philosophical tradition is a story of the ongoing rejection of simple solutions. The overall process has a perfectly standard structure—it is a matter of ever-greater complexity, of adding distinction after distinction, moving toward ever-greater complexity. There is always more to be said. More problems can always be raised, further objections made and countered. The scholastic treatise with its dialectic of objections and replies and its sequential deployment of useful distinctions is therefore a good paradigm. The labor is potentially infinite.

There is an "arms race" in philosophy fueled by a technological escalation of sorts. One cannot fight the battles of the present with the armaments of the past. Those who want to propound old positions in the changed circumstances of the disicpline can no longer put them forward satisfactorily in the old way. The discussion must be pressed forward to a new level of sophistication. (Of course, the fact that old positions demand new formulations does not mean that they must be abandoned *in toto*.)

No doubt there is something uncomfortable about this situation. Technical progress is not an unquestionable benefit. As the articulation of a philosophical position becomes more subtle, nuanced, and sophisticated, it also becomes increasingly complex. It requires more and more conceptual machinery that piles epicycle on epicycle. It is far from clear that such complexity deserves an unqualified welcome. A veritable labor of Sisyphus confronts us. An ever-receding horizon separates where we are from where we would ideally like to be in philosophy. We cannot bring matters to a satisfactory conclusion; philosophical disputes never reach the point of natural closure. It is only the disputants that become exhausted, never the issues.

This never-ending debate often repels younger workers coming into the field. It explains the perennial popularity of a Descartes or a Hume or a positivist sceptic who offers to sweep all the old rubbish away and to free us from having to bother with all those endless discussions and arguments and distinctions. The voice of the philosophical iconoclast is welcome in every age. But his impact is always transitory. In philosophical deliberation there simply is no satisfactory way to liberate ourselves from the burdens of increasing complexity.

Is this increasing technical sophistication to be lamented? Progress in cognitive technology, like progress in ordinary technology, doubtless has its dark side and is not always unqualifiedly welcome.[10] But there is little we can do save accept the inevitable.

The library shelves of philosophy are bound to multiply no less than those of science and of scholarship. Progress is only possible through complication. Once we are embarked on the journey of inquiry, there is no way of returning to the comfortable simplicities of an earlier age.[11] Evolving complexity is not sought for its own sake; it is

---

10. Cf. chap. 1 of Kekes, *The Nature of Philosophy*, for an expression of dismay about some aspects of philosophical "progress."

11. For an interesting discussion of these issues, see William J. Rapoport, "Unsolvable Problems and Philosophical Progress," *American Philosophical Quarterly* 19 (1982): 289–98.

the inevitable consequence of the nature of the problems and of the intellectual instrumentation available to us for dealing with them. And of course in philosophy, as elsewhere, progress takes its toll. To unqualifiedly embrace the theses and arguments of an earlier era—ignoring the debates and discussions that have intervened between that day and ours—is to mark oneself as incompetent, as unable to put the tools of one's discipline to good effect.

Philosophy certainly does progress in forcing the discussion of the issues through to new levels of difficulty and sophistication. Amidst the vexation of controversy and the disappointment of failures to convince, we do arrive at increasingly less deficient formulations. The crucial fact that the old moves in the game cannot effectively be repeated unchanged in the newly attained state of the art shows that philosophers have not labored in vain. The controversy may be inconclusive, but it is so only because our opponents are forced to ever higher levels of sophistication through the development of our own position, with the result that this position itself is articulated in an ever less unsatisfactory and more fully developed way.

## 6. Is Consensus Dispensable?

We must confront the pivotal question of whether a branch of inquiry can possibly be worthwhile given that we cannot expect it to issue in agreement among its practitioners.

The proper answer in the case of philosophy is an emphatic *yes*. For only by engaging in the venture are we able to secure for ourselves well-wrought answers to those important "big questions"—answers that can yield rational satisfaction, if not to everyone, at any rate to us. Those monumental conceptions of "truth," "knowledge," "value," "beauty," "justice" are things we want to know about; nay, as rational creatures *need* to know about. No doubt philosophy is born in wonder and puzzlement and is destined always to remain there to some extent. But better this than the vacuity of ignorance—even the sophisticated ignorance of uncommitted polymathy.

Nothing inherent in the realistic appreciation of the situation offered by orientational pluralism need undermine the sense of legitimacy of those who cultivate this field in the pursuit of substantive solutions. They are entitled—fully and rationally entitled—to maintain an assured confidence in the validity of this enterprise. Nothing about the fact that *their* solutions are destined not to emerge as *everyone's* solutions need give them pause.

To be sure, the community does not "solve" the problems of philosophy any more than it "solves" the problems of life. Those basic disputes about knowledge and reality, value and duty, and so on, that constitute the extraphilosophical basis of philosophizing are ever with us. In philosophy we generally continue to play the same old games, but we play them at ever-increasing levels of difficulty and sophistication. The progress made in philosophy is of a kind that does not yield widened consensus but deepened understanding.

# 12

# Reactions to Pluralism

## 1. An Inventory of Responses

The most serious indictment of philosophy, so we are told, is its own history.[1] Dilthey wrote: "Claims to the universal validity of philosophical systems are destroyed by this unfolding of historical awareness even more thoroughly than by the strife of (contemporaneous) systems."[2] Every philosophical system lays implicit claim to the unrestricted validity of its assertions. Yet the claims of each are countermanded by the no less emphatic and confident claims of its rivals. The discipline seems to be destroyed by its own fertility; the plurality of competing systems makes a mockery of their pretensions.

What is one to make of this pluralistic proliferation of philosophical doctrines?

It is, of course, possible to deny pluralism outright. One can adopt the dogmatic view that only one philosophical position exists—at any rate, only one worth taking seriously. Kant put the claims of this position squarely:

One must ask whether there can really be more than one philosophy.... Objectively, inasmuch as there can be only one human reason, so likewise there cannot be many philosophies; that is, only one true system of philosophy based on principles is possible, however variously and often contradictorily men may have philosophized over one and the same proposition.... When, therefore, someone announces a system of philosophy as a new creation of his own, this amounts to his saying that there has been no other prior philosophy at all; for if he were to admit that there was another (real) philosophy, then

---

1. "Der ärgste Feind aller Philosophie ist ihre eigene Geschichte" (Leisegang, *Denkformen*, p. 455).
2. Wilhelm Dilthey, *Gesammelte Schriften*, vol. VIII (Stuttgart and Göttingen, 1960), p. 121.

there would be two distinct philosophies on the same subject, and this is self-contradictory.[3]

Reason is by its very nature *universal*.

The post-Kantian tradition gave a special twist to this "one reason, one philosophy" dogma. Striving for generality through inclusiveness, it took the stance that there is but a single grand "position of reason as such" that somehow embraces all meaningful alternatives in one overarching whole.

On such a view, there is actually only one body of philosophy. Disagreement is simply the result of error—usually the product of too superficial a scrutiny of the issues. The various disputants in philosophical controversy are really saying (or *trying* to say) the same thing; their basic agreement is masked by mere differences in formulation or emphasis. Ultimately, with sufficiently careful and sympathetic efforts at understanding, all the quarreling parties are bound to come to realize their fundamental agreement. Though small minds of myopic vision may fail to recognize this because they lack the breadth of vision to see the whole, the fact remains that all of the great thinkers who have contributed to *philosophia perennis* agree on the essentials of the great tradition. Those who stand outside the grand consensus are just so many ships that have lost their way in the fog of loose thinking; they are drifting about aimlessly while the grand consensus of genuine philosophy sails majestically on its true course.

A pretty vision, this! But hardly one that grasps the realities of a situation in which different schools of thought all too plainly arrive at radically conflicting positions with equal fervor and dedication. Disagreement is simply a fact of life in philosophy, because different cognitive orientations lead to different, mutually inconsistent ways of resolving the aporetic conflicts in which philosophical problems are rooted.

This circumstance is illustrated by the very issue that concerns us in this book. For there is no getting around the fact that the pluralistic approach to philosophical conflict is itself only one among others. Confronted with a choice among alternative positions, three basic lines of response lie open (see table 4). These several approaches exhaust the spectrum of possibilities; any response will fall somewhere within this range.[4] Let us examine these positions more closely.

3. Immanuel Kant, *The Metaphysic of Morals*, pt. II (vol. VI, Akad. ed., p. 207).
4. This tripartite division was initially proposed by the young German philosopher, Eberhard Rogge, who was killed at the age of thirty-three in the course of military service during World War II. His posthumous *Axiomatik alles möglichen Philosophierens* (Meisenheim am Glan, 1950) is an interesting book that does not deserve the oblivion which has heretofore been its fate. The three positions here characterized as scepticism, doctrinalism, and syncretism were designated by Rogge as positivism, rationalism, and hermeneutics (respectively).

*Table 4*
AN INVENTORY OF POSSIBLE APPROACHES TO A CHOICE AMONG RIVAL PHILOSOPHICAL POSITIONS

The view that there simply are no (genuine) alternatives at all is DOGMATISM. The view that there indeed are viable alternatives, however greatly they may differ in merit, is PLURALISM. It has many varieties.

Faced with a plurality of distinct alternatives, one's approach may be:

I. To adopt *none*. To say "a plague on all your houses," refusing to commit oneself, and abstaining from taking any definite position whatsoever. This is the stance of SCEPTICISM which has two main versions:

—AGNOSTIC SCEPTICISM, which sees the issues as beyond the powers of human reason to resolve.

—NIHILISTIC SCEPTICISM, which sees the issues as inherently meaningless and the conflict between positions as a mere sham.

II. To adopt *one* particular alternative. This "one-to-a-customer" approach may generically be characterized as DOCTRINALISM. It can be implemented in many different ways:

(1) By an ARATIONALISM that looks to the rationally indifferent adoption of one alternative. The distinction of right or wrong is seen as inapplicable; there is just no room for any substantively preferential considerations, no question of being rationally well grounded or ill grounded. This sort of view can take many different forms. For it can hold that the range of alternatives is effectively reduced to one by nonrational constraints that are inherent in

(A) the psychology of the individual: his temperament or disposition or such

—PSYCHOLOGISM

(B) the cultural-social-intellectual context; the social constraints of the particular place and time (Zeitgeist)

—HISTORICISM

(C) the general course of historical tendencies

—HISTORICAL CONVERGENTISM

(2) By taking the stance that one particular theory within the range of alternatives can be shown by considerations of reason to be superior to all the rest (RATIONALISM), and specifically that this can be done by:

(A) considerations of evidential reason alone

—ABSOLUTISM or EVIDENTIAL MONISM (impersonal and presuppositionless objectivism)

(B) considerations of axiological (normative or evaluative) reason relative to the value orientation of the individual

—VALUE-ORIENTATIONAL MONISM (personalistic and relativistic)

III. To adopt *all*. To try for a grand supersynthesis that conjoins all alternatives.

—SYNCRETISM

*Notes to Table 4:*

There is also the somewhat more relaxed version of II, which is based on the approach: adopt *some but not all;* simply pick and choose. This response is too eccentric to be worth taking seriously, but it would, in any event, simply yield a series of less determinate counterparts to the spectrum of II-positions.

RELATIVISM and PERSONALISM are cross-classifications. Personalism collects together those doctrinalist approaches that provide for person-variable ("subjective") preferability, namely II(1), II(2)A, and II(2)B; relativism collects those doctrinalist approaches that exclude preference on objective evidential grounds, namely all of II apart from II(2)A.

ECLECTICISM is a form of DOCTRINALISM: it constructs a single uniform position by selecting and combining elements from several alternative doctrines. It thus differs crucially from SYNCRETISM which proceeds not by way of a discriminating *selection* but by a brute-force *conjunction.* (Cf. the article in Lalande's *Vocabulaire de la philosophie,* 9th ed. [Paris, 1962].)

## 2. Scepticism

The sceptic holds that the various rival alternatives simply kill each other off, that when all is said and done, no party to the controversy remains alive to claim victory. The sceptic's approach toward the contending positions is thus even-handed and egalitarian: they are all equally good because equally worthless.

In particular, the Sceptics of Greek antiquity maintained that a situation of "balancing out" (*isostheneia*) obtains in most cognitive disciplines—philosophy preeminently included. For every argument in favor of a doctrinal contention, some intrinsically no less cogent, equally plausible case can be built up for the contrary, and they insisted that this indicates that none of the alternatives merit acceptance.[5] Mutually opposing doctrines are mutually annihilating. And so the only rational course is a total suspension of judgment (*epochē*).[6]

It might seem that a metaphilosophical pluralism must inevitably lead to such a scepticism regarding philosophical issues. Since distinct positions are always available on any given philosophical issue, it might appear that resolving problems is at best a matter of arbitrary choice

---

5. The ancient sceptics backed this position by the analogy of vision: "Since, then, all apparent objects are viewed in a certain place, and from a certain distance, or in a certain position, and each of these conditions produces a great divergency in the sense-impressions, as we mentioned above, we shall be compelled . . . to end up in suspension of judgment. For in fact anyone who purposes to give the preference to any of these impressions will be attempting the impossible" (Sextus Empiricus, *Outlines of Pyrrhonism,* bk. 1, 121).

6. As Sextus Empiricus put it (in the special case of philosophical theology): "Different people have different and discordant beliefs about the gods, so that neither are *all* of them to be trusted, because of their inconsistency, nor *some* of them, because of their equipollence (*isostheneia*)" (*Adv. Math.,* bk. IX, 192).

among rationally equivalent alternatives. If there were always a canceling balance or equivalence among rival solutions, there would indeed be no justification for coming down on one side or the other. A sceptical suspension of judgment would then be the appropriate response. But this, of course, is not so—at any rate as orientational pluralism sees the matter. For once we assume a probative-value orientation, the purported equivalence disappears. The plurality of "available" alternatives notwithstanding, one of them is uniquely appropriate.

The theme of scepticism revolves about the following inconsistent triad:

(1) Reason can (in principle) settle all meaningful questions decisively.
(2) Reason cannot resolve philosophical questions.
(3) Philosophical questions are meaningful.

Committed to item (2) of this aporetic cluster, the sceptic offers us a choice between:

(1)–rejection: The issues involved in philosophical controversies lie beyond the limited powers of human reason—they are simply *ultra vires* for us. Rational warrant for taking any particular stance cannot in principle be provided (agnostic sceptics: Montaigne, Hume).

and

(3)–rejection: Controversy regarding philosophical issues is a mock battle. Taking a substantive position in philosophy is *senseless* because the issues involved are actually *meaningless* (nihilistic sceptics: Kant, positivism, Wittgenstein's "bewitchment by language" theory).

The sceptic jumps from the consideration that philosophical positions cannot be justified by appeal to absolute and uncontroversial standards to the conclusion that they cannot be justified at all. (Or, differently viewed, he insists that only impersonally objective justification, which is unavailable in philosophy, could ever qualify as acceptable justification.) He fails to see that rationalism and relativism are compatible, that rational justification can be evaluative, orientation-relative, multiform. He does not see (or does not admit) that the ground rules for *evidential*, scientific, impersonally objective reason cannot settle matters on the side of *normative*, evaluative, commitment-presupposing deliberations. In sum, the sceptic fails to recognize that (2) should give way to:

(2') Strictly evidential reason cannot resolve philosophical questions; but normative reason can indeed do so—albeit only in a way that is commitment relative and not invariant with respect to evaluative presuppositions.

Scepticism of the *agnostic* mode concedes that there may be a truth of the matter but insists that we cannot possibly come to know it. The questions at issue are legitimate questions, but their pursuit is pointless since their resolution is in principle beyond our grasp. The most we can learn from philosophy is something about the limits of our understanding.[7] As the agnostic sceptic sees it, philosophy teaches one useful lesson, at any rate—the ultimate futility of philosophizing. It has always been a characteristic sceptical device to argue on both sides of a question, as is indeed always possible in philosophy.[8] Then, once all the pro-considerations are matched with reciprocal con-considerations, the agnostic sceptic insists that cancellation occurs and that suspense of judgment—*epochē*, total abstinence from any endorsement—becomes the only sensible course. The questions of philosophy lie beyond our capabilities; we cannot answer them and have little alternative but to stand before them in awe. We thus achieve a once-and-for-all resolution of all philosophical problems—for if we accept nothing, there can clearly be no conflict among the things we accept. And so the venture is not pointless, for what we gain in philosophizing is not new knowledge but rather an insight into the limits of our knowledge and the rationale for their existence.

By contrast, *nihilistic* scepticism holds that there just is no truth of the matter in philosophy and that its questions are altogether illegitimate. The very fact that philosophical problems do not admit of any objective and standpoint-free resolution is taken to indicate that they are improper—literally senseless. They must be dismissed holus-bolus as mere pseudoproblems, so that philosophy, as traditionally conducted, is inappropriate and irrational. The whole discussion is literally senseless because there's actually nothing to disagree about. Kant put the problem as follows:

Nothing seems to be clearer than that since one of them (viz., metaphysicians) asserts that the world has a beginning and the other that it has no beginning and is from eternity, one of the two must be in the right. But even if this be so, none the less, since the arguments on both sides are equally clear, it is impossible to decide between them. The parties may be commanded to keep the peace before the tribunal of reason; but the controversy none the less continues.

---

7. "It may be true that some philosophical problems have no solutions. I suspect that this is true of the deepest and oldest of them. They show us the limits of our understanding. In that case such insight as we can achieve depends on maintaining a strong grasp of the problem instead of abandoning it, and coming to understand [the reasons for] the failure of each new attempt at a solution, and of earlier attempts. (That is why we study the work of philosophers like Plato and Berkeley, whose views are accepted by no one.) Unsolvable problems are not for that reason incorrect" (Nagel, *Mortal Questions*, p. xii).

8. See Charlotte L. Stough, *Greek Scepticism* (Berkeley and Los Angeles, 1965), p. 28 and passim.

There can therefore be no way of settling it once and for all and to the satisfaction of both sides, save by their becoming convinced that the very fact of their being able so admirably to refute one another is evidence that they are really quarrelling about nothing, and that a certain transcendental illusion has mocked them with a reality where none is to be found.[9]

As Kant saw it, theoretical reason is simply tilting at windmills in speculative metaphysics:

Instead, therefore, of rushing into the fight, sword in hand, we should rather play the part of the peaceable onlooker, from the safe seat of the critic. The struggle is indeed toilsome to the combatants, but for us can be entertaining; and its outcome—certain to be quite bloodless—must be of advantage as contributing to our theoretical insight. . . . [For] reason is . . . of itself confined and held within limits by reason. . . . In this dialetic no victory is gained that need give us cause for anxiety.[10]

Given this situation, the traditional traffic in philosophical doctrines should be abandoned.

The stance of positivism in general and logical positivism in particular illustrates this nihilistic position: all of speculative philosophy is simply nonsense (*Unsinn*). Ludwig Wittgenstein's "bewitchment by language" approach represents another version of this position. What is needed, in his view, is not to answer philosophical questions but to "cure" people of asking them. Philosophizing of the traditional sort is regarded as a psychological malady—a mental aberration. The only valid sort of philosophizing is that which endeavors to provide an antidote to traditional philosophy.

In recent years such a position has been defended by Morris Lazerowitz. He sees metaphysics as ensnared in deep misunderstandings about ordinary language: "A metaphysician is a verbal magician who is taken in by his own tricks; he is both subtle and inventive with words and blind to what he does with them."[11] Nihilistic scepticism does not propose to *reform* philosophy but to *abandon* it. Using historical stalking horses, Richard Rorty has advocated this position in the following terms:

[Heidegger] does not, like Descartes and Hegel and Husserl and Carnap, say "This is how philosophy has been; let philosophy henceforth be like *this*." Rather, like Nietzsche and Wittgenstein and Dewey, he asks "Given that this is how philosophy has been, what, if anything, can philosophy now be?" Suggesting, as they did, that philosophy may have exhausted its potentialities, he

---

9. Kant, *CPuR*, A501 = B529.
10. Ibid., A 747 = B775.
11. *The Structure of Metaphysics* (London, 1955), p. 79.

asks whether the motives which led to philosophy's existence still exist and whether they should.[12]

Agnostic scepticism holds that philosophizing is a waste of time; nihilistic scepticism holds that it is outright error. But either way, the upshot is substantially the same—we are unable to take any position because "taking a position" is a rationally indefensible step. The great historical body of philosophical discussion may inspire different reactions. Some see it as an interesting conversation piece (Rorty), some as a useless encumbrance (positivists), some as a dangerously infectious substance (Wittgenstein). But in no case is any part of traditional philosophizing worth reckoning with seriously on its own terms in an endeavor to carry the venture forward.

In the sceptic's opinion, the absence of a standpoint-transcending process for resolving the battle of the schools indicates the ultimate futility of the whole enterprise. If *that's* what philosophy is, the game is not worth the candle. The rational course is a refusal to engage, to depart the arena of philosophical controversy and refrain altogether from forming doctrines and endorsing theses by remaining opinion-less, *adoxastos,* as the ancient Sceptics put it. We would do well to abandon the whole project and go on to something more profitable.[13]

The sceptic will be no man's dupe. The road to scepticism is paved with good intentions. But once we arrive there, we are left empty handed. Philosophical scepticism requires us to forego any attempt to provide answers to those momentous questions we have about the world and our place in it. In thus abandoning the project as a rational enterprise, we defeat the purposes for which philosophy was instituted in the first place, thereby frustrating our deepest cognitive aims and aspirations.

In controversy, the sceptic always has an easy time of it. His denial that there is any adequate criterion or standard of probative cogency means that there is nothing we can use in opposing him without begging the question against him. His position is secure from assault. But it is only secure because of its vacuity; the fact that the citadel is

---

12. Rorty, *Consequences of Pragmatism,* p. 40.
13. For the ancient sceptic, this "something more profitable" was the ordinary beliefs of the aphilosophical plain man. "For it is sufficient, I think, to live by experience and without subscribing to [theoretical] beliefs (*adoxastos*), according to common practices and preconceptions, suspending judgment about those statements that issue from dogmatic subtlety and are further of recoursed from the usage of ordinary life" (Sextus Empircius, *Outlines of Pyrrhonism,* bk. II, 246.) With Renaissance sceptics, it is not to mundane life that we should turn, but to religion. Modern sceptics would have us turn to science, and those of the future perhaps to *belles lettres.* There is nothing fixed about cognitive values!

impregnable is immaterial because there is nothing in it to defend. The great advantage of rejecting scepticism is that this step alone enables us to reclaim for rational inquiry important questions that would otherwise be intractable.

To be sure, the option of *abandoning* philosophy is always there—and the sceptic licks his chops at the prospect. He is only too eager to have us turn to other pursuits—to history or literature or mathematics or woodworking. But we must not fool ourselves into thinking that in *ignoring* the problems of philosophy we have somehow dealt with them. Life without philosophy is undoubtedly possible, as is life without science or art or religion or other such major projects of human endeavor. But this is so only at the cost of intellectual impoverishment—of stunting our nature as rational animals and resting content with being less than we could or should endeavor to be. The life of the mind, of which rational inquiry is an integral component, is an essential constituent of our conception of the human good. And rational inquiry leads inexorably to philosophizing. For we engage in philosophy not (merely) because it is intellectually diverting—a game one can play for its own sake. It orients our thought, clarifies our values, guides our actions. Philosophy matters because it clarifies and systematizes our thought about issues that matter.

Moreover, if we want to think coherently and consistently—if those cognitive values of rational inquiry that underlie orientational pluralism matter to us—then there is no getting away from philosophy. The discipline is embarked on an inquiry to resolve problems regarding the coherence of our beliefs. To abandon philosophy is to rest content with incoherence.

Scepticism roots in the following apory:

(1) Adopting a solution (to a philosophical problem) is appropriate.
(2) It is never appropriate to pay an epistemic price (to risk error or court controversy in taking a "controversial" stance).
(3) No solution is available that does not require us to pay an epistemic price.

Now, (3) is simply a fact of life; there is no way of getting around it. And so we face the dilemma of a choice between abandoning (1) or (2). The sceptic hews to (2) and jettisons (1)—with dubious consistency he adopts the posture of nonadoption.

Orientational pluralism, by contrast, drops (2) and asks us to be prepared to "pay the price" of taking a perspectival, potentially person-differential stance. It does so because it sees the sceptic's alternative of (1)-rejection as unrealistic and unpalatable. In the standard cases we begin with a question and proceed to consider *all* of the conceivable

# THE STRIFE OF SYSTEMS
*Reactions to Pluralism*

*Table 5*
ALTERNATIVES FOR A GLOBAL EXPLANATION OF NATURAL LAWS
(Why Is Nature's Law System as It Is?)

1. The question is illegitimate (rejectionism).
2. The question is legitimate but inherently unsolvable (mystificationism).
3. The question is legitimate and solvable. But the resolution lies in the fact that *there just is no explanation*. The world's law structure is in the final analysis reasonless. The laws just are as they are; that's all there is to it. And this brute fact eliminates any need for explanation (arationalism).
4. The question is legitimate and solvable, and a satisfactory explanation indeed exists. But it resides in an explanatory principle that is itself outside the range of (normal) laws—as it must be to avoid vitiating circularity (transcendentalism).

lines of response thereto (see table 5). We survey all of the possibilities and "box the compass" of available alternatives. And if this is competently done, the sceptic is left with no option; there is simply no way to get outside the range of alternatives, no *further* direction in which to turn. Whatever balancing there is occurs only at the higher, metaphilosophical level when we abstract from our cognitive values and consequently from our doctrinal commitments as well.

An orientational pluralist certainly recognizes that alternatives to his position exist. And he acknowledges that when one "steps backward" (so to speak) from the arena of controversy and abstracts from one's commitment to a particular evaluative orientation, then one must recognize that a case can also be built up for other, conflicting positions. But *this* sort of disengagement at the *communal* level—which *brackets out*, as it were, our own orientational commitments—does not constitute a cogent reason for a suspension of judgment (*epoché*) at the *personal* level of philosophical deliberation itself, where these commitments are very much in place. It shows that philosophy at large must suspend judgment, but not that philosophers should do so. Orientational pluralism accordingly rejects scepticism. It insists that at the ground-floor level of philosophical controversy—where we do and must possess an evaluative plausibility orientation—a situation of indifference or balance does not obtain.

## 3. Arationalism

Faced with a plurality of alternative doctrines, the sceptic rejects all alike, the doctrinalist endorses just one of them. But why this particular possibility? One line of response here is that of an arationalism that runs roughly as follows:

Philosophy is a valid cognitive enterprise, and in such matters we do indeed want to have answers. Not wishing to go empty-handed, we must take a position. But reason alone does not dictate any one position; from the standpoint of rationality as such, it is a matter of complete indifference which alternative is adopted. So you just "pays your money and takes your choice." At bottom, all the alternatives are of equal value, and so it ultimately doesn't really matter which one we pick. We cannot choose among doctrines for rationally cogent reasons. To be sure, this does not mean that we cannot choose at all. After all, the starting point that serves as a basis of reasoning can, as such, never itself be justified by reasoning; it is simply a matter of arbitrary decision. We simply choose this or that, making a selection that is indifferent, at any rate from the *rational* point of view—there may be psychological or historical or sociological constraints but not ones that bind in the order of probative rationality. The selection of one alternative over the others hinges on an extrarational basis of preference. Nothing more fundamental is at stake.

This is the position of *arationalism*. It sees the philosopher's adoption of one alternative as something arbitrary and indifferent from the rational point of view, being ultimately grounded not in *reasons* but in some determinative facet of a philosopher's situation, such as

—the psychology of the individual (psychologism),
—the sociocultural context or Zeitgeist (historicism), or
—the siren call of economic interest (Marxism).

We are enjoined to the view that people are led to their doctrinal positions through factors that operate in the order of causes rather than reasons—that they are induced to take particular positions not through reasons (which are always a matter of rationalization and "false consciousness") but through motivating forces that operate extrarationally in the order of efficient causality. As arationalism sees it, reason mongering and the development of arguments and rationales are simply delusive irrelevancies—a matter of "false consciousness." "Philosophy is nothing more than the sham-battles of systems of rationalizations, a clash of personalities masquerading as rational discussion."[14]

Arationalism accordingly holds that we can seriously espouse a particular position but that the justification for doing so does not proceed through *reasoning*. It is closely cognate to scepticism, but it represents a scepticism of process rather than product. Human reason is seen as inadequate—too feeble to accomplish the task on its own. Some fundamentally extrarational impetus ("will," "instinct," "sensibility," "natural inclination," or some such) is the appropriate instrument of validation. Popular in the last century in reaction to the exaggerated rationalism-

---

14. John Passmore, "The Idea of the History of Philosophy," *History and Theory*, Supplementary Volume 5 (1965), p. 26. Passmore is here stating a possible view, not his own.

of Hegel, this sort of line was espoused by such thinkers as Schopenhauer, Kierkegaard, Nietzsche, James, and Bergson.

It is difficult to bring oneself to see arationalism in a favorable light. Its decisive defect is that it commits an unjustifiable assimilation of *values* to mere *tastes*.

After all, the issues controverted between philosophical positions are transparently important; indeed they are the most *momentous* issues that confront us in the intellectual endeavor. A view that regards resolving these massive issues as lying outside the sphere of reason, as the product of rationally immaterial factors, is patently problematic.

To abstain from rational deliberation about philosophical issues is to take a step that is by no means costless. It requires us either to take no position at all (and thus to have no answers to our questions) or else to espouse a position without due rational warrant, thereby adopting a stance that we (as rational creatures) cannot regard as reasonable. Either way we act against our own desires and interests.

The shortcoming of such a position thus lies in the impossibility of reconciling it with the whole rationalist tradition of philosophy. Given arationalism, the very nature of philosophy as a venture in rational inquiry goes by the board.

The position also faces problems of inconsistency. Even those philosophers who endorse some other mode of thought different from reason have always used reasoning to show the fundamental status of this other mode and to attack the idea that reason is ultimate. The *status* of those "good extrarational reasons" as good reasons must always itself be shown by reason. Philosophy is not just a matter of taking positions but one of maintaining purportedly *justified* positions. It is inextricably rational. There is no way to do philosophy and to reject reason as the ultimate arbiter at the same time. A dilemma arises: the *ultimate* grounding of a position is either rational or one must concede that the position itself is simply not held on philosophically appropriate grounds. The difficulty with arationalism is that we cannot have it both ways, even if we would like to do so.

Orientational pluralism certainly does not underwrite any sort of arationalism. Even though philosophical problems generally admit of several distinct solutions, each of which is optimal from a particular evaluative orientation, this certainly does *not* mean that it is a matter of rationally arbitrary choice what one accepts; that one can simply pick at random because "it makes no difference." There is no universally appropriate diet, but that does not make it a matter of indifference what a person eats; there is no globally correct language, but that doesn't mean it is a matter of rational indifference how a particular person in a particular situation goes about communicating with others. In none of these cases is it a case of "anything goes." Relativism does *not* authorize arationalism.

Orientational pluralism accordingly holds that we are bound to see the alternatives to our own position in a very different light and deem them "available" only to others (misguided souls!) and not to ourselves. It maintains that we can indeed validate our philosophical claims, though, to be sure, only on the basis of a particular set of cognitive values. Such a stance is emphatically opposed to arationalism. It maintains that once we assume a particular cognitive-value orientation (as indeed we must), we are impelled by due rational constraints to adopt one particular resolution as uniquely appropriate and "correct."

The existentialist says: "Decide for yourself! Devise your own answers. You are mistaken to think that you can find answers through inquiry. There are no answers! The choice is yours to make! Be brave and face up to it."[15] Orientational pluralism utterly rejects this sort of view. It insists that an answer can indeed be found; that the issue is one of rational inquiry, not of decisional fiat. It does, however, see the inquiry as proceeding via a normative stand based on cognitive values. Yet this recourse to normative reason certainly does not leave the matter at the level of arbitrary decision. (The values we have are not objects of choice.)

### 4. Historical Convergentism

One might attempt to vindicate a particular philosophical position by discerning an evolutionary pattern favorable to it within the course of historical developments. Faced with the embarrassment of diversity and change throughout the history of philosophy, some theorists have sought to rise above these contingent variations to a higher plane by exploiting the idea of historical tendencies. Yearning for transcendence, for a way of overcoming the unending succession of different systems, they hope to find it in an overall evolutionary direction within the constantly changing succession of systems. As did Hegel, they find the hidden hand of rationality working its way

---

15. Compare the quote attributed to Donald Kalish in the "TIME Essay: What (If Anything) to Expect from Today's Philosophers," p. 24.

through the succession of conflicting positions.[16] This is the position of historical convergentism.[17]

Adherents to this position interpret the history of philosophy as an ongoing succession of conflicting positions gradually converging toward one favored doctrine of ultimate and absolute validity.[18] Thus, Peirce saw history as favorable to scientific truth, Marx as favorable to dialectical materialism, Hegel as favorable to Hegelianism. History is on the side of the angels; it is not a matter of fortuitous contingency—of just one thing after another—but a great eschatological trend toward one final, decisive, and definitive conclusion. Necessity prevails as a fundamental tendency at work within the merely seeming contingency of events. Convergentism is a mode of eschatological absolutism, looking to the emergence of some one theory that will ultimately assert itself so compellingly as to compel the assent of all right-thinking people. Its reaction to diversity is: sit tight, it will go away.

This position involves great difficulties. For one thing, it is always difficult to validate as real the trend one *seems* to discern; on all the evidence, the point of convergence very much lies in the eye of the beholder. Moreover, even if there were a clearly establishable trend (which in philosophy there is not), it would be difficult to show that this in its nature betokens validity, that convergence is not simply fortuitous, a matter of people's joining a bandwagon to accommodate themselves to a majority view, say. The question of validation, of rational legitimation, would still remain as an unresolved philosophical issue. Historical convergentism not only fails to fit the observed facts to date, but, more seriously, lies open to theoretical difficulties its advocates have never been able to overcome. For even if (*per impossibile*) convergence occurred, there is no way to cash in on it without the use of independently validated metaphysical machinery.

---

16. Although undoubtedly the most prominent exponent of this tendency of thought, Hegel was not its sole discoverer. The 1796 prize essay of the undeservedly neglected philosopher August Ludwig Huelsen (1775–1810) was a seminal work which maintained the gradual emergence of an increasingly clearly distinguishable Science that grasps the real truth across the conflict of systems. The strife of systems simply represents the transitory birth pangs of a gradually emerging cognitive order in which this conflict is progressively transcended. For a compact summary of Huelsen's views, see Braun, *Histoire de l'histoire de la philosophie*, pp. 284–87.

17. One of its prime exponents was Bernard Bosanquet, who labored to exhibit how the history of philosophy manifests the emergence of an ever more distinct consilience of positions, and looked to the crystallization of an increasingly definite consensus. See *The Meeting of Extremes in Modern Philosophy* (London, 1924).

18. Cf. Braun, *Histoire de l'histoire de la philosophie*, p. 92.

## 5. Rationalistic Doctrinalism in Its Absolutistic and Orientational Versions

The stance of rationalistic doctrinalism is straightforward. Though confronted by a plurality of positions, we can choose from among them on rationally cogent grounds. These grounds might, in principle, be of two kinds:

(1) of a purely evidential sort (evidential monism or demonstrative absolutism)

or

(2) of a partly normative sort (normative relativism or orientational monism).

Little need be said at this stage about an *evidential* monism that contends that considerations of objective evidential rationality will decide in favor of one position. The whole history of philosophy speaks against this absolutistic view, as does a theoretical analysis of the nature of philosophical problem solving. These are issues we have already considered at length; they form the recurrent leitmotiv of this entire book.

The orientational approach acknowledges that alternative positions exist in philosophical matters and can be supported by plausible argumentation. But it recognizes that the choice among the alternatives is something momentous, something that matters enormously. And it insists that this choice be made on the basis of good reasons and cogent arguments, even though these belong to the sphere of normative rather than evidential reason. Despite its name, orientational pluralism is thus essentially monistic in maintaining that, while various alternative positions will always exist with respect to any philosophical issue, the choice among them can be resolved on a perfectly cogent basis, albeit one that ultimately hinges on matters of evaluation. Holding that "purely evidential" considerations cannot of themselves validate a particular position, the doctrine nevertheless insists that we should not allow ourselves to be daunted by this consideration, because the issues can be resolved on the basis of evaluatively grounded considerations. Orientational monism thus finds its own support as a philosophical position in exactly the sort of methodology it itself endorses: the identification of one particular alternative as optimal in the light of cognitive values.

Yet in taking this stance, one must acknowledge the impossibility of rationally dislodging others from where they stand in a categorically presuppositionless way. One recognizes that other positions continue to be seen as tenable on other evaluative bases. It is, after all, a truism that other people who proceed from a variant basis of fundamental commitments will see matters differently from ourselves. However, this recognition nowise constitutes a rational impediment to our seeing them as we do.

## 6. *Syncretism: Against the Averroist Theory of Multiple Truth*

Syncretism maintains that it is mistaken to think that the conflict among discordant positions must be resolved by the doctrinalist procedure of adopting one or the other of them and rejecting the rest. Confronted with contradictory beliefs or doctrines, we need not see ourselves as constrained to make a choice among them—we can and should *conjoin* them. Properly speaking, there should not be a *pluralism* of positions at all, but one single, all-inclusive conjunction of positions, a grand superposition that embraces the lot. Each individual system represents but one sector of the whole—only the totality of systems, only philosophy-as-a-whole captures the whole truth.[19] The incompatability of claims does *not* mean that one or another of them must be denied. We must be open to "the recognition of the *equal or nearly equal adequacy* of a number of world theories and to a recommendation that we do not fall into the dogmatism of neglecting anyone of them" and persist "in holding these . . . [rival] theories in suspended judgment as constituting the sum of our knowledge of the subject."[20]

Acting on this generous sentiment, syncretism sees all of the rival positions as justified. Truth is somehow large enough to accommodate contradictions. With Hegel (and Nicholas of Cusa before him) we should reject the "principle of noncontradiction," to the effect that the truth is self-consistent. On the contrary, every party to a conflict of contradiction, duly counted by its opposite, is thereby also an essential part of the overall body of truth. Each self-consistent component is in itself imperfect, for the very reason limited by its very lack of contradictoriness from providing for the truths embodied in its contraries. On such a view, reality is a fusion of many worlds, and the synoptic philosophy that describes it is the superposition of many systems. (This theory of multiple truth is an enlarged version of the medieval "Averroist" theory of double truth, which held that reality embraces two incompatible world pictures, that of Aristotelian thought and that of Christian teaching.) Syncretism propounds a massive synthesis, a superdoctrine that lets all of the contesting parties have their own ways throughout the entire range of doctrinal divergence.

---

19. The conjunctionist agrees with Tristram Shandy's father: " 'Tis a pity, said my father, that Truth can only be on one side, brother Toby—considering what ingenuity these learned men have all shown in their solutions" (Laurence Sterne, *Tristram Shandy*, bk. III, chap. 41).

20. Pepper, *World Hypotheses*, p. 342.

Such a position-*conjoining* approach is *not* a position-*combining* eclecticism that takes the stance that each lower-level doctrine is right in some very partial respect though wrong in others, a position that is simply a complicated, internally diversified sort of doctrinalism. Rather, it insists on a conjoining of alternatives that lets everyone be right *on the whole*. The syncretist proposes to accept everythiing *as it stands*, without resorting to the "interpretative" qualifications or emendations that reconcile discordant views via distinctions. (The syncretist is akin to the religious fundamentalist in this regard.)

The conjunctionist program of syncretism is guided by the model of the book and the library. The book should be consistent; it should tell its own internally coherent story. But, just as the library as a whole contains many diverse and discordant books, so reality is a complex of many different and discordant "worlds." Each has its own consistent and coherent rational structure. But reality is a complex and diversified whole that encompasses them all. Each particular philosophy presents its own thought world, and reality as a whole is ample enough to embrace them all without being captured by any of them, refusing to be captured in any one-sidedly self-consistent frame of thought.

Syncretism is the approach of the overly open-minded philosopher who, carried away by Hegel or Marx, simply "refuses to take contradiction seriously." Declining to be intimidated by mere inconsistency, he accepts mutually exclusive alternatives and revels in their very inconsistency, regarding it as a sign of the fecundity of the real. Presented with the choice between having his cake and eating it, he tries to do both.

On such a view, the philosopher need not make up his mind between alternative views, he can accept them all (perhaps with varying degrees of enthusiasm). His task is to create an all-embracing system of systems—a macrosystem that somehow accommodates *all* of those alternative possibilities. The aim is not the resolution of problems but "enlightenment"—a nonparochially cosmopolitan appropriation of the entire range of possibilities. Philosophizing is now not an inquiry aimed at achieving definite answers but an encyclopedic compilation of all possible answers. The philosopher is not a craftsman creating a work of his own but a museum manager displaying the range of workmanship.

Generous though it may sound, syncretism is not a very promising position. For there just is no rationally sensible way in which to "have it all ways at once."

The grand idea of an intellectual symphony, where each player contributes to the overall harmony by playing his own score, is in deep difficulty simply because diverse philosophical positions are, as they stand, logically inconsistent with each other. The result of juxtaposing them is bound to yield not music but cacophony.[21]

The crucial fact is that the community as a whole is bound to adopt inconsistent views. The *conjunction* of these mutually incompatible positions is not a philosophical position—it is just a mess. We don't get a philosophical position until we clean the mess up, until we remove the inconsistency and fashion some coherent doctrine out of it. Whatever the communal product of philosophers at large may be, it is not a philosophy, any more than the product of diplomatists at large is a diplomacy.

Syncretism's facade of openness and liberality hides from view the awesome cost of taking this sort of position. It purchases the advantage of being liberal and nonjudgmental at a substantial price. In being over generous, it is self-defeating. Seemingly it allows everything, but actually, when all is said and done, it leaves us with nothing![22]

## 7. Coda

To adopt *any* alternative to metaphilosophical doctrinalism (be it scepticism, indifferentism, psychologism, historicism, or syncretism) is, in effect, to abandon philosophy as a significant rational enterprise. For all these other doctrines deny that we are taking a definite position for good and sufficient reasons. Rationalistic doctrinalism is not a mere matter of "business as usual" for philosophy, but an essential precondition to conceiving of it as an inquiry that represents a serious cognitive venture.

The upshot of these deliberations is emphatically not that the mode of doctrinalism endorsed by orientational pluralism has no viable rivals. For there certainly are some, and we have now systematically examined them. But in considering their claims, we have seen that orientational pluralism emerges as victor in a cognitive cost-benefit analysis of just exactly the sort that it itself envisions as the appropriate method of conflict resolution in philosophy.

A philosophical position cannot be self-exemptive; it cannot say of itself that "others abide our question, thou art free." And this has important applications. A scepticism that denies all doctrines cannot itself be doctrinal; the sceptic's philosophical denial of all philosophizing annihilates itself. A Humeanly positivistic insistence that all cognitively significant discourse must be either mathematical or "experiential" cannot survive the admission that it itself is neither. Here lies a

---

21. A useful and historically well informed critique of syncretism is given in the section, "Allegemeiner Nachweis der Unmoeglichkeit einer all-umfassenden Einheitsphilosophie" in Kröner, *Die Anarchie*, pp. 131–52.

22. The whole of chap. 2, sec. 5 above is relevant to this issue as well.

cardinal merit of orientational pluralism *vis-à-vis* its rivals: it is able to live by the philosophical methodology it advocates.

Among the various metaphilosophical alternatives (scepticism, arationalism, conjunctionism, and so on), the rationalistic doctrinalism represented by orientational pluralism is alone self-applicative. Scepticism is, at this level, a position that does indeed endorse one particular line of resolution—contrary to its own stance. (It advocates but does not exemplify *epochē,* suspension of judgment.) Arationalism inconsistently argues for one particular alternative among others. A syncretist conjunctionism would of course include itself among the alternatives, but that would not entitle it to a privileged position that enables it to present itself as the optimally appropriate response. The objectivistic position of evidential monism is also in difficulty on this score because it is unable to deliver what it promises: a rationally incontestable demonstration of its own appropriateness. Absolutism (which has problems of its own) apart, none of these rival positions are self-sustaining—none are in a position to practice what they preach.

Given the orientationalist approach, such pluralism at the methodological level is exactly what one would expect to encounter. But while orientational pluralism does indeed grant that other approaches are also "available" and that there is much to be said on their behalf, it insists that from its own methodological stance this fact is actually confirmatory seeing that, from its own perspective, the price of taking them is unrealistically high. Orientational pluralism has the clearly important merit of being self-sustaining by emerging as duly legitimated on its own telling. And this is as it should be. As a metaphilosophical doctrine that is, as such, itself philosophical, orientational pluralism must and can view itself in its own terms.

An objector may well protest:

But all this simply means that orientational pluralism is superior from *your* orientation. On your own principles, you are bound to recognize that it need not prove superior from *mine.*

And this objection is in essence correct. Orientational pluralism's approach to philosophical appraisal is indeed predicated on certain cognitive value commitments that implement the idea of philosophy as rational inquiry. All that the operational pluralist can say is: "If you share my values, then you ought by rational rights to share my position. If not, you can look elsewhere—indeed, you must do so." If he is to be live to his own principles, this is the stance he must take. Seeing these metaphilosophical issues as themselves philosophical, the orientational pluralist cannot claim more for his own doctrine than its emergence as comparatively optimal in a cost-benefit analysis based on certain principles of cognitive value—and thus as resting on an evaluatively normative basis that is essentially contestable. He is himself the first to acknowledge, and indeed to stress, that he cannot compel acceptance of these particular values through a course of reasoning that is value-free, simply because his own doctrine has it that rational inquiry in this domain essentially presupposes a basis of cognitive values.

The quarrel about the nature of philosophy itself represents a quintessentially philosophical discussion. As such, it clearly reflects our cognitive values. Various modes of "serious intellectual endeavor" exist, and the question of which is the archetype for philosophy is paramount—in particular, is it a matter of *inquiry* or of "enlightenment"? Orientational pluralism, true to its doctrinalism, comes down squarely on the side of inquiry. To see this not just as a *possible* account of philosophy but as the *correct* one is to take a doctrinal stance, one that ultimately rests on an evaluative assessment of the alternatives. And this, so orientational pluralism holds, is exactly as it should be.

The orientational pluralist is gladly willing (and perfectly able) to view the theoretical availability of competing approaches at variance with his own—and the seeming plausibility of some of them—as a point of *substantiation* of his theory rather than as a *refutation* of it.[23] But as he sees it, no alternative approach can rival his doctrine in this regard, because none is comparably self-substantiating—absolutism the least of all, considering the inability of variant absolutisms to reach agreement. This important intellectual merit of rational cogency—that pivotal cognitive value!—is optimized by orientational pluralism alone.

---

23. This view is reminiscent of Protagoras' reported contention that everything can be disputed equally on both sides, pro and con—even whether everything is disputable on both sides (*Protagoras ait de omni re in utramque partem disputari posse ex aequo, et de hac ipsa, an omni res in utramque partem disputabilis sit* [Seneca, *Epistles*, 88, 43]. One may, to be sure, wonder whether "equal *force*" or "equal *validity*" is at issue—a question which Seneca's "equally" (*ex aequo*) leaves frustratingly obscure.

# 13

# More on Scepticism and Syncretism

## 1. The Kinship of Scepticism and Syncretism

Confronted with a plurality of rival philosophical doctrines, the sceptic accepts *none* of the alternatives, the syncretist *all* of them. The former finds acceptability nowhere, the latter everywhere. Both approaches are wholly egalitarian: each assigns merit to all the rival alternatives and rejects the discriminatory idea of endorsing one rival and rejecting the rest.

Scepticism and syncretism both represent a reaction against the strife of contending systems. Their ultimate motivation roots in dismay about the Byzantine rivalries brought to light by philosophical doxographers—Dilthey's "boundless chaos."[1] Both say, "If *that's* the sort of thing philosophy is, I don't want any part of it." Each demands something less adversarial and contentious, yearning for the harmony of agreement and settled opinion. At a deeper level, the theories are thus closely akin in their determined refusal to discriminate and "take sides" in the disputes. It is worthwhile to consider them more closely in this light.

## 2. Agnostic Scepticism

The sceptic regards all philosophical doctrines as equally worthless. He holds that insofar as the aim of the enterprise is to answer questions and provide information, it fails abysmally. Philosophy is no longer viewed as an *informative* enterprise; at best it can usefully be an *educational* one whose aim is not to answer our questions but to "raise our consciousness"—not to enlarge our knowledge but to enhance our

---

1. "Grenzenlos, chaotisch hegt die Mannigfaltigkeit der philosophischen Systeme hinter uns und breitet sich um uns aus" (Dilthey, *Gesammelte Schriften*, vol. VIII [Stuttgart and Göttingen, 1960], p. 75).

awareness. Philosophy comes to be seen not as a venture in rational understanding but (at most) as a *noncognitive* undertaking whose proper task is to enlighten rather than to instruct, to be broadening without being literally *instructive*.

The sceptically agnostic approach to philosophy accordingly proposes a radical reorientation of the program of philosophy along something like the following noncognitivistic lines:

| *Abandon* | *Cultivate* |
|---|---|
| Knowledge | Insight and awareness |
| Doctrines | Vistas (aperçus) |
| Truth | "Meanings" |
| Reality | Possibility |
| Inquiry | Appreciation of alternatives |
| Information | Awareness |
| Discursive argumentation | Perceptiveness |
| Reason | Sensibility |
| Discrimination | Openness |

This approach calls for a radical *reconceptualization* of philosophy as an intellectual enterprise. It envisages a transvaluational reorientation of philosophy that totally abandons its traditional role as a rational inquiry that endeavors to answer questions, hold positions, offer teachings, maintain doctrines, and the like.

The exponents of such a position hold that the fundamental lesson of philosophy is that "philosophy" (in the traditional sense) is simply *impossible*. The history of the discipline is a sort of intellectual "optical illusion" that we must get rid of. To study philosophy may be useful, but to philosophize is not. The enterprise represents a difficult quest ultimately leading to a realization of its own infeasibility.[2] The study of philosophy is seen as a means for attaining higher-level wisdom without ground-level knowledge. Philosophy becomes a matter of intellectual history, of cultural enrichment. We can examine and discuss philosophical issues without anything so serious as actual commitment. The "correct" way to view philosophy is as a venture not in *learning*, but in consciousness expansion and *enlightenment*:

In this experience [of sympathetically reading the great philosophers] I did not find a stimulus to devising some grand synthesis (i.e., to forming some doctrinal position of my own that takes some account of them). Rather, I began to ask myself if philosophy should still undertake such synthetic tasks at all. Should it not rather open itself in a radical way to the furtherance of the

---

2. The wise man, as Ludwig Wittgenstein has put it: "must transcend these [philosophical] propositions, and then he will see the world aright. What we cannot speak about we must consign to silence" (*Tractatus Logico–Philosophicus*, ad fin).

hermeneutical experience [of interpreting and explaining rather than propounding doctrines]. . . . Philosophy is enlightenment, and, in particular, enlightenment against its own dogmatism.³

Such a view proposes to transcend philosophy by taking the somewhat paradoxical step of replacing the discipline with the study of its past. The history of philosophy becomes a replacement for philosophy itself. We embark on the path of post-Kantian idealism: "Which system is reasonable? None at all! Rather, the critical consideration of all systems is alone reasonable."⁴

The sceptic is tempted to the historical approach because it affords him the chance to discuss the issues without commitment. He sees the work of philosophy not as an inquiry aimed at getting answers to questions but as an exposure to "the great tradition" aimed at appreciation—a branch of *belles lettres* that affords cultural enrichment. Philosophy becomes the inherently nonpartisan and uncommitted study of the historical course of speculation. Its aim is not a product (knowledge) but a process (cultural exposure), and its model is not the scholarly treatise but the academic discussion or conference—the consideration of certain themes from different points of view.

Such an approach is based upon wholly misguided hopes and expectations.

Philosophical erudition tells us only what people *think* about issues; philosophy as such deals with the issues themselves. To grapple with philosophical issues meaningfully, one cannot simply *examine* positions, one must *take* a position. The philosopher asks, "Are there *good* grounds for maintaining the position *P*?" His interest is directed to the issues, *ad rem*. The mere student of philosophy disengages from the issues and deliberates *ad hominem*. He asks, "What did *X* intend when he maintained *P*, and what were *his* grounds for maintaining *P*?" The intellectual historian speaks not for himself but for others; his natural expression is "*X* maintains." But the philosopher's is "I maintain." Matters of the formal proprieties of exposition apart (e.g., logical consistency), the historian of philosophy as such, that is, as historian, can offer no *assessment* of the issues he describes.

But once we become involved with the questions of truth, correctness, adequacy, and so on, and enter the domain of normative deliberations, we are at once back on the battlefield, doing philosophy. The scholarly historian attains his "higher" vantage point, his externality,

---

3. Hans-Georg Gadamer, in L. J. Pongratz, ed., *Philosophie in Selbstdarstellungen*, vol. III (Hamburg, 1977), p. 78.
4. "Welches *System* is vernünftig? Keins! Sondern die prüfende Überlegung aller Systeme ist vernünftig" (Herbart, *Sämtliche Werke*, vol. II, p. 592).

by stepping outside the domain, by ceasing to do philosophy and taking up another line of endeavor. The discipline is converted from inquiry into intellectual tourism and Alexandrian polymathy. Its practitioners become cultured and learned but not informed; they *know about* views without *having* any. We are carried back to the burden of Kant's complaint that "there are scholarly men for whom the history of philosophy (both ancient and modern) is philosophy itself."[5]

The history of philosophy is not a substitute for philosophy. To study philosophy is not to philosophize; to become informed about philosophies is something very different from having a philosophy—from philosophizing effectively. Having a philosophy is a matter of *doing*, of problem solving, and here as elsewhere doing something oneself is one thing and learning about what others have done another. Knowing how X and Y and Z answer a question does not in the final analysis afford *us* an answer to it. However helpful the study of philosophy may prove by way of preparation for the work of philosophizing, it is not a way of doing it. Two errors are possible here. One is to mistake the scholarly history of philosophy, which should be strictly factual and descriptive, for a part of actual philosophy. The other is to think that philosophy, which must be normative and evaluatively committed, can be replaced by its history.[6]

To be sure, all this does not prevent the subject's history from being an indispensible tool for the conduct of philosophical work. For in this field (unlike the sciences) it is only by knowing the background of a problem—only by knowing something of the dialectical evolution through which the issue has come to have the form that it does—that we can understand what the issues actually are. We cannot assess the philosophical significance of our questions unless we know something of the genealogical filiation through which they have come to figure on the agenda of discussion. These considerations explain why philosophers tend to communicate in terms of the history of their subject. "Ah yes, what you mean by a 'sense datum' is much like a Humean *impression*" or "I see, your 'observation statements' are much like the protocols of the logical positivists." The history of the subject is available to all its practitioners alike. Historical doctrines become tokens of exchange, code words by which philosophical ideas are conveyed. But

---

5. Kant, *Prolegomena To Any Future Metaphysics* (Akad., p. 255).

6. Neither of these was committed by Hegel. He wanted the history of philosophy to be provided *more philosophico*—to create a philosophical history which did not merely detail the historical developments, but to evaluate their contributions to philosophical truth. Such an enterprise in effect absorbs the history of philosophy into philosophy itself. But it thereby ceases to be scholarly in the strict sense (it is no longer purely factual and value-free) and becomes *engagé*, partisan, and "whiggish."

the fact remains that to study the history of philosophy is by no means to philosophize.

The sceptic, to be sure, is perfectly content with all this. "Quite so," he says. "In examining the history of philosophy we are not philosophizing at all. That's exactly what I want. We should just stop doing philosophy." This position must be dealt with.

## 3. Scepticism in Its Neo-Hermeneutic Guise

The sceptical approach represents a thin, red line running through the history of philosophy. The Cynics and Sceptics of antiquity, the medieval mystics, Renaissance antirationalists of the stamp of Montaigne and Sanchez, and such later thinkers as Kierkegaard and the contemporary hermeneuticists all exemplify this tendency of thought. There is no doubt about the respectability of its lineage, since it goes back to the Socrates of Plato's early dialogues, who stands committed to the pursuit of discussion and inquiry (*elenchos*) but feels that the process is unlikely to issue in any particular teaching or lesson (*mathesis*). "I have never been anybody's teacher," Socrates reassures his judges in the *Apology* (33A). Inquiry is its own reward and "Inquiry Without Doctrine" a plausible motto. This view continues to be maintained with vigor and erudition in our own day by the German hermeneuticist Hans-Georg Gadamer and by many others.[7]

Richard Rorty is the principal importer of this neohermeneutic approach into English-language philosophizing. His books *Philosophy and the Mirror of Nature* and *Consequences of Pragmatism*[8] gleefully envision a "post-philosophical" culture in which "one would no longer think of the standard list of Cartesian [i.e., traditionally philosophical] problems as a *Fach* [a discipline of substantive inquiry]: rather, one would think of the study of the concern that once was felt about these problems as a *Fach*. The best analogy available is the shift from 'theology' to 'the study of religion' " (*CP*, p. 32). The philosophizing of the post-Cartesian mainstream tradition is roundly criticized by Rorty: "the more 'scientific' and 'rigorous' philosophy became, the less it had to do with the rest of culture and the more absurd its traditional pretensions seemed" (*PMN*, p. 5).

In effect, Rorty's analysis sets out from the following aporetic cluster with respect to traditional or, as he terms it, "normal" philosophy:

(1) Philosophy aims at knowledge.
(2) The only valid mode of knowledge is objective knowledge.

---

7. For an interesting discussion of its *institutional* implications see W. Hochkeppel, *Mythos Philosophie* (Hamburg, 1976), esp. p. 162.

8. These books are here cited as *PMN* and *CP*, respectively. The former was published in Princeton, 1979; the later in Minneapolis, 1982.

(3) Philosophy cannot attain objective knowledge.
(4) The aims of philosophy are realizable.

Rorty proposes to exit from this contradiction by dropping (1) and insisting that philosophy should not aim at knowledge. He urges us to reject philosophical cognitivism and adopt a different, edificationist approach to the goals of philosophy. (This revision of [1] also, of course, revolutionizes [4].)[9]

According to Rorty, philosophy should simply abandon the traditional problems. Or, put differently, one should simply abandon the subject and welcome "an end to philosophy" as philosophy has heretofore been understood and practiced (*CP*, p. 31). Orthodox philosophy has been a failure—a would-be "science" without results, and indeed without any agreement, even on fundamentals. In foresaking it we can put all those frustrating controversies behind us. "The [very] possibility of alternative theories ends only when interest in the subject has lapsed so far that no one cares what anyone else might say about it" (*CP*, p. 25). As though when people reached the point of exhaustion in considering them, the issues themselves had perforce to vanish!

On such a view, philosophy's cognitive efforts at establishing and consolidating systems must be abandoned, and we should exchange "normal," information-oriented philosophizing for the efforts of "philosophers whose aim is to edify—to help their readers, or society as a whole, break free from outworn vocabularies and attitudes" (*PMN*, pp. 11–12). Philosophy should become a venture whose aim is not *teaching* but enlightenment. It should be taken out of the knowledge business altogether. Following in the footsteps of sceptics since antiquity, we should simply give up on knowledge in the philosophical domain:

> It would make for philosophical clarity if we just *gave* the notion of "cognition" to predictive science, and stopped worrying about "alternative cognitive methods." The word *knowledge* would not seem worth fighting over were it not for the Kantian tradition that to be a philosopher is to have a "theory of knowledge," and the Platonic tradition that action not based on knowledge of the truth of propositions is "irrational." (*PMN*, p. 356)

The aim is not to establish theses and answer questions but to liberate people from making cognitive demands, to induce them to abstain from having those intellectual concerns that philosophy heretofore endeavored to address; to *dissolve* rather than *resolve* the traditional philosophical issues.

Philosophy should cease to be *inquiry* concerned with matters of

---

9. Note that orientational pluralism resolves this aporie by rejecting (2). It sees philosophical inquiry as normatively conditioned and hence as exponent-relative in a way that precludes strict objectivity.

*truth* and become a *conversation* concerned with matters of *interest*—its aim not to produce theories regarding facts but creative proposals regarding issues of interest: "To see keeping a conversation going as a sufficient aim of philosophy, to see wisdom as consisting in the ability to sustain a conversation, is to see human beings as generators of new descriptions. . . . To see the aim of philosophy as truth . . . is to see human beings as objects rather than subjects" (*PMN*, p. 378). Since "the facts of the matter" are as they are regardless of our wishes and efforts, there is something debilitatingly passive and conformist about a concern for them. The job of the philosopher is not to *inquire*, to address questions and seek to give good reasons for his answers, but merely to *stimulate*, to voice interesting and provocative opinions, to be an engaging companion.

The aim of Rorty's sceptical enterprise is to render philosophy obsolete—to have us turn our back on that entire "collection of the principal topics discussed by most of the 'great philosophers'—subject and object, mind and matter, utilitarian and deontological ethics, free will and determinism, language and thought, God and the world, universals and particulars, meaning and reference, etc., etc." (*CP*, pp. 29–30). We are enjoined to stop doing philosophy—to cease philosophizing. To be sure, this does not mean that we should cease to *study* philosophy—after all, such study has various useful lessons to teach us (not only about the futility of the enterprise of philosophizing but also about the culturally broadening history of ideas). But philosophy as an *inquiry*—a discipline to be cultivated with serious cognitive intent—should simply be abandoned as a childish venture that we sophisticates should put away with other childish things.

It is understandable that Rorty should labor mightily to sever the link between philosophy and reasoned inquiry. For the sceptic faces the aporetic cluster:

(1) If rationality matters, then philosophy matters.
(2) Rationality matters.
(3) Philosophy does not matter.

Committed to (3), the sceptic faces the choice between rejecting (2) and dismissing rationality itself, or rejecting (1) and trying to sever its link to philosophy.

An "edifying" postphilosophy should be summoned into being to free us from the issue-oriented concerns of old: "The point of edifying philosophy is to keep the conversation going rather than to find objective truth" (*PMN*, p. 377). Its goal is not *understanding* but *liberation*, not the intellectual satisfaction that comes from comprehension but that of "the sort one feels when no longer oppressed by a need to answer unanswerable questions" (*CP*, p. 36). We should realize the same sort of contentment we get when we end a childish game, not by following its rules and winning, but simply by not playing the game at all.

Calling this sort of position "pragmatism," Rorty declares that its exponents

> think that the history of attempts to isolate the True or the Good, or to define the word "true" or "good," supports their suspicion that there is no interesting work to be done in this area. . . . They do not think we should ask those questions anymore . . . they would simply like to change the subject. . . . Pragmatists keep trying to find ways of making antiphilosophical points in nonphilosophical language. (*CP*, p. xiv)

This pragmatism, while having "things to say about truth, knowledge, morality . . . [does] not have *theories* of them in the sense of sets of answers to the textbook problems" (*CP*, pp. 161–62). Systematic philosophizing in the manner of the traditional mainstream must be abandoned (*PMN*, pp. 367–68). The tradition-abandoning, liberationist ethos of the 1920s represented by the later Dewey, Wittgenstein, and Heidegger should be our model, seeing that they rightly "called into question Western metaphysics as a theoretical discipline" (*PMN*, p. 368). Confronted by traditional philosophical disputes, we should not come down on this side or that but should turn our attention elsewhere.

## 4. Why Not Abandon Philosophy? A Reply to the Sceptic

Scepticism is a kind of liberation philosophy or, perhaps better, a liberation *from* philosophy. It frees us from involvement with all those problematic issues and lifts from our shoulders the burden of having to take sides in all those abstruse controversies. This would be very nice indeed if it were not for one awkward fact. Those competing doctrines *span the entire range of available alternatives* for getting answers to our questions. To obtain answers, to have any view at all, we must come down someplace or other in this range; we must take sides. We can, of course, abandon this whole idea of taking sides, and so of having answers, positions, views. But abandoning philosophical subjects is a leap into nothingness. We can indeed escape from grappling with philosophical issues—into the history of philosophy, into technical minutiae, into issues of process and machinery, and so on. But all this is simply an abandonment of the subject and not a way of coming to grips with its issues. To avoid cognitive vacuity, to secure answers to our questions, we must be prepared to take sides in the controversies of the field.

"You ought not to philosophize," says the sceptic. "But you must," cries our nature as inquiring beings (*homo quaerens*). The issues matter too much for their dismissal to be comfortable; they are too pressing and important. We have questions and want to answer them as best we can. Noncognitivism is not a realistic option.

Herbart mentions the dictum that one must have a metaphysic even as one must have a house, and this observation is correct in spirit.[10] Our need for *intellectual* accommodation in this world is no less pressing—no less *practical—than our need for physical* accommodation. But in both cases, we do not want just some house or other but one that is well built, that will not be blown down by the first wind that sweeps along. Sceptics from antiquity onward have always said, "Forget about those abstruse theoretical issues; focus on your practical needs." They overlook the crucial fact that an intellectual accommodation to the world is itself one of our deepest practical needs—that in a position of ignorance or cognitive dissonance we cannot function satisfactorily. We are creatures for whom intellectual comfort is no less crucial than physical comfort. The human condition is such that we are going to have some view (after all, scepticism itself is just one such). The question is simply whether we are going to have one that is well thought out or not.

The sceptical stance of the modern thinkers commemorated by Rorty simply pours more wine into the old bottles already used by the Pyrrhorian Sceptics of classical antiquity and their latter-day successors from Montaigne to Hume, as well as the logical empiricists of the Vienna Circle. In striving to transcend the human condition (be it in life or in philosophy), we merely proceed to exemplify it. Seeking to *overcome* philosophy, the sceptics actually adopt a well-defined position within its serried ranks. Scepticism itself is no more than just another philosophical stance, simply another member of the spectrum of ongoingly available alternatives—and a problematic one at that. The Groucho Marx of *Horsefeathers* notwithstanding, ("Whatever it is, I'm against it"), one cannot adopt the position of opposing *all* positions with consistency, let alone with intellectual satisfaction.

The sagacious sceptic—Rorty himself, for example—is worried by this. How, after all, can the sceptic "decry the very notion of having a view, while avoiding having a view about having views" (*PMN*, p. 371)? Rorty recognizes this question without ever resolving it. He throws out dark hints about saying things without really quite meaning them—about the paramount need "to prevent [philosophical] conversation from degenerating into inquiry, into an exchange of views" (*PMN*, p. 372). But he never succeeds in explaining how this position itself avoids being just another view. In the end, it comes

---

10. Herbart, *Sämtliche Werke*, vol. II, p. 290.

down to this, that "to think of . . . [edificationist philosophers] as having views about how things are is not to be wrong about how things are, exactly; it is just poor taste. It puts them in a position which they do not want to be in, and in which they look ridiculous" (*PMN*, p. 372). It is not without shrewdness that a philosophical view that cannot offer a more cogently reasoned defense than this rejects the necessity of providing rational defenses.

It sounds deep to say things like:

> No system can encompass reality. The delimited compass of any one system induces us to the illusion that we have got at the truth and blocks the view of the chasm—the mystery and dreadfulness of an open-endedly complex reality that mocks our feeble efforts at understanding.

But the philosopher who sends us this sort of message is not a thinker who annihilates doctrine but a fellow theorist with a highly problematical doctrine of his own.

No matter how we struggle against taking a philosophical position, once we enter the arena of substantive discussion we occupy some position. Even the view that one should espouse no philosophical doctrines whatever is simply another view that has been with us since antiquity. *Any* view about "the real nature of philosophy" or about "the proper work of the philosopher" is just another view, another position in the spectrum of possibilities. As a philosophical position or doctrine, scepticism is ultimately self-defeating. The only way to avoid being caught up within the network of alternative views is to keep silent altogether and turn to other pursuits. The best the rational sceptic can do is set us the good example of stolid silence in philosophical matters.

Rorty is quite prepared to embrace this consequence. He contemplates with relish a postphilosophical culture in which philosophy as we have known it occupies the same status in informed quarters that nowadays falls to the lot of alchemy, astrology, and divination (*CP*, pp. xxxvii–xxxix). But the costs of this position are not counted up. For in abandoning philosophical inquiry for the heady atmosphere of the free-wheeling postphilosophical era we have a lot to lose.

The discomfiture of ignorance looms large among the unpleasant consequences of philosophical scepticism. As a reward for our labors we are left at the end of the day with . . . nothing. The sceptic is gladly willing to accept this consequence (after all, it represents his enlightening "insight")—but there is no reason why others should see the matter in this light and try to fool themselves into thinking that this cost is no cost. For both theoretical and practical reasons, we want and need answers to our questions—to satisfy our questioning minds and to guide our actions in the light of accepted beliefs. Scepticism requires us to forego answers to our questions—to live in a cognitive limbo. But our philosophical problems are important and urgent. We have a real *interest* in their solutions—in every sense of this term. We cannot just dismiss them and expect to walk away with easy consciences.

Rorty's scepticism flows from a deep-rooted disaffection from professional philosophy. As he sees it, philosophers' issues and problems are *only* philosophers' issues and problems (*CP*, p. 54). If we give them all up, lock, stock, and barrel, it just doesn't matter, it simply makes no difference. But to take this view of philosophical problems is to fail to realize that philosophers' theses and distinctions are not an idle parlor game invented for the sake of amusing the players but issue from real concerns, real questions arising entirely outside the technical sphere of philosophy. Even the most technical of philosophical issues is linked to the big questions of extraphilosophical concern. We address them in order to resolve questions whose resolutions in turn facilitate answers to other questions in a chain that ultimately leads back to those big extrasystemic questions of prephilosophical concern.

Moreover, Rortyan scepticism invites objection in its proposal to take philosophy out of the reason business. The key division of labor was already fixed in Plato's contrast between the philosopher and the poet. The latter, too, may portray possibilities and project views, but the former is concerned with their rational evaluation—with developing and initiating the arguments for and against adopting them. Without reasons and arguments we may have insight, appreciation, and even culture—but never wisdom. Philosophy—love of wisdom—is concerned not simply with the statement of views but with their *rationalization*—with the development and evaluation of reasons for or against their adoption. Philosophy is inextricably bound to the life of reason, and to do away with this part of it is to do away with the whole.

In withdrawing from the strife of doctrines and the clash of issues, we abandon philosophizing as a rational enterprise. Once "rationally justified opinion" in this domain is abandoned, with the alternatives seen as either indistinguishable in point of merit or distinguishable only by such extrarational criteria as "taste" or "congeniality" or whatever inclination or "heightened sensibility" induces, our deepest intellectual aspirations are profoundly frustrated.

The critical shortcoming of the sceptic's position lies in its failure to recognize the seriousness of the issues. We cannot, in the final analysis, rest content—*rationally* content—with leaving the arena of philosophical controversy empty handed. Our intellectual stake in the great questions about life in this world that are philosophy's stock-in-trade is simply too great to allow us to be comfortable in foregoing this whole inquiry. Philosophy is an inquiry that seeks to resolve problems regarding the coherence of our beliefs in those great matters, and to abandon philosophy is to rest content either with ignorance or with incoherence, or both. In adopting the sceptic's stance, we reap a bitter harvest. We lose the chance to make sense of things—and that is a lot to lose.

The noncognitivist posture of a sceptical approach to philosophy can itself be seen as a doctrinal response to an aporetic cluster:

(1) Philosophy is a worthwhile enterprise.
(2) Worthwhile intellectual enterprises establish theses.
(3) Philosophy cannot establish theses.

There are three initial lines of response to this antinomy:

(1)–denial: an abandonment of the entire philosophical project (nihilistic scepticism).
(2)–denial: An insistence (in the way usual among sceptical agnostics) that worthwhile intellectual enterprise can issue in orientational *insight* rather than informative *knowledge* (noncognitivism).
(3)–denial: The orthodox view and that of orientational pluralism (doctrinalism).

The first two alternatives take a noncognitivist turning. Orientational pluralism, by contrast, takes the third exit. It insists that we can indeed "establish" philosophical theses, albeit only relative to a certain cognitive-value orientation. We can avert its (3)–denial, to be sure, but at a substantial price.

Admittedly, there is no evaluatively presuppositionless demonstration of one particular solution as uniquely tenable in philosophy. But to see this as a basis for dismissing the whole enterprise, bears the aura of petulance. It means that we are unwilling to play the game simply because we cannot have it all our own (deeply misconceived) way—a stance reminiscent of Aesop's fable of the fox and the grapes.

## 5. Syncretism

Facing a plurality of contending rival answers to philosophical questions, the sceptic embargoes *all* of the available options and enjoins us to reject the whole lot as meaningless or otherwise untenable. A more radical option, though equally egalitarian, is to proceed in the exactly opposite way and view all the alternatives positively, embracing the whole lot of them. The guiding idea of this approach is that of *conjoining* the alternatives. Such a syncretism represents an attempt to "rise above the quarrel" of conflicting doctrines, refusing to "take sides" by taking all the sides at once. It is a Will Rogers kind of pluralism that never met a position it didn't like. Confronted by discordant possibilities, it embraces them all in a generous spirit of liberalism that sees them all as essentially correct. Each alternative is held to carry its small burden of truth to the general and all-embracing amalgam of the Truth.

The discordant doctrines of philosophers are seen by syncretism as no more than individual contributions to a communal project whose mission is not a matter of *establishing a position* at all but one of *examining positions, of exploring the entire space of alternatives*. The key question is now not (as with the hermeneutic approach described above) the history-oriented "What positions *have been* taken?" but the possibility-oriented "What positions *can be* taken?" It is a matter of the comprehensive appreciation of possibilities in general and not one of trying to substantiate some one particular position as rationally appropriate. On this approach, the real task of philosophy is to inventory the possibilities for human understanding with respect to philosophical issues. In studying the issues we widen our sensibilities, enhance the range of our awareness, and enlarge the range of our cognitive experience. Philosophy once again becomes a matter of horizon broadening rather than problem solving—a matter not of *knowledge* at all but of the sort of "wisdom" at issue in an open-endedly welcoming stance toward diverse positions. To take philosophy as *judging* its theses and theories—deeming these acceptable and those not—is seen as a corruption. Philosophy properly understood is essentially nonjudgmental. Its task is to enlarge our views and extend our intellectual sympathies by keeping the entire range of possibilities before our mind.

This approach represents a vision that has been at center stage in German philosophy since Hegel. And it was in this frame of mind that the Bertrand Russell of the pre-World War I era wrote: "Philosophy is to be studied, not for the sake of any definite answers to its questions, since no definite answers can, as a rule, be known to be true, but rather for the sake of the questions themselves; because these questions enlarge our conception of what is possible, extend our intellectual imagination, and diminish the dogmatic assurance which closes the mind against speculation."[11] Robert Nozick advocates a revival of this tendency of thought.[12] Traditionally, philosophers have sought to es-

---

11. Russell, *Problems of Philosophy*, pp. 249–50.
12. See his *Philosophical Explanations* (Cambridge, Mass.: 1981). Hereafter cited in the text.

tablish conclusions on the basis of arguments. But Nozick sees this as socially unpalatable. For cogent argumentation is coercive; it seeks to constrain acceptance of a conclusion; it uses (intellectual) "force" and endeavors "to bludgeon" people into acceptance (p. 10). Philosophizing by way of rational argumentation is authoritarian and coercive: "A philosophical argument is an attempt to get someone to believe something, whether he wants to believe it or not. A successful philosophical argument, a strong argument, *forces* someone to a belief" (p. 4). Even rational coercion is wicked; given cogent arguments, someone who accepts the premises *has to* accept the conclusion—and may thus be *forced* to believe something he may not want to believe. And this "is not a nice way to behave toward someone." Philosophy should abandon rational coercion and turn to "morally better" ways (p. 13). It should forego arguments and would-be proofs and offer "explanations," which should be put forward tentatively and uncommittedly in the guise of explanatory *hypotheses* (p. 14).

As Nozick sees it, the task is to explore the spectrum of possible explanations for what we know or accept on extraphilosophical grounds (p. 11). The aim is not securing answers to philosophical questions but gaining insight and "understanding" through the comparison and contrast of various possible explanations. He tells us that "When this book explores hypotheses depicting eccentric possibilities, as it sometimes does, even a reader who is convinced the hypothesis fails, who will not take the possibility seriously, even a reader who does not enjoy (as I do) the playful exploration of possibilities for its own sake, may see benefit in the increased understanding gained" (p. 12). In philosophy we should not seek to find and establish specific *answers* to our questions; we should seek to explore the range of alternatives: "Treating philosophy as a black box, we might view its 'output' not as a single theory, not even as one set of theories, but as a set of questions, each with its own set of associated theories as possible answers" (p. 20). Perhaps we should "view the highest products of philosophy as the philosophical questions themselves, the theories and systems being commentary to exhibit the value of the questions" (p. 20). In any case, it is the *questions* that matter, it being neither possible nor even desirable to try to arrive at definite *answers* to them. At the level of answers, it is with possibilities rather than actualities that we should be concerned: "Perhaps, as knowing a subject (such as logic or physics) involves seeing the different ways it can be organized and viewed, the different ways [of getting] around [in] it, so too (only this time the views are incompatible so the analogy is imperfect) knowing the world involves seeing the different ways it can be viewed" (p. 21).

Accordingly, it should be the mission of philosophizing to explore what Nozick calls "the network of possibility" (p. 12). Rather than seeking to consolidate a particular position or to validate a particular answer to a philosophical question, philosophy should deliver an entire "basketful" of alternative views (pp. 21–24). Philosophizing should aim at understanding rather than rational conviction and reflect "a desire to understand, not a desire to produce uniformity of belief." Academics are presumably open-minded liberals in political matters, and they should be so in philosophical matters as well. Taking a philosophical position up is just too primitive, too partisan, too parochial. We should simply be "too proud to fight." We must recognize that reality is too manyfaceted to be encompassed in the framework of any one theory (p. 21).

Induction upon the history of philosophy shows that there is no point in *adopting* any of the available theories; each is destined to succumb to the onslaught of critical assault. No amount of refurbishing will help matters: "When position X succumbed to difficulty Y, any position aptly described as 'neo-X' will, after a time, with probability .942, succumb to neo-Y, if not to the same old Y" (p. 558). There's no such thing as getting at (or near) the truth in this domain.[13]

And that's all to the good. The real truth is too restrictive and confining, because we cannot make it up as we go along. We should channel our concern into more rewarding and satisfying directions.

Nozick is the devotee of doctrinal syntheses (*Vermittelungsansichten*, or bridging views) in just the sense mocked by William James in his caricature of Wilhelm Wundt:

> He isn't a genius, he is a *professor*—a being whose duty it is to know everything and have his own opinion of everything. . . . He says of each possible subject "Here I must have an opinion. Let's see. What shall it be? How many possible opinions are there? three? four! Yes! Just four! Shall I take one of these? It will seem more original [and less parochial!] to take a higher position, a sort of *Vermittelungsansicht* between them all. That I will do, etc., etc."[14]

As Nozick sees it, philosophy should aim not at resolution but at mediation. It becomes a venture in intellectual combinations—in familiarizing ourselves with the multiplicity of alternatives on various issues. To opt for a particular position within the spectrum of alternatives manages to be all the wrong things: old fashioned, parochial, divisive, and unchic. It combines all sorts of defects: intellectual, political, and (perhaps worst of all) social.

---

13. What lessons Nozick would draw from the infeasibility of securing permanent triumphs in theoretical physics—let alone in life—is a matter for intriguing conjecture.
14. William James's letter to Karl Stumpf (February 6, 1877), in Henry James, ed., *Letters of William James* (Boston, 1920), pp. 263–64.

To be sure, Nozick makes the reluctant concession to our human weakness by allowing that we need not regard all alternative views on philosophical matters as having altogether equal merit. He grants that a total neutrality of a wholly undiscriminating egalitarianism is perhaps too much to ask for:

> Are we reduced to relativism then, the doctrine that all views are equally good? No, some views can be rejected [but why?], and the admissible ones remaining will differ in merit and adequacy, though none is completely lacking. Even when one view is clearly best, though, we do not keep only this first ranked view, rejecting all the others. Our total view is the basket of philosophical views, containing all the admissible views. . . . This position is not relativism, for the views are ranked, but neither is just one view settled upon. (Pp. 21–22)

Nozick's discussion is extremely skimpy, however, on the pivotal normative issues that arise here. How are we to go about judging which views are admissible and which are not? And by what criteria are we to rank the admissible ones? Nozick's heart just is not in this matter of comparative appraisal and evaluation. In fact, he is unsure whether rational appraisal is even at issue. Perhaps the matter is one of merely aesthetic preferences. The scruples Nozick initially expresses in the introduction ("I feel discomfort, though, with the aesthetic view of philosophy" [p. 20]) seem to have been overcome altogether by the time he reaches the final page: "An artistic philosophy would welcome (and appreciate) other shapings, other philosophical visions as part of the basketful, while striving itself for a prominent position in the ranking" (p. 647). Whatever the criterion of ranking is, it is apparently something in the sphere of extrarational appeal.

The cardinal virtue is a cosmopolitan tolerance, and the cardinal sin is dogmatism. Perhaps we cannot manage to abandon commitment altogether—the inner impetus to cognitive discrimination is too strong. But we should strive for inclusiveness and a cosmopolitan openness to variety. "Assent will . . . be more tentative, perhaps more transient" (p. 20). After all, "there is no compelling need to settle upon only one philosophical view" (p. 643). The thing to be avoided at all costs is not error, nor even silliness, but *parochialism*. The philosopher is not a business man who sets up shop in a particular line but a merchant banker who diversifies his investments and hedges his bets by placing his money into various diversified enterprises.

Such a flight from commitment is ennobled in the name of open-mindedness. The prime desideratum is to keep on good terms with as many possibilities as possible: "[Since] a neutral beginning is chimerical, the alternative of starting just where we are seems parochial and dogmatic, especially if there are some theoretical places where we can't get to from here. We can [and should!] build modes of change into a view, hoping parochialism is avoided when any theory can be reached. . . . The treatment for philosophical parochialism, as for parochialism of other sorts, is to come to know alternatives" (p. 19). Presumably the available possibilities are all good chaps—to know them is to like them and to give them some degree of credit and credence. Dedication, commitment, and conviction divide men into separated groups; ergo they are inappropriate and wrong.

## 6. A Critique of Syncretism

Its obvious attractions notwithstanding, the view of philosophy as possibility exploration is not without its defects. The prime difficulty is that possibility mongering fails to accommodate the central project of serious inquiry. Possibilities don't answer questions. To *engage in* the enterprise, rather than merely to deliberate *about* it, we must ask, "What position *shall* we take?" and not merely "What position *can* we take?"

The standard view of philosophy sees the aims of the enterprise in terms of answering "the big questions" concerning man and his place in nature's scheme of things. The object of philosophizing is to remove ignorance and puzzlement, to resolve cognitive problems—to provide *information*, in short. To abstain from taking a definite position, to refuse to take sides (be it through sceptical abstention or through open-minded conjunctiveness) is simply to abandon the enterprise. To endorse a plurality of answers is to have no answers at all—an unending openness to various possibilities, a constant yes-and-no, leave us in perpetual ignorance.

We can *study* philosophy to expand our horizons, to learn what sort of positions are available—what sort of stories can be told about the issues. But we *engage* in philosophizing because we want to have answers to the questions and solutions to the problems of the field—answers with which we ourselves can rest rationally content, even if they do not form the focus of a universal consensus. If we wish to *philosophize*, to arrive at answers to our questions, we cannot avoid taking a position. We must be committal and espouse views and positions in a selective, discriminating way that endorses some alternatives at the expense of others.

By their very nature, philosophical disagreements resist being transcended by way of conjunction. Conjunctionism is an invitation to indifference, to refraining from the serious business of making up one's mind.

The individual laborer in the domain of philosophy *cannot* transcend his individuality and adopt the diversified labors of the community into his own doctrine. Conjunctionism is a grand notion that founders on the recalcitrant fact that there is just no way of making the library over into a single book—of conjoining the multiplicity of discordant philosophies into a meaningful whole. Individual philosophers can do no more than take one stance among others, arriving at a position that unavoidably remains controversial. They cannot at once engage in the enterprise and enjoy the security of a higher vantage point above the din of battle.

To project one's pacifist ideology into the sphere of philosophy is to emasculate the subject. It is not by accident that Athena, goddess of wisdom and patroness of philosophy, presides over the arts of war as well. The strife of systems is relentless—the destiny of philosophy is not peace but the sword.

## 7. The Flight from Commitment

To refuse to discriminate—be it by accepting everything or by accepting nothing—is to avert controversy only by refusing to enter the forum of discussion. This is not a way of taking a (particularly sophisticated) position, it is a way of avoiding the subject—of addressing the *ideas* of philosophy, perhaps, but not the *problems* of philosophy. In trying to be equally open (or closed) to all the alternatives, we get nowhere. To transmute philosophy into the study of alternatives is indeed to avoid doctrinal commitment, but it is also to abandon the project as a serious inquiry aimed at securing answers to questions. And this is something we do not—and should not—want to do, because the questions matter too much—the issues are simply too important to us.

To obtain informative guidance from philosophy, it is not enough to *contemplate* philosophical positions—be it as historical actualities or as theoretical possibilities. We must actually *commit* ourselves to one. We can only get answers to substantive questions if we do our philosophizing in the doctrinalist manner—only if we are willing to "stick our necks out" and take a position that endorses some answers and rejects others.

This seems to go against the ethos of the age. Contemporary philosophers, including some of the most influential, are often unwilling to philosophize in the traditional way of taking a substantively committal position. They deem it beneath them to "take sides"—to formulate a position and defend it against all comers by rational argument. Adopting one limited alternative is somehow too partisan, too parochial for their taste. In consequence, taking refuge in an egalitarian scepticism or syncretism, they refuse to commit themselves to philosophical positions.[15]

The aversion to taking a doctrinal stance indicates a profound failure of nerve, a debilitating reluctance to take a stand, to come down on one side or the other. It inflates the importance of consensus to the point where the fact that we cannot obtain it *within* the field but might obtain it *about* the field becomes decisive. In doing so, however, it thinks nothing of the consequence that in taking this externalistic stance we destroy the enterprise as traditionally conceived.

Sartre deplored the attempt to secure rationally validated knowledge. He saw this quest as a way of avoiding responsibility for *making* something of oneself, for "choosing one's own project," seeing that the real truth is not something one can make up as one goes along. But this view turns the matter topsy-turvy. Not the pursuit of truth but its *abandonment* represents a failure of nerve and a crisis of confidence. The avoidance of responsibility lies in an indifferentism that sees merit everywhere and validity nowhere (or vice versa), thereby relieving us of any and all duty to investigate the issues in a serious, workmanlike way. We are driven back to the view of the pre-Platonic Sophists, who maintained that with respect to the great issues of human concern something is to be said on all sides and that in consequence there is no such thing as a true position. To take this stance is to shirk one's responsibility as an inquirer.

There is nothing admirable in the present-day inclination to philosophical detachment with its concomitant reluctance to trust one's personal judgment in matters of human significance. There is nothing praiseworthy about the widely felt need of philosophers for the security of the support and backing of others. Scepticism and conjunctionism alike manifest a wishy-washy unwillingness to adopt a position, to stand up and be counted. They reflect a regrettable unpreparedness to take intellectual responsibility—to say: "I've investigated the matter as best I can, and this is the result at which I've arrived. Here I stand, I can do no other. If you wish to stand with me, then welcome to you; if not, then please show me how my position is untenable." They represent recourse to an uncritical open-mindedness that comes close to empty-mindedness. In philosophy, as in politics and religion, one does well to prefer someone who has views and sticks by them to the per-

---

15. The result is a defect that even the layman can see: "Men turn for guidance to scientists, psychiatrists, sociologists, politicians, historians, journalists—to almost anyone but their traditional guide, the philosopher. Philosophy, in revolt against its past and against its traditional function, looks inwards at its own problems rather than outward at men" ("TIME Essay: What (If Anything) to Expect from Today's Philosophers," pp. 24–25).

son who rejects the whole project or (equally wrongly) tries to ride off in every direction at once.

The question of intellectual seriousness is pivotal. Do we care? Do we *really want* answers to our questions? And are we sufficiently committed to this goal to be willing to take risks for the sake of its achievement, risks of potential error, of certain disagreement, and of possible obloquy and reproach? If we lose the sense of legitimacy and become too fainthearted to run such risks, we must pay the price of abandoning the inquiry.

This of course can be done. But to abandon the quest for answers in a *reasoned* way is impossible. For in the final analysis there is no alternative to philosophizing as long as we remain in the province of reason. We adopt some controversial position or other, no matter which way we turn—no matter how elaborately we try to avoid philosophical controversy, it will come back to find us. The salient point was well put by Aristotle: "[Even if we join those who believe that philosophizing is not possible] in this case too we are obliged to inquire how it is possible for there to be no Philosophy; and then, in inquiring, we philosophize, for rational inquiry is the essence of Philosophy."[16] To those who are prepared simply to abandon philosophy, to withdraw from the whole project of trying to make sense of things, we can have nothing to say. (How can one reason with those who deny the pointfulness and propriety of reasoning?) But with those who *argue* for its abandonment we can do something—once we have enrolled them in the community as fellow theorists with a position of their own. F. H. Bradley hit the nail on the head: "The man who is ready to prove that metaphysical knowledge is impossible . . . is a brother metaphysician with a rival theory of first principles."[17] One can abandon philosophy, but one cannot *advocate* its abandonment through rational argumentation without philosophizing.

---

16. *Aristotelis Fragmenta Selecta,* ed. W. D. Ross (Oxford, 1955), p. vii (for the text see. p. 28). But cf. also Anton-Hermann Chroust, *Aristotle, Protrepicus: A Reconstruction* (Notre Dame, 1969), pp. 48–50.

17. Bradley, *Appearance and Reality,* p. 1.

# 14

## Prescriptive Versus Descriptive Metaphilosophy

### 1. Modes of Metaphilosophy

It is essential for present purposes to heed carefully the crucial distinction between evaluatively *normative* and observationally *descriptive* approaches to metaphilosophy. The descriptive issue of how philosophy *has* been done is one of factual inquiry largely to be handled in terms of the history of the field. But the normative issue of how philosophy *should* be done—of *significant* questions, *adequate* solutions, and *good* arguments—is something very different.[1]

*Normative* metaphilosophizing regarding the *correct* or *appropriate* problems, methods, and theses of philosophy is a part of philosophy itself. That a certain way of doing philosophy is appropriate, successful, effective, superior, or the like—that philosophy is *properly* done in a certain way—is patently a philosophical thesis. And this sort of substantive philosophical contention itself turns on matters of cognitive evaluation and is thus bound to be every bit as controversial as any other issue of the field. What philosophy might "really" be is resolvable only within the framework of a philosophical position and cannot be settled extraphilosophically.[2] As Franz Kröner cogently put it: "The dialectic of 'intraphilosophical' and 'extraphilosophical' and of 'theoretical' with 'atheoretical' shows that given a finger philosophy at once takes the whole hand. It is an autonomous whole that provides its own

---

1. This point is forcibly argued by Robert Nozick: "A metaphilosophy will be part of a total philosophical view rather than a separate neutral theory above the battle" (*Philosophical Explanations*, p. 19). As we have seen, however, the conclusions he draws from this consideration are very different from those of the present book.

2. This is the burden of Franz Kröner's dictum that "there is no such thing as philosophy *überhaupt*" (*Die Anarchie* p. 59).

boundaries."³ *Descriptive* metaphilosophy, on the other hand, is not a part of philosophy at all. At this level we are dealing with a branch of *factual* inquiry—with the history of philosophy and perhaps its sociology. It is a matter of the observational scrutiny of a certain enterprise within the wide framework of human intellectual endeavor. And this is primarily a branch of *historical* studies, not fundamentally dissimilar in spirit from that of characterizing the historical development of the conduct of warfare or of techniques of communication.

In consequence, *descriptive* metaphilosophy is not controversial in the manner of philosophy itself, but is disputable, at most, in the manner of any interpretation of historical facts. There is every reason to think that one particular descriptive position should alone be tenable. And in this regard—that of a merely descriptive account—the claims of orientational pluralism are clearly substantial. That conflicting positions are in fact maintained and that their different justificatory backings trace back to different probative value orientations are circumstances spoken for by the plain facts of the history of philosophy.

The question of what philosophy actually *is*—that is, what it has become at the hands of its recognized practitioners—is thus a straightforwardly factual question whose answer is to be found by examining the course of historical developments. Dilthey, to his great credit, saw this clearly: "What philosophy is is a question that cannot be answered conformably to the views of individuals. Its nature and tasks must be determined empirically from the historical facts."⁴ This essentially descriptive issue is a part of the shared reality of objective fact. All philosophers, regardless of their doctrinal commitments, should be able to agree about the history and sociology and psychology of philosophical work. At the level of descriptive metaphilosophy it should be possible to reach consensus, since we are here in the domain of factual rather than philosophical inquiry.

But once we come to the normative question of what is *good* philosophy, matters stand on a very different footing. For this is a deeply value-laden and thus an eminently philosophical issue.⁵

---

3. Ibid., p. 273.
4. Wilhelm Dilthey, *Gesammelte Schriften,* vol. VIII (Stuttgart and Göttingen, 1960), p. 185.
5. Some writers find a "historiographic circle" in the purported fact that one can only decide what belongs to philosophical history if one knows what "philosophy" is, but can only find this out from a study of philosophical history (see Maria Assunta del Torre, *Le origini moderne della storiographia filosofica* [Florence, 1976], esp. p. 67). But to make much of this is to become involved in needless mystification. What belongs to the "history of philosophy" is simply everything that belongs to the history of what people *call* "philosophy" (a purely factual matter) and this is enough to enable us to decide what belongs

Theses about the *appropriate* nature, methods, standards, and goals of philosophy are always philosophical themselves. Any methodological precept for philosophizing—any thesis to the effect that "X constitutes an effective way of addressing a philosophical issue" or "any adequate solution of the problem Y must satisfy the condition C"—will itself be philosophical. The character of *genuinely* philosophical questions and the character of *successful* philosophical problem resolutions are thus themselves always potentially controversial issues of substantive philosophy. What constitutes successful philosophizing is a matter of (perfectly legitimate) dispute. It is a characteristic feature of philosophy; that is, the one intellectual descriptive whose very nature is one of philosophy's key problems.[6] Alone among cognitive disciplines, philosophy finds itself in a state of *permanent* "foundation crisis" (*Grundlagenkrise*). There is always dispute and controversy about fundamentals. Neither method nor any other alternative provides a "neutral" Archimedean fulcrum for the weighing of philosophical issues.

Descartes' proposal to overcome philosophical conflict by means of the right *method* envisaged the plausible sequentialism of settling on a philosophical method first and then using it to resolve philosophical conflicts. But as Hegel emphasized, this approach is ineffective because the question of "the proper method" of philosophizing is itself a part of philosophical work; the methodological mechanism by which our discussion is to be conducted is itself a party to the dispute. The question of the proper mission of philosophy is inevitably one of the central issues on the philosophical agenda.[7]

On the normative question of how the business of philosophy is properly to be conducted, we must therefore always expect to find a plurality of diverse and discordant positions. It should come as no surprise that, seen as *normative* doctrines regarding how philosophy is appropriately conducted, doctrinalism, arationalism, conjunctionism, and scepticism each have their own characteristic view of what philosophy properly amounts to. At this normative level, metaphilosophy is just as controversial and aporetic as philosophy itself because it constitutes part and parcel of philosophy.

The mere facts of the matter do not enable us to substantiate the

---

to "philosophy" so-called. What is not resolved by this (since normative issues are now involved) is what philosophy *ought* to be. But of course this normative question of philosophy proper is not a historical question at all, but one of substantive philosophy.

6. Cf. Arthur Danto, *What Philosophy Is* (New York, 1968), p. 2; Rorty, *The Linguistic Turn*, pp. 1–2.

7. "Über die Frage nach dem Wesen des Philosophie wurde soviel nachgedacht das man geradezu sagen konnte 'Philosophie ist diejenige Forschungsarbeit, die immer nach ihrem eigenen Wesen fragt' " (Rogge, *Axiomatik,* p. 18).

normative claim that the real is rational—that the historically preponderant way of philosophizing is indeed correct (proper, appropriate, and so on). We cannot validly move from the descriptive analysis of how philosophy *is* done to secure normative conclusions as to how philosophy *should be* done. The reverse also holds good; we cannot validly move from a particular normative theory as to how philosophy should be cultivated to substantiate conclusions about the actual practice of the enterprise. One cannot infer "ought to be" from "is," but one cannot infer "is" from "ought to be," either.

This means, in particular, that specific doctrines about the nature of philosophy can indeed make exclusions from their own precincts, but not from the subject as such. A philosopher can reject the concerns, methods, and doctrines of his rivals, but he cannot exile them from the community—cannot expel them from philosophy as such. What belongs to philosophy as the field has in fact been cultivated, rather than to the more limited range of *good* or *adequate* philosophy, is a matter of strictly factual investigation at the position-detached level of "the profession" or "the tradition" as a whole—on which no one sector has a monopoly. People may remove themselves from philosophy by turning to other activities (literature or mathematics, for example), but no power on earth can excommunicate from the discipline as such the person who grapples with any of the traditionally relevant issues.

The distinction between descriptive and normative metaphilosophy is crucial to the tenability of orientational pluralism. For two very different things are at issue. As a *descriptive* theory, orientational pluralism holds that people do in fact hold different standards of cognitive evaluation and extract different positions from them. As a *prescriptive* theory, it holds that people are (locally) justified in holding the different standards they do (or might)—albeit justified in ways that involve these standards themselves, since no globally validatable standards are available on a basis free of evaluative committments.

The question of the *descriptive* adequacy of orientational pluralism will have to be deliberated on factual grounds. There is no real room for normative disagreement here; the historical facts must speak for themselves.

But what of the *normative* aspect of the matter—the question of the adequacy of orientational pluralism as a (philosophical) theory of what proper philosophizing is "really" like? This is clearly an evaluative (and actually *philosophical*) issue. This question of the acceptability of orientational pluralism as a position in normative metaphilosophy will, by its own lights, have to emerge as controversial.

To manage this controversy we must face the following challenge:

The present analysis presents orientational pluralism as the correct account of *normative* metaphilosophy—as substantively appropriate for characterizing what philosophizing should be: a venture in rationalistic doctrinalism. One cannot (on its own telling) justify this through its adequacy at the merely *descriptive* level. How then can one support it?

The answer must be sought in a cognitive cost-benefit analysis *vis-à-vis* orientational pluralism's rivals along the lines contemplated in the preceding chapters. As a substantive doctrine of normative metaphilosophy, orientational pluralism will have to be defended by the sort of evaluative cost-benefit appraisal that characterizes the validation of philosophical positions in general. The defense of its rationalistic doctrinalism must lie in the fact that it proves superior as a substantive theory of philosophizing in the light of the relevant cognitive values. We must, in sum, look to the relative advantages that this position has over absolutism, scepticism, arationalism, conjunctionalism, and so on. And the salient consideration here is that it is the only account within this range that enables us to see philosophizing as a viable cognitive activity while yet accommodating its humanistic commitment to values. On its basis alone are we able to avoid succumbing to the unattainable promises of absolutism and yet maintain for philosophy the status of a rigorous inquiry (*Wissenschaft, scientia*) that endeavors to provide rationally justified answers to significant questions.

## 2. Orientational Pluralism Is Not at Odds with Doctrinal Commitment

Orientational pluralism in its role as a theory of normative metaphilosophy takes a dualistic, two-tier stance.

(1) *At the doctrinal level*, it envisages a one-sidedly dogmatic commitment made "from where one stands." It holds that from the vantage point of one's *own* cognitive-value perspective—the only one that one has—only one optimally adequate position on philosophical issues is rationally warranted.

(2) *At the metadoctrinal level* of the objectively descriptive realities (in contrast with one's own normative idealities), it envisages a pluralism that recognizes that other perspectives exist and are "available" (albeit only to others!).

This two-tier approach requires us to consider philosophy at two levels: (1) at the "internal," substantive level where actual commitment to philosophical doctrines takes place, and (2) at the "external," noncommittal level of strictly factual and descriptive considerations, where we consider metaphilosophical issues in a way that abstracts from our own substantive commitments.

At the substantive level of philosophical inquiry we can work out our own favored position and develop "our own stand" on the issues. In doing so, we take sides—we accept a definite position. We say, "Here I stand, and these are my reasons for so doing. . . . That's how I see the issue, and I am convinced that any reasonable person who saw the matter as I do, in its true light (without distorting biases and predispositions), would come to agree." But we do this even while realizing that when we step back from this doctrinal level to survey our own work (and its rivals) descriptively, with commitment-suspensive detachment, then other positions will also emerge as tenable "from other points of view."

To be sure, this open-minded recognition that alternatives, too, have their place in the larger scheme of things only happens "at a remove," when we step back from *engagement* in substantive philosophy and assume a descriptive metaphilosophical stance in which our own perspectivally conditioned commitments are suspended and "bracketed."

At the level of commitment-detached, descriptively metaphilosophical consideration we can, indeed, take a broader perspective that encompasses also other alternatives alongside our own. Such a stance recognizes that "our truth"—the truth as we see it—is part of a larger complex that also includes conflicting positions. But of course this is the stance of the detached *historian* of philosophy and of the deliberately impartial *expository teacher*. When one *studies philosophy*, one examines many alternative positions—one wanders down the street and looks in the windows, so to speak. Only when one *philosophizes* does one develop a position and secure an intellectual habitation of one's own.

Historical studies do not establish philosophical positions. The Hegelian claim "History is on my side—and against yours" cannot be made good. The (descriptive) history of philosophy is a common resource on which everyone can draw for materials and for inspiration—to mix metaphors, it is a many-edged sword that cuts in various directions.

Only the detached, "scientific" historian can tell the story fairly, because he has no ax to grind. But he must tell that story in the full complexity of its discordant variety—as a tale full of sound and fury that signifies nothing by way of substantive conclusions. At this level of "scientific" detachment, the history of philosophy must remain an account related with a clinical detachment that makes no attempt to make sense of it all. Someone who finds sense and extracts lessons is *thereby* transformed into a fellow philosopher with a particular position—someone who does not just describe the history but reworks its materials in order to grind an ax of his own.

Even the orientational pluralist can say that he who abandons "dogmatism" in philosophy is a traitor to the spirit of the enterprise, because this is what good philosophical work demands at the substantive level. In abandoning universalistic claims for his position, the orientationalist can perfectly well say:

> I take philosophical inquiry seriously because I am eager to discover what qualify—from the vantage point where I myself stand—as the proper and correct answers to these questions. That these should also prove to be *your* answers would be very nice but is not necessary. Nor need this failure daunt my own confidence. After all, I do not feel the less persuaded of the rightness of my own standards of judgment in moral or political matters because I realize they are not shared by everybody.

Metaphilosophical pluralism need nowise impede dedicated partisanship on matters of philosophical doctrine. Orientational pluralism at the descriptive metalevel is perfectly consonant with orientational monism at the substantive ground level; there is no clash or conflict between the two. Philosophical partisanship is not incompatible with metaphilosophical tolerance and need not be undermined by it.

It cannot be emphasized too strongly that a metaphilosophical recognition that there are other positions that are, abstractly speaking, "available"—though only from the standpoint of an orientation that one may not share—constitutes no reason whatsoever for giving up a firm adherence to the philosophical position to which one stands committed. If we do not take our values seriously, then the whole enterprise doesn't matter. (But what does?) If we do, then the prospect of bringing our commitments into rational consonance with them should be attractive—indeed, decisive.

## 3. On Replacing Philosophy with Its Own History

Confronted by the "anarchy of systems," philosophers often yearn for the law and order of scientific inquiry. We are urged to avert the inconveniences of disagreement in philosophizing itself by escaping into the *study* of philosophy (even as some theologians would have us withdraw from religion into the study of religions). It was in just this light that Dilthey saw the comparative history of philosophy as a latter-day surrogate for philosophy.[8] He proposed to implement Hegel's grand dream of a "scientific" systematization of worldviews in the light of world history. Accordingly, Dilthey sought to fuse the history of

---

8. "The same surgical knife of historical relativism, which has dissected all metaphysics and all religion alike, must also be used for healing. But the key is thoroughness. We must make philosophy itself the object of philosophizing. What is needed is an inquiry which takes philosophical systems themselves as its objects through the comparative analysis of their historical development. This inquiry would stand to the history of philosophy as comparative philology stands to the history of languages—and if someone wants to transcend the separation of the two, I shall be the last to object" (Dilthey, *Gesammelte Schriften*, vol. VIII, pp. 234–35).

# THE STRIFE OF SYSTEMS
*Prescriptive Versus Descriptive Metaphilosophy*

philosophy to a psychologically informed study of the human condition in an endeavor to devise a Mendeleeff-reminiscent periodic table to coordinate all possible philosophical positions into a systemic rational framework that would allocate each metaphysical position a place in the grand scheme of things. As he saw it, such an endeavor to provide a systematic typology of worldviews holds forth the promise of finding an implicit rational order amidst the confusing phenomena.[9] The promise of a meta-metaphysical substitute for metaphysics is held up before us, a theory able to explain the strife of systems in terms of a "philosophy of life" that allows us to view philosophical differences as arising from different approaches to the complexities of human life.

In the German-language orbit especially, this line of thought fell on fertile ground. Dilthey's ideas were carried forward by his pupil Max Frischeisen-Koehler in an important 1907 essay.[10] He tells us:

Each philosophical epoch seems to be filled with an illusion, each great philosopher believes himself to be the one who has succeeded in solving the final riddle, but each epoch is succeeded by another, which recognizes anew how little permanent the achievements of the preceding one are; each philosopher finds his successor and opponent, who refutes him, at the same time; each philosophy carries the seed of its own death. The history of philosophical thought shows no connection, no continuity, no progress, but is all the more a chaos of opinions, an anarchy of viewpoints and of theories, of which none can be proved, and yet each of which makes the same claim to general validity.[11]

And so Frischeisen-Koehler too proposes to replace philosophizing of the traditional sort by a new mode of higher-level inquiry along Diltheyan lines.

Franz Kröner was an especially important link in the chain, and his 1929 book titled *The Anarchy of Philosophical Systems* treats many of the themes that have occupied us here.[12] He proposed to replace philosophy by *systematology*, a metaphilosophical examination of *philosophical systems* conducted descriptively, from the outside, as it were. In this

---

9. Dilthey's project was put into execution by (his pupil?) Heinrich Gomperz in his monumental *Weltanschauungslehre*, vol. I, (Jena, 1905). An important later contribution to the same project is Erich Rothacker's *Logik und Systematik der Geisteswissenschaften* (Munich, 1927).

10. Max Frischeisen-Koehler, "Die historische Anarchie der philosophischen Systeme und das Problem der Philosophie als Wissenschaft," *Zeitschrift für Philosophie und philosophische Kritik* 131 (1907): 131–35. Born in 1878, this prolific author was a pupil of Dilthey's and Professor of Philosophy in the University of Halle.

11. Ibid., pp. 66–67.

12. Franz Kröner (1889–1958) was born in Vienna and taught in universities in Graz and in Zürich. For a presentation of his ideas, see the "Symposium on Systematology" in *Metaphilosophy* 13 (1982): 240–66. Kröner was influenced by Dilthey and, as the introduction to his book makes clear, by Frischeisen-Koehler as well.

way, he believed, it would become possible "to create a cosmos out of chaos."[13] By focusing upon the fundamental theses of philosophical systems, we can discern the nature of their problems and their interrelationships. Moreover, we can analyze the alternatives to each system by altering its fundamental theses in various combinations and permutations. The inherent task of systematology is a descriptive analysis—effectively a phenomenology—of philosophical systems, conducted in the spirit of the geometer who studies alternative systems by varying the usual axioms. To be sure, unlike mathematical systems, philosophical systems are "imperfect"—their concepts are never fully exact and their theses develop dialectically so that no definitive axiomatization is possible. The prospect of variation makes pluralism inevitable. The aim of systematology is a typology of philosophical systems (reminiscent of Dilthey's theory of types of worldviews), based on differences rooted in theoretical possibilities rather than psychological inclinations.

Kröner's own solution to the problem of the strife of systems leaves something to be desired. Instead of simply accepting the phenomenon of conflict and moving on from there, he tries to dismiss it as itself a pseudoproblem rooted in imperfect understanding.[14] However, while his diagnosis is deficient, his remedy—to forget about this strife and get on with the work of addressing concrete philosophical problems—is altogether right-minded.[15]

Kröner himself ultimately became disillusioned with his systematology because he came to recognize that the study of philosophy cannot provide a substitute for philosophizing.[16] His theory ran into the following apory:

(1) There is no absolute philosophical system, and so there are no unconditionally acceptable philosophical propositions.
(2) Theses about the nature of philosophy are themselves philosophical.
(3) Thesis (1) itself is unconditionally acceptable.

Kröner tried to extricate himself from this aporetic conflict by dropping (2): "The proposition that there can be no philosophical system is in the strict sense not a 'philosophical' proposition; that is, it cannot stand in such a system and does not belong to the context of such a system, just as the proposition that it is not the only possible geometry does

---

13. Kröner, *Die Anarchie*, p. 8; cf. also pp. 42, 287.
14. "Das Phaenomen der Anarchie der Systeme [ist] als oberflaechlich und einseitig aufgefasstes schlechthin zum Verschwinden zu bringen" (ibid., p. 320).
15. "Die einzige und beste Antwort . . . ist also der Uebergang zur konkreten Arbeit an den konkreten Problemen" (ibid., p. 323).
16. Cf. Georg Janoska's contribution to the "Symposium on Systematology," p. 253 (see n. 12 above).

# THE STRIFE OF SYSTEMS
*Prescriptive Versus Descriptive Metaphilosophy*

not belong to the contents of Euclidean geometry."[17] He thus stood committed to the doctrine that systematological theses stand outside philosophy—(2) itself included. This forced him to acknowledge that systematology cannot commit itself to any philosophical issues as such and so is precluded from resolving any philosophical questions. It succeeds in replacing strife by order only by abandoning the subject. As our deliberations have made all too plain, if systematology is a matter of systematizing the materials made available by the history of philosophy, it becomes a study in alternative possibilities and never manages to arrive at a determinate study of the issues. Kröner's theory came to shipwreck in the course of its search for an Archimedean *pou stō*. The methodological commitments of a purely descriptive metaphilosophy (which Kröner saw as necessary to avert chaos) also preclude the enterprise from becoming properly philosophical, and this defeats its deepest aspirations.

In fairness to Kröner, it should, however, be said that his aims were entirely right-minded: "Our battle will have to be fought on two fronts, for a way must be found for navigating between the Charybdis of one-system absolutism and the Scylla of a nihilism that relegates philosophical systems to providing materials for cultural history or for psychology."[18] This statement could serve to formulate the aims of this book as well.

A further link in the chain was the German philosopher Eberhard Rogge, who, still in his thirties, was killed in 1941 while fighting on the Russian front. His posthumous book, *The Axiomatic of All Possible Philosophy*, was an attempt to identify the fundamental theses of the different modes of philosophical system building. The basic idea, as with Dilthey and Kröner, is to proceed on a factual basis, on analogy with the work of bibliography: "The librarian must know, for serious purposes, what philosophy really is, so that he can avoid putting a philosophical book into the category 'miscellaneous.' Library classification is a significant cognitive endeavor, quite distinct from philosophy itself, in which one seriously asks: 'What is philosophy?' "[19] In this vein Rogge embarked on the project of metaphilosophy in the spirit of bibliographic taxonomy, an approach that has the same defects as its predecessors. By examining philosophy *more bibliothecario* we are to learn not merely what philosophy has been but also what it should be. The idea sounds promising, but it does not work. Descriptive metaphilosophy cannot venture into prescriptive methaphilosophy; it cannot

17. Kröner, *Die Anarchie*, p. 278.
18. Ibid., p. 55.
19. Rogge, *Axiomatik*, p. 48.

inform us about what is significant or adequate. It runs up against the cardinal difficulty of this whole Diltheyan tradition; that is, that the study of philosophy is not a satisfactory surrogate for philosophy itself.[20] The *study* of philosophy, however valuable, cannot of itself provide us with a determinate philosophical position.[21]

It has been the great, ambitious dream of German philosophers since Hegel to tell a story about the whole history of philosophy that makes it clear how everything within it has contributed usefully to the constituting of one grand synoptic view of the nature of things. In principle, there is no reason why this cannot be done. But also, alas, there is no reason to think that it cannot be done in many different ways—and in favor of many different positions.

As this brief review of Germanic reflections on "the anarchy of systems" suggests, the present discussion continues an ongoing tradition of metaphilosophical thought deriving from Hegel and his congeners. It differs from this tradition primarily in its willingness to maintain a clear line of distinction between the descriptive and the normative aspects of metaphilosophy, with the upshot that pluralism is seen as wholly devoid of implications for the conduct of philosophy itself.

## 4. Does Orientational Pluralism in Metaphilosophy Carry Lessons for Philosophy Itself?

It deserves stress that an orientational pluralism in descriptive metaphilosophy has no implications for, and indeed no material bearing whatever upon, the actual *substance* of our philosophical doctrines themselves. There is no lesson we can draw for the appropriate *content* of our own substantive position from the fact that different positions are available to others who see the issues differently.

We must, in particular, avoid any temptation to project metaphilosophical pluralism into a ground-level, substantive doctrine about the

---

20. This difficulty also pervades the analysis of Pepper's *World Hypotheses*, which is an American cousin to these German efforts. Cf. Mark Williamson, "Stephen Pepper's *World Hypotheses* and Metaphilosophical Evaluation," *Transactions of the Charles S. Peirce Society* 19 (1983): 255–71. Williamson rightly notes the internal conflicts of a theory that distinguishes between "historical" and "speculative" typologies while engaging in practice in an effort that hopelessly conflates the two, seeking to avoid metaphysical doctrines while yet providing a metaphysics.

21. To be sure, there is history and history. The *standard* mode is a merely *descriptive*: history which presents the development of what people generally *call* "philosophy." But there is also *normative* history: the account of *good* philosophy with special reference to those of its features that mark it as such. This enterprise is of course philosophical to the very core. But the very fact that it is substantively *engagé* sets it apart from the mode of "scientific" history which seeks to be purely descriptive and "value-free."

nature of reality—a support for a doctrine of manyfaceted reality (along the lines sketched in chapter 10). Nothing in orientational pluralism enjoins any one particular substantive position regarding the availability or unavailability of particular doctrines regarding the nature of the real. Metaphilosophical doctrines cannot preempt substantive issues—they are ontologically neutral.

Hegel dreamed the grand dream of sublimating the whole history of philosophizing into the ahistorical contemporaneity of the absolute spirit—of rising above the limitations of historically conditioned doctrines to a higher plane where all doctrines were absorbed into one grand ahistorical superdoctrine. This dream, though indeed grand, is no more than a grand illusion.

The great error of Hegelian theory consists in a twofold conflation of levels: the descriptive/normative and the individual/communal. Hegel slid from the valid insight that the process of philosophizing has the structure of a dialectical pluralism at the descriptive metaphilosophical level to the inappropriate normative conclusion that the same situation should obtain prescriptively at the ground level of concrete philosophizing—that the proper structure of a philosophical doctrine should also be inherently pluralistic and dialectical. Such a view confuses the actual work of the community, *descriptively* considered, with the work proper to the individuals that constitute it, *normatively* considered.

In philosophy, evaluative appraisal (as correct, proper, appropriate, valid, and so on) always demands an appeal to cognitive values. We are not able to assess positions from a basis void of evaluative commitments but can only appraise them by assuming a determinate value posture. In philosophy we cannot free ourselves from the restrictive pressure of limiting commitments; no one doctrine, no substantively *philosophical* account (as opposed to a descriptively metaphilosophical one) can embrace the whole spectrum of alternatives.

Orientational pluralism does, however, carry a useful lesson for philosophers, a lesson not, to be sure, for the *substance* of their ground-level philosophical positions but for the *conduct* of their philosophical inquiries—a lesson for *method* rather than *doctrine*.

The individual philosopher must do the best he can to elaborate and substantiate his solution to a philosophical issue—to work out his own position and defend it against all comers. But when he "steps back" and detaches himself from his commitments through a provisional suspension of belief, he should recognize that his own position is merely one alternative among others (a very privileged alternative, to be sure, in being—as he himself sees it—the *correct* one).

It should be noted that communal diversity—the absence of consensus in philosophy—is not an unmitigated disaster. A good case can be made out for seeing it as socially beneficial. It is not all that implausible to take the view that intellectual strife, while fatal to the prospect of "a public philosophy," might nevertheless be advantageous to the public weal and that "the strife of systems" has its positive side.[22] For there is good reason to think that positive consequences flow from the fact that the arena of philosophy presents a scene of discord rather than consensus.

Dissonance is a prod to effort. Opposition and conflict operate as a stimulus to exertion, to self-development. Pluralism is cultural evolution's solution to a problem—that different people have different needs and must develop in different directions. Uniformity would mean not only stagnation for the group but impoverishment for many of its individuals.

Thus, there are compensating gains for the loss of the reassurance of consensus. The fact that no single position preempts the domain of acceptable possibility establishes the need for reaching a deeper, more intensely personal level of thought—for working things out for ourselves and arriving at our own answers. It means that philosophical work is not a matter of *scholarship,* of mastering a particular body of objectively validated doctrines, but of *philosophizing,* of discerning how to navigate one's way among the rocks and reefs of rival possibilities. As Kant rightly emphasized, philosophy is, in the final analysis, not a matter of *learning* but of *thinking.*

The lesson is that we should be prepared to give other points of view their due in a nondismissive way. We should be prepared to take them seriously, take account of them, learn from them, and (above all) respond to them, defining our positions against the background they afford and defending it against them. Parallel to Peirce's famous injunction not to bar the path of inquiry runs the no less important injunction not to block the channels of communication.

Orientational pluralism in metaphilosophy accordingly sees philosophy at large as a communal venture—a competitive yet quasi-cooperative endeavor to build up as good a case as possible for a diversified spectrum of discordant possibilities. What counts as crucial from this overarching metaphilosophical standpoint is not the matter of "getting at the absolute truth," but rather of enhancing the quality

---

22. "Everywhere society's health depends on the simultaneous pursuit of mutually opposed activities or issues. The adoption of a final solution means a kind of death sentence for man's humanity. . . ." (E. F. Schumacher, *A Guide for the Perplexed* [New York, 1977], p. 127).

of the argumentation and gaining a deepened understanding of the structure of alternative positions.

We cannot put our philosophical theories to the test by experiment and observation as one can in the natural sciences. But even as science develops as a dialectic of interchange between theorists and experimentalists, so philosophy develops as a dialectic of interchange between theorists and countertheorists. The only way we have of testing our philosophical doctrines is by exposing them to the trial of counter-argumentation in order to see how cogently objections can be met. The way to "progress in philosophy" lies through opposition—through a dialectic of challenge and response.

The development of philosophy as a *field* of inquiry involves a division of labor that requires each era to have its Platonists and Aristotelians, its nominalists and conceptualists and universalists, its empiricists and its rationalists, its sceptics and its dogmatists, and so on. At the metatheoretical level, the philosophical enterprise exhibits a prismatic many-sidedness that provides each worker with collaborators and adversaries, endowing the communal process of philosophical work with an interactionism and creative tension that engender a dialectical movement across the whole doctrinal spectrum.

The world spirit does not engender a Hegelian succession of limited positions gradually moving toward a wider vision of the ultimate truth. The history of the philosophical enterprise does not have a structure that enables us to look across the battleground of history to discover where it all leads, to catch some dim glimpse of a limiting consensus position toward which all change gradually converges. Rather, the historical process maintains an ongoing plurality of discordant positions. We can already discuss how it will end, not because we can detect some great, ultimate convergence, but, more mundanely, because we are already there. It will end where it began—in disagreement and controversy.

Pluralism thus has important consequences for philosophical method. It implies the value of reasoned discussion, of arguing with our opponents in the endeavor to articulate, develop, and refine our own position through the dialectic of controversy.

At this point we can effect the transition from descriptive to prescriptive metaphilosophizing by means of a transcendental argument to the possibility of fruitful disagreement. There must be common language, common foci of attention, common issues, and, above all, a shared matrix of rational deliberation, a common standard of deliberation and argumentation. That is why it is important to facilitate contact through the maintenance of at least some rudimentary probative constraints at the level of logic. No profitable discussion is possible among those who cannot even agree on $P$'s following from $Q$ or on $R$'s being incompatible with $S$—who cannot see eye to eye on matters of implication and counterindication, consensus and discord. The basic principle of cognitive rationality—of probative process—is part of the *lingua franca* that philosophers of otherwise varied views do and must to some extent share. The principles of reasoning are communally agreed—not as a matter of contingent good fortune but because those who do not share them stand outside the community—and outside the subject. We cannot rationally engage those who do not play the game by the rules of rationality. However interesting their deliberations may be as *belles lettres,* we cannot count them as belonging to philosophy. Even those who see reason as secondary and subordinate must—if they are to participate in the work of philosophy—substantiate their positions by rational means.

Various imperatives—imperatives not *of* philosophizing but *for* philosophizing—inhere in this situation: be open to contacts, listen to objections, conduct dialogues with opponents, respect their efforts, and so on. In philosophy, we should come to recognize our opponents as unwitting collaborators. Where the constructive impetus of reasoned disputation is absent, something fundamental to the process of philosophizing is lacking. For philosophizing is, at bottom, a striving not for *consensus,* but for a consolidation and sophistication of our own doctrinal position that is best achieved in the stimulating school of controversy. Nothing is as conducive to the deepening of philosophical expiation as debate. The salient lesson is that of maintaining a respectful contact with the work of competitors—a preparedness to reckon with them in a certain antagonistic yet cooperative colleagueship. Meaningful disagreement is possible only where there is also community—a fundamental accord on issues of "logic" in the broad sense—on what constitutes a relevant consideration or counterconsideration and a good argument or counterargument. Disagreement on matters of substance is fruitful only against the background of an agreement on probative standards—on the methodology of reasoning.

But of course these deliberations relate to process rather than product. This process reflects a commitment to reason—to rationality, discussion, disputation. It urges a willingness to listen, to commune, to respond, to learn, to keep open lines of communication—to see the doctrines of others as serious though wrong-headed attempts to deal with the issues in ways worthwhile taking account of and responding to. It is, in sum, a matter of procedure rather than substance—of the way in which one argues in deploying one's cognitive values rather than of the values themselves that underlie the argumentation.

Philosophers accordingly have a great stake in rationality. Their concern is not only for answers but for *defensible* answers to philosophical problems. And this line of thought yields an immediate reply to the question of why *I* should be what *you* call reasonable and rational. For only in this way can I commune (discuss, debate, deliberate) with you. The commitment to rationality is the salient precondition for keeping the argument (discussion, debate) going. To abandon rationality is to withdraw from the arena of deliberation and in effect to exile oneself from the community. The need to maintain contact with others engaged in the communal enterprise makes for a significant pressure toward intersubjectivity. To be sure, this sort of communal uniformity is a matter of argumentation and not of substance. (We need not *agree* in order to have an interesting and mutually profitable discussion—save in matters regarding the ground rules of discussion itself.)

Thus, while our substantive philosophical position has its personalized basis in our cognitive values, its articulation and defense always proceeds in the public forum. Notwithstanding the value relativity of our doctrinal commitments, our processes of communication and reasoning must be unrestrictedly communal. The impetus to universalized rationality is decisive and links the practitioners of philosophy into a professional community committed to an enterprise of publicly accessible inquiry. The imperatives of reason are the fundamental guidelines of philosophy.

All this, to be sure, relates to the *process* of philosophizing rather than to the *substance* of philosophy. That great question of post-Hegelian German philosophy "What are the *philosophical* implications of philosophical pluralism?" is far simpler than its exponents ever dreamed. For the answer is simply that there aren't any. The strife of systems is simply irrelevant from a doctrinal point of view. That great project of trying to absorb all of philosophy within the single grand structure of an all-inclusive philosophy is a fraud and delusion. There is no good reason why, in philosophy, we should not be doctrinaire, devising our own positions and resolving the issues in our own way. There is no good reason why, in building up a structure of our own, it should deter or worry us that others might find a building of a different sort more suitable for themselves.

From Hegel's day to ours, philosophers of all persuasions have seen the strife of systems as something to be overcome—somehow to be put behind us once and for all. Some, following Hegel himself—that

Napoleon of Philosophy[23]—use the approach of conquest and annexation, of seeking to absorb all of philosophy into one great synthesis. Others, following Comte, see it as a matter of putting childish things aside and turning to the real issues—the issues of science. The present approach takes a very different line. It sees pluralism and strife as acceptable—as part of the ground rules of the enterprise that we simply have to take in stride. Its stance is, roughly: "Agreement is not in prospect—the comfort of consensus is not available. The task is one of devising a position satisfactory not to everyone, but to ourselves. If we can manage that, responsibly and in good scholarly conscience, we have achieved all that is reasonable to ask for."

For centuries, most philosophers who have reflected on the matter have been intimidated by the strife of systems. But the time has come to put this behind us—not the strife, that is, which is ineliminable, but the felt need to somehow end it rather than simply to accept it and take it in stride. To reemphasize the salient point: it would be bizarre to think that philosophy is not of value because philosophical positions are bound to reflect the particular values we hold.

23. Kröner, *Die Anarchie*, p. 5.

# Name Index

Agrippa, 3n
Albert, Hans, 29n
Anaxagoras, 22, 65, 71, 92
Anaximander, 70, 92
Anaximenes, 70, 71
Apel, Karl-Otto, 143n, 208
Aquinas, St. Thomas, 33, 138n
Aristotle, 7, 14, 17, 20n, 22, 33, 35n, 39, 73, 100, 127, 138n, 260
Assunta del Torre, Maria, 262n
Austin, J. L., 56n, 106
Ayer, A. J., 10, 179

Baumgarten, A. G., 75n
Bergson, Henri, 232
Berkeley, 13, 32, 37, 64, 87, 92, 124, 211, 226n
Bosanquet, Bernard, 234n
Bossuet, J. B., 93
Braun, Lucien, 13n, 82n, 118n, 203n, 234n
Bradley, F. H., 13, 130–31, 260
Brandom, Robert, 43n
Broad, C. D., 81

Carnap, Rudolf, 13, 92, 211, 227
Cassirer, Ernst, 141n
Castaneda, Hector-Neri, 31n
Cavell, Stanley, 36
Chroust, Anton-Hermann, 260n
Cicero, 33, 191
Collingwood, R. G., 8, 32, 34, 62n
Comte, Auguste, 16, 92
Croce, Benedetto, 161

Danto, Arthur, 263n
Darwin, Charles, 47n
Democritus, 72, 73, 92
Derrida, Jacques, 16, 106
Descartes, René, 3–4, 26, 27, 33, 65, 92, 112, 154, 162, 218, 227
Dewey, John, 16, 106, 195, 227
Dilley, Frank B., 98n, 121
Dilthey, Wilhelm, xi, 5, 6n, 7n, 8, 12n, 30n, 48n, 85, 87, 90, 91, 97, 120, 131, 134, 136, 175, 221, 241, 262, 267, 268, 269, 270, 271
Doppelt, Gerald, 104n

Eckhart, Meister, 154
Empedocles, 70, 71
Epictetus, 25
Esposito, Joseph L., 195n
Euclid, 48

Feyerabend, Paul, 38n
Findlay, J. N., 55n
Frege, Gottlob, 35n
Frischeisen-Koehler, Max, 268

Gadamer, Hans-Georg, 106, 242–43, 245
Gallie, W. B., 123n
Gassendi, Pierre, 65, 124
Gettier, Edmund, 110
Glanvill, Joseph, 118
Gödel, Kurt, 110
Gombrich, E. H., 60n
Gomperz, Heinrich, 268n
Goodman, Nelson, 106, 174–75

Hegel, G. W. F., xi, 5, 6n, 55n, 84, 90, 106n, 125, 136, 138n, 141n, 227, 232, 234, 234n, 236, 237, 244n, 253, 267, 271, 276
Heidegger, Martin, 13, 197, 227
Heim, Karl, 6
Hempel, C. G., 74n
Heraclitus, 25, 65, 70, 71, 154
Herbart, J. F., xi, 84–85, 98n, 243, 249
Herbert of Cherbury, 5
Hippias, 30
Hobbes, Thomas, 26, 35n, 65, 92
Hochkeppel, W., 245n
Huelsen, August Ludwig, 234n
Hume, David, 4, 6, 14, 16, 33, 34, 104, 130, 203, 218, 225, 238, 244, 249

279

# THE STRIFE OF SYSTEMS
*Name Index*

Husserl, Edmund, 5, 10n, 178, 227

James, William, 7, 10–11, 80, 133–34, 154, 174, 176, 197, 211, 232, 255
Janoska, Georg, 269n
Johnson, Samuel, 13
Johnstone, Henry W., Jr., 22n, 31, 100n, 106n, 123n

Kalish, Donald, 233n
Kant, Immanuel, 5, 14, 15, 24n, 32, 33, 34, 35n, 60, 61, 75n, 86, 92, 106, 108n, 111, 127, 128, 138n, 144, 176, 179, 208, 221–22, 225, 226–27, 244
Kekes, John, 18–19, 35n, 119, 123n, 218n
Keynes, J. M., 101n
Khayyam, Omar, 15
Kierkegaard, Soren, 154, 232
Kröner, Franz, 12n, 16, 83n, 179n, 238n, 261, 262, 268–70, 277n
Kuhn, Thomas S., 104n, 106

Lange, John, 143
Lazerowitz, Morris, 8, 134, 227
Leibniz, G. W. von, 26, 27, 32, 64, 91n, 93, 99n, 104, 119, 138n, 215n
Leisegang, Hans, 106, 108, 221n
Lewis, C. I., 211
Lewis, David, 110
Locke, John, 35n
Lovejoy, A. O., 116
Luther, Martin, 118, 150

MacIntyre, Alasdair, 193–94
McTaggart, J. M. E., 81
Magnus, Simon, 154
Marconi, Diego, 54n
Marcus Aurelius, 25
Marx, Groucho, 249
Marx, Karl, 41n, 234, 237
Mates, Benson, 114
Meiland, Jack, 179n
Mill, J. S., 35n
Montaigne, Michel de, 4n, 225, 245, 249
Moody, Todd, 143, 202n
Moore, G. E., 13

Nagel, Thomas, 193n, 226n
Neurath, Otto, 114–15
Newman, John Henry, 134n
Nicholas of Cusa, 42, 79, 236
Nietzsche, Friedrich, 175, 227, 232
Nozick, Robert, xi, 118–19, 253–57, 261n

Ockham, William of, 97

Parmenides, 37, 65, 71, 72
Pascal, Blaise, 154, 158
Passmore, John, 91, 110n, 123n, 231
Pierce, Charles S., 5n, 6, 190, 208, 234, 273
Pepper, Stephen C., 78n, 104n, 106, 139n, 236, 271n
Plato, 14, 22–23, 26, 28, 33, 35n, 49, 61, 67, 68, 72, 73, 92, 97n, 104, 127, 138n, 154, 226n
Plotinus, 36
Popper, Karl, 35n
Protagoras, 109, 191, 240n
Pyrrho, 92
Pythagoras, 71, 73

Quine, W. V. O., 35n, 57n, 106

Ramsey, Frank P., 69
Randall, J. H., Jr., 32–33
Raphael, 12
Rapoport, William J., 218n
Reichenbach, Hans, 9, 140, 179
Rescher, Nicholas, 43n, 52n, 101n, 211n, 214n
Rogers, Will, 253
Rogge, Eberhard, 100n, 222n, 263n, 270
Rorty, Richard, xi, 8, 15–16, 58n, 108n, 110, 111, 128n, 227, 228, 245–48, 249–51
Ross, J. R., 101n
Rousseau, J. J., 38
Russell, Bertrand, 11–12, 13, 53n, 97n, 253

St. Paul, 154
Sanchez, Francisco, 245
Sartre, J.-P., 35n, 259
Saxe, John Godfrey, 173
Schelling, F. W. J. von, 13n, 106
Schiller, F. C. S., 6, 7, 8n, 134, 135
Schlegel, Friedrich von, 75n, 82
Schlick, Moritz, 10, 68n
Schoemaker, Sydney, 57n
Schopenhauer, Arthur, 113, 154, 232
Schumacher, E. F., 273n
Seneca, 240n
Sextus Empiricus, 3, 38n, 92, 191n, 224n, 228n
Shakespeare, William, 76
Skinner, Quentin, 32
Socrates, 23, 69, 105, 245
Spencer, Herbert, 85, 128
Spinoza, Benedictus de, 22, 26, 27, 35n, 65, 104, 106, 112, 138n
Sterne, Laurence, 236n
Steuchus, Augustinus, 91n

280

Stough, Charlotte L., 226n
Stumpf, Karl, 255n

Thales, 15, 70, 71
Thrasymachus, 23, 25, 26
Tidedmann, Dietrich, 203n
Tinner, Walter, 99n
Turienzo, Saturnio Alvarez, 91n

Unger, Peter, 49n, 115n

Waismann, Frederick, 6n, 48, 96, 123n
Weitz, Morris, 123n

Wiggins, Davie, 57n
Williamson, Mark, 271n
Wilson, Daniel T., 116n
Winch, Peter, 195n
Wittenstein, Ludwig, 5, 9, 55n, 225, 227, 228, 242n
Woehrmann, K. R., 99n
Wolff, Christian, 52n, 75n

Xenophanes (of Colophon), 38n

Zeno, 65, 67, 71

# Subject Index

absolutism, 223
analogy, 98–107
antinomies, 28–31, 45–63
aporetic cluster, 21–31
apory, 21–31, 78–90, 95–97
appraisal, value-free, 214–17
arationalism, 223, 230–33
atomism, Greek, 70–72
Averroism, 236–38

belief, 46–47
bodily continuity, 46–47, 50–51

charity, principle of, 36
cognitive incommensurability, 31–37
cognitive values, 95–115, 116–38, 170–72, 277–79
commitment, 258–260
common denominator, 30
concepts, fact-coordinated, 50–57, 60–61
consensus, 125–38, 202–20
consistency, 38–44
convergentism, 233–36

dialectics, 69–72, 78–90
disagreement, philosophical, 3–16
distinctions, 64–75

edification, 247–48
epoche, 224, 239
esoteric argumentation, 99
evidential monism, 223
exoteric argumentation, 99
experience, limits of, 60–63

fact-coordinated concepts, 50–57, 60–61

*Geisteswissenschaften*, 113

hermeneuticism, 245–48
historical convergentism, 223
historicism, 223

*homo quaerens*, 42
human sciences, 113

incommensurability, cognitive, 31–37
inconsistency, 38–44
indifferentism, 145–51
inquiry, 39–40
inventiveness, philosophical, 75–76
irrationalism, 151–53
*isostheneia*, 224

limits of experience, 60–63

metaphilosophy, 261–79
method of relations, 85
monism: evidential, 223; value-orientational, 223
multifaceted-reality view, 173–75

no-reality view, 175–76

objectivity, 111–15
orientational pluralism, 118–38, 147–58, 159–72, 177–79, 221–40, 265–67, 271–79
overdetermination, 22

perennial issues, 33
perspectival-reality view, 176–78
*philosophia perennis*, 91
philosophy: applied, 162–65; autonomy of, 139; data of, 18–20; history of, 267–71; mission of, 17–21, 45, 58–63, 246–52, 277–79; Platonic ideal of, 9–13; progress of, 202–20; science, 210–17
plausibility, 21
pluralism, orientational, 147–58, 159–72, 238–40, 265–67, 271–79
Protagorean relativism, 191–96
pseudoproblems, 132–33
psychologism, 223

282

rational selection, 47n
rationality, 40–44, 139–58
reason, taxonomy of, 155
relativism, 173–201; Protagorean, 191–96; self-consistency of, 180–86

scepticism, 78–79, 224–30; agnostic, 223, 226, 241–45; nihilistic, 226
schools of thought, 33
significance, 130
Socratic questioning, 23
standards, 142
syncretism, 223, 236–39, 241, 245, 260

tabula rasa, 17–18
taxonomy of reason, 155
traditions, convergence of, 78–79
truth, pursuit of, 186–91, 196–201

unique-reality view, 176–78

values, cognitive, 129–38, 170–72, 277–79
value-free appraisal, 214–17
value-orientational monism, 223
*Vermittelungsansichten*, 255

wisdom, proverbial, 60